LENIN, 1918

THE LETTERS OF

LENIN

TRANSLATED AND EDITED BY
Elizabeth Hill AND *Doris Mudie*

HARCOURT, BRACE AND COMPANY, NEW YORK

DK
254
L4
A36

20597

Designed by Robert Josephy

PRINTED IN THE UNITED STATES OF AMERICA
BY QUINN & BODEN COMPANY, INC., RAHWAY, N. J.

Foreword

Owing to the political and conspiratorial nature of the letters, Lenin's correspondence is far from complete. It was conducted under great difficulties. The "chemical" letters which would now be invaluable to the historian are irretrievably lost. Such communications, bound inside book covers or written between the lines of non-committal letters, or often between the printed lines of books and periodicals, were destroyed immediately after the contents had been read. Dangerous letters, sent by ordinary methods, were also frequently destroyed by the recipient. Others, travelling by roundabout ways, never reached their destination. A number were intercepted by the Tsarist authorities.

In spite of these destructive agents, however, about a thousand letters have been preserved. No doubt a few more will eventually come to light. Of those that are known, 289 letters to Lenin's relations were published in Soviet Russia in a single volume by the Lenin Institute, Gosizdat, in 1931, and 515 political letters were published by the Marx Engels Lenin Institute, Moscow, in 1932 and 1933 as Volumes XVIII and XIX of his collected works. The rest were printed in other volumes of his collected works, in the "Lenin Miscellany" and in various Russian newspapers and periodicals.

With the exception of a very few letters, Lenin's correspondence has never before appeared in English. The present volume of 340 letters has been taken direct from the three Russian volumes of collected letters. Those translated from the volume to relations are marked (R) and their number in that publication retained, while those from the two volumes of political letters are marked (P¹) and (P²) respectively.

The bulk of available material has naturally necessitated a selection for English readers. On what principle has this selection been made? On the principle of completeness as consonant with the size of the volume. Each letter has been faithfully translated in its entirety, retaining as far as practicable Lenin's peculiarities of style and punctuation, his use of brackets, repetitions, allusions, nicknames and a certain vagueness in places owing to the need to veil activities from a vigilant censor. The selection has also been motivated by the wish to present those letters which will cast as varied a light on Lenin himself and which will be as representative of his activities as possible. The volume has been divided into ten sections, each one preceded by a concise chronology showing Lenin's life correlated with the course of the revolutionary movement in Russia. Brief notes have been added, explaining details and personalities as they occur; editorial insertions in the text are in square brackets.

Lenin's letters need no introduction. They speak for themselves. Lenin neither kept a diary nor wrote his autobiography. His letters therefore are the most intimate of all his writing. They are a revealing self-portrait, an invaluable contribution to a fuller understanding of his personality. It is not so much Leninism that emerges from his letters. This is to be found in the collected volumes of his theoretical works and other writings available to English readers in translation. There emerges above all the vivid figure of Lenin himself.

The letters cover a period of a quarter of a century of Russian revolutionary activity. It is the background to them. It is the reason why they were written. Year by year they show the part he played in that historical process. Lenin stands out in them as the indefatigable realist, the leader, the strategist, the tactician of the Russian Social Democratic Labour Party, as a man wholeheartedly and single-mindedly devoted to his cause.

The importance of these letters to the historian, biographer and the general reader cannot be exaggerated.

Elizabeth Hill, Ph.D.

Contents

Illustrations

THE PRE-EXILE PERIOD
1870–1895
1896

SUMMARY

1870
24th March. Marx says to the Russian Section of the I International: "Your country also is beginning to participate in the general movement of our age."

1870's
Government reaction sets in after Karakozov's unsuccessful attempt to shoot Alexander II (4.4.1866). Revolutionary-Narodnik movement among the intelligentsia.

1872
Russian translation of Marx's "Capital," Vol. I.

1874
Spring. Government crushes Narodnik movement.

1876
Revolutionary-Narodniks form "Land and Liberty" (or "Will") Secret Society.

1877
Revolutionary-Narodniks advocate political struggle and terrorism. "South Russian Workers' Union" formed.

1878
"North Russian Workers' Union" formed.

1879
Lipetsk and Voronezh Congresses of Socialist Narodniks. Organisations of the Executive Committee of "The People's Will" Party. "Land and Liberty" Party splits into (1) "The People's Will" Party, (2) "The Black Partition" (i.e., Agrarian revolution) led by G. V. Plekhanov.

1881
March 1st. Assassination of Alexander II by order of "The People's Will" Executive Committee. The Government crushes "The People's Will" Party. "The Black Partitionists" emigrate abroad.

1870
April 10/22. Lenin (Vladimir Ilyich Ulianov) born in Simbirsk. His father, I. N. Ulianov, was a civil servant, inspector of primary schools in the province of Simbirsk.

1879-87
Lenin at the Simbirsk High School.

2

SUMMARY 3

THE RUSSIAN REVOLUTIONARY MOVEMENT

LENIN'S LIFE

1883-4

Plekhanov, Axelrod, Zasulich and others found "The Liberation of Labour" group in Switzerland (the first foundations of a Russian Workers' party). The group publishes the "Library of Contemporary Socialism" and Plekhanov's "Socialism and the Political struggle" (which urges the necessity for Russian Socialists to organise a Social Democratic Labour Party in Russia).

1886

Terroristic group of "The People's Will" Party formed with P. Shevyrev and Lenin's brother, Alexander Ulianov, at the head.

1886

January. Lenin's father dies.

1887

March 1st. Unsuccessful attempt to assassinate Alexander III. Arrest of the terroristic group. Alexander Ulianov, Shevyrev and others hanged (May 1887).

1887

Lenin finishes at the Simbirsk High School and receives the first prize.
Matriculates in the Kazan University and enters the Law faculty in the Autumn. December: Expelled from the University for participation in student disturbances. Exiled to village Kokushkino, his maternal grandfather's estate in the Kazan province. Joins sister Anna, then under police surveillance. Lenin studies Marx's "Capital."

1888

Autumn. Liberation of Labour group founds the "Russian Social Democratic Movement." First Marxist groups formed in Russia.

1888

Lenin refused re-admission to University. Police forbid him to go abroad. Winter in Kazan. Contact with student circles for study of Marx.

1889

Plekhanov attends 1st (Paris) Congress of the II International as S.D. Delegate.

1889

Summer. Moves to Samara. Marxist activities. Refused the right to sit for final University examinations.

1891

Famine. Oppositional and revolutionary spirit grows.

1891

Lenin passes final law examinations as external student of the St. Petersburg University.

1893

Formation of the Narodnik party "The People's Right."

1893

Lenin in Samara. First group of Marxists in Samara: Lenin, Sklyarenko (Popov) and Lalayants. In August Lenin moves to St. Petersburg. Admitted to the Bar in September. Secret activities among workers with Krupskaya, Krzhizhanovsky etc.

THE RUSSIAN REVOLUTIONARY MOVEMENT	LENIN'S LIFE
1894	**1894**
Narodniks in Berne form "The Union of the Russian Revolution," their newspaper being "The Russian Worker." Attempted strikes in main industrial centres of Russia. Social Democrat, Struve, writes "Critical remarks on the question of the Economic development of Russia" (legal Marxism). November: Death of Alexander III.	Lenin joins St. Petersburg circle of S.D. propagandists, the central group for leading the workers' movement. Lenin's first literary work, an illegal pamphlet "Who the 'Friends of the People' are and how they fight against the Social Democrats." Lenin's lecture "The reflection of Marxism in bourgeois literature" (debating Struve's book).
1895	**1895**
January 17. Nicholas II makes a speech on the stability of autocracy. Literary conflict between Marxists and Narodniks. The Union of Russian Social Democrats is formed abroad on the initiative of the Liberation of Labour Group.	April. Lenin abroad (4 months). Relations with Plekhanov, Axelrod, Zasulich (Liberation of Labour Group). November. He returns to Russia after arranging for the transport of illegal literature to Russia. Organises the "Union for the struggle of the liberation of the working class." Writes leaflets to the St. Petersburg workers. Encourages strike at Thornton's factory. Prepares for publication of illegal newspaper the "Rabocheye Delo" ("The Workers' Cause"). December 9: Lenin and other members of the Union arrested and imprisoned.
1896	**1896**
June: First strike of textile workers (30,000) in St. Petersburg, who demand reduction of working hours to 10½.	Prison (14 months). Works on "The Development of Capitalism in Russia." Sends out leaflets from prison, pamphlets (one on "Strikes") and a draft programme for the Russian Social Democratic Party.

1895

1. (3 R). TO M. A. ULIANOVA, LENIN'S MOTHER

Salzburg, 2/14th May, 1895 [1]

I am taking advantage of a two hour wait in a small Austrian town (not far from my destination, slightly more than twenty-four hours), to keep my promise to write to you on the way.

---

[1] On April 25, 1895, Lenin went abroad, where he established links with the Liberation of Labour Group—with Plekhanov, Axelrod, Zasulich. The letter is necessarily non-committal.

I have been travelling abroad for two days now and am practising the language; I find I am quite weak at it. I understand the Germans with the greatest difficulty, or rather, I do not understand them at all. I do not understand even the simplest words—their pronunciation is unusual and they talk so fast. I ask the conductor a question—he answers; I do not understand. He repeats his answer louder. I still do not understand; he gets angry and goes away. In spite of such a disgraceful fiasco, I do not lose courage and fairly assiduously distort the German language.

Greetings to all our people,

Your, V. Ulianov

I shall probably not be able to write my next letter to you for some little time.

2. (5 R). TO HIS MOTHER

Paris, 27th May/8th June, 1895

I received your letter just before leaving for Paris. I am terribly sorry there is such a stupid business over Mitya's illness; I do not understand how a person can be refused postponement of an examination if he has a medical certificate. Why does he not want to make further enquiries? What is the good of losing a year?

Manyasha's exams are probably finishing now or are already over. She should have a good rest in the Summer.

I am only just beginning to look round Paris a little; the town is enormous and spread over a wide area, so that the surrounding districts (where I am more often) convey no idea of the centre. It makes a very pleasant impression—wide, light streets, many boulevards, much greenery; the crowd behaves quite unrestrainedly, so that at first one is slightly surprised, having grown used to Petersburg respectability and severity.

One would have to spend several weeks here to see it properly.

Flats are very cheap here; for instance, 30-35 francs per

month for two rooms and a kitchen; 6–10 francs a week for
a furnished room—so I hope to live inexpensively.

Greetings to all our people,

Your,

V.

Are you all pleased with the Summer villa?
[The end of this letter is cut off.]

3. (6 R). TO HIS MOTHER

[*Switzerland*], *6/18th July, 1895*

If I am not mistaken, I wrote my last letter to you on the
8th. Since then I have wandered about a good bit and find
myself now in a Swiss health resort: I have decided to take
the opportunity of attending seriously to my tiresome stomach
trouble, especially as the specialist who runs this place has
been strongly recommended to me as an expert. I have been
living here for the last few days and feel all right; the pension is excellent and the cure is evidently sensible, so I hope
to get away from here in four or five days' time. Judging
from all appearances, life here will be very expensive; the
cure still more expensive, and I have already exceeded my
budget and cannot hope to manage on my resources. If it is
possible, send me another 100 roubles to the following address:
Suisse, Zürich Parterre, Seilergraben 37, Hn. Grünfest [1]
(*nothing else*, "c/o" and so forth is not necessary). The best
way of sending the money is by money order through the
post. In any case I shall expect letters to be sent to that address;
I am not giving you my actual address, because it is useless:
I shall leave here before I can receive an answer.

Are you pleased with your trip down the Volga? What is
the news from there? Are all well? Probably a letter has been
posted to me, but I have not yet received it (the last letter I
received was from Mark in Paris—a postcard) because I have

[1] Saul Grünfest took part in the organisation of the Minsk printing press.
In 1882 he emigrated abroad, joined the Liberation of Labour group where at one
time he did administrative technical work. Later, in Zürich, he took part in the
Social Democratic movement. Died 1906.

been on the move all the time. But if it has been sent to the Paris address, then I will receive it.

Is your Summer hot? It is very hot here, but I am now living in a good place far from the town amid greenery and near a large lake.

Greetings to all our people,

Your V.

4. (7 R). TO HIS MOTHER

Berlin, August 29th/September 10th, 1895

I do not know whether you have received my last letter which I posted from here a week ago. In any case I repeat my address: Berlin, Moabit, Flensburgerstrasse 12 (bei Frau Kurreick), Herrn. W. Ulianoff.

I am quite happily settled here: the Tiergarten is only a few yards away (it is a beautiful park, the best and largest in Berlin), also the Spree, where I bathe each day, and the railway station. The railway here runs through the whole town (over the streets); the trains run every five minutes, so it is very convenient for me to go to "town" (Moabit where I live is considered to be a suburb).

The only trouble is the language: I understand German conversation infinitely worse than French. The Germans have such an unusual pronunciation that I cannot understand the words they use even in a public speech; whereas in France, I understood almost everything in similar speeches and from the outset. The day before yesterday I went to the theatre; they were playing Hauptmann's "Weavers." In spite of the fact that I had re-read the whole of the drama before the performance in order to follow the acting, I could not catch all the phrases. However, I do not lose heart and I am only sorry that I have far too little time to learn the language thoroughly.

Greetings to all our people,

Your, V.

If you have already sent me money then please write to me

about it immediately. If you have not, then send some to me here.

Probably the reason why I have not had any letters from you for so long is that they (the letters) are wandering about the places where I have been.

5. (8 R). TO HIS MOTHER

[Berlin], 17th/29th August, 1895

The other day I received your letter, darling Mother, and today a letter from Mark to whom I shall add a short note.

My life goes on as usual and so far I am pleased with Berlin. I feel quite well—it must be the regular way of living, the bathing and so on, together with following the doctor's prescriptions which are having their effect (I am very tired of moving from place to place, and besides, during these moves I never managed to eat regularly or properly). I study as usual in the Königliche Bibliothek and in the evenings I usually wander about different places studying Berlin manners and customs and listening to German. I have grown more used to the language now and understand somewhat better, although still very, very badly.

I am very idle about visiting the Berlin "Sehenswürdig-keiten," I am not particularly interested in them and I usually go by chance. In general I prefer to prowl around various popular evenings and amusements to visiting museums, theatres, arcades and so on.

As for staying here for some time—I do not think so; "visiting is all very well, but home is best." Well, I shall live here for a while yet, but, to my great horror, I see I have again money difficulties; the temptation to buy books etc., is so great that my money goes the devil knows where. Again I have to turn to you for assistance: if you can, send me 50-100 roubles.

Mark writes that your affairs with regard to the flat are in a positively tragic condition: that there are no flats. Evidently in this respect Moscow is worse than Petersburg. It is terribly

FACSIMILE OF LENIN'S WRITING, 1895

unpleasant to have all this bother about a flat. I hope you will soon be rid of it.

Greetings to all our people,

Your,

V. Ul.

6. (10 R). TO HIS MOTHER

[Petersburg], 5/17th October, 1895

Yesterday, darling Mother, I received your letter of the 2nd/14th October. At last I have found a good room for myself, or so it seems: there are no other lodgers, the landlady's family is not large and the door leading from my room to their drawing room is papered over, so that sounds are muffled. The room is clean and light. The entrance to the house is good. Also, as it is not far from the centre of the town (for instance, it is only fifteen minutes walk to the library), I am perfectly satisfied.

I saw Tillo[1] both yesterday and today. He has not obtained the ticket and unfortunately cannot get it, as the person on whom he relied is not there. He says he may be able to get it when his own position in the temporary management of the railways becomes more stable. But this evidently will not be soon.

I went to the Volkovo cemetery[2] soon after I arrived: everything is in order—both the cross and the wreath.

Your loving,

V. Ulianov

I would ask you to send me some money: mine is coming to an end. I hear from Samara that the Grafov case money (my Kazan law suit in Samara) has been promised to be paid in November. This will give me about 70 roubles (if the promise is kept—but how far that is certain I do not know).

---

[1] A. E. Tillo, a railway official and engineer. Accused in 1896 of aiding the transit of "criminal publications" over the frontier. A Social Democrat since the '80's.

[2] Lenin's sister, Olga, who had died of typhus in Petersburg in 1891, was buried in the Volkovo cemetery.

I am promised work here in a lawyer's office, but when it will be actually settled (if ever) I do not know.

Write and tell me what your financial position is. Have you received anything from our Aunt? Have you received the September rental from Krushvits? [1] Was there anything left over from the deposit (500 roubles) after the expenses of the removal and the settling in?

For the first time in Petersburg I have been keeping a debit and credit account book to see how much I spend. It appears that for the month beginning 28th August to the 27th September, I have spent in all 54 roubles and 30 kops, not counting payment for things (about 10 roubles) and expenses over a legal matter (also about 10 roubles) which I may pursue. Out of these 54 roubles there are items which will not be repeated each month (galoshes, clothes, books, accounts etc.), but even deducting these (16 roubles) the expenditure is still excessive—38 roubles a month. Evidently I have been living uneconomically: on trams alone, for instance, I have spent 1 rouble 36 kops in the month. Probably when I have got used to living here, I shall spend less.

7. (11 R). TO HIS SISTER, M. I. ULIANOVA

[Petersburg, October, 1895]

I have read your letter of the 27th August/9th September with interest and I should be very glad if you would write to me occasionally. I have neither visited the Hermitage Gallery nor the theatres; somehow I do not feel like going alone. When I am in Moscow, I shall go with you to the Tretiakov Gallery and other places with pleasure.

I read the "Russkiye Vedomosti" in the public library (the news is always two weeks old). I may subscribe to the paper when I have found some work here. It is not worth while keeping them for me, but I think it would be helpful if you did not tear them up too soon, for there might be something of interest in them, something useful.

I see from your story of the French master, that although

[1] Lenin's mother had let her farm Alakaevka (now Leninka).

the Moscow school girls have overtaken you, they cannot be very far ahead of you. Probably the average pupils do not know any more than you. Write and tell me if you spend much time over your homework.

Tell Mitya that he ought to send the bookseller to the devil, I mean the one who asks 25 roubles for Klyuchevsky [1]; it should not cost more than 4 roubles. How are Mitya's studies progressing?

Goodbye,   Your

                                             V. U.

P.S. Can you read my handwriting?

8. (1 P[1]). TO P. B. AXELROD IN ZÜRICH

[Petersburg, early November, 1895]

You are probably cursing me for the delay. There were good reasons.

I will tell you everything in the right order. First of all, I was in Vilna.[2] I discussed the "Miscellany" [3] with our crowd. The majority agree that there is an urgent need for such a publication and promise their support and supply of material. On the whole, their attitude is mistrustful, (I remembered your remark about the provinces being politic): "Let us see," they said, "whether it will conform with the agitation tactics and the tactics of economic strife." I emphasised particularly that that depended upon us.

Next: I was in Moscow. I did not see anyone, as there was not a sign or sound from the Master of Life.[4] Is he all right? If you know anything about him and have his address, write to him and tell him to send us his address, otherwise we cannot establish any links there. There were serious raids

---

[1] V. O. Klyuchevsky: "A course of lectures on Modern Russian History."

[2] Vilna and other place names in the letter were written in code.

[3] "The Worker" started in 1894 by the Social Democrats in Russia and on the initiative of Lenin.

[4] The "Master of Life"—E. I. Sponti, Social Democrat and active member of the Moscow Workers' Union. In the Spring of 1895 he and Lenin had been abroad to establish links with the Liberation of Labour Group. Sponti was arrested on the 12th December, 1895, and in 1897 was exiled to the North of Russia for two years.

there,[1] but I think a few people are left and that the work is going on. We have information from there—an account of several strikes. If you have not had any information, write, and we will send it to you.

Then I was in Orekhovo-Zuevo. Such places, frequently found in a central industrial region, are most interesting; it is one of those typical small factory towns with some tens of thousands of inhabitants, and where the life of the town depends on the factory. The factory administration is the sole authority. The factory management "rules" the town. The people are very sharply divided into workers and bourgeois. The workers are consequently somewhat oppositionally inclined, but after the recent raid there are so few of our own people left, and these are all so closely watched, that communication is very difficult. However, we shall manage to get the literature through to them.

Next: the delay was caused by local trouble. That explains the paucity of the material I am sending.

I do not like the Zürich address. Cannot you find another— not in Switzerland but in Germany? That would be much better and safer.

Next: in sending us an answer—*the book on technology*—use the address: Mr. Luchinsk, Chemical Laboratory, Alexandrovsky Cast Iron Foundry, Petersburg.

If there is room in the parcel, add the other material; the small pamphlets which came out in Geneva, interesting cuttings from "Vorwärts" and so on. Write as fully as you can about the "Miscellany"; tell me what material is ready, what the plans are, when the first number is to appear and what exactly is lacking for the second number. As for the money, we shall probably send it, but later on. Reply *as soon as you can*, so that we may know whether this method is all right.

Give the Pole [?] an address for a personal call. Preferably let it be as soon as possible, for we are in need of means of communication. The address: the same town, Technological Institute, Student Michael Leontievich Zakladny—ask for

---

[1] This refers to arrests among the Social Democrat groups in Moscow and the province of Moscow.

Ivanov. The money for publishing the Russian edition of his "Geschichte etc." has been promised.

Next: a request; we urgently need paint—find out what sort of paint it is from Mögli, who has some. Could you find some means of getting it to us? Will there be an opportunity? Please think about this and tell your "practicians" to think about it. By the way, you asked us to refer to them direct. Then let me know: (a) do they know our method and code? (b) do they know who is sending these letters?

I now send: (a) information about the expulsion of the Dukhobors, (b) the story about the agricultural members in the South and (c) a description of Thornton's factory—of which so far only the beginning, about a quarter of the whole.

You must write in Indian ink. It would be better, if you were to add a small crystal of potassium bichromate ($K_2Cr_2O_7$); then it would not wash off. Use *thinner* paper.

Greetings,

Your . . . . .

Greetings to your comrade.

9. (2 P[1]). TO P. B. AXELROD (ZÜRICH),

A RUSSIAN SOCIAL DEMOCRAT

[Petersburg, Middle November, 1895]

I have received the Breslau report.[1] We opened it with indescribable efforts, tearing the greater part of it (the letter, thanks to the good paper, remained whole).[2] You have evidently not yet received the second letter. It is essential to use liquid paste: not more than a teaspoonful of starch to a glass of water (and moreover, potato flour, not the ordinary flour, which is too strong). The ordinary (good) paste is only necessary for the top sheet and for coloured paper, because the paper holds well together under a press, even with the thinnest of pastes. In any case, it is a suitable method and ought to be used.

---

[1] Report of the Breslau Parteitag (congress) of the German S.D. party in 1895.

[2] Correspondence from abroad was often sent over to Russia hidden inside the bindings of books.

I am sending you the end of Thornton.[1] We have material
about the strike: (1) at Thornton's, (2) at Laferme's, (3) the
Ivanovo-Voznesensk strike, (4) the Yaroslav strike (a letter
from a worker, very interesting, about the Petersburg factory
for the mechanical production of boots). I am not sending it
yet, because there has not been any time for copying it and
because I am not reckoning on being in time for the first number of the "Miscellany." We have established links with the
People's Will Printing Press,[2] which has already published
three things (not ours) and which is taking one of ours. If you
have any material for workers' pamphlets, send it to us. They
will print it with pleasure. We are thinking of publishing a
newspaper [3] and the material will go into it. This will be definitely settled in about 1½ to 2 months. If you think the
material will be in time for the first issue—let me know at once.

Your
Il'in

Are you managing easily with our parcels? We must both of
us improve the method.

10. (12 R). TO HIS MOTHER

[Petersburg], *5th/17th December, 1895*

I received a letter yesterday, darling Mother, from Anyuta
saying you were thinking of going to Kazan with the Ardashevs [4]—and I hasten to write to you.

---

[1] A description of Thornton's factory in Petersburg.

[2] A group of young Narodovoltsy (People's Will) was formed in S.P.B. in 1895.
In ideology they approached Marxism. In the autumn of 1895 the Social Democratic
group (subsequently the Petersburg Union for the Struggle for the Liberation of the
Working Class) arranged for the Narodovoltsy to print literature for the workers.
Lenin conducted the negotiations. "One of ours" is Lenin's pamphlet: "An explana-
tion of the Law about fines."

[3] The first number of the newspaper was ready to go to press in December. It
was to be called "The Workers' Cause." The main article, written by Lenin, out-
lined the programme and explained the necessity of forming an independent Labour
Party and struggling for political freedom as a means of attaining Socialism. However, on 9/21 December a number of raids were carried out and the leading members of the "Union for Struggle," with Lenin at the head, were arrested.

[4] The Ardashevs—his cousins.

The Ardashevs were thinking of leaving today. Ts. A. Ardashev has suggested I should take over the case of establishing the right of inheritance of a relation of his, but so far we have not come to any definite agreement.

Life goes on as usual here. I am not very pleased with my room; first because the landlady finds fault, and secondly, I have discovered there is the thinnest partition between my room and the one next door, so that everything is overheard and sometimes I am forced to escape from the balalaika with which my neighbour amuses himself immediately under my ear. Fortunately this has not happened very often. He is usually out and then the flat is quiet.

I do not know yet whether I shall stay here another month [1] —I shall see. In any case at Christmas when the agreement for my room expires, it will not be difficult to find another.

The weather here is very fine and my new coat is quite suitable.

(The second page of the letter has not been preserved.)

---

[1] Lenin was arrested on the 9/21 December.

THE PERIOD OF EXILE
1897   1898   1899

SUMMARY

1897

June 2. Law limits working day to 11½ hours. Zürich Summer Conference reuniting all S.D. groups into one party. Unions for the struggle for the liberation of the working class formed in Kiev, Ekaterinoslav, Nikolaev.

1898

Formation of the R.S.D.L.P. I Party Congress in Minsk. Its activities: (1) Struve composes the manifesto of the Party: (2) Organisational Statute; Unions for the liberation of the working class, the "Workers' Newspaper" group and the Bund of Jewish S.D. groups form one Party. Central Committee is the executive organ of the Party and is elected by the Congress: (3) the Union of Russian Social Democrats is part of the Party and its representative abroad. "The Workers' Newspaper" is the official Party organ. The Party is crushed by the Government and most Party members are arrested. The development of Economism (the Economists were the Trade Unionist wing of Russian Marxism).
November: Congress of "The Union of Russian Social Democrats."
December: General Strike of Ivanovo-Voznesensk Workers.

1899

S.D. legal Marxist journals "Zhizn" and "Nachalo." Conflict between economists and politicians. "Rabocheye Delo" ("The Workers' Cause") is the journal of the economists abroad.

1897

Jan. 29.-Feb. 10. Exiled for 3 years to Eastern Siberia, Shushenskoye village, Minusinsk district. In close secret contact with Russian Social Democrats, the Liberation of Labour group. Writes articles in "Novoye Slovo," "Nachalo" and other periodicals against the ideology of the Narodniks and legal Marxism. Translates Webbs' "Theory and Practice of Trade Unionism."

1898

In Shushenskoye, continues work on "The Development of Capitalism in Russia." Writes articles under signature of "N. Lenin." Krupskaya sentenced to Siberian exile.
July 10: Lenin and Krupskaya marry. "The Tasks of the Russian Social Democrats" published abroad.

Lenin fights Economism; writes declaration which is signed by 17 Social Democrats exiled in the Minusinsk district.

1899

Exile in Siberia continues.
April: "The Development of Capitalism in Russia" is published. Contributes articles to legal Marxist Journals.

1896

11. (13 R). TO A. K. CHEBOTAREVA[1]

Petersburg. The house of preliminary detention
2nd/14th January, 1896

I have a plan which has been interesting me intensely ever since my arrest and the interest is increasing. For a long time I have been studying a question in economics (the sale of goods produced by industry within the country).

I have collected some books on the subject, formed a scheme of work and I have even written something about it with a view to issuing a book, if the material exceeds the length of an article for a periodical. I do not want to give up this work, but I am faced with the alternative either of writing it here or of giving up the idea altogether.

I realise that the idea of writing it here will be faced with many obstacles. However, I think I ought to make an attempt. Some of the obstacles, the so to speak independent obstacles, are being set aside. Those who have been detained are allowed to do literary work. I made a point of asking the Public Prosecutor about this, although I knew about it before (even those in prison are allowed this). He also confirmed that there was no limit set on the number of books permitted. Also, books can be returned; consequently one can make use of libraries, which means that in this particular matters are satisfactory. Other obstacles are more serious—procuring the books. Many books are necessary and I append a list of those which I need at once, and it will require a good deal of trouble to get them. I do not know whether it will be possible to get them all. The Library of the Free Economic Society can probably be relied upon. If

[1] A. K. Chebotareva was the wife of a close friend of the Lenin family, where Lenin used to board. Actually, the letter was meant for his comrades, Krupskaya among them. The book list contained the names of a number of works Lenin really needed for writing his work on "The Development of Capitalism in Russia." The titles marked with a question mark were either real or fictitious, but they concealed the names or nicknames of those comrades about whose fate he was anxious. E.g., Mayne-Read "The Mynoga," Russian for lamprey, a fish, was an inquiry about Krupskaya, whose nickname was Minoga. A reply to this list, which unfortunately is lost, was sent in the same conspiratorial way.

you leave a deposit, books can be borrowed for a period of two months, but this library is very incomplete. If through some writer or professor[1] one could make use of the University Library or the Library of the Scholars' Committee of the Ministry of Finance, then the problem of obtaining books would be solved. Some of the books will have to be bought and I think I can allot a certain sum of money for this.

The last and most difficult obstacle is the delivery of the books. It is not like bringing a couple of books now and again; it will be essential to have them brought regularly over a long period, to have them fetched from the libraries, brought here and then returned. I do not know how this can be arranged. It might be done this way: some porter, messenger or lad could be chosen and I would pay him to fetch the books. Of course there would need to be an accurate and regular exchange of books both because of the conditions of my work and because of the library regulations. All this must be properly arranged.

"The tale is soon told. . . ."

I feel that the scheme will not be so easy to carry out and that it may turn out to be a chimera. Perhaps you will not think it useless to hand this letter over to someone else to seek advice—while I will wait for an answer.

The list of books is divided into two parts, just as my work is divided into two parts: (a) the general theoretical part, which requires fewer books, so that I hope to write it whatever happens, but it will require more preparatory work; (b) the application of theoretical situations to Russian facts. This part needs very many books. The main difficulties will be: (1) provincial editions: however, I have some of them and others can be ordered (minor monographs), while others can be obtained from friends who are statisticians, (2) Government editions— works of Commissions, reports, protocols and Minutes of Congresses, Meetings, etc. These are important and are more diffi-

[1] Lenin is hinting at P. B. Struve and A. N. Potresov. P. B. Struve, a Social Democrat in the '90's. The most outstanding representative of "legal Marxism" in the '90's, an economist and publicist. Became a Menshevik. A. N. Potresov, a Social Democrat, contributor to Marxist journals. At II Congress of R.S.D.L. Party joined the Mensheviks.

cult to procure. Some are in the Library of the Free Economic Society—perhaps all of them.

I append a long list because I intend to cover a wide field. Of course, if I can keep to the plan, the list may become longer as the work progresses. It may not be possible to get certain books and then I shall have to narrow the theme correspondingly. This is quite possible, especially in regard to the second part.

I have omitted books from the list which are in the library here and those which I have are marked with a cross.

As I am working from memory, I think I may have muddled some of the titles and where I am not certain, I have used a question mark.

12. (14 R). TO A. I. ELIZAROVA, LENIN'S SISTER

Petersburg. The house of preliminary detention
12th/24th January, 1896

I received some provisions from you yesterday and just before that someone brought me a number of different things to eat, so I am accumulating quite a store: for instance, I could almost begin trading in tea, but I don't think I should be allowed to do so, because, if I were to compete with the little shop here, the victory would undoubtedly be mine. I eat very little bread. I try to keep to a certain diet—but you have brought such an enormous quantity of bread, I think it will last a week and will probably become as hard as the Sunday cake in Oblomovka.[1]

I have everything I need and even more than I need. For instance, someone has brought me a suit, waistcoat and shawl, all of which being superfluous have been sent at once to the Military Depot. My health is satisfactory. I can have mineral water here; it is brought to me from the chemist on the day I order it. I sleep about nine hours a day and dream about the various chapters in my next book. Is Mother

[1] A reference to Goncharov's novel "Oblomov."

well and the rest of our people at home? Give them my love.

From,

V. Ulianov

P.S. If you happen to come again, please bring me a pencil which has the lead inserted in a holder. The ordinary wooden pencils are inconvenient: penknives are not allowed. The warder has to sharpen the pencils and he does this unwillingly and takes his time over it.

It would also be good to receive the oval box containing an enema: it is in the drawer of my clothes cupboard. You may be able to do this without a certificate. Give the housekeeper a tip and tell her to take a cab, bring the box here and hand it over in exchange for a receipt. Unfortunately she is as obstinate as Korobochka.[1] There is no immediate need for this so it is not worth buying one.

13. (15 R). TO A. I. ELIZAROVA

Petersburg. The house of preliminary detention
14th/26th February, 1896

Yesterday I received your letter of the 12th/24th and I am sending you a second letter of authorisation, which may actually be superfluous, but I am not sure. I also received some of my things yesterday and it made me think my first letter had probably been received. In any case I am sending you the authorisation according to your letter and the one from Alexandra Kirillovna [Chebotareva]. I have enough underclothes and everything; do not send any more underclothes, because I have nowhere to put them. However I could pass it over to the Depot, so as to finish with the matter once and for all.

I am very grateful to Alexandra Kirillovna for the trouble she took over the dentist: I am quite ashamed to have caused so much bother. No special pass is required for the dentist, for I have the Public Prosecutor's permission to see him and I

---

[1] A character in Gogol's "Dead Souls."

THE FOUNDERS OF THE ST. PETERSBURG UNION FOR THE LIBERATION OF THE WORK-
ING CLASS. *Sitting, from left to right:* V. V. Starkov, G. M. Krzhizhanovsky, Lenin, Y. O. Martov.
Standing: A. L. Malchenko, P. K. Zaporozhets, A. A. Vaneyev.

wrote to him only after I had received the permission. The day and time when he comes does not matter. Obviously I cannot guarantee not to be absent if, for instance, I am up for interrogation, but I think the sooner he comes the more chance there will be of avoiding such a happening. I am not writing to Mr. Dobkovich (dentist, Vazhinsky's assistant): He lives next door to my former flat—(Gorokhovaya 59) and perhaps you will call and explain the position to him.

With regard to my books, I have already sent a short list of those I should like to receive. I am very grateful for the books by Golovin and Schippel received yesterday.[1] From my own books I must add *dictionaries* to the list. I am now translating from the German and would ask you to send me Pavlovsky's dictionary.

Some underclothes have been sent to me evidently belonging to someone else. They are not mine and ought to be returned; when you come, please ask for them and I will hand them over to you.

I am quite well,

V. Ulianov

P.S. I am very glad to hear that Mother and Mark have recovered.

14. (16 R). TO A. I. ELIZAROVA

Petersburg. The house of preliminary detention
16th/28th January, 1896

Yesterday I received your letter of the 14th/26th and I hasten to answer it, although I have little hope of your receiving my reply before Thursday.

I have already written to you about returning the other person's underclothing. I have gathered it together and you must ask for it when you come, or else tell whoever comes here to ask for it in my name. I am not returning all of it,

---

[1] K. Golovin: "The Peasant Without Progress, or Progress Without the Peasant." M. Schippel: "Technical Progress in Modern Industry" or "The Circulation of Money and Its Social Significance."

because some of it is in the wash (perhaps you will ask somebody to collect the rest of it later on). For the time being I
am taking the liberty of keeping the travelling rug which is
very useful here.

Next, I have been making enquiries about books: a small
box may be left in the Depot here. Some clothes may also be
put in it: an overcoat, a pair of trousers and a hat. The waistcoat, jacket and shawl which were brought here can be taken
back. Of course it is no use having all my books brought here.
In the list which you sent me there are some books which are
not mine: for instance "Factory Industry" and "Kobelyatsky"
["A reference book for factory inspectors and manufacturers,"
S.P.B. 1895] belong to Alexandra Kirillovna and I borrowed
some other book from her. Also the "Sborniki of the Saratov
Zemstvo" and the "Zemsko Statistical Sborniki of the Province
of Voronezh" were lent, I believe, for a short time by some
statistician. Perhaps you will find out if I may keep them for
a time: it is no use bringing them here now. Also, I do not think
Pogozhev ["Factory Life in Germany and Russia," M. 1882]
or the "Collected Edition of Compulsory Decrees for St.
Petersburg" are mine either (aren't they library books?). The
codes of law and law text books are obviously not necessary
here. I would ask you to bring Ricardo ["On the Principles
of Political Economy and Taxation," 1895], Beltov ["On the
Question of the Development of the Monistic View on History," S.P.B. 1895], N.—on ["Outlines of Our Post Reform
Social Economy," S.P.B. 1893], Ingram ["History of Political
Economy," 1891], Foville ["La France Economique, Statis-
tique raisonnée et comparative," 1887-89], Zemstvo official
publications (of the Tver, Nizhegorod, Saratov Provinces). Tie
them into one bundle, count them; it is no use making a list: I
think the bundle could be left in the Depot. In this way the
question of books would be settled and there would be no need
to bother any more. I shall be able to take books from the Depot
(after inspection).

I am so afraid I am causing you too much trouble. Please
do not worry too much about it, especially about sending the

books on the list; there will be time for this later, for I have enough books for the present.

Your,

V. Ulianov

P.S. About linen: I would ask you to add some pillow cases and towels. I am re-reading Shelgunov with interest and I am studying Tugan-Baranovsky ["Industrial Crises in Contemporary England, their Causes and Influence on National Life," S.P.B. 1894]. His research is solid but his plan is vague (for instance, at the end) and I confess I don't understand him. I shall have to get the second volume of "Capital."

1897

15. (17 R). TO HIS MOTHER

Ob' station, 2nd/14th March, 1897

I am writing to you, darling Mother, once more while I am on my way. We have a long wait here.

There is nothing to do, so I have decided to write you a letter from my journey—my third. There are still two more days to travel. I have just crossed the River Ob' on horseback and I have taken a ticket for Krasnoyarsk. As the traffic is only "temporary" on this line, payment was according to the old tariff and I had to pay ten roubles only for the ticket and five for my luggage covering some 700 versts! ! And the speed of the trains here is absolutely impossible. It will take two days to cover these 700 versts. Beyond Krasnoyarsk the train only goes as far as Kansk, which is 220 versts farther, but it is about 1000 versts to Irkutsk. This means we shall have to travel there by horses, *if we must go there.*[1]

To cover these 220 versts will take another day: the farther we go, the slower the trains.

We had to cross the River Ob' on horseback, because the

---

[1] Lenin was permitted to travel to exile in Siberia at his own expense. He did not travel to Irkutsk, but remained in Krasnoyarsk, awaiting further orders.

bridge is not yet finished, although its framework is erected. The ride was not so bad but I managed it without a warm (or rather the warmest) suit, only because the crossing was short, under an hour. If I have to ride on horseback to my destination (and in all probability I shall have to), then presumably I shall have to get a sheepskin coat, felt boots and perhaps a fur cap (this is what it means to have been spoilt in Russia! ! And on horses!).

In spite of the devilish slowness I am far less exhausted by the journey than I expected; indeed, I am not at all tired, which seems strange, for a three days' journey between Samara and St. Petersburg used to wear me out. The fact is, that without exception I sleep splendidly through each night. The land through which the Western Siberian Railway runs and which I have just covered (1300 versts from Chelyabinsk to Krivosh-chekovo, three days) is extraordinarily monotonous: bare and desolate steppe. Neither towns nor dwellings, only a very few villages, an occasional wood, but the rest all steppe. Snow and sky—and so for three whole days. Further on they say there will be first the taiga [marshy Siberian forest] and then hills from Achinsk. But the air here is good; it is easy to breathe. The frost is intense; over 20 degrees Réaumur, but it is much easier to bear than in Russia. I should not have thought it was as much as 20 degrees. The Siberians assure me that it is because of the "softness" of the air which makes the frost more bearable: that may be so.

In the train I came across the "Arzt" [V. M. Krutovsky, a revolutionary] whom Anyuta visited in Petersburg. I heard some useful information from him about Krasnoyarsk. According to him I shall definitely be able to stay there for a few days. I am thinking of doing this, so as to find out what I shall have to do next. If I send you a telegram "staying a few days" it will mean I do not know how long I shall have to stay there. So I shall wait there until the doctor [Ya. M. Lyakhovsky] arrives.[1] I shall meet him and if we have to travel as far as

---

[1] Ya. M. Lyakhovsky, arrested at the same time as Lenin, Krzhizhanovsky and others, was exiled to Verkholensk, Siberia, for 3 years. He subsequently dropped revolutionary activity and practised medicine in N. America.

Irkutsk, then we can go there together. According to the same person, there is no need to anticipate any delay in regard to a decision concerning my destination, for it is probably already decided, since necessary measures for this are usually taken in advance.

Well, until the next time I write,

Greetings to all our people,

Your,

V. U.

P.S. Now you can blame me for anything else, but not for not writing to you often! When there is *something* to write about, I write twice as often! Thanks to my conversation with the doctor, I am much clearer (though only approximately clear) about many matters and I therefore feel quite calm: I have left my nerves in Moscow. The reason for nerves was the uncertainty of the position and nothing else. But now that there is less uncertainty, I feel well.

16. (18 R). TO M. I. ULIANOVA

Siberia, Krasnoyarsk, 10th/22nd March, 1897

The doctor has given me your letter and I am glad to have news from home. I have received the bag which Mother sent, it will be very useful. I shall probably take advantage of your offer to take notes for me from books in the Rumyantsev Library.[1] Yesterday I went to the local and famous library belonging to Udin[2] who welcomed me and showed me his book treasures. He gave me permission to study in the library and I think I shall be able to manage this (there are two obstacles: first, his library is outside the town, but the distance is not great, only two versts and it is a pleasant walk; secondly, the library is not completely arranged, so it may be a nuisance to Udin if I ask for books too often). We must see how it

---

[1] These notes were necessary for Lenin's work "The Development of Capitalism in Russia."

[2] Udin was a well-known Krasnoyarsk merchant and bibliophile. His extensive library was sold to America in 1907 and is the Slavonic section of the Washington Library of Congress. Krutovsky had given Lenin a letter of introduction to Udin.

works out in practice. I think the second obstacle will be removed. I did not get a complete idea of what is in the library, but in any case it is a remarkable collection of books. For instance, there are complete sets of periodicals (the principal ones) dating from the end of the 18th century up to the present day and I hope I shall be able to use them for the references necessary for my work.

I see from the newspapers that in the Spring express trains are to start running here—eight days from Paris to Krasnoyarsk, which will mean six days from Moscow. It will then be much easier to correspond.

Your,

V. U.

17. (19 R). TO HIS MOTHER

Krasnoyarsk, 15th/27th March, 1897

I have been waiting all this time, darling Mother, for a letter from you, but so far in vain. Enquiries at the post office yield nothing and I am beginning to think you have not written to me because you are expecting a telegram which I could not send you as soon as I arrived. In view of the great length of time it takes for letters to pass between us, you should write without waiting for an address. If I am sent away from here, then I shall leave word at the post office to forward letters to my new address. So do write oftener to the last address which you have—for I am depressed without letters from home. I have received only one note through the doctor and that was from Manyasha.

Today I saw the doctor off; he has gone to Irkutsk. He was not allowed to stay here any longer, i.e. the local authorities would not allow it. So far they have not disturbed me, but then I do not think they can, because I have sent a petition to the Governor-General and I am now waiting for a reply. However, it is not absolutely impossible that I too will have to make the same journey. The people here reckon that from today the season of bad roads will begin because of the floods and travel by post horses will then be dearer and more difficult. The weather is perfect, it is real Spring. I spend my time in two ways: first, I visit Udin's library and secondly, I am getting to know the town of Krasnoyarsk and its inhabitants who are for the most part prisoners. I go each day to the library, and as it is two versts out of town I have to walk about five versts, that is about an hour's walk. I am very pleased with this walk and enjoy it, although it often makes me drowsy. It turns out that there are fewer books in the library on my subject than might have been expected, judging from its size, but there are some which are useful to me and I am glad I can spend time here not entirely uselessly. I also visit the Town Library where one can look through periodicals and newspapers; they get here after eleven days and I am not yet used to such late "news." If I have to live a few hundred versts (by horse) from here, then the post will take even longer and it will be still more essential to write without waiting for a reply; for if one were to wait for an answer, then it would take over a month!

I am terribly sorry that nothing is known about the party.[1] I have given up waiting for a telegram from Anyuta, having decided that she cannot find out anything or that there has been a hitch. They say here that the halting places for transported convicts have been changed, which means the party will arrive by train and if that is so, then I cannot understand why it is being detained in Moscow. Can you manage to hand over any books, food, letters? If these enquiries are not too late, then I shall be very glad if Anyuta will answer them.

16th/28th March

I was too late to post the letter yesterday. The train from here leaves for Russia late at night and the station is far away. I kiss you and send greetings to all our people. Tomorrow

---

[1] The group of exiles who travelled at the Government's expense and which included Lenin's close comrades of the Petersburg Union of Struggle: G. M. Krzhizhanovsky, Y. O. Tsederbaum (Martov), A. A. Vaneyev and V. V. Starkov. The delay was due to transport difficulties. The group arrived by train at Krasnoyarsk on the 4th/16th April, 1897.

I may return to Anyuta the books which were borrowed for a short period.

Your,

V. U.

P.S. Did my letter with the address reach you? In case not, I repeat it: Bolshekachenskaya Ulitsa, The House of Claudia Popova. You can also write Poste Restante to the Post Office, where I enquire. When I leave here, they will forward my letters.

18. (21 R). TO HIS MOTHER

Krasnoyarsk, 5th/17th April, 1897

There was good news today, darling Mother, and I hasten to send it to you. First, I received a telegram from the doctor at Irkutsk: "Have heard your destination Minusinsk"; secondly, A. M.[1] has at last heard the Governor-General's decision; Gleb [G. M. Krzhizhanovsky] and Basil [V. V. Starkov] are also exiled to the Minusinsk District. E. E. [Elvira Rosenberg] arrives tomorrow and will work for their release and also for them to be allowed to travel at their own expense. It looks as though it will be possible to succeed in this (judging from available precedents).[2]

I am very pleased with my destination (if the rumour turns out to be true—and I do not think it is false), for Minusinsk and its surrounding district are the best, both because of the excellent climate and the cheapness of life. The distance from Krasnoyarsk is not very great. There is a post two or three times a week, so that instead of the present twenty-two or twenty-three days, it will probably take some thirty to thirty-five days and not more to receive the reply to a letter. I do not think I shall be able to set out before the steamers begin to

---

[1] A. M. Rosenberg, G. M. Krzhizhanovsky's sister who followed her fiancé, V. V. Starkov, into exile. Worked as a nurse in Krasnoyarsk.

[2] Krzhizhanovsky, Starkov, Martov and Vaneyev were kept in the Krasnoyarsk prison till 23 Apr./5 May, 1897. Starkov and Krzhizhanovsky were then exiled to Tesinskoye in the Minusinsk district, and both were allowed to travel with Lenin at their own expense by steamer to Minusinsk on 30 April/12 May.

run, because the season of bad roads is at its height and the whole party intended for Irkutsk is being detained here until May. But when navigation begins I shall be able to reach Minusinsk by steamer.

I am very sorry that they did not try to get permission for Anatole Alexandrovich [Vaneyev] to be sent to the Minusinsk district. It would have been most beneficial for him to have come after his pleurisy. We have sent a telegram to St. Petersburg telling them to make enquiries about it: in view of the delay of the whole party, there is plenty of time and it is to be hoped they will manage to get permission for him if they set about it energetically.

Letters for me should be sent to the old address: if I go away from here, then I shall leave my new address and letters can be forwarded to me. My case of books can be sent to me at once, I think, without waiting for the new address: whatever happens you cannot send them to Minusinsk (there is no goods office there) and it will take a long time by rail. So send it here, say to A. M.'s address, or better, send it as goods to be delivered to the one who presents the receipt which you will send by registered post to A. M. From here the goods can then be forwarded by steamer in the Spring.

They say that Gleb and Basil look very ill; pale, yellow and terribly exhausted. Let us hope they will recover when they come out.

I am quite well and I live comfortably; the weather is marvellous. I am thinking of writing a letter to Manyasha with "literary" contents, only I do not know whether I can summon enough energy to do so. I have seen the "Novoye Slovo" [1] and I read it with real pleasure.

Greetings to all our people,

Your,

V. U.

---

[1] "Novoye Slovo" ["The New Word"], a journal of the Right Narodniks from 1894-97; from April 1897 it became the journal of the "Legal Marxists." Banned in December 1897. Lenin, Martov, Struve, Zasulich, Tugan-Baranovsky, Bulgakov and Gorky were all contributors.

19. (22 R). TO HIS MOTHER AND A. I. ELIZAROVA

Krasnoyarsk, 17th/29th April, 1897

Darling Mother, I received three of your letters yesterday. Today I have collected some more detailed information about the villages to which we shall be exiled (officially I have not yet been informed). I am being sent to the village of Shushenskoye (I think in my former letters I spelt it wrongly—Shush*in*skoye). It is a large village with more than 1500 inhabitants and has a volost administration office and a resident rural assessor, (a rank corresponding to our commissary of rural police, but with wider powers), a school etc. It lies on the right bank of the Yenisei, 56 versts South of Minusinsk. As there is a volost administration office, the post will be fairly regular: I hear there is one twice a week. To get there I shall have to travel by steamer to Minusinsk (steamers do not go any higher up the river) and then by horse. Today the ice on the river has begun to move, so that in about seven or ten days' time the steamers will run again and I am thinking of travelling either at the end of April or the beginning of May, but you can, or rather should, write to my present address, because when I leave I shall tell them to forward my letters. I cannot possibly fix the exact day when I shall leave. Gleb and Basil are exiled to the village Tesinskoye, also with a volost administration office etc. It is thirty-seven versts North of Minusinsk on the River Tuba (a right tributary of the River Yenisei). A telegram has been sent today about them to the Police Department with a petition to allow them to travel at their own expense. I hope they will be allowed this at the request of their mother [E. E. Rosenberg] who is always ill here, and then we can all travel together to Minusinsk. Consequently I shall spend the Summer in "Siberian Italy," as the South of the Minusinsk district is called here. I cannot yet judge of the accuracy of its name, but they say that the Krasnoyarsk district is not as good. But the country round the town here and along the River Yenisei reminds me slightly of Zhiguli or views of Switzerland. The other day I took several walks (it was quite warm and the roads were dry) and I was very pleased with them and would

have been even more pleased had it not been for remembering
our people at Turuhansk [Martov, Vaneyev] and our prisoners
at Minusinsk. [Starkov, Krzhizhanovsky and Lepeshinsky.]

I live well here, am comfortably settled in my flat, especially
as I live en pension. For occupation I have some books on
statistics (I think I told you about this), but I do little studying,
I idle about more.

Thank Manyasha for her letter. I have given her so much
work, that I am afraid to bore her with figures. My books must
be sent to Krasnoyarsk to be given to the person who presents
the receipt (as goods or through the transport office whichever
is best) and I will ask my friends to send them to Minusinsk
where I shall have to find more friends—there is no other
way.

Why has Mitya thought of going to where the plague is? [1]
If he has such a passion for trains and medicine, then I would
suggest he should take a job in some emigrant centre in Eastern
Siberia, for instance. By the way, I have heard that an emigrant
centre is being opened in "my" village Shushenskoye, Minusinsk
District, Yenisei Province. . . . He would be very welcome.
We could hunt together, if only Siberia succeeds in turning me
into a hunter and if he does not find work (and hunting) in
places not so far away. Aha! If in a little over three weeks I
can become such a Siberian that I invite you to come from
Russia, what will happen in three years' time? But joking apart,
I was very surprised to hear of his plans concerning "the
plague." I hope there will be neither a plague, nor that he will
have to go to where the plague is.

Your,

V. U.

To Anyuta.

About books: how to send them—see above. What to send?
If I receive 150 roubles [2] (perhaps in three instalments—a

---

[1] Mitya: Dymitry, Lenin's brother, a Moscow University medical student.
[2] Payment for Lenin's article "Towards the Characterisation of Economic Romanticism," the first part of which appeared in the April, No. 7 of "Novoye Slovo."

spoonful each hour, that is each month?) then you can allot some for books. Buy the three last issues of "Industries of the Vladimir Province" for me (3.75 roubles). "The Influence of Harvests etc" by Chuprov and Posnikov (5.00 roubles); "A Handbook of Factories and Works," 1890 (St. Petersburg 1894, 5.00 roubles). Then I will write again to you according to the amount of payment which it would be useless to send in one lump sum (to "Schwester" [A. M. Rosenberg] of course). Please write to "the Writer" [P. B. Struve] and say I should be glad if instead of sending me all the money he would send me some books, both Russian and foreign, for review and otherwise. He knows which subjects interest me and he could send books to you. I would also be glad to undertake all sorts of translation work, which I could distribute among our exiles at Minusinsk and Turuhansk (not very urgent translations). I would be responsible for the supervision of the translation and their satisfactory execution. This is of course another matter, but I should like to arrange for payment to me in books, *if only it would not be too much of a burden to "the Writer"* (tell him this literally). I rely entirely on his choice; the payment in books interests me because it is the only way of immediately receiving important new books and because the timeliness of articles and reviews is most important in periodical work. If, however, I first find out about them and then write for them, there will be a minimum delay, say five weeks.

I think I shall have to subscribe to some periodicals and newspapers: there will probably be nothing in Shushenskoye. According to my finances I may subscribe to "Russkiye Vedomosti,"[1] "Russkoye Bogatstvo,"[2] "Vestnik Finansov"[3] (without any supplements), "Arkhiv fur Soziale Gesetzgebung und Statistik."[4]

[1] A Moscow academic Liberal paper founded in 1863. From 1905 the organ of the Right wing of the Cadets.

[2] A St. Petersburg monthly founded in 1876. From 1892 it expressed Narodnik views. From 1906 title altered to "Sovremennye Zapiski." In 1918 appeared again under its original title.

[3] A weekly official organ of the Ministry of Finance.

[4] This periodical gave much space to Labour Legislation and the Labour movement. The leading critics of Marxism: Sombart, Struve, Bulgakov and others contributed to it.

This is quite a lot and only in case there is a large payment, but if there is only a small payment I must, I suppose, limit myself to "Russkiye Vedomosti," but you will see, especially when I let you know from Shushenskoye what my budget is (I believe you are cross with "the Writer," but when you write to him on my behalf do not show him this—I have absolutely no rancour against him for the loss of my "literature." After all, he had nothing to do with it).

My greetings to the Bulochkins.[1] Why don't you write more details about them? What has happened to them? [i.e. their sentence]. Isn't there one? That would be splendid. If you have an opportunity, give my greetings to other acquaintances, to the bookseller [A. N. Potresov] and others.

V. U.

P.S. I hope you will let me know in advance when you have decided to go to the West, so that I can have time to write to you and ask you to do several things for me.

20. (24 R). TO HIS MOTHER

[*Shushenskoye*], *18th/30th May*, *1897*

Darling Mother,

I received two of your letters this week (the 20th April/2nd May and the 24th April/6th May) and I answer the latter by the first post which leaves tonight. Write to me and tell me on which day you receive this. Your letters took so long to reach me because they were forwarded from Krasnoyarsk and a "mass" of time was wasted in the forwarding. About my finances:—I do not remember your having asked me twice about this, as you say in your letter of April 24th/May 6th; perhaps I have forgotten. While my finances were good, I did not write about them. But before I left Krasnoyarsk (about the 26th or 28th) I sent a *registered* letter with a request for money to be sent. Probably the money is coming here from Kras-

---

[1] Bulochka was Zina Krzhizhanovsky's nickname. By Bulochkins Lenin evidently means a group of friends arrested on Aug. 9th, 1896: Krzhizhanovsky's sisters, Zina and Sophia, and N. K. Krupskaya in particular.

noyarsk. I also wrote to you from here that I would have enough money for another two weeks.

As for your coming here just for the purpose of begging a transfer for me, it is definitely not worth while; first I can probably get permission for a transfer if I set about it, and secondly, I doubt whether Tesinskoye is better than Shushenskoye. According to information obtained beforehand, Tesin- skoye is much worse than Shushenskoye as regards its locality, hunting etc; and, thirdly, the journey here is not such a simple matter. I have written about this before and today I am writing in greater detail to Manyasha who is blaming me (I am joking) for "terrible inhospitality." So far I have not had a letter from Tesinskoye and not knowing anything about it, I shall of course do nothing; they may ask to be transferred to another place, if it is as bad as the accounts we have had.

Shu-shu-shu is not a bad village. True, it lies in a fairly bare place, but there is a wood not far away (about one and a half to two versts) although much of it has been cut down. There is no way of getting to the Yenisei, but the River Shush flows close by the village and there is also a fairly large tributary of the Yenisei not far away (one to one and a half versts) and there I shall be able to bathe. On the horizon lie the Sayan hills or their offshoots. Some of them are all white and the snow on them hardly ever melts, so that there is even something artistic about them and it was not in vain that I composed a poem in Krasnoyarsk: "In Shusha, at the foot of Sayan . . ." Unfortunately I have not composed any more than the first line!

I am surprised you do not say a word about sending me the rest of the books. It is a pity if they have not yet been dispatched (I wrote long ago about this from Krasnoyarsk). The steamers are now able to reach Minusa (the water is rapidly rising!) and it would be very easy to send them. Later it will be difficult again, for the Yenisei forms many shallows and high water does not last long. However, perhaps the books have been sent?

As for my complaints that you write seldom to me—that is ancient history and is explained by the amazing (because we are unaccustomed to it) slowness of receiving an answer to a letter. I seem to have said this a month or six weeks ago, therefore it refers to those letters which you wrote at the end of March! But I am now receiving letters oftener than before and I do not think any are going astray, because I should know of their loss when I received the next batch. Evidently not a single one has gone astray, with the exception of the letter sent by Anyuta to the railway station. Now that I am in this village, more attention should be paid to correspondence and it would be better if letters were to come oftener from "Russia."

You write that "Anya says she has already read the editor's reply," but I do not understand: do you mean she has read the reply, or has the editor had time to read it? Does Anya know any details about the dispute with the editor's office concerning the attack on it by the gold digger and company? [P. Maslov and the editorial board of the Samara "Vestnik"]. Has she heard "the other side," that is from someone in the editor's office? I shall await a letter from her. Have you subscribed to a newspaper for me? I sit here without any newspapers; they are also wanted in Minusa, for there is no reading room there.

Greetings to Mark. He does not send any news about himself. Tell him and Mitya that shooting is apparently not so bad here. I rode out twelve versts yesterday and shot duck and snipe. There is plenty of game, but without a dog and I being such a bad shot, shooting is a difficult sport. There are even some wild goats and on the hills and in the taiga (about 30 to 40 versts away, where the local peasants go shooting) there is squirrel, sable, bear and deer. I am sorry I did not bring a mackintosh cape, for it is essential to have one here. Could you send me one in a small parcel? I do not know when I shall go to town and anyway would I find anything suitable in such a town-village as Minusinsk? I may also ask Mark (if I have the money) to buy me a good revolver—meanwhile, however, I do not foresee any real need for one.

Your,

V. U.

P.S. What news is there of Columbus [I. Kh. Lalayants]? [1]
I heard he was married and ill. Do you know anything about
him? Anatole [Vaneyev] and Julius [Martov] have again been
put into prison. They did not want to leave before the steamers
were running and so the Governor-General gave orders for
them to wait in prison. The steamer from Krasnoyarsk was to
leave for Yeniseisk round about May 20th.

21. (28 R). TO HIS MOTHER AND A. I. ELIZAROVA

[Shushenskoye], 8th/20th June, 1897

Darling Mother, I received your and Manyasha's letter from
Warsaw on the 6th, that is the day before yesterday. Only then
I learnt that you had at last set aside all your doubts and had
started on your journey. It is splendid and I send you my
good wishes for a comfortable and more restful Summer. I do
not know why you are afraid of feeling homesick. Is it because
of a trip in the Summer? Surely not. I will write just as often
as before and the extra three or four days' delay in the post
caused by the distance from Moscow, will not make much
difference.

You will have received by now all my earlier letters from
Shusha and know that my life here is not at all bad. It is exactly
a month today since I came and I can repeat that I am completely satisfied both with my food and rooms; as for the mineral water about which you ask, I have forgotten about it and
I hope I shall soon forget even its name. At present I am
expecting visitors: a friend from Minusa [S. G. Raichin] wants
to come and see me and after that Gleb is coming for some
hunting and shooting. So I shall not be bored. Julius left
Yeniseisk for Turuhansk on May 27th/June 8th. But Anatole
has remained; the doctor who had to certify him by order of
the Governor-General found him to be weak. Probably he will
be sent to the Minusinsk district. Possibly to me. The doctor
[Ya. M. Lyakhovsky] has also not been sent to Yakutka. He is
being exiled to Kirensk.

---

[1] I. Kh. Lalayants, an active revolutionary.

M. A. ULIANOVA, LENIN'S MOTHER, 1902

Thank Manyasha for her postscript.
I kiss you and her.

Your,

V. U.

For Anyuta:—

I believe I have already written to you about newspapers and periodicals. I am sorry I have not written to Mark. There may be great delay because of this.

Send me more "literary manifestations"—all sorts, even catalogues and prospectuses. You should write to many different places to collect as many as possible. I should much like to obtain the classics of political economy and philosophy. It would be as well to find out the cheapest editions (people's editions etc) and their price. You will probably not find many of these, except in secondhand bookshops. Well, I shall wait to hear how you have arranged matters for yourselves and then there will be time for me to write to you.

Gleb sends you his greetings. They are all living in Tes and A. M. also (she has given up her work). They have had a crowd of visitors lately, so it was jolly. They write that they are fairly comfortably settled.

I am still without any newspapers. I have also not received the May number of "Novoye Slovo." Send me your newspaper after you have read it and any odd numbers which you happen to buy. At least I can look through them.

Well, goodbye for the present.
Do write more.

Your,

V. U.

22. (30 R). TO HIS MOTHER AND M. I. ULIANOVA

[Shushenskoye], 19th/31st July, 1897

Yesterday, darling Mother, I received your and Manyasha's letters of the 17th/29th June: thank you for them.

With the extraordinary length of time our letters take, the answers arrive so long afterwards that it becomes superfluous to answer many points. For instance, you are still worried in your last letter about the money and the bundle of books—but by now you have received my letter which explains all this: I received the money long ago. I did not receive any for a long time, because I did not need any and there was no need to take any from A. M. I have not yet had the bundle of books: I do not know if it has arrived in Krasnoyarsk (it was expected there at the end of June) and it will be sent from there when an opportunity occurs, which I expect will be soon. It would probably cost a fair amount to send by post from there, for the post is not taken by steamer, but by rail to Achinsk and from there by horse to Minusa.

In the same way you of course know by now not only about the offer made to Mark to move to St. Petersburg, but also his decision: he wrote to me that he was waiting for your answer from abroad.

I have received your letter with an account of the Kokushkino affair [1] and have already answered it. Yesterday I also received Mitya's first letter where he describes his journey to Kazan.

From the point of view of hygiene I have probably fixed myself up here hardly any worse than in Spiez [Switzerland]: I bathe in the Yenisei (sometimes twice a day). I walk and hunt. I protect myself by a net from mosquitoes. There are swarms of them here. But that is trifling, in comparison with the North! True, there are no suitable places for walks, but sometimes when I go shooting I happen to wander far away into places which are not so bad.

I received news from Tes that there is to be a wedding— Basil [Starkov] and A. M. [Rosenberg]. I am invited to be best man. But it will not be yet awhile, of course. [2]

I am terribly sorry for Peter Kuzmich [Gutsul]! [3] I learnt about him only from your letter!

---

[1] Kokushkino, an estate belonging to Lenin's maternal grandfather [Alexander Dmitrievich Blank]. Lenin spent his first exile there in 1887-88. Dymitry, Lenin's brother, was sent to sell it up after the death of their aunt. Lenin had written to his mother on the 15/27 June that it would be a good thing to be rid of the business, only it would be a pity if his mother inherited not only the estate, but the debts too!

[2] The wedding took place on the 11/30 August, 1897, and Lenin was allowed to be present.

[3] P. K. Gutsul (1872-1905), an active revolutionary who was arrested in 1895,

I kiss you and ask you not to worry about me.

Your V. U.

I had a letter from the doctor [Lyakhovsky] from Verholensk (Irkutsk Province), where he has been exiled. N. E. Fedoseyev [1] is also there.

23. (3 p[1]). TO P. B. AXELROD IN ZÜRICH

[Shushenskoye], 16th August, [1897]

My dear Pavel Borisovich,

I am very, very glad that after all I have managed to receive a letter from you (I received it yesterday, i.e. 15th August) with news of you and of G. V. [Plekhanov]. His and your remarks about my literary attempts (for the workers) [2] have encouraged me considerably. I should not like anything better; I have never dreamt of anything so much as of the possibility of writing for workers. But how is it to be done from here? It is very, very difficult, but, in my opinion, not impossible. How is V. Iv's [Zasulich] health?

I know only one way—the way in which I am writing this letter.[3] The question is whether a copyist could be found to carry out this difficult task. Evidently you think this impossible and the method altogether unsuitable. But I do not know any other. . . . It is a great pity, still I do not lose heart: if it does not succeed now—it may succeed later. Meanwhile, it would be satisfactory, if you would write occasionally by the method which you use with your "old friend" [A. I. Elizarova]. Then we would not interrupt our relations, and that is the main thing.

Enough has of course been told you about me, so there is no

---

at the same time as Lenin, but he went mad in prison. He was handed over to parental care. He was put in a mental home where he died of consumption.

[1] N. E. Fedoseyev (1871-98) a leading and energetic early Marxist in Russia. Organised student circles. Lenin belonged to one of them when he was in Kazan.

[2] Lenin's pamphlet, "An Explanation of the Law on Fines."

[3] Lenin's letters to Axelrod were usually sent bound inside the spine of a book. After passing through the hands of two or three people, they would reach A. I. Elizarova, Lenin's sister, in Berlin, who then copied them and forwarded them to Axelrod.

need for me to add anything. I am living here in solitude. I am quite well and am working a little, both for the periodical ["Novoye Slovo"] and at my big work ["The Development of Capitalism in Russia"].

I send warm greetings. Sincere greetings to V. Iv. [Zasulich] and G. V. [Plekhanov]. I have not seen Raichin [1] for over a month. I hope to go soon to Minusinsk to see him.

Your
V. U.

24. (33 R). TO HIS MOTHER

[Tes. Minusinsk District.] 30th Sept./12th Oct., 1897

As promised, I am writing to you, darling Mother, from Tes. I arrived here last night. The journey took a fairly long time, because there were three of us travelling (Basil, I and a boy I took with me), also a horse to carry our things; and the horse moreover was very lazy.

The Tes people [Starkov, Krzhizhanovsky and his mother, E. E. Rosenberg] are very comfortably settled. They live in a splendid flat in a large two-storeyed house (in Shusha there isn't even such a house), the best in the village. They have the entire top floor, four large rooms with a kitchen, and a hall into the bargain. The rooms are large, light, high, clean, the furniture is good; in fact, it is a beautiful flat for six roubles a month. Gleb has some work of sorts, thanks to which they are able to manage somehow, and the financial crisis is over—but at one time things were rather difficult for them. A. M. has taken a place as district nurse in Sagai village, which is in the same district as Tes, but a good many versts away. She will probably not work there for long, for her health will certainly not allow her to do such work: she is expected back within a month. Gleb does not look well, he is constantly ailing and nervous. Basil is

---

[1] Raichin, a worker type-setter in charge of the "Liberation of Labour Group" printing press in Geneva. In 1892 he was sent by the group to Russia with illegal literature and to form links with Social Democrat groups in Russia. Arrested. Sentenced to 2 years' prison and 10 years' exile in E. Siberia. At the time of this letter Raichin was in Minusinsk, but he managed to escape in the Spring of 1898.

flourishing. On the whole E. E. feels well, surrounded by her family and busy with the household, although in the Summer it was rather hard for her, and even now life is not too easy: she has to do all the work herself. There are no servants to be found here, and in the Summer it is quite impossible to find anyone. Now a woman comes to help them.

Today we all went out shooting together. The weather is glorious and we are spending our time delightfully. I have a permit for five days and I shall leave here on Friday or Saturday straight for Shusha. Shusha is seventy versts away from here.

Some time ago I received a letter (of the 12/24 Sept.) from Mark. I will wait for news about how he completed his "liquidational journey" to Kazan. By the way, he wrote to me about a dog. I took a pup to Shusha and I hope to have a sporting dog next year. To send one from Russia would be terribly expensive. He also asks me about my book ["The Development of Capitalism in Russia"]: it is still at freezing point. But when I return to Shusha, I hope to work at it more industriously and then I shall write to him in greater detail.

I kiss you and Manyasha.

Your V. U.

People here also think I have grown fat during the Summer. I am sunburnt and look quite a Siberian. See what shooting and village life can do! All Petersburg illnesses vanish at once!

All our people at Tes obviously send lots of greetings.

25. (34 R). TO HIS MOTHER

[*Shushenskoye*], *12th/24th October, 1897*

Darling Mother, on the 7th/19th I received your letter and Mitya's letter of the 20th Sept./2nd Oct. Last time I was in a great hurry and therefore, I seem to remember, I did not write much. I shall have to catch up today.

I thank Mitya for his letter. I am answering his questions:

I am receiving "Questions of Philosophy and Psychology" [1] for the year 1897, and have also received one number for 1896. I shall return it when I have read it (meanwhile I have given it to them in Tes).

I still go in for shooting. The sport is much less successful now (shooting rabbits, grouse and partridge is a new sport for me and I must therefore get used to it) but it is no less pleasant. As soon as it is a fine Autumn day (and they are frequent this year) I take my gun and set off to prowl about the woods and fields. Prominsky [2] and I generally go together; I take the landlord's dog, which I have trained to come with me and which has certain (it is true, not great) sporting instincts. I have got a dog of my own—I have taken a pup from one of my local friends, and I hope to train it by next Summer: only I do not know if it will turn out to be a good dog and whether it will have any scent. I do not know how to discover this and it is not possible to form a definite opinion from the origin of my "Pegasus." The kind of wadded jacket we all bought in St. Petersburg is most useful for shooting, and I cannot cease praising it. Altogether, I must say, in regard to Winter clothing and such like (about which you ask me), I have more than enough. When I was in Minusinsk, I bought many things for the Winter, but there are still one or two other things I must buy. It is not at all easy to buy things in Minusinsk: the choice is very poor, the shops are of the village type (all sorts; the goods arrive periodically and I happened to be there just when the old goods were sold out and the new had not arrived), so that when you are used to town shops, it is rather difficult to find what you want. Still, it is high time one threw over town habits: they are quite out of place here and one should get used to the local ones. I think I am quite used to them, but when shopping, I still argue in the Petersburg manner: go into a shop, so to speak, and buy . . .

I will tell you about my trip in greater detail. I spent only

---

[1] A quarterly published by the Moscow Psychological Society (1889-1918). V. Klyuchevsky, P. Struve, L. Tolstoy were among the contributors.

[2] I. L. Prominsky (1859-1923), a Polish worker exiled to E. Siberia in 1895 for participating in the Lodz organisation of the Social Democrats of Poland.

two days in Minusinsk; the whole time went in running about
the shops, in looking into Basil's affair (I helped him to write
a complaint about the sentence passed by the justice of peace,
and this judge himself agreed that his sentence was too severe.
We shall see what the second instance will decide) and in visiting friends. There is a fair number of political exiles in Minusinsk: A. V. Tyrkov (for the affair of 1st March, 1881); N. S.
Tyutchev and E. K. Yakovlev (Narodopravtsy), S. I. Mel-
nikov (a Narodovolets), Blazhievsky (a Polish worker), S. Gr.
Raichin (my nearest friend, also a political comrade), F. Ya.
Kon (a Polish intellectual; has served a term of hard labour),
Stoyanovsky (for the Ginsberg affair; has served a term of hard
labour). I have seen nearly all of them. I think I shall manage
to visit them once again in the Winter. Such temporary visits
are probably even better than to live in Minusinsk, which does
not attract me at all. There is one advantage in it—the post (in
Achinsk this is a still greater advantage and of course I would
prefer Achinsk). But this is only by the way, for I am quite
accustomed to Shusha and to spending the Winter here; I am
not trying to get a transfer and I do not advise you to try
either.

I went to Tes together with Basil. I spent the time very
pleasantly there and was extremely pleased to see friends and
to live in a crowd after my Shushensk solitude. But I think the
crowd is probably worse off than I, not in respect of accommodation but in regard to contentment.

Gleb's health is bad, he is often melancholy; Basil I found
was also not at all "flourishing," although he is the most bal-
anced of the Tes group. E. E. looks after the housekeeping and
is very pleased with her life in Tes; she too is ailing. It is not
easy for her to do the housekeeping, for they have no servant;
in Siberian country districts it is very, very difficult to find a
servant, and quite impossible in the Summer. Therefore to live,
as I do, on full board, is quite convenient, but it is very difficult
when one has to do one's own housekeeping.

The Tes crowd live much more "sociably" (so to speak) than
I: they know the district nurse in Tes, then some former women

students live not far away (about 15 versts) and they often see them. I am not giving up hope that their gloomy mood will also pass. Gleb and Basil have work: they could not exist without it, for the Government allowance is only 24 roubles (they will not allow anything for Basil's wife [A. M. Rosenberg] for he married only after coming into exile).

More about the library: from which library did Mitya borrow "Questions of Philosophy and Psychology"? Was it from the Petrovsky one? If so, cannot he send me its (new) catalogue? I believe they issue books without a definite time-limit.

Your V. U.

P.S. I am quite well. I study; and I feel quite all right.

The doctor (from the North) [A. P. Sklyarenko] has asked me to send his greetings to all (I correspond fairly regularly with him and with the Columbus [I. Kh. Lalayants] family).

26. (39 R). TO HIS MOTHER AND M. I. ULIANOVA

[*Shushenskoye*], *27th Dec. 1897/8th Jan. 1898*

Darling Mother, I received the money, both the first and second sums (i.e., sent on 16/28 Nov. and 8/20 Dec.). We also receive the Government allowance regularly, so that money matters are quite normal, and I think for a long time (comparatively) I shall not need any extra additions.

Gleb has been staying with me for the last few days. He was given permission to visit me for ten days. We live here splendidly and do a great deal of walking. Fortunately for the most part the weather is very warm. After one day, when the frost, they say, reached 36° R. (about ten days ago) and after a few days of snowstorm ("weather," the Siberians call it) the days have become very warm, and we go out shooting assiduously, although with not much luck. What sort of shooting can there be in the Winter! But the walks are pleasant. As a result of the Christmas holidays no post left here this week on Wednesday (and there was no delivery on Friday). It is the third time in my life in Shusha that I have missed the post—not so often; thanks to my visitor I hardly noticed it.

I kiss you warmly,

Your V. U.

P.S. I am sending a small article for the periodical. It would be a good thing if you could forward it as quickly as you can: perhaps it would be in time for the January number.[1]

Gleb sends greetings to you all. He asked me to tell Manyasha that he expects he and she will have much to argue about.

Manyasha, do not take so much trouble over Stange:[2] in all probability I made a mistake. How can I remember so many years back? You have found one small article, and thank God for that. I even thought the second article was not in the "Economic Journal"—but in the "Severny Vestnik" for 1891 (at any rate, I recently found a reference to that effect somewhere). In any case you need not go through the "Economic Journal" before 1885.

I am very glad about the preparations for the journey to come to me. It is quite another matter now, and I have no particular reason to start dissuading. By waiting for the steamers to run up the Yenisei, one can get here without great inconvenience. It is quite possible that Nadezhda Konstantinovna [Krupskaya] will also come to me: this question will probably be decided soon, and perhaps will have been decided by the time you read this letter. But if she is permitted to take Shushu-shu as her place of exile instead of the North of Russia, then of course she will not be allowed to put it off until the Spring and she will have to travel at once.

I send you greetings,

V. U.

I remember that Mark once wrote to me offering to buy me a sporting dog in Moscow. I treated the matter very coolly

---

[1] "The Inheritance Which We Renounce," an article for "Novoye Slovo." The periodical was banned and Lenin's article was printed subsequently in "Economic Studies and Articles," in 1899.

[2] A. Stange's article on "How to Help the Locksmiths of the Pavlovsk Region," published in Nos. 7 and 8 of the "Economic Journal," 1899.

then, for I was relying on Pegasus, who has betrayed me so cruelly. Now of course I should be very sympathetic towards such a plan—but it is apparently purely Utopian and hardly worth while. The cost of sending a dog would be incredibly expensive. Gleb suggests having a small pup sent in a basket! We had a good laugh over such a scheme, which of course is not much better than any other. No, Mark has probably just had "a fling" and you can see by this postscript what trifling matters sometimes amuse the inhabitants of Shu-shu-shu and Te-Te-Tes.

1898

27. (40 R). TO HIS MOTHER

[Shushenskoye], 4th/16th January, 1898

Darling Mother, I have received your letter of the 15th/27th December. There was one post less this week (January 1st), so I do not know the result of Anyuta's enquiries.[1] However, they will probably end well, for if the case has already been transferred to Petersburg, it means the matter is not important and there will be no need for any more delay.

Your fears about the fur-lined coat are quite unnecessary. My Winter suit (which each of us brought from Petersburg) and the coat is quite sufficient *even for drives* (and I seldom go for drives). The coat is far too hot to walk in and I wear a padded coat—except on a few cold days (yesterday and the day before yesterday). Altogether, the Winter here is unusually warm. Your worrying about my going out shooting is also unnecessary: there is nothing dangerous in it. However, all shooting will soon cease; probably until the Spring. (I have received the money, both the first and second amounts.)

It is 55 versts from Shusha to Minusinsk, but the road is shorter in the Winter—50 versts. Gleb left me the day before yesterday, having spent 10 (ten) days with me. That was a

---

[1] Lenin is referring to his brother Dymitry, who had been arrested on 7/19 Nov., 1897, in connection with the Moscow "Workers' Union." He sat in prison until 20 Oct./2 Nov., 1898, was expelled from the University and exiled to Tula for about one month, and then lived under police surveillance in Podolsk, Moscow Province, during 1898-99, after which he was allowed to enter Yuriev University, where he completed his studies in 1901.

real holiday in Shu-shu-shu and I did not notice how the ten days passed. Gleb liked Shusha very much, he assures me that it is much better than Tes (and I who talked as I did about Tes! I teased him saying that it is always better where one is not), for there is a wood close by and in the Winter there are excellent walks in it and a beautiful view of the Sayan hills. Gleb raved about the Sayans, especially in a good light on clear days. By the way, he has become very keen on singing, so that my silent rooms became gay as soon as he arrived and are silent again now he has gone. But he has neither much music nor songs. I believe we have lots of such rubbish (left from the days when we too used to "screech"). If no one wants it, it would be nice to send some to him: he would be glad. Basil is a musician (guitar) and would transpose the songs for him. While Gleb was staying with me his health improved somewhat, thanks to the regular régime and the many walks, and when he left he was quite cheered up.

I seem to remember having written to you that Nadezhda Konstantinovna [Krupskaya] is thinking of asking to be sent here (she has been exiled for three years to the Northern Provinces). If this plan is realised it will be a good opportunity to send books, notes, and anything else by her.

I kiss you.

Your V. U.

28. (42 R). TO HIS MOTHER AND A. I. ELIZAROVA

[Shushenskoye], 24th January/5th February, 1898

I have received letters from Manyasha and Anyuta and two books: "Semenov," Volume III ["A Study of Historical Information about Russian Foreign Trade and Industry from the Middle of the XVII Century to 1858."] and the "Yuridichesky Vestnik" ["The Legal Messenger," a monthly]. Many thanks to Manyasha for the latter. I have also received a postcard from Basil [Starkov].

I would ask you to buy two more books for me: Kablukov's "Lectures on the Economy of Farming" and V. V.'s [Vorontsov's] "Outlines of Home Industries" (1.50 roubles). You may find the latter in a secondhand bookshop; the former was recently published for students and Manyasha will probably be able to get it, even if it is not on sale (judging by the absence of announcements in the "Russkiye Vedomosti").

I have nothing new to say about myself. It is much jollier now that the three of us go out shooting together. The weather is just like the Spring: it is even thawing today.

Nadezhda Konstantinovna has had her hopes raised that her three years' exile in the Province of Ufa will be altered to two years in Shusha,[1] and I am expecting her, together with Elizaveta Vasilievna [Krupskaya's mother]. I am already looking for quarters for them—the room next to mine. I am having an amusing competition with a local priest who is also asking the landlord for a room. I protest and insist that they should wait until my "family affairs" are finally settled. I do not know whether I shall succeed in overcoming the competitor. If visitors come in the Summer we shall be able to occupy the entire house (the landlord would then move into the old hut in the yard, and that would be much more convenient than equipping one's own house).

But I am not sure whether N. K.'s case will be settled before the Spring; they say it should be finished by February, but after all many things can be said.

It is annoying that Mitya's case is so protracted: it will be unpleasant for him to lose a year. Still, he will probably be allowed to enter another University or sit for his examinations as an external student.

Your

V. U.

P.S. The enclosed letter is for Columbus [I. Kh. Lalayants].

For Anyuta.

I read in the papers about the publication of your translation of [E. de] Amichis's "School Friends." If you have any available copies, please send them to me. On what conditions

---

[1] N. Krupskaya's term of exile was not reduced. She was allowed to live in Shushenskoye together with Lenin. She arrived on 7/19 May, 1898, and had to remain in exile in Ufa for a year after Lenin had left Siberia.

did you do the translation? Was there a contract with a publisher, and what sort?

My head is full of plans about the publication of my articles as a separate book ["Economic Studies and Articles"]. The other day I received N. Vodovozov's "Studies in Economics" and they gave me the idea. It is very inconvenient to publish the article about handicraft workers as a pamphlet: it would be better to combine the articles on Sismondi ["Towards a Characterisation of Economic Romanticism" (Sismondi and our Russian Sismondists)] and the one on handicraft workers. Then it could be published without any preliminary censoring (for this it is necessary to have ten printed sheets and these would make twelve, namely, about two hundred pages) and that would be much more satisfactory. The title could be "Towards an Evaluation of the Romantic Theories of the Narodnik Movement."

The contents of such a book would be more interesting and varied. Will the censor pass the reprint of an article taken from a banned periodical? That is the principal question in my opinion, but I should think it would be allowed, for the article is of an abstract character and was printed a fairly long time ago, long before the periodical was suppressed. I am also writing to N. K. about this, so that she can ask the Writer's [Struve] advice. I do not feel like waiting until their new plans are realised. Besides, both articles are unsuitable for a periodical, because of their length. The other articles can go into the periodical, for I consider it dangerous to add them to the book (they would not be passed) and they would not be suitable (they are quite different in character).

The article about the handicraft workers is inoffensive, containing an abundance of statistics. As for the financial aspect, this in my opinion is much easier than the question of censorship. Taking the price at, say, 1.50 roubles and only 1,000 copies (with 2,000 copies one could reduce the price to 1.25 roubles) one can reckon 500 roubles for the publication and the same amount to booksellers and the author. Five hundred copies should pay for the edition and probably that number would be sold.

Question: who will take the responsibility of publishing? There is no one in Petersburg on whom we can rely. Perhaps Mark would undertake the arrangements (the buying of the paper, the agreement with the printers) and Manyasha the proof-reading? There will not be any complicated proof-reading for ½ the book is a reprint and the other ½ is printed from manuscript which has been carefully copied out by me. If this plan were to be realised I should immediately send you the alterations for the Sismondi article (it is essential to break it up into paragraphs and to correct important misprints). Then *wire* me: "Send alterations." I reckon that if we are successful we may be in time to publish the book in April, if not earlier. It seems to me that we ought to try by ourselves, without waiting for the "Novoye Slovo" people—"the snail crawls . . ." It is annoying to feel one is writing uselessly and, besides, I need the money. Perhaps they will retort that there is too much difference between the two articles, but in my opinion that does not matter: Vodovozov's articles are also varied in character and, besides, there are plenty of collections of articles published. Also, there is a similarity between them: both are a criticism of Narodnik economics: one is abstract and the other is based on Russian facts.

Please answer quickly about this question: is the plan feasible or no? If "yes," then I must tackle it without losing any time.

N. E. F. [Fedoseyev] does not write to me, does not even answer me, although I have written him two letters. Reproach him for this when you write to him. I heard about the row in Verholensk: some disgusting scandalmonger [I. A. Yukhotsky] who attacked N. E. [Fedoseyev]. No, better not wish me to have comrades among the intellectuals in Shusha! When N. K. [Krupskaya] arrives even that will be like a colony!

Greetings to all our people.   Your V. U.

29. (43 R). TO HIS MOTHER

[Shushenskoye], 7th/19th February, 1898

Yesterday, darling Mother, I received letters from you and from all our people (22-23 Jan./3-4 Feb.); I was very glad to get them, and send my thanks for all the good wishes. Of course I expected that you would write to Nadezhda Konstantinovna to ask her to come and see you on her way; it is to be hoped she will be allowed to do so. Well, so far I know nothing about the transfer to Shusha: she keeps on writing that it will be decided "one of these days," but the matter is still dragging on. However, we have not long to wait for a final decision.

About sending things by N. K.—I think she should be fairly heavily loaded with books, for I do not know if there will be an opportunity in the Summer. Manyasha is thinking of going abroad (and that, of course, is a little more interesting than Shusha and Siberian mosquitoes), while you and Mitya will probably be going to Kokushkino. . . . It is a bad thing that after only two and a half months Mitya should be showing signs of swelling. First of all, is he keeping to a diet in prison? I am sure he is not. But in my opinion it is essential to keep to one there. And secondly, does he do any physical exercises? Also, probably not. They are also essential. At any rate I can say from experience that *each day* I used to do exercises before going to sleep with great pleasure and benefit. They loosened my joints so that I used to get warm even on the coldest days, when my cell was icy cold, and afterwards one sleeps much better. I can recommend this to him, as well as a fairly easy exercise (though a ridiculous one):—fifty prostrations. It is exactly what I used to make myself do—and I was not in the least perturbed that the warder, on peeping through the little window, would wonder in amazement why this man had suddenly grown so pious when he had not once asked to visit the prison church. But he must not do less than fifty prostrations, without stopping, and touch the floor each time without bending the knees—write and tell him this. You know that doctors for the most part only know how to talk about hygiene.

Then with regard to clothes, I have already written to you something about this. You might send me some socks. As for our local tailors, I cannot rely on them. It is very inconvenient to have clothes made in Minusinsk—as one has to go there. There is a tailor here and he makes clothes for everyone (he told me so today), he sews for the old political exiles and even for the priests—(he boasted to me about it). Although it sounds very effective, it would be better to buy a ready-made suit in Moscow, and to give Mitya or Mark the cloth which you had got ready for me. I ask for only one thing particularly —a devil's skin, for I tear my clothes terribly when I go out shooting. If my straw hat is still in existence (after all, it is from Paris! The devil take it!), let her bring it. It is true, Prominsky has begun to make hats here (sometimes they look like felt boots), but his are for the Spring and Autumn, and not for the Summer. And then, there is one more thing—a pair of kid gloves, if they can be bought without knowing my size (I doubt it). I have never worn them, neither in Petersburg, nor in Paris, but I want to try them in Shu-shu-shu—in the Summer, against mosquitoes. You can put a net over your head, but the hands are always attacked. Gleb assures me that the local mosquitoes bite through gloves—but I do not believe it. Of course, one should choose suitable gloves, not for dancing, but for mosquitoes. I also want some paper, *ruled in squares:* I doubt if there is any in Minusinsk, but I do not need very much—about four quires with squares of various sizes, from the smallest to the largest.

Anyuta asks when is the wedding and whom "are we inviting?"! She is in a hurry! Nadezhda Konstantinovna must first arrive, then we must get a permit for the marriage from the authorities—after all we are people wholly without rights. And only then can we start "inviting"!

About "verbalisme" and "phraséologie," it seems to me that they should be translated as verbalism (with an explanation) and phraseology. . . . Although it is not the exact translation, but merely a transcription, what else can we do? "Dilettantism" instead of verbalism is not at all right, rather the reverse. Verbalism, perhaps, is nearer to scholasticism, i.e., to a surplus of (pseudo) learning, than to dilettantism. However, I do not remember in what sense exactly Labriola uses these words [in his "On the Question of the Materialistic View of History"].

LENIN, AFTER HIS ARREST IN DECEMBER, 1895. (*A Police photograph*)

Thank you for Bogdanov ["A Short Course of Economic Science"]. I have already read half. Very interesting and sensible. I am thinking of writing a review of it.[1]

In answer to Manyasha's questions: what kind of a voice has Gleb? . . . Hm. Hm! . . . I believe a baritone—I am not certain. But he sings the same things Mark and we used to "screech" (as Nurse used to call it).

The other question: will she go mad in Paris?—Quite possibly. But she has already been abroad and she can judge for herself. I spent only a month in Paris, and did very little studying there; I did more sightseeing. It is also not clear to me if Manyasha wants to go abroad to study, or only for the Summer.

I thank Mark for his letter. Let him, however, not forget Gogol's character, Ivan Andreich.[2] I do not know what progress there is in Russia, but undoubtedly they are flourishing here, and they are interested not only in whether the soldier is galloping by or whether the young ladies are skipping.

I am surprised that you have heard nothing about "Syn Otechestva." I saw in the "Russkaya Mysl" today (Nov. or Dec. 1897) that that paper is being announced as the organ of the Narodnik *pur sang*.

Until the next time I write.

Your V. U.

P.S. We have real frost now, so that we have given up shooting and only go for walks—also into the wood. But my rooms are warm and my clothes still warmer.

Let Manyasha send Nadezhda Konstantinovna the list of books which I should like to have—she will look for them in St. Petersburg, if, of course, it is not too late.

If we have any children's books with pictures, let N. K. bring them for Prominsky's youngsters.

(Here follows a list of Russian books on Economics.)

[1] Lenin's review was printed in the April number of the periodical "Mir Bozhy," 1898.
[2] Lenin means Ivan Kuzmich, the Postmaster in Gogol's comedy "The Government Inspector," who read all the letters out of curiosity. This was evidently Lenin's hinted warning to Mark to be more careful in correspondence.

30. (44 R). TO HIS MOTHER AND MARK ELIZAROV

[Shushenskoye], 14th/26th February, 1898

Darling Mother,

I have received a book from Manyasha (Bulgakov) ["On Markets under Capitalist Production," M. 1897] and I thank her for it. She asks me if I have received the registered packet sent by Anya (27th December/8th January). I have received No. 3 "Neue Zeit." It is difficult for me to remember for certain, because it was such a long time ago. I seem to remember receiving "Neue Zeit"[1] and some foreign catalogues. Manyasha wrote on the 26th January/7th February, so it is quite possible my answer to her letter of the 27th December/8th January had not reached Moscow. I received the Bogdanov book still earlier; I liked it very much and I wrote a review of it. Bulgakov's little book is also not bad, but I did not like the chapter on circulation and his formulation of the question of the foreign market is not quite accurate. Of course I was very glad it had been sent to me.

There is again delay over our allowance—because of the New Year. As to news—a new district police superintendent has arrived from Yeniseisk (the same man who confiscated guns there). So far he has evidently done nothing to distinguish himself here. For some unknown reason Prominsky's allowance has been reduced from 31 roubles a month (he has five children) to 21 roubles. Seven people cannot possibly live on such a sum in Shusha and hat-making (his profession) will not flourish here. Another comrade [O. A. Engberg] has gone to Minusinsk to be cured and is in hospital there.

The weather is still very, very cold: the Siberian Winter means to make itself felt. But I seem to have grown used to the frost to a certain extent, for every day I walk a fair amount.

Your

V. U.

Did you send N. K. [Krupskaya] any money for a subscription to the "Vestnik Finansov"? I was not expecting it

---

[1] "Neue Zeit," a theoretical organ of the German Social Democrats from 1883-1922. K. Kautsky was its editor before the war.

at all (for I asked you to subscribe to it for me only if my finances were brilliant), but now I receive it from her as usual.

I am sending Anyuta the library books today together with the technical reports in a registered packet.

31. (47 R). TO HIS MOTHER AND M. I. ULIANOVA

[*Shushenskoye*], *24th February/8th March, 1898*

Darling Mother,

I received a pile of letters today from every corner of Russia and Siberia and therefore felt in a holiday mood all day.

I received letters of the 9th/21st February from Manyasha and Anyuta; also the "Yuridichesky Vestnik" and the "Statistichesky Vremennik," as well as the Report of the Congress (of technicians).[1] Thank you for everything. The last was most interesting and special thanks to Anyuta for it. She writes that Amichi's book is childish. I did not know that— but even a childish book will be useful here, for Prominsky's children have nothing to read. I have even thought of doing this: subscribing to the "Niva."[2] It would be very jolly for Prominsky's youngsters to see it (weekly illustrations), while I would get the complete works of Turgenev promised by the "Niva" in twelve volumes as a free gift. And all this for seven roubles, including postage. Very tempting! If only the Turgenev is bearably published (i.e. without distortions, omissions, or bad misprints), then it would be well worth it. Has anyone among our friends seen the "Niva" gifts of recent years? I think they once gave Dostoevsky? Was it any good?

I am now definitely counting on mending my finances, for the separate publication of the articles must bring in something, and then I am to be given a long translation from the English (from Petersburg) of a work by Adam Smith, for

---

[1] This report evidently contained a chemical letter.
[2] The "Niva," an illustrated weekly, founded in 1869, well known for its free gifts to subscribers of the works of classical authors.

which I shall be paid something.[1] I shall therefore pay back all my debts (only they must not be forgotten). So I consider I can also subscribe to "Niva"—let our people decide whether the Turgenev is any good, they have more information from which to judge.

Today I received No. 1 of "Russkoye Bogatstvo" for 1898. I have been receiving "Vestnik Finansov" for some time now.

Of course I shall have to ask you to send some money with N. K. (it is not necessary to send it sooner. My allowance was paid today) for expenses then may be considerable. So my debt will grow somewhat.

My life is the same. No news whatsoever—no visitors at all— also no new acquaintances as yet.

Anyuta writes that N. K. has written that "a publisher has been found in St. Petersburg." She wrote to me, however, that they only "promised to find one." Possibly there is an amusing misunderstanding: that the plan originated independently in St. Petersburg before the arrival of my letter, and I also came independently by it, before the Petersburg letter. So we go on dancing side by side, like people walking along the same street, who collide when face to face and do not know whether to allow their vis-à-vis to pass to the left or to the right.

However, the matter is probably settled by now.

I kiss you and send greetings to all our people.

Your
V. U.

I understood from Manyasha's letter that both books (the "Yuridichesky Vestnik" No. 12—1887 and the "Statistichesky Vremennik") have been bought, which means they do not need to be returned.

N. K.'s case is progressing very badly. She will probably have to leave her case about the reduction of her term of

---

[1] The translation of Adam Smith is not known. It may be that Lenin did not know which book was being sent him for translation, for in subsequent letters he speaks only of the Webbs' "Theory and Practice of English Trade Unionism" which he translated in exile.

exile in somebody's charge, but they promise to allow her to come here.

I enclose a letter for her, for perhaps she is already in Moscow. If not, then please forward it.

For Manyasha. Send me, Manyasha, the following things:—

(1) A Hardmuth pencil No. 6. (Anyuta bought me one last year and I liked it very much, but it has unfortunately served its purpose.)

(2) A small box of sealing wax and some sort of seal for sealing letters. (If you have not an old seal at home, then either buy one or order a cheap one.) A name is not necessary on the seal, not even initials—just a picture of something or some design that can be remembered easily and passed on to the others.

(3) A penwiper. ⎫I had both these things, but alas, I lost
(4) Small scissors.⎭them somewhere on the way.

Now instead of a penwiper, I use the lapel of my jacket; I have decorated it beautifully; I borrow the landlord's scissors—sheepshears. Their merit is that they always cause laughter and amusement.

Au revoir,

V. U.

32. (49 R). TO HIS MOTHER AND A. I. ELIZAROVA

[Shushenskoye], 8th/20th March, 1898

Darling Mother,

I do not think I have had a single letter from any of you this week; I conclude from this that Mitya is still sitting in prison—it is very sad.

I do not know whether this letter will find N. K. still in Moscow. If so, then I add one more forgotten commission. Send me one of our sets of chess: I have found several partners among our friends at Minusinsk and I suddenly remembered the past with great pleasure. I was wrong in thinking that Eastern Siberia was such a wild country where chess would not be needed. There are the most varied places in Eastern Siberia!

Life goes on as usual. The people in Tes write that E. E.
has had her allowance stopped. "Mothers are not considered
members of a family" (new explanations!). Prominsky's allowance has also been reduced from 31 roubles to 19 roubles a
month. Anatole [Vaneyev] has at last rescued his wife [D. V.
Trukhovskaya] after many trials and tribulations. Julius
[Martov] writes from Turuhansk that his life is bearable—
fortunately the lad is not one to lose heart.

Your

V. U.

I enclose a letter for N. K.

Please send me a little more money by N. K., but if she has
left, then send it in Eliz. Vas's name [Krupskaya's mother].
I may have to incur considerable expense, especially if we are
going to start our own household, so that I expect I shall have
to have recourse to a considerable increase in my debt and
to another domestic loan. By the Autumn I shall probably receive enough from the translation [Webb, "Theory and Practice
of English Trade Unionism," Vol. I.] to cover my debts: I
believe more than five hundred roubles [£50].

For Anyuta. I want to ask you to get me a textbook on the
English language. I have let myself in for a translation and
have received a fat book by the Webbs. I am afraid of making
mistakes. I ought to have:

(1) An English Grammar, especially *syntax* and especially
a section on the idioms of the language. If N. K. has not got
Nurok ["A Practical Grammar of the English Language together with Prose Extracts and a Vocabulary"] then you
might send it for the Summer, if you (or Manyasha) do not
need it. If you can get hold of a good textbook on English
it would be splendid.

(2) A dictionary of *geographical* and proper names. The
transcription and translation from English are very difficult
and I am afraid of making mistakes. I do not know if there
are suitable dictionaries? If there is no reference in the "Book
of Books" [A bibliography] or in some other reference book
or catalogue, then perhaps it might be possible to find one

from some other source? Of course if you can find out this
and procure it (I am not concerned about money, for the payment will not be small and the first attempt must be done
sensibly) but it is not worth troubling about it specially. I shall
also get a German translation of the book, so I shall always be
able to manage.

Your

V. U.

What are your plans for the Summer? Will Mitya be
allowed to go to Kokushkino? Are you thinking of staying
there or no? Is not Moscow a rotten town? Life there is rotten,
book publishing is also rotten there—and why are you clinging
to it? I was really amazed to hear from Mark that you are
against moving to St. Petersburg.

33. (52 R). TO HIS MOTHER

[*Shushenskoye*], *10th/22nd May, 1898*

Darling Mother,

My visitors have at last arrived. They arrived on the 7th
May in the evening, and of course it was the very day I had
cleverly gone out shooting, so they did not find me at home.
I found Nadezhda Konstantinovna looking not at all well, she
will have to look after her health a little better here. But
about me, Elizaveta Vasilievna said: "Gracious! how you have
spread!" so you see, you do not need a better report.

I am terribly sad they have not brought better news of Mitya.

I have received both the letter sent by them and the one
dated 20th April/2nd May. Many thanks for the things you
have sent. About the books that are supposed to arrive:—N. K.
has already spoken about them in Minusinsk and I hope to
receive them soon and without any bother. Perhaps I shall
bring them myself, for I am thinking of going "to town."

As regards the steamers: N. K. was brought only as far as
Sorokin (about 70 versts from Minusinsk); they waited a week
in Krasnoyarsk. The water is still low and it will not be high

water until about the end of May, or the beginning of June. It is 55 versts from Minusinsk to Shusha. The local steamers are irregular in their service: there are no timetables, but when navigation is running smoothly then probably they will run more or less regularly and without any extraordinary delays. I would very, very much like you to try to come here—if only they would release Mitya soon.

Of course Anyuta asks me whom I am inviting to the wedding: I invite you all, only I do not know if it would not be better to send the invitation by telegram!! As you know, N. K. has had a tragi-comic condition made to her: if she does not marry *immediately*, she is to return to Ufa. I am not at all inclined to allow this and we are therefore beginning "to fuss" (mainly about the petition for the documents, without which one cannot get married in order to be in time to marry before the Fast) (the Fast of St. Peter, midsummer): however, it is permissible to hope that the strict authorities will find it a sufficiently "immediate" marriage! I am inviting the people from Tes (they have already written, that surely, I shall need witnesses)—and I hope they will be allowed to come.

Greetings to all our people,

I kiss you warmly,

Your

V. U.

Oh! I almost forgot: Nadya told me, that some books on philosophy arrived for me, but they have gone past here, somewhere to Irkutsk. Why did I hear nothing about it, *not even once*? Has a letter gone astray? I would ask Anyuta to explain what is the matter.

34. (54 R). TO HIS MOTHER

[Shushenskoye], 7th/19th June, 1898

Darling Mother,

The day before yesterday I received your long letter of the 20th May/1st June. Thank you for it. Last time I forgot to tell you that I had received the case of books in Minusa and brought it back with me.[1]

I cannot understand how it is you have had no letters from me for a long time; from "time immemorial" I have been writing to you every Sunday.

The question of our wedding is somewhat delayed. I presented the petition for sending me the necessary documents almost a month ago and when I was in Minusa I made enquiries from the district police superintendent about the reasons for all the delay. It appears (Siberian methods!) that my paper is not in Minusa *to this day*—although it is already my second year of exile!! (the paper in question is the document about an exile; without that document the district police superintendent does not know anything about me and cannot issue any certificate). They will have to write for it to the prison at Krasnoyarsk, but I am afraid the district police superintendent will waste time over that. In any case the wedding cannot take place before July.[2] I asked the district police superintendent to allow the Tes people to come to our wedding, but he categorically refused, on the grounds that one political exile in Minusa (Raichin) took leave to go to the country in March of this year, and disappeared. . . . My contention that there was absolutely no need to fear the disappearance of any of the Tes people did not have any effect.

The Tes people have been allowed to stay in Tes until the Autumn and after that they move to Minusa.

I believe I have written to you about the steamers along the Yenisei. It is still high water, and is even increasing. It is very hot and the snow is probably melting in the taiga on the hills. There are no timetables for the steamers (which are all steam tugs); the steamer takes two days—sometimes longer—to come from Krasnoyarsk to Minusinsk. The distance by horse from Minusa to Shusha is 55 versts.

I hope to receive a telegram from you when Mitya is released and you decide to visit us.

[1] Lenin visited Minusinsk at the end of May, O.S., when there was a meeting of exiled Norodovoltsy and Marxists at Minusinsk in connection with C. G. Raichin's escape.

[2] The wedding took place on the 10/22 July, 1898.

Elizaveta Vasilievna is afraid the journey might tire you too much. But if you could travel second class by train, then I think it would not be too tiring.

Greetings to all our people. I am waiting for a letter from Anyuta. Has she received "Questions in Philosophy"?

I kiss you warmly,

Your

V. U.

35. (59 R). TO HIS MOTHER AND A. I. ELIZAROVA

[Shushenskoye], 16th/28th August, 1898

Darling Mother,

I received Anyuta's letter of the 30th July/11th August, in Minusa, where I went to have my teeth attended to [10/22-13/25 August]. I was very surprised to receive that letter, which apparently came by express train. However a delay was caused by the transfer of letters from the express (going to Tomsk) to the ordinary train: on Tuesday, 11th/23rd August, I received a newspaper from Moscow (dated 29th July/10th August) by the ordinary train, whereas the letter (dated 30th July/11th August) came by express—which means, not so very much faster.

But I cannot send letters from here by express, because to do so one must have friends in Ob' to whom the letter should be sent for posting in the letter box on the express train.

However, make another experiment with the express and we shall see when the letter arrives.

Today I am posting the Webb translation to St. Petersburg. I have written to say that the money for this should be sent to you: if the Writer [Struve] does not know your address, then send it to him.

There ought to be news about the book of articles, but I have not had any yet, and Nadya and I are beginning to think it is a fiasco. . . .

In my opinion, Manyasha is unnecessarily hesitant. It would do her good to go and live and study abroad in one of the capital cities, and in Belgium it is particularly easy to study. On which particular subject does she wish to attend lectures?

And so, it was not in vain I put off complaining about the "Questions": it appears they were not lost, although they were so delayed that sending them became pointless.

For Anyuta.

I am sending you, Anyuta, by registered post [Ada] Negri, Tempeste [Book of poems] and the catalogue for which you asked. The address—the same as in this letter. Let me know when you receive it.

When I received your letter, I also had news from Archangel that M. G. (Hopfenhaus) had shot herself (18th/30th July). What a terribly tragic story! And the fantastic slander of that scoundrel Yukhotsky (*a political!!* exile in Verholensk) has played one of the principal parts in that finale. N. E. [Fedoseyev] was terribly upset about it and depressed. As a result he made up his mind not to take help from *anyone* and suffered terrible hardship. They say that 2-3 days before his death, he received a letter in which the slander was repeated. The devil only knows what it all means! There is nothing worse in exile than these exile scandals, but I never thought they could go to such a length! The slanderer has been exposed long ago and definitely condemned by all his comrades, and I had no idea N. E. (who had had certain experience of exile scandals) was taking it all so terribly to heart.

I received Shakhov ["Lectures on 19th century French literature"], Gumplowicz ["System cocyologii," Warsaw] and "Izvestiya" [A book catalogue] (2 numbers, the January and March) two days ago: the delay of one post was due to our postman.

Julius [Martov] hopes to get out of Turuhansk soon.[1] They are having their wedding in Tes and then moving to Minusinsk. Basil has found work as a technician in a local [salt] works.

Your

V. U.

---

[1] Martov did not receive the necessary permission, and had to stay in Minusinsk till the end of his term of exile.

36. (62 R). TO HIS MOTHER

Krasnoyarsk, 16th/28th November, 1898

Darling Mother,

I have been living here for the last few days and tomorrow I am thinking of leaving, if the steamer is not delayed for a day. I shall have to travel without A. M. [Rosenberg] and E. E. [Rosenberg] (I believe I wrote to you from Minusinsk telling you how we had arranged a trip together). E. E. has gone into the local hospital; one of the doctors is a friend of A. M. and E. E. is, I believe, quite comfortable and happy there. The doctors are still unable to give an exact diagnosis: it may be merely pain from a blow, (she fell from a carriage about six or eight weeks ago) or it may be an abscess on the liver, a very serious illness, lengthy and difficult to treat. I am terribly sorry for poor A. M., who has not yet recovered after the death of her child and her own illness. At times she is so nervous that she almost has nervous seizures. I do not want to leave her here alone, but my permit will soon expire and I shall have to go. I shall ask our comrades here to visit her. As a result of this trip, the need to help A. M. and certain purchases I have to make, my money is at rather a low ebb. Please send Elizaveta Vasilievna [Krupskaya's mother] (from whom I borrowed some money) about half the sum which should have been sent to me for the whole of my Webb translation (posted to St. Petersburg on the 15th/27th August).[1] If they have not sent it to you yet, I think it would be better to wait a little (or to take payment, should such an occasion arise). But there will be no crisis for me and there is no particular hurry.

I am very pleased with my trip here; my teeth have been attended to and after eighteen months' sitting in Shushensk I have enjoyed a good airing! No matter how few people there are in Krasnoyarsk, after Shusha it is pleasant to meet people and talk to them about other things than shooting or the "Shushensk News." The journey back will take fairly long (five days or thereabouts): up-stream, the steamers move devilishly slowly up the River Yenisei. I shall have to keep to

---

[1] Lenin gives a different date in Letter 35.

a cabin, because the weather is extremely cold. (Obviously I am wearing Winter clothes and have bought a sheepskin coat for Nadya, so that the cold will not penetrate.) I have got a supply of candles and books so as not to die of boredom on the steamer. Lepeshinskaya, the wife of an exile, who is going to take up work in the village Kuraginskoye (about 40 versts from Minusinsk, where Comrade Kurnatovsky [1] lives) will probably travel with me; her husband has been transferred to the same place. I heard some good news yesterday: that Julius [Martov] has been transferred, but I do not yet know where to. The last letter from home was from Anyuta dated 24th August/5th September. Thank her very much for it and for the books ("Neue Zeit," a reprint from "The Arkhiv," a biography of Kohanskaya [2] and others). I shall answer her from Shusha, namely in about ten days' time: this will mean a considerable delay, but it cannot be helped.

Your

V. U.

I kiss you warmly and send greetings to all our people.

I have just seen A. M. and heard that E. E. is much better. The doctors say there is no danger and promise that in about eight days she will leave hospital feeling quite well and in a fit condition to travel to Minusinsk. This is good news.

37. (68 R). TO M. I. ULIANOVA

[Shushenskoye], 11th/23rd November, 1898

We have received your letter, Manyasha, and were very glad to have it. We immediately took out our maps and began to hunt for Brussels. We found it and began thinking how close it was to London, that Paris was near and also Germany—one could call it the centre of Europe. Yes, I envy you. At the beginning of my exile I decided never to touch a map either

---

[1] V. K. Kurnatovsky (1867-1912), an active Social Democrat. Exiled to Siberia for participation in the "Liberation of Labour" group and writing an agitational pamphlet "The Workers' Day."

[2] N. S. Sokhanskaya (1825-87). Her autobiography, published in 1896, was evidently used by his sister, Anyuta, for sending Lenin an "illegal" letter. "Kohanskaya" was her pseudonym.

of European Russia or even of Russia; it would mean too much bitterness, as I looked at those various black spots. But it is not so bad now; I have grown patient and can examine maps more calmly. Sometimes we even dream into which of the "spots" it would be interesting to land later on. During the first half of my exile I must have been constantly looking back, now I look forward. Ah well, "qui vivra—verra."

With regard to newspapers and books, please get what you can. Send all sorts of catalogues both from bookshops, and secondhand bookshops, and in all languages. Today I thought of asking you to do something for me, but I have decided to postpone it until next time. May I remind you that last year I wrote either to you or to Anya saying that newspapers and official documents containing verbatim reports of parliamentary debates were particularly interesting. It would be splendid if you could find out where such newspapers or journals are sold (are there only Belgian ones for sale in Brussels or also English and French?) and if you were to send me any interesting issues (you read the newspapers, I hope?). I advise you not to limit yourself to Belgian newspapers, but to subscribe also to some German ones; then you will not forget the language and will have excellent reading matter (also the prices for newspapers are not high).

Are you going home for Christmas?

Your

V. U.

After waiting a long time I have at last received my Miscellany. I will ask Anyuta to send you a copy.

38. (69 R). TO HIS MOTHER AND A. I. ELIZAROVA

[Shushenskoye], 15th/27th November, 1898

Darling Mother,

How are you spending the Winter in Podolsk? It is probably not a happy Winter for you—Mark has had to be away from you and Mitya is chained to Podolsk. He does not write in answer to my question: how will he have to do military service:

in the ranks or in the medical Corps? Have you any information
about his case? For instance, when is it likely to end and how?
Or do you not know? How is Mark's health? Is he not bored
alone in Moscow? Or is he smothered under work in his job
and with the evening lectures? (Does he read the lectures?) [1]
We have absolutely no news, only our diversion has changed,
now that the Winter has come: instead of shooting I am beginning to skate. I am reminded of the old days and I do not seem
to have forgotten how to skate, although I have not done any
for some ten years. Nadya also wants to learn, but I do not
know if she will succeed.

Greetings to all our people,
    I kiss you warmly,

Your

V. U.

1899

39. (78 R). TO HIS MOTHER

[*Shushenskoye*], *3rd/15th January, 1899*

Darling Mother,

Yesterday Nadya and I returned from Minusa where we
spent a happy week with Gleb and Basil, greeting the New
Year among comrades. There was a number of toasts when
the New Year came in and one comrade's toast to Elvira
Ernestovna and to absent Mothers was particularly warmly
received.

Today we find it difficult to get back to our routine life, but
tomorrow we shall have to set to work again. The sixth chapter
of my book is finished (not yet copied): I hope to finish the
whole book in about four weeks' time. I answered Anyuta's
letters of the 5th/17th and 8th/20th December from Minusa
and I agreed to the immediate handing over of the first chapters to the printers; to correct proofs without sending them to
the author (preferably three, and not two proofs); to sending
only the fair-copied pages to him, and in general that Anyuta

---

[1] A reference to Mark's activities in the Sunday and evening schools for workers.

should supervise the publication as she thinks best. I hope she has received my letter. At the same time I sent a letter to Mitya, asking him to buy me a gun. Will there not be some money difficulties? There seems to be a hitch with the money that is due to me. I keep on taking and taking books from Kalmykova's shop and I am quite ashamed.

I kiss you warmly and send greetings to all.

Your

V. U.

P.S. E. V. and Nadya send their love.

40. (83 R). TO M. I. ULIANOVA

[Shushenskoye], *24th January/5th February*, *1899*

I have received some catalogues from you Manyasha—many thanks for them. There are some interesting things in them. I am thinking of sending you a small list of books which I should like to have. Write and tell me if you have got to know Brussels well and particularly its book trade. It would be interesting to read the verbatim reports of some of the important debates in the different Parliaments. In Paris, for instance, they can be found in the Journal Officiel which is sold in separate numbers. I do not know if you can get it in Brussels. Probably you can. Similar reports are printed in the Belgian Government newspapers. Where did you find the English catalogues? Are there some English bookshops in Brussels or did you send to London for them?

At present I am busy with some urgent work: there is a little more of my book to be done and after that I shall probably have to write for some of the periodicals. That is why I am not writing much for the moment, especially as Nadya says she is going to write in greater detail about our life. If you come across any literature in the secondhand bookshops on the economy of farming in England, France etc. (agricultural statistics, enquêtes, reports of English commissions) or on the history of the forms of industry (by the way, [Charles] Babbage and [A.] Ure are well known writers on the subject), then buy them, if the prices are reasonable.

LENIN IN DISGUISE

Have you much work? When are you thinking of returning home?

I send you my greetings,

Your

V. U.

41. (5 P[1]). TO A. N. POTRESOV IN ORLOV, VYATKA PROVINCE

[Shushenskoye], 26th January, 1899

I have received your letter of the 24th December. I am very glad to hear that you have at last got rid of your illness. Rumors of it had reached even us: I heard about it during Xmas, when I was in Minusinsk and I kept wondering how I could find out more. (I did not like to write to you direct, for they said the illness was a serious one.) Well, you have been resurrected just at the right time, when a certain literary undertaking is also resurrecting. Of course you know about "Nachalo"[1] ["The Beginning"] which is to appear in the middle of February. I hope you have quite recovered—a month has gone by since you wrote your last letter, in which you said you would be able to work. Surely you are not badly provided for in the way of books; are you ordering the most important new ones? If you are not too hard up to order books, then I should imagine you could work even in the back-woods. I am judging at any rate from my experience—when I compare my life in Samara about seven years ago, when I read other people's books almost exclusively, with now, when I have begun the habit of ordering books.

As for "Nasledstvo" ["Heritage"], I agree with you that it is a bad tradition of the bad years ('80's)[2] to consider it as something unique. Perhaps I ought not to have touched

---

[1] "Nachalo," an organ of legal Marxism under the editorship of P. Struve, M. Tugan-Baranovsky, V. Bogucharsky, A. Kalmykova. It began appearing in Jan. 1899, and was banned in June. Lenin contributed several reviews and one chapter of his work "The Development of Capitalism in Russia."

[2] Lenin's article: "The Inheritance Which We Renounce" where he criticised Skaldin's (pseudonym for F. P. Elenev) work "In the Remote Provinces and in the Capital" (1867). In the 1890's Skaldin became an extreme reactionary and a member of the Chief Censorship Committee.

literary-historical themes. . . . My only justification is that I do not propose in any of my work to admit inheritance from Skaldin. It is indisputable that one must inherit from other people. It seems to me that my defence (from possible inimical attacks) will be a note on page 237, where I have Chernychevsky in mind and where I give reasons for the inconvenience of taking him as a parallel. I also admit there that Skaldin was a Liberal-Conservative, that he was not typical of the 1860's, that it was "inconvenient" to take typical writers—I had neither then, nor have I now, any of Chernychevsky's articles—the main ones have not yet been republished and, even if I had them, I doubt if I would be able to avoid the submerged rocks.

I would also defend myself by saying, that after all I had given an exact definition of what I meant by the word "inconvenience." Of course, if the article still produces the impression that the author proposed to accept his inheritance from Skaldin, then nothing can be done. I have almost forgotten to mention my main "defence": if Skaldin is "a rarity" then bourgeois Liberalism, which is more or less consistent and is purely derivative from the Narodnik movement, is not "a rarity" but a broad current of the 1860's and the 1870's. You object that "the distance between coincidence and derivation is enormous," but after all, the point of the article is that it is essential to cleanse bourgeois Liberalism of "Narodnichestvo." If that is correct and is *realisable* (a very important condition!) then the residue after the cleansing will be bourgeois Liberalism, not only coinciding with Skaldin's Liberalism, but also derived from him. So, if I am to be criticised for accepting inheritance from Skaldin, then I shall have every right to answer that I take upon myself only the *cleansing* of it from admixtures, and, apart from this cleansing of Augean stables, I have more pleasant and more positive things to do. Well, I think I have been carried away and I have imagined myself really defending myself!

Our correspondence has been so long at a standstill that I must confess I have already forgotten when exactly I wrote to you last about the articles "Die historische Berechtigung"

[Axelrod's articles in "Neue Zeit"]. I believe I wrote before receiving them? Now that I have made myself familiar with them, I have discovered that the author's basic thought fully deserves acceptance (especially at the end, about the two extremes or the submerged rocks which ought to be avoided.[1] The class character of that movement should be made to stand out more. The author did speak of it (but only in passing and very briefly). He should also not be so lenient towards "fronderising" Agrarians: in their Liberalism there is more Frondism and "injured feeling" for 1861 [Emancipation of the peasants] than the wish for a most rapid industrialisation of the country. One needs only to remember their attitude towards migrant labour etc. The author ought to state his problem more clearly; he should extricate whatever is progressive from the junk of Narodnichestvo and Agrarianism and utilise it in such a cleansed condition. In my opinion "utilise" is much more accurate and suitable than support and union. The latter points to the equal rights of these united comrades, whereas they should (and in this I quite agree with you) bring up the rear, sometimes even with a "grinding of teeth"; they have definitely not grown yet to the stature of equality and will never do so with their cowardice, disunion etc. However, there will be support not only from the intelligentsia and the progressive landowners, but from many others, from the Jews and merchants and industrialists (these last the author has omitted quite unnecessarily: it is an open question whether they form a smaller percentage in their social sphere than our supporters amongst the landowners). Support will also come from those peasants who are inclined to think of "Judgment" and not "Prejudice," the future and not the past of their class, and from many, many others. In two respects the author has exaggerated in the other direction: firstly, in fighting the economists, he has neglected the practical, immediate demands,

---

[1] Axelrod pointed out that two extremes might have a harmful effect on the attitude of the educated class towards the workers' movement. (1) If that movement did not go outside single conflicts between the workers and individual capitalists; (2) (which would be even worse) if the workers' movement under the influence of Bakunin's or Blanc's ideas would see their immediate task in an anarchist or communist revolution.

important both for the industrial workers, handicraft workers and agricultural labourers etc.; secondly, he fought against an abstract, disdainful attitude towards the moderate progressive elements (that is quite right, they should in no way be disdained, but they should be used) and he, as it were, put thereby into the shade the independent and more definite position occupied by the movement which he was presenting. In the historical philosophic sense it is impossible to dispute the position which he presents (and earlier Inorodzev had presented this in his "Social Practice"),[1] namely, that among our present comrades there are not a few disguised Liberals. After all, this could also be said about Germany, when compared with England. It is actually our good fortune, for it helps us to count upon an easier and swifter beginning; and this compels us to make use of all these disguised individuals. The author's formulation will probably give rise to certain misinterpretations (one old believer told me that it meant "humiliation") on the one hand, and a feeling of mistrust and confusion among the comrades on the other. In this respect I consider that Inorodzev also was unsatisfactory in his statement of the problem.

But in the main issues, I do not think I disagree with the author.

As for Parvus [A. L. Helfand], I have not the slightest knowledge of his personal character and in no way deny that he has really great talent. Unfortunately I have read very few of his works.

Are you hoping to get hold of Kautsky's "Die Agrarfrage" which appeared recently?

So far as Vert, Eugene Soloviev and M. Filippov[2] are con-

---

[1] P. Inorodzev said in his article, "The Workers' Movement in Russia," printed in the German weekly "Soziale Praxis," 1896, that a time may come when the foremost elements of society will be moved so forcibly by the necessity of political freedom, that no Liberalism will satisfy it. And just because of the industrial backwardness of the country and the political backwardness of the industrial bourgeoisie that the political strivings may assume a social-democratic form.

[2] Possibly O. A. Vert; Eugene Soloviev, a Russian literary historian who tried to analyse the history of Russian literature from a Marxist point of view; M. Filippov, a literary writer, who was somewhat of a "legal" Marxist.

cerned, I must tell you that I do not know the first named at all and have read very little of the other two. There will be and is already a loss of authority, of that I have not the slightest doubt. Therefore it is particularly essential to have not only disguised literature, but . . .

Greetings,

V. U.

42. (88 R). TO HIS MOTHER

[Shushenskoye], *7th/19th February, 1899*

Today I am sending another small packet (registered) addressed to you, darling Mother,—first, the number of "Isvestia" which you asked me to return,[1] and secondly, a review[2] which I ask you to send on to "the Writer." By the next post I will send you another small addition to the seventh chapter. I hope it will not be too late. Last time I wrote, I believe I forgot to say that according to my calculations there are about 934,000 letters [of the alphabet] in the whole book. That is not much; about 467 printed pages, reckoning 2,000 letters to a page. If, however, there are fewer letters to a page, for example 1680 (as for instance in Tugan-Baranovsky's "Crises"), then that would, of course, make it a more expensive publication, for then it would have about 530 pages.

Anyuta has probably not yet received my letter (written long ago) in which I asked her to send me: (1) some decent German translation of Turgenev, (2) a detailed German grammar, (even in German for Germans, for the grammars written for Russians are usually too short). I want to begin studying German thoroughly. Will you also send me a Russian-German dictionary, one of those we have at home, either Lenström or better still, Reiff, with the Russian into three European languages? I ordered Pavlovsky's Russian-German dictionary

---

[1] A book catalogue, evidently with a chemical letter.

[2] A review of Parvus's book: "The World Market and the Agricultural Crisis." It was printed in "Nachalo," No. 3.

from Kalmykova, but it appears it is still coming out in parts and only about half have so far been published.

Greetings to all our people,

Your

V. U.

43. (93 R). TO HIS MOTHER

[*Shushenskoye*], *7th/19th March, 1899*

Darling Mother,

This week I have received three small books by Turgenev in German. Thank you for them; it is excellent that you bought the Reklam Edition, for it is the most useful. I shall now expect the Russian-German dictionary (I remember we had two; Lenström and Reiff,) and also some sort of grammar. I have already written to Anyuta about this; Mark has "the Book about Books" [bibliography] in which certain detailed German grammars *in German* are mentioned. I wanted to buy Pavlovsky's Russian-German dictionary and ordered a copy from Kalmykova, but it seems it is not yet finished and is being published in separate parts.

I am now finishing a short article ["On the Question of the Theory of Realization"] in answer to one by Struve: in my opinion he has thoroughly muddled matters and by this article may cause some misunderstanding among supporters, also malicious satisfaction among antagonists. I think if I fail to place my article in the periodical (in view of the fact that Tugan-Baranovsky or Bulgakov may forestall me with their answers, I have not been sent the January number of the "Nauchnoye Obozreniye"!), I shall include it as a fourth appendix in "The Markets" (the article is no more than one printed sheet). Of course it would be better in a periodical.[1]

Our life goes on as usual. The weather is warm. Spring is in the air.

There is little good news from our comrades. Apollinaria Alexandrovna [Yakubova] has been allowed to go to Yeniseisk

[1] Lenin's article appeared in "Nauchnoye Obozreniye," August, 1899.

for three weeks. Poor Anatole [Vaneyev] is still ill; his
temperature goes up to 120°. They say he has consumption but,
of course, they are carefully hiding this from him. The question of his being transferred to the Minusinsk district is still
not settled.

Your

V. U.

I kiss you warmly. E. V. and Nadya send greetings to all.

44. (96 R). TO M. I. ULIANOVA IN BRUSSELS

[Shushenskoye], 17th/29th March, 1899

I apologise, darling Manyasha, for writing so briefly this
time, but I am adding my good wishes to Nadya's letter. The
fact is, that a number of letters have accumulated today: I
have to write to Turuhansk (the post goes once a month) [to
Martov] and I must send Anyuta a list of misprints in the
proofs [of Chapters II, III. "The Development of Capitalism
in Russia"].

We have very little news. There is a lull in literature for the
present—we are still waiting. Foreign newspapers mention
events in Petersburg and Finland (judging from the "Frankfurter Zeitung") but these passages are blocked out,[1] so that
we know very, very little.

I send you greetings.

Perhaps we shall meet soon.

Your

V. U.

45. (99 R). TO HIS MOTHER

[Shushenskoye], 11th/23rd April, 1899

Darling Mother,

I received Mitya's parcel on Tuesday. Many thanks for the
trouble. I am pleased with the gun. So far the weather is bad:
the usual Spring squalls of these parts—the strongest winds

---

[1] A reference to student disturbances in Petersburg in February, 1899.

because of the Yenisei, so that there has been hardly any shooting. The cartridges, size 2¾, seemed to me too large— the gun recoils, so I have begun to use size 2½. I cannot understand how they could put three divisions in the barrel! So far I have not yet noticed better firing from the left barrel, perhaps because I tried at too great a distance, namely about sixty paces.

If you come here, bring with you some smooth black tulle for a mosquito net: I cannot go about without a net. The district round about is fairly boggy. Also, please bring with you about 200 wads for gunpowder and shot (similar to those which Mitya sent. We cannot get any here and they are very light and easy to pack).

I am thinking of going on a shooting expedition at Easter to better places.

I kiss you warmly,

Your V. U.

Next Sunday there will not be any post—Easter. Also the Yenisei ice may start moving: this usually happens about the 20th of April. It is possible, therefore, that there will be breaks in our correspondence, and you should not worry about this. However, I believe there was hardly any break last year.

For Anyuta.

By the next post and addressed to Mother I shall send a short article on Kautsky and Bulgakov.[1] Please forward it to "the Writer" [Struve] with a request to let you know as quickly as possible whether they can accept it for the periodical. I consider it quite possible that they will refuse it, because "the Writer" is probably on Bulgakov's side and will consider polemics unsuitable—especially sharp polemics. As far as I could, I tried to soften down my tone, but all the same I cannot speak calmly about that revolting professorial and clumsy article which introduces such a terrible discord. Of

---

[1] "Capitalism in Agriculture" (on Kautsky's book and Bulgakov's article "On the Capitalistic Evolution of Agriculture," in Nos. 1-2 "Nachalo." S. N. Bulgakov, a representative of Legal Marxism, was a Marxian critic like Tugan-Baranovsky and Struve. Later he turned away from Marxism to idealism and to mysticism after 1905. He became a priest in the Greek orthodox church.

course I cannot restrict the publishers in "their right to make corrections," but there is no need to write about it, for this follows of itself if the author does not find fault particularly. If it is not accepted, please let me know as soon as possible; and send the article if you can to "Zhizn" or "Nauchnoye Obozreniye" (I doubt if "Mir Bozhy" would take it). We have no literary news from "the Writer" and we do not hope to receive any. Meanwhile, correspondence without a constant and regular exchange is devilishly awkward. For instance, ages ago, as far back as January, I wrote to them (Nadya wrote) that I was thinking of writing on Kablukov. They did not inform me that they already had another article [by Tugan-Baranovsky]. Do you know anything about the reviews? (The review of Kautsky should be cancelled, or placed elsewhere in view of the article against Bulgakov). I do not know what they have or what they have not got. It would be helpful if you could begin a correspondence with the Chicago individual [V. A. Ionov] whom you know and who is fairly sympathetic, so that he could easily answer you on all points and altogether keep you in touch with periodicals. I do not know if that is practicable?

How am I to send the manuscripts if you (and Mother) leave [for Shushenskoye]? In any case leave word at the Post Office where and to whom letters and newspapers are to be sent.

Yes, in my article ["Capitalism in Agriculture"], I refer to my markets. If my book ["The Development of Capitalism in Russia"] has not appeared when you forward the manuscript, then please cross out those references or write on the MS. that they should be deleted.

I send you greetings.   V. U.

46. (100 R). TO HIS MOTHER

[Shushenskoye], 1st/13th May, 1899

Darling Mother,

On Tuesday I received Anyuta's letter dated 12th/24th April and on Friday my book (three copies) and the manuscript of the translation. I am writing separately to Anyuta.

We are having a particularly early Spring. The leaves on the trees are beginning to come out and the water is rising considerably. The steamer could come now as far as Minusa, but whether this high water will stay and for how long—nothing definite can be said.

Mik. Aleks. (Silvin) wrote to me that his fiancée wants to come to him at the end of May (not before 23rd): Her name: Papperek (Olga Aleksandrovna)—address: Egorievsk, Ryazan Province. She is an elementary schoolteacher there. If you decide to come too, you might travel together. In any case it will be a good opportunity. Mik. Aleks. asked her to come to Podolsk on her way, but of course it is essential to write to her, for circumstances might prevent her. Ermakovskoye is forty versts away from us. (M. A. lives there); the way there from Minusa is through Shusha.

Your

V. U.

I kiss you warmly and send greetings to all our people. How are you settled now? How is your health? When are you expecting Manyasha back?

For Anyuta.

1st/13th May, 1899

I received your letter of the 12th/24th April, my book and the Webb translation (three registered packets).

I am very pleased with the outside appearance of the book. It is beautifully published, thanks to the great trouble you have taken over the proofs. And I think you did well to raise the price. If students can have a 25% discount—that is quite sufficient. Have you sent the book round to all our friends? I think "the Writer" [Struve] should have another fifteen spare copies: they will have to be given in exchange for various books etc. I have already written to you about the "Studies" asking you to get a few more copies (send only two copies here, but there is no hurry). I am fully satisfied with the title: "the Writer's" corrections are good. If any payment is sent—it is not worth forwarding it for the present. (I am writing soon to Mother, telling her of a good opportunity.)

I agree to undertake the editing of the Webb translation. I shall edit it, taking my translation of the first volume into consideration. Now that the editing has been entrusted to me— there is no need to wait and the first volume should go to print at once. Is not that right? Or will that again depend on the decisions of Peter Bernarovich [Struve]?

For the editing *I must have:*

(1) *The English Original*—Vol. II (I have only the first volume) and (2) *the German translation,* Vol. II. (K. Hugo, I have only the first volume.) The second has also appeared. If these books have not been sent yet, please write soon to tell them to send them at once. Will that also cause a delay? Cannot someone be asked to take these books from them and post them?

I was not very pleased that P. B. sent my reply to his article to the "Nauchnoye Obozreniye." Is he wanting perhaps to avoid polemics in "Nachalo"? [1] If that is so, then my article on Bulgakov ["Capitalism in Agriculture"] will probably not be accepted. I have at last received "Nachalo," both books, and complete. Altogether I liked it very much. But the Bulgakov article is revolting. He is *simply distorting* Kautsky, and then too that attack against the Zusammenbruch [2]—an echo of Bernstein "criticism" (the shop has refused to send Bernstein's book ["Die Voraussetzungen des Sozialismus und die Aufgaben der Sozialdemokratie," 1899]. I asked Manyasha: I do not know if she will bring it. Could you perhaps get hold of it?) I am writing a second article against him. [3] Of course polemics are unpleasant among one's own people, and I tried to tone it down, but it is not only unpleasant but *positively harmful* to be silent about the differences—and besides, one cannot be silent over those root differences between "orthodoxy" and "criticism" which have appeared both in German and Russian Marxism. In any case, the opponents are making use of those differences.

[1] "Nachalo's" position was unstable, the April number had been confiscated and Struve therefore handed over Lenin's article "On the Question of the Theory of Realization" to "Nauchnoye Obozreniye."

[2] Bulgakov refutes the Marxist theory of a Socialist revolution.

[3] "Capitalism in Agriculture," "Zhizn," Feb., 1900.

(Mikhailovsky No. 4. "Russkoye Bogatstvo").[1] After all, it is possible in polemicising among ourselves to censure the general solidarity against the Narodniks. I want to do this at the end of my article. One of Bulgakov's many defects is that he did not point out exactly in what he solidly supports Kautsky against the Narodniks.

I greet you warmly,

V. U.

I saw in the "Nauchnoye Obozreniye" No. 3, Maslov's note against my article on inheritance. It seemed quite interesting.

I am sending Negri. And what agricultural report was it?

One should give a copy of "The Development of Capitalism" to Maslov. Do this please, through the editors of the "Nauchnoye Obozreniye" or through P. B. or through V. A. [Ionov].

Please send all reviews of the book and ask V. A. to send those which have appeared in the Petersburg papers.

47. (101 R). TO HIS MOTHER

[*Shushenskoye*], *9th/21st May, 1899*

Darling Mother,

I received a letter from Manyasha in which she writes that she is thinking of coming home soon. I shall be waiting to hear what you have decided about your visit to us here.

We have been having the "strongest" weather here, as the Siberians say. They call "weather" the *wind* that blows from the Yenisei, from the West, cold and as strong as a whirlwind. There are always whirlwinds here in the Spring, they break fences, roofs, etc. I have been out shooting and walking in the forest these last few days and I saw the whirlwind break enormous birch trees and pines. However, such unpleasant "weather" happens only in the Spring and Autumn. But in the Summer if there is a wind, it is never a strong one, so there is no need to fear it. It is a little better today; it is probably turning to Summer. From the middle of May to the middle of August there is no need to fear Siberian "weather."

[1] In which Mikhailovsky criticises the direction of both "Nachalo" and "Zhizn."

Next Sunday I shall send addressed to you the manuscript of my article ["Capitalism in Agriculture"]: if you leave, arrange for it to be forwarded.

All our people are well and send greetings to you and to all the rest,

Your

V. U.

For Anyuta.

Today I finished the second article against Bulgakov. When it is revised and copied I will post it, addressed to Mother. I am impatiently waiting for an answer about the first article: there should be an answer in the middle of May.

Many "disciples" [1] are going over to "Zhizn." Do you know who is the actual editor there?

The debates now in Germany about Bernstein's book ["Die Voraussetzungen des Sozialismus und die Aufgaben der Sozialdemokratie"] are very interesting—but I have not seen either that book or anything written about it, (except some casual remarks in the "Frankfurter Zeitung"), and I am very sorry.

Did Mitya dispatch my book to everyone on my list? If V. A. was to send it to some of them, then please ask him if he sent it to *everyone;* for instance P. N. Lepeshinsky (village Kuraginskoye, Minusinsk district, Yenisei Province) writes to me that he has *not received* the book, although he was on my list. I think one ought to have another fifteen spare copies (but it is not worth sending them here).

I send you my greetings.

V. U.

Greetings to Mark.

---

[1] By disciples Lenin means Marxists, i.e., Social Democrats. He uses the word "disciples" for conspiratorial reasons.

48. (102 R). TO A. I. ELIZAROVA AND HIS MOTHER

[Shushenskoye], 29th May/10th June, 1899

For Anyuta,

I received your postscript to Mark's letter.

About the offer that I should write a short course on political economy:—you have not mentioned this to me before. I have decided to decline this offer: it is difficult to write to order, (and particularly to compete with Bogdanov; why not reprint his ["Short Course of Economic Science"])? It would be difficult to have it ready by the Autumn and I want to write less and to read more. As our correspondence with "the Writer" has come to a standstill please tell him about my refusal.

I have not touched Webb yet. I am *still waiting* for the original (Volume II) and for the German translation (Volume II). If there is any delay—the fault will not be mine. However, we ought to be more anxious about "the Writer" causing delay. Is the first volume being printed? I have just learnt from your letter that you sent me a telegram about the publication of my book. I am writing to the Minusinsk Post Office to ask them to trace the telegram. Was the address correct? (You must write "Minusinsk, Shushenskoye. By post for Ulianov," and prepay 7 or 14 kopecks for postage. If the words "by post" are omitted then the telegram might be held up at the post office). I have not noticed before that the sending of telegrams here was a hopeless undertaking; others have reached me punctually. A telegram ought to be sent so that it reaches Minusinsk in the evening, on either a Sunday or a Wednesday; then I should receive it on the Tuesday or Friday morning.

I am sending you my article about the Sismondists, for which you ask, and my reply to "Nezhdanov." It would be better if the latter were to appear in "Zhizn."[1] If however "Nachalo" were to revive, which would be contrary to expectation, then of course I should prefer it to appear there.

I am doing some reading and am studying languages a

---

[1] It appeared in "Zhizn," No. 12, 1899.

little. I do not work much and I do not intend to write anything.

I was very disappointed "the Writer" did not write anything to me about Gvozdev. I too should like to swear at him, but I saw he was a collaborator in the same periodical and I felt compelled therefore to be as gentle as possible. It would have been strange to quarrel in the same periodical; perhaps "the Writer" wanted to get rid of the matter in this way, namely to get rid of the "Gvozdevism," as I now call such things. I do not definitely know this, nor do I know what kind of man Gvozdev is. It is difficult to judge at a distance.

Your
V. U.

P.S. Darling Mother, I am sending my article to you by registered post and a reprint of the article about the Sismondists for which you asked. I am writing in greater detail to Anyuta and Mark, from whom I received a letter this week. It is strange that their letter of the 14th/26th May was stamped "Krasnoyarsk." Was it sent by the Siberian Express?

I kiss you warmly,

Your
V. U.

49. (103 R). TO HIS MOTHER AND D. I. ULIANOV[1]

[Shushenskoye], 20th June/2nd July, 1899

Darling Mother,

I have received your letter of May 31st/June 12th. Thank you for it. With regard to the statistical publications of the Tver and Vyatka Provinces, I seem to remember having written before *that you do not need to send them all to me:* I am not studying this subject now and do not intend to until the end of my term of exile. If I happen to need the first or second book, it would be better to write separately for them, for as it is, I shall have to bring back a large number of books. However, you will probably not send many of the statistical publications.

---

[1] Lenin's brother Dymitry or Mitya.

Mikh. Al. writes that he is not expecting his fiancée before the end of the Summer.

We do not think it would be worth asking for a transfer to Krasnoyarsk. We happened to speak about it to El. Vas. who thought of seeking permission for me to go this Autumn to Ufa in view of the difficulty of the Winter journey for her and Nadya. If she succeeds, then I will write and tell you.

The allowance has been paid to us.

They write from Ermakovskoye about Anatole and say he is no better. They wrote that Lyakhovsky worked as a doctor in Chita.

It is a great pity you are having such bad weather and that you cannot rest as you should in the country. June here is also rainy. Our life goes on as usual. I study little and when the shooting season begins, I shall probably study still less.

I received the May number of "Nachalo"—much cut. There does not seem to be anything particularly interesting in it. I am losing hope of this journal ever recovering. They wrote to me, saying the Ministry of the Interior had insisted on the editors revealing the authors' pseudonyms in the January and April numbers; it would be interesting to know if any of our mutual friends were among those "revealed."

I kiss you warmly and send greetings to all our people,

Your

V. U.

For Mitya.

I found an article ["The Fundamental Mistake in Marx's Abstract Theory of Capitalism"] by Tugan-Baranovsky in No. 5 of the "Nauchnoye Obozreniye." It was monstrously stupid and absurd, he simply introduces at random an alteration in the norm of additional cost, so as to refute Marx and thus presupposes an absurdity: a change in the productivity of labour without a change in the cost of the product.

I do not know whether it is worth replying to each of these rubbishy little articles: let him first fulfil his promise to develop it more thoroughly. I am becoming a firm opponent of the newest critical trend in Marxism and *Neo-Kantianism* (which by the way has given birth to the idea of separating sociological from economic laws). The author [G. Plekhanov] of "Beiträge zur Geschichte des Materialismus" is perfectly right in pronouncing Neo-Kantianism to be a reactionary theory of the reactionary bourgeoisie and in revolting against Bernstein. Bogdanov's new book ("The Basic Elements of a Historical View on Nature," S.P.B. 1899) has aroused my interest. I wrote for it—there is a review of it in the May number of "Nachalo," written most stupidly, with grand phrases and neglecting the main ideas. I am very sorry I somehow missed the announcement of the book when it appeared. I think it must be an important book and such a review should not be allowed to remain without a reply. I am pleased with the gun. I did little shooting in the Spring. It will begin soon and I am thinking of doing more shooting this Summer.

I greet you warmly,

V. U.

P.S. Please send me a list of the three statistical publications you have sent me, i.e., their titles and brief contents (tables or tables plus text, nothing else).

50. (7 P¹). TO A. N. POTRESOV

[Shushenskoye], 27th June, 1899

Last Friday I received your letter of June 2nd but I have *not received* either the Mehring or the Karelin books which you say you have sent me. At first I waited for them, thinking there was some delay in the post, but now I am beginning to think the parcel has gone astray or else you have delayed posting it. If the first surmise is correct then make enquiries at once at the post office.

Your remarks about my book ["The Development of Capitalism in Russia"] made me happy, but all the same I think you exaggerate the importance of having it translated: it is doubtful whether the Germans would read a book full of purely local and detailed facts. Certainly N.'s [N. F. Danielson

"Outlines of our Post-reform Social Economy"] has been translated, but he had a wide reputation and probably a recommendation from Engels, although the latter (according to the Monist [G. V. Plekhanov] was intending to pull it to pieces. Have you seen any reviews of it in the German press? If I am not mistaken, it has been translated into French. I was rather surprised to read, that you "had at last managed to get hold of" my book. Did you not get a copy from Moscow or Petersburg? I asked them to send you one as well as to my other friends, and they have all received theirs. If you have not yet had your copy, let me know and I will write again to Moscow. So far, I have not seen any reviews of it in the press, but I am not expecting to see any before the Autumn— however, the only Russian newspaper I read is the "Russkiye Vedomosti" which continues its "tactful silence."

I have read Bulgakov's article in "Arkhiv" [a review of Kautsky's "Agrarian Question"]—I do not intend to reply to it for German readers yet. First, because I cannot write it in German—and secondly, even if I found a translator from the Russian, the article as written for the Russian public, with a detailed exposition of Kautsky's book, is quite unsuitable for the German public. I cannot answer Bulgakov's special citations (based on German statistics) for I have no information. Nor would I undertake to write for Germans about his general point of view (Kantian and Bernsteinian, if I may use such an expression) I think it is necessary to correct the Germans' ideas about Russian scholars, but to do this (if no one will undertake to write a separate article) it would be sufficient to make a simple comment about my article against Bulgakov ["Capitalism in Agriculture"] when it appears in a Russian journal. If it never appears . . . because of the extinction of "Nachalo," or because of the refusal of "Zhizn" to print it, or because of the censorship, then the matter would take on quite a different aspect.

As for the "staggering discoveries" made by Russian scholars and their Neo-Kantianism, I am becoming more and more incensed. I read Tugan-Baranovsky's article in Number 5 of the "Nauchnoye Obozreniye" . . . ["The Fundamental Mistake in Marx's Abstract Theory of Capitalism"] the devil only knows what such stupid and pretentious rubbish means! Without any historical study of Marx's doctrine and without any new investigations—it is based on mistakes in the schemes (the random alteration of the norm of additional cost) and the author makes a general rule out of an exceptional case (the increase of the production of labour *without* a decrease in the price of the product: an absurdity, if it is taken as a general phenomenon). On such a basis to announce a new theory! To talk about Marx's mistake . . . and suggest reconstruction . . . ! No! I cannot believe your remark that Tugan-Baranovsky is becoming more and more of a comrade. Mikhailovsky was right when he called him an "echo of a man." Do you remember his short article in "Mir Bozhy" (1895) "According to Beltov [= Plekhanov]" which confirms the severe strictures of a partial critic? It also confirms what I have heard of his personal qualities both from you and Nadya [Krupskaya]. Of course all this is not enough for a final decision and I may be altogether mistaken. It will be interesting to hear your opinion of his article.

And this idea of differentiating the "sociological" and "economic" categories launched by Struve ["On the Question of Markets in Capitalist Industry"] ("Nauchnoye Obozreniye" No. 1) and also repeated by P. Berzin (in "Zhizn") and by Tugan-Baranovsky! In my opinion it promises no more than an empty scholastic game of definitions to which the Kantians give the grand name of "Critique of Pure Reason" or even "gnoceology." I absolutely cannot understand what sense there can be in such differentiation. How can the economic be outside the social??

By the way, about Neo-Kantianism, which side are you taking? I have read and re-read with real pleasure "Beiträge zur Geschichte des Materialismus"; I have read articles by the same author [G. Plekhanov] in "Neue Zeit" against Bernstein and Konrad Schmidt (in Number 5 "Neue Zeit" 1898-99. I have not seen any further numbers). I have read Stammler ("Wirtschaft und Recht") much praised by our Kantians (P. Struve and Bulgakov) and I have definitely taken

the same side as the Monist. Stammler, in whom I refuse
to see the slightest hint of anything new or valuable, has infuriated me. Nothing but gnoceological scholasticism, stupid
definitions made by a most obtuse lawyer (in the very worst
sense of that word) and no less stupid deductions. After
Stammler, I re-read Struve's and Bulgakov's articles in
"Novoye Slovo" and I saw how essential it is to take Neo-
Kantianism seriously into account. I could not restrain myself
and I slipped in some remarks against him both in my reply to
Bulgakov and in my reply to Struve (his article in the "Nauchnoye Obozreniye." Why and by whom the printing of the reply
is being delayed I cannot understand!! They said it would appear in Number 6 of the "Nauchnoye Obozreniye" but it is
not there. Meanwhile my silence is becoming awkward for me;
for instance, Nezhdanov's article in Number 4 of "Zhizn")
I say I could not restrain myself, because I realise my lack
of philosophic education and I do not intend to write on such
themes until I have done some more reading. And that is
what I am studying now, having begun with Holbach and
Helvetius [French materialist] and I intend to pass on to
Kant. I have got hold of the most important classics of philosophy but I have no Neo-Kantian books (I have ordered
only Lange ["Geschichte des Materialismus und Kritik seiner
Bedeutung in der Gegenwart," 1896]). Please let me know
whether you or your friends happen to have any such books
and whether you could lend them to me.

A review of Bogdanov's book ["The Main Elements of a
Historic View of Nature"] in No. 5 of "Nachalo" (the May
number—suffering from consumption in its last stages!) interested me very much, being on the same subject. I cannot
understand how I could have missed an announcement of this
book. I have only just written to order it. After reading
Bogdanov's first book ["A Short Course of Economics"] I suspected the Monist [Plekhanov] and the title and contents of
his second book confirm my suspicions. And how indecently
empty and indecently arrogant the review is! Not a word on
the substance and . . . then censure for ignoring Kantianism,
although from the reviewer's remarks it is apparent that

Bogdanov does not *ignore* Kantianism, but *rejects* it, since he takes another viewpoint in philosophy. . . . I think (if I am not mistaken about Bogdanov) that this review cannot possibly be left unanswered. There is only one thing I cannot understand: how *could* Kamensky [Plekhanov] leave Struve's and Bulgakov's articles against Engels in the "Novoye Slovo" unanswered? Perhaps you could explain this to me?

Your information about the reaction against Marxism which has begun in Petersburg was news to me. I can't believe it. "Reaction"—does that mean among the Marxists? What kind of Marxists? Like Struve? Perhaps it is Struve and Co. who are developing the tendency of uniting with the Liberals? I shall await an explanation from you with great impatience. I quite agree that the "critics" only muddle the public *without saying anything at all*; also, I quite agree that a serious war with them (especially about Bernstein) is essential. But shall we have a paper in which to fight them? If Struve "completely ceases being a comrade"—then it will be all the worse for him. Of course it would be a great loss for all comrades, for he is a very talented and well-informed man, but obviously "friendship is friendship and work is work" and on this account the necessity for war will not disappear. I quite understand and share your "frenzy" (caused by the epithet "repugnant" sic ! ! !) [used by Struve in a letter to Potresov] with regard to the Monist. Why this? Was it because of the article in the "Neue Zeit" or the open letter to Kautsky about who is to bury whom? I am interested in his reply to your letter which expresses this fury (I have still not seen Bernstein's book ["Die Voraussetzungen des Sozialismus und die Aufgaben der Sozialdemokratie," 1899]). A thorough analysis is, of course, necessary, but it cannot and will not appear either in "Nachalo" or "Zhizn"; only special articles against "critics of Marxism" will appear. For this we need a third type of literature [illegal, party orthodox literature] and a platform (if I have understood you correctly). It will be then only that the real comrades will be differentiated from the "camp-followers" and then only will no personal caprices and staggering theoretical

discoveries cause confusion and anarchy. Cursed Russian disorganisation is entirely to blame here!

How your article about inheritance (I have read only No. 1)
was directed against the Petersburg people—is not clear to me.
I have not seen the article "Not in turn." Send it. I should
like to talk in greater detail and more fully about the Lightning
Conductor but I shall have to postpone that to another time.
My term ends on the 29th January 1900: that is, if they do not
increase it—which is the greatest misfortune and not infre-
quently happens to exiles in Eastern Siberia. I am dreaming
about Pskov. And what are you dreaming about?

Nadya sends greetings,
    I send you mine,

                                    Your
                                            V. U.

P.S. I have just re-read the rough draft of the conclusion of
my article against Bulgakov—and I see that the tone of it is
conciliatory. . . . I am an "orthodox" and a definite antago-
nist of the "critics" (I said this plainly), *but* these differences
should not be exaggerated (as Bulgakov does) in face of common enemies. Possibly the "conciliatory" tone (I did my best
to soften the tone and to polemicise as a comrade) will prove
to be inappropriate and even ridiculous if such expressions as
"repugnant" become current and if the "critics" bring about a
final differentiation. I should then prove to be innocently
guilty: not having seen Bernstein's book, not knowing all the
views of the critics and being at a safe distance (when I wrote
the article), I still held the old ideas as a collaborator in
"Nachalo." It seems that my assertion that the theory of class
warfare has not been touched by criticism is wrong?

            51. (107 R). TO HIS MOTHER

            [*Shushenskoye*], *1st/13th August, 1899*
Darling Mother,

    I believe we have scarcely any news this week. Summer has
come, the heat is intense and interferes somewhat with the

shooting in which I indulge all the more because it will probably soon come to an end.

I cannot remember whether I wrote to you about the doctor
(Y. M. Lyakhovsky) who is working as a doctor in Chita,
and is thinking of taking a similar job in Stretensk.

We have guests: M. A. and his wife and others.

Forgive me for ending this letter. We are all well and send
our greetings. I shall soon write to Anyuta in greater detail
about the Credo [1] (which interested and infuriated me and all
of us).

I kiss you warmly.

Your

V. U.

52. (112 R). TO HIS MOTHER

[Shushenskoye], 25th August/6th September, 1899

Darling Mother,

We came home last Sunday and received Manya's letter and
the cuttings (many thanks for them), also "Neue Zeit" from
Anyuta and offprints (two) of my articles against Levitsky.
I was particularly glad to receive them. Anyuta writes that
you are still undecided about making a trip out here and that
you would probably come, if you could be certain the steamer
would take you to Minusa and back again. When we read this,
we decided to send you a telegram that the steamers will run
until the middle of September (last year a steamer brought
me up to Minusa itself—true, it was the last—about the 20th
September), so that you would have sufficient time to come
here if, of course, you are quite well and Mitya's case is not
detaining you. I hope you have received the telegram in
time: sent on the 22nd August/3rd September. In reply we
shall expect either you in person or a letter. So far (two years)

---

[1] E. Kuskova's "Credo" which placed the views of the Russian Marxists on a
theoretical foundation of Bernsteinianism. Lenin disapproved strongly of this Credo
of the economists, drew up a protest in the name of 17 Social Democrats and called
a meeting of exiles in the village Ermakovskoye.

the Autumns have been pleasant here; I do not know what it will be like this year after a rainy Summer.

Of the books sent by Anyuta I was particularly glad to have Mehring ["Zur Geschichte der Deutschen Sozialdemokratie"]; I have only just got the second volume and was very, very pleased with it. As for the Credo of the young, I was simply astounded by the emptiness of its phrases. It is not a Credo, but merely a paltry collection of words! I am thinking of writing about it in greater detail.

"The Writer's" silence disgusts me. They have not sent Webb. They have not printed my article about the Markets and there is not a sound about the article against Bulgakov. Not a sound. I think all the manuscripts ought to be taken away from him and handed to the editor's office, so as to get punctual and accurate answers about their having been placed and to be able to have direct contact. Of course it is not possible for me to do this, but I think Anyuta might, if only her other activities would allow her to devote time to it. Surely it would be better to send them direct than to send them to "the Writer." If he has kept back my article against him, simply because he has not yet finished his reply to it,—then that is absolutely disgusting! [1] There is no point in writing to him— he does not reply.

I kiss you warmly and send greetings to all our people,

Your

V. U.

53. (113 R). TO HIS MOTHER

[*Shushenskoye*], *1st/13th September, 1899*

Darling Mother,

This time I could not write to you on Sunday, so I am writing to you in the middle of the week.

We received Bernstein's book yesterday; also "Vandervelde" and two numbers of the Moscow "Vedomosti." The

---

[1] Lenin was correct in his surmise. Struve published his "Reply to Lenin" in the same No. 8 of the "Nauchnoye Obozreniye" as Lenin's article "On the Question of the Theory of Realization."

Bernstein book was wrapped in one number of the newspaper and half of the other (No. 223) was in a separate wrapper, which surprised us greatly. Has something gone astray, or was it a mistake?

I have come to the conclusion that I can look upon Bernstein's book as belonging to me. Manyasha did not definitely say it had to be returned by a certain date, but she said she had taken steps to procure another copy. However, I badly need this book: if contrary to expectation Manyasha has to have it returned, let her write *at once* to me about it.

Nadya and I both sat down at once to read Bernstein's book ["Die Voraussetzungen des Sozialismus und die Aufgaben der Sozialdemokratie"] and we have read more than half of it; its contents astound us more and more. Theoretically, it is incredibly weak; a repetition of other people's ideas. There are mere phrases about criticism and no attempt at serious and independent criticism. Practically, it is opportunism (or rather Fabianism: the original source of a number of Bernstein's contentions and ideas is in the latest books written by the Webbs). It is indifferent opportunism and "possibilism" and cowardly opportunism at that, for Bernstein simply does not want to get anywhere near a programme. There can be no doubt about his fiasco. His statement that many Russians support him (Notes to pages 170 and 173) absolutely infuriated us, but then we have probably grown "old-fashioned" and are lagging behind the "new ideas" to be found in Bernstein. I will write presently and more fully to Anyuta on this subject.

We received Webb yesterday (at last!), the second volume in English (but not the German copy; we are ordering it today)—without any letter or any news whatsoever about the first volume!

I consider it is *essential* to alter my article against Bulgakov and to expand it. I shall do this from the manuscript which I have here. Will Anyuta ask at once for the immediate return of the *second article* ["Capitalism in Agriculture"] and keep it until she receives the corrections from me?

We have not much news. Anatole is getting worse and worse. Gleb is moving one of these days to Nizhneudinsk

(Irkutsk Province) to work on the railway. Eliz. Vas. received the money order yesterday for 100 roubles.

I kiss you warmly,

Your

V. U.

Greetings from all to all.

P.S. It appears that the "Frankfurter Zeitung" is being received not far from here, so there is no need to subscribe to it. I would ask Manyasha to try and get for me (by writing to Dresden, or by finding out from friends) copies of the "Sächsische Arbeiter Zeitung" for 1898 ((1) containing the articles by Parvus against Bernstein and (2) numbers 252-255 for 1898).[1]

54. (114 R). TO HIS MOTHER

[Shushenskoye], 11th/23rd September, 1899

Darling Mother,

I have to send you some very sad news: Anatole [Vaneyev] died on the 8th/20th September and we buried him in Ermakovskoye village on the 10th/22nd September. We had long given up hope of his recovery and latterly his illness developed very rapidly. His wife is staying for the present in Ermakovskoye. Mikh. Al. Silvin is faced with military service: he has already received a paper, ordering him to present himself in Minusinsk, and he is to go there on the 14th/26th September. If they take him, he will have to serve for two years—two months longer than his term of exile.

Nadya and I have begun work on the Webbs' second volume without waiting for the proof sheets of the first (which would be very useful for editing the translation of the second volume), or the second volume of the German translation. The work will probably take a fair amount of time. I am sending with this letter and under registered cover the correc-

---

[1] Containing G. Plekhanov's article: "Why We Ought to be Grateful to Him." An open letter to Karl Kautsky, in which Plekhanov fiercely criticises Bernstein.

tions of my article on Bulgakov. Ask Anyuta to make these alterations in my manuscript (by cutting out the old and pasting in the new), and to get into touch with the editors about placing it.

I should like to know the fate of my article as soon as possible. We are all well.

I kiss you warmly, my darling, and send greetings to all our people.

Your

V. U.

55. (115 R). TO HIS MOTHER

[Shushenskoye], 17th/29th October, 1899

Darling Mother,

This week I have had many interesting things from home, and I thank you for them.

I was exceedingly glad to make the acquaintance of that new French periodical ["Le Mouvement Socialiste"] which promises to be interesting. Its appearance under the editorship of Longue [1] is significant. I am also finishing reading the Stuttgart Protocols, also with great interest.[2] Finally, the book about the Professional Congress in Moscow (which came on Friday) is also very interesting and instructive.[3]

On the subject of literature, a lull. I think I have already told you that I saw an announcement in the papers about the publication of the Webbs' first volume and I *ordered a copy*, because they evidently think it is superfluous to send me one! I have heard of a new newspaper in Petersburg "Severny Kurier" [The Northern Courier].[4] I intend ordering it as

---

[1] G. Longue, an active member of the French Socialist party, was at one time the leader of its left wing. The grandson of K. Marx. Adopted a pacifist position during the war; one of the organisers of the II International, and later a member of the Bureau of the II International.

[2] The protocols of the Stuttgart Congress of the German Social Democracy. 3-8 Oct., 1898.

[3] Lenin's sister Anna evidently used this book for sending a chemical letter.

[4] A social, political and literary daily, in Petersburg from 1899-1900. It was Marxist. Its contributors, among others, were P. Struve, M. Tugan-Baranovsky, S. and Z. Vengerov.

soon as I see an announcement in the papers. Julius wrote to me from Turuhansk, saying that there was a feuilleton in "Novosti" by M. Engelhardt[1]: "Uncovered Cards," containing a cruel slashing of Il'in's book on capitalism. It would be interesting to see it—but only if the finding and buying of it in Moscow does not mean too much trouble. I see "Zhizn" occasionally; No. 7 was sent me absolutely unexpectedly, straight from Petersburg and almost direct from the editors (sic ! ! ? ! !) "Nauchnoye Obozreniye" is occasionally sent to me by some people who live near and whom we sometimes manage to see.

Everything goes on here as usual. Are you now settled in Moscow? And who is going abroad and when? Anya or Manyasha? Has Mitya remained alone in Podolsk?

I kiss you warmly and send greetings to all our people.

Your

V. U.

[There is a postscript to this letter written by Krupskaya in which she says that Lenin is busy on the Webb translation, working on it alone, as it takes longer when they work together; that the work is fairly dull, because the German translation is bad and they have almost to retranslate it. Only three months and thirteen days of their exile remain and Krupskaya has petitioned the Department of Police for permission to go to Pskov (this was refused).]

[1] Engelhardt attacked the representatives of "Neo-Marxism" (V. Il'in and Tugan-Baranovsky), as he called the Russian Marxists, and reckoned them among the ideologists of the bourgeoisie.

THE "ISKRA" ("THE SPARK") AND "ZARYA" ("DAWN") PERIOD

1900–1903

SUMMARY

1900

Feb.: Plekhanov's "Vademecum" criticises economism. Liberation of Labour Group proclaims struggle against anti-revolutionary elements in the Party. The majority of the Union of S.D. support economism. The difference of opinion between economists and politicians results in the "Liberation of Labour Group" leaving the Union of Russian Social Democrats in March, and in April they form a revolutionary organisation of Social Democrats.

Dec.: No. 1 "Iskra" appears. Its epigraph: "From the spark will come the flame." "Iskra" defends the political and revolutionary side of Marxism.

1901

The struggle against economism and Narodnik ideology continues. The "Iskra" group publishes "Zarya" ("Dawn") for working out theoretical problems.

June: Geneva Conference (draft project prepared for agreement between S.D. organisations abroad. Decision to call a general Congress).

1900

Feb.: Siberian exile ends. Vain attempt to renew the publication of the Central Party organ, "The Workers' Newspaper," with Martov and Potresov as editors. Decision for Lenin and Potresov to publish a S.D. newspaper abroad in co-operation with the "Liberation of Labour Group."

Residence in S.P.B. forbidden. Settles in Pskov.

Pskov Conference: attended by Lenin, Martov, Potresov, Radchenko, Struve, Tugan-Baranovsky, who work out a plan for publications abroad. Illegal visits to S.P.B., Moscow, Nizhny-Novgorod and Ufa to form links with local S.D.'s. Arrested on S.P.B. visit in May. Three weeks prison.

July: Goes abroad. Contact in Switzerland with the "Liberation of Labour Group," led by Plekhanov.

Autumn: Agreement reached between Lenin and "Liberation of Labour Group" re-publication of newspaper, but the Group keeping its organisational independence. Secret links with underground political groups in Russia. Begins publication of "Iskra" in München; editor and collaborator.

1901

Lenin abroad is the leader of the "Iskra" organisation. Krupskaya is its secretary.

October: Zürich Congress. Agreement between S.D. organisations not reached.
Under pressure from Lenin, the "Iskra"
group breaks off negotiations with economists and forms a "League of Russian
revolutionary Social Democracy abroad."

1902

Growth of Workers' S.D. organisations.
Beginning of demonstrations.
April: Belostok Conference to decide
question of convening II Party Congress.
Election of Organisational Committee to
prepare for Congress. Police interfere;
"Iskra" transferred to London.
June: Editors of "Zarya" and "Iskra"
publish programme of the R.S.D.L.P.,
which becomes the official Party programme at the II Congress.
October: II Belostok Conference: election of second Organisation Committee of
the "Iskra" direction.

1903

The Organisation Committee for the II
Congress is very active, and by the Sum-
mer most local Committees support
"Iskra" principles.

1902

Editor of main Party organ. Works out
Party programme. Writes book, "What is
to be Done?" (criticism of the Right
Wing of the Russian S.D.). Publishes
"Letter to a Comrade on Our Organisational Tasks" (re the organisation of local
cells of the R.S.D.L.P. subordinated to
the directives of a conspiratorial centre
of professional revolutionaries). Summer
holiday, North Coast of France, with his
mother and sister, Anna.

1903

Feb. and March: Lectures in Paris at
the Russian Ecole des Sciences Sociales
on the Agrarian question.
April: Moves to Geneva where "Iskra"
has been transferred.

1900

56. (117 R). TO HIS MOTHER

[Pskov], 15th/28th March, 1900

Darling Mother,

The other day I received your letter! On the 10th/23rd
I sent a petition for Nadya and I expect an answer soon. If it
is unfavourable (contrary to expectation), I am seriously
thinking of asking you (if you are well) to go personally to
present a petition, but that will be later on. We must wait
and see.

I received "Zhizn," so do not send it.

Ask Anyuta to send the "Arkhiv" to Nadya (I find I have

a second copy here for the time being). I am living quite comfortably here. I often visit the library and go for walks.

Forgive this brief letter; I am late for the post.

I kiss you warmly and send greetings to all our people,

Your

V. U.

P.S. A certain doctor is praised here and I want to consult him about my catarrh. They say, that with the approach of Spring in Petersburg there are various epidemic illnesses.[1]

57. (119 R). TO HIS MOTHER

[Pskov], 6th/19th April, 1900

Darling Mother,

Today I received a letter from Manyasha, dated the 3rd/16th March, in which she blames me for my silence. I am guilty —I did not even congratulate you and Manyasha on April 1st. The fact is I was again "twisted up" (as Nadya expressed it to our Siberian comrades) on the arrival of a long awaited traveller [Martov][2] who has probably reached his home by now.

My life goes on as usual; my health is satisfactory and today I tried giving up taking "the waters." I walk—it is quite pleasant to go for walks here—and in Pskov (as well as in the surrounding district) there are apparently a number of pretty places. I bought some picture postcards of Pskov in the local shops and am sending three: for you, Manyasha and Anyuta.

I received a letter from M. A. [Silvin] yesterday: he writes (on the 4th/17th April) that tomorrow or the day after he is again going to Siberia (with O. A.) [Olga Silvin]—the military authorities have again altered his place of service. He has promised to send their new address from Achinsk.

Nadya is probably laid up; the doctor has found (as she

---

[1] By epidemics Lenin means arrests.

[2] Yu. Martov came to the Pskov conference on his way from Siberia, and then left for Poltava.

wrote a week ago) that her illness (gynæcological) requires persistent treatment and that she must go to bed for two to six *weeks*. (I sent her some more money (I received 100 roubles from Vodovozova), for the treatment will mean considerable expense. I shall have sufficient for the time being and, if I run short, then I will write to you.) This means she would not have been able to come to me, even if she had been granted permission. (I have still no reply and have almost given up hope of expecting one.)[1] I am thinking of visiting her in the Spring in about six weeks' time—perhaps sooner.

My friend here[2] is taking out a passport for abroad and is thinking of going for a cure round about the 20th April; I shall be fairly dull when he goes.

I am taking German lessons at 50 kopecks a lesson from a local German. We translate from the Russian, converse a little—we are not progressing very quickly and I am wondering whether to give it up—however, we shall see. Altogether I am not doing much studying: I have not finished the index to the Webb translation yet. I go to the library and read the newspapers. I see few new books; I have not seen Davydov's book ["What is Economic Materialism?"]. Will Manyasha send me a copy if she has one? I am not thinking of replying to P. Struve. (I have sent a small paragraph directed against him to be inserted into my article in answer to Skvortsov). I have seen Kachorovsky's book ["The Russian Commune"] and I am thinking of replying to him. Has Manyasha seen numbers 3 and 4 of the "Nauchnoye Obozreniye"? It contains a splendid article on Pisarev [by Vera Zasulich].

So Mitya has thrown up his work and settled down to studying? That is excellent. Is Manyasha working hard? How and where have Anyuta and Mark settled?

I send you congratulations, my darling, and kiss you warmly.

---

[1] Lenin was granted police permission to go to Moscow for a week, but Krupskaya's permission to move from Ufa to Pskov was refused.

[2] A. N. Potresov went abroad in April, 1900, to get into touch with Plekhanov and Axelrod and to see about the possible publication of a theoretical journal abroad. Potresov also had to find out from German Social Democrats whether it would be possible to print secretly a newspaper in Germany.

Thank Manyasha for her letter,   Greetings to Mitya.

Your

V. U.

58. (121 R). PETITION

TO HIS EXCELLENCY THE DIRECTOR OF THE DEPARTMENT OF POLICE

A Petition presented by the hereditary noble, Vladimir Ilich Ulianov, residing in the town of Pskov, in Archangel Street, in the house owned by Chernov.

His Excellency the Minister of the Interior has issued instructions that I be forbidden residence in certain districts, including the Ufa Province. At the present time my wife, Nadezhda Ulianova, who is under police surveillance, is living in the town of Ufa and it was not considered desirable to grant the permission which I sought (in my petition of March 10th of this year) for her to be transferred to the town of Pskov.

According to the latest news concerning my wife, she has fallen ill and is being treated by the local specialist in women's diseases, Dr. Fedotov; I give the doctor's name so that my statement may be corroborated; and in case it is essential to check my statement, I have the honour humbly to beg that the enquiry be made by telegraph. My wife's illness necessitates consistent treatment, which, in the words of the doctors, will require not less than six weeks and, as my wife's mother, who is with her, has soon to leave Ufa, my wife will be left alone, which may have a very harmful effect upon the cure.

On the basis of the above statement, I have the honour humbly to beg permission to reside for six weeks in the town of Ufa.

Hereditary nobleman,
Vladimir Ulianov.
Pskov.

20th April, 1900.

59. (122 R). TO HIS MOTHER

[Pskov], 5th/18th May, 1900

Darling Mother,

It was only this morning that I received your letter of the 2nd/15th, with Manyasha's postscript. Why the letter was late I do not know (you expected me to receive it on the 3rd/16th or not later than the 4th/17th); the postmarks on it are "Postal Waggon of the 2nd" and "Pskov 4th/17th" so there was probably no delay. The letter arrived on the 4th/17th in Pskov and was delivered this morning. Probably letters from Podolsk cannot come as quickly as from Moscow.

You are worrying about me, my darling, quite unnecessarily: my health is considerably better. I have given up taking the waters long ago and not once have I felt the wish or need to start taking them again. I received a certificate yesterday from the Chief of Police stating that for his part he has no objection to my going abroad. I paid half my deposit today (10 roubles) and in two hours' time I shall receive my passport endorsed for abroad. This means that I shall move in the Summer to warmer parts; I cannot leave here immediately, because I must come to some arrangement with editors and certain publishers of translations and also wind up certain money affairs (by the way, I am hoping to receive a small sum from Filippov: if I do not receive it from him or from Popova, then I shall write and ask you to send me a little). Besides, I must wait for an answer to my petition to the Department for permission to spend six weeks in Ufa on account of my wife's illness. I sent the petition on the 20th April/3rd May and there ought to be a reply in about a week's time. I shall certainly go and see Nadya, but I do not know yet whether I shall spend six weeks with her or whether, (which is more likely), I shall have to content myself with less time. In any case I shall not be hampered by having my passport endorsed for abroad. I had to get it in Pskov, where I have been living lately, for by law such passports when issued in the provinces do not expire for three months, which means it will not be too late, even if I were to leave Russia on the 5th/18th

August. Therefore as I have already told you, I am thinking of leaving here on the 15th/28th or the 20th May/2nd June, but of course I shall try to get away before that. Write what I am to do with my things; shall I leave them in Moscow (is Mark there and in which flat? Will he be staying long in Moscow and does he often come to visit you?) Or am I to take them straight to Podolsk (I do not know whether that will be convenient. I think I shall have to take all my things with me including my books). I would ask Manyasha to write to me in greater detail as to how I am to find you in Podolsk.

I embrace you warmly and send greetings to all our people. I shall see you soon,

Your

V. U.

Nadya writes that her health is better. I have just received a passport from the Governor General's Chancellery and have made enquiries about my petition asking for permission to go to Ufa. Apparently it has been refused ! ! ! [1] I did not expect that and I do not know what to do now.

60. (123 R). TO HIS MOTHER

[Pskov], 10th/23rd May, 1900

Darling Mother,

I have just received your letter of the 8th/21st and am settling down to answer it at once. I am very glad to say I have received permission to see you and I shall obviously make use of it; unfortunately I cannot leave at once, for I should not like to return here and I have to spend another five or six days or thereabouts so as to settle certain money matters and business with editorial offices. But it is unimportant whether I arrive a week or so later. On the whole I agree with your and Anyuta's arguments, (by the way, thank you for the work on town statistics received today). I think I shall do as you

---

[1] Lenin was granted permission to visit Krupskaya in Ufa, and he, his mother, and his sister Anyuta spent over a month there in the summer of 1900. Lenin returned to Podolsk soon after the 10th July.

suggest, only I shall have to give up a personal trip to St. Petersburg and I must ask you to go there instead of me, if you can get there by Thursday[1] the 18th/31st; if you are too late then by Thursday, 25th May/7th June, all according to whether we shall see each other.

Goodbye until we meet,

Your

V. U.

61. (125 R). TO HIS MOTHER

[Ufa], 2nd/15th July, 1900

Darling Mother,

Unfortunately I have to tell you that our meeting must be somewhat delayed: I am compelled to go for a short visit to a comrade in Siberia[2] and I shall not, therefore, be coming through Podolsk before the 20th July/2nd August or the 21st July/3rd August (I should think the latter). I shall then have time simply to collect my things, have my passport viséd, and then go on. If my things are not there yet—I beg Mitya to do what he possibly can and before he goes on his own journey. All our people are well and send you greetings.

I embrace you tenderly, my darling, and send love to all our people,

Your

V. U.

62. (127 R). TO HIS MOTHER

[Nüremberg], 18th/31st August, 1900

Darling Mother,

I am surprised not to have received a single letter from you: I wrote to you twice from Paris[3] and am writing en route. I

---

[1] His mother did succeed in getting police permission in Petersburg for Lenin to go to Ufa, as requested in his petition.

[2] Lenin did not go on a visit to Siberia: he visited Podolsk on July 10/23 and left Russia on 16/29 July to go abroad in order to establish the paper "Iskra." ("The Spark.")

[3] Lenin did not live in Paris in 1900, and if he did visit it, it must have been only for a short while. But for conspiratorial reasons he sent his letters to Russia via Paris.

have been taking a trip down the Rhine.[1] I am well and am spending the time quite pleasantly: I saw Anyuta the other day and we went boating on a very pretty lake and enjoyed the exquisite views and fine weather; but fine weather seems to be unusual here, only rain and thunderstorms. The Summer is as unsatisfactory for tourists as it is in Russia.

I kiss you warmly and send greetings to all our people. Ask Manyasha to send as soon as possible all the books which are addressed to me. I hope to write to you soon about the boxes.

Your

V. U.

You can write to me at the same address, or to Anyuta, who will forward letters, although that is slower than sending them to Paris.

63. (9 P[1]). TO AN UNKNOWN ADDRESSEE

Nüremberg, 5th September, 1900

Dear Comrade,

And so, I suppose, we shall not be able to see each other: we do not intend going either to Mainz or to Paris. We are leaving here tomorrow.[2] It is a great pity, but one has to be resigned and be content with conversation in letters.

Firstly, I hasten to introduce a correction into a remark in your first letter—a correction which I would ask you to pass on to *him* who gave you the message about my apparent "promise" to meet. That is not true. I did not promise to meet, but said that we would *officially* (i.e. in the name of our group) get into touch with the Union [of Russian Social Democrats abroad], when we were abroad, *if a need for that should arise.* It is a pity that G. ["Grishin" = Ts. Kopelson] forgot this condition and also forgot to add that I spoke to him personally and not officially and consequently *could not* promise anything definite, which would forestall the decision of our group. After we had listened here to the other side [i.e. the

---

1 Lenin visited Germany in August, 1900, to see Adolf Braun, the German Social Democrat who helped considerably in establishing "Iskra" in Germany.

2 For München, the place chosen for the "Iskra" headquarters.

Liberation of Labour Group] and learnt about the Congress and the split,[1] we saw that there was no need for an official communication. That is all. The Union *has absolutely no right* to take exception to me, but I take exception to the fact that G. passed on the gist of our conversation to superfluous people, although he gave me a *formal* promise that he would not tell *anyone anything excepting the arrested person* [?] before dealing with the Union of our group. Since you have passed on to me his complaint,—I hope, as you are in Paris, you will not refuse to pass on to him this my rejoinder. If the rumour [about the proposed "Iskra"] has spread very far, then it is G. who is to blame.

Secondly—another little digression from the main point:— I have heard what G. (*whom I saw for a few days*) has to say and also what the other side has to say. You, however, have heard only the Unionites; you have not heard any sufficiently influential or authoritative representatives of the other side. It therefore seems to me that the rule "audiatur et altera pars" has been broken by you rather than by me.

Now, let us pass on to the main matter. Fusion *is impossible*. Federation is also impossible; if we are to take the word in its real sense, i.e., a certain agreement, a part, mutual undertaking etc. "The striving to help one another to the utmost" —that, I think, is not connected with federation; it can exist without it, and is quite possible, although I do not know whether it is easily realisable—if the Union really sincerely desired it, then I doubt if it would have issued ultimata against us from the outset and threatened us with boycott (that was the very meaning of the words of the person who delivered your letter): that will not bring about an improvement in our relations.

We are an independent literary group. We wish to remain independent. We do not consider it possible to conduct matters without such forces as Plekhanov and the Liberation of Labour

---

[1] At the Congress of the Union of Russian Social Democrats abroad, held in April, 1900, the Liberation of Labour Group left the Union on the grounds of principial differences. The Liberation of Labour Group were orthodox Marxists and acted on the principles of revolutionary Social Democracy, whereas the majority of the Union went over to economism and the criticism of Marxism.

Group, but *no one has the right to conclude* from this that we are losing even a *particle of our independence:* that is all that we can say at present to people who wish to know what our attitude is towards the Liberation of Labour Group. He who is not satisfied with this, must be told only this: "Judge us by our deeds, if you do not believe our words." But if we were to speak of the more or less immediate *future* and not of *the present moment,* then of course we would not refuse to tell those people with whom we will have close relations further detailed facts about the *form* of the relations between us and the Liberation of Labour Group.

You will ask: what will our relations be with the Union? *For the present we will not have any,* and we shall not have any because of our *irrevocable* decision to remain an independent group and to make use of the closest co-operation with the Liberation of Labour Group, but this decision is causing the mistrust of the Union, which is afraid that we shall not be able to preserve our complete independence and that we shall fall into an "impossible" (your expression) polemical tone. If our activity dispels this mistrust on the part of the Union, then we shall be able to establish good relations; if not, then not. Voilà tout. You write: "The eyes of the Union are turned on you"; but it is obvious that we could help the Union only in a literary way; and it is no less obvious that at the present time, when all our vital energies must be devoted to the nourishing of our infant ["Iskra"] which is about to be born, we cannot undertake the feeding of other people's children.

You write, that (1) there are no differences of opinion where principles are concerned and that (2) the Union is actually ready to prove its determination to struggle against the "economic direction." We are *convinced* that *you are mistaken* on both those points. Our conviction is based on such *literary* works as the *afterword* to the "Anti Credo," the *answer* to the "Vade mecum"; No. 6 of the "Rabocheye Delo"; the *preface* to the pamphlet; the turning point in the Jewish workers' movement and others. We intend to appear in literature with a refutation of the opinion that there is no difference of principles (so that we shall have *certain* connections with the Union: such as exist between polemists).

Now the last and the *main* thing is: are we right or wrong in observing a very sharp change of view in you? Let us recall what happened in Russia. You *knew* we wanted to establish an *independent* literary undertaking. You *knew* we were on Plekhanov's side. Consequently, you knew *everything* and not only did you not refuse to participate, but you yourself used the expression "our venture," "our undertaking," (do you remember our last conversation à trois and in your flat?). And by this attitude you caused us to expect the closest collaboration from you. Now, however, there is *not a word* from you about participation. You give us "the task, no matter what happens, to settle the conflict abroad," namely a task which we never undertook and which we will not undertake now—without, of course, losing the hope that the formation of an *independent* undertaking with the collaboration of the Liberation of Labour Group may create the basis for settling the conflict. You are evidently doubtful of the expediency of our group creating an *independent venture*, for you write that the existence of two organisations "the one leaving the other to act as the spirit moves" would be harmful to the cause. It seems to us indisputable that your views have altered radically. We have stated with complete frankness how our affairs stand at present and shall be glad if our exchange of opinions on the subject of tasks ahead of us will not end with this.

Address Nüremberg,

Ph. Roegner

64. (30 P[1]). TO N. K. KRUPSKAYA IN UFA

[München, September, 1900]

I have long been thinking of writing to you about various matters, but a number of obstacles has prevented me. I am living in such a chaos and this (N.B.) in spite of the extraordinary measures I have taken to preserve myself from any disturbance. I live practically in solitude and yet the disturbance is not any less. We must admit that this is inevitable

and unavoidable in every new situation and it would be wrong
to complain, because I am not nearly as nervous as our dear
"bookseller" [A. N. Potresov] who falls into black melancholy and becomes prostrate on account of this chaos. There
are, however, several good things as well as chaos! Well, I
will now tell you about events in the Union of Russian Social
Democrats abroad and I will tell you about them on the basis
of facts and tales from the *other* side. . . .

First of all, there is quite a wrong idea in Russia about the
"Vade mecum"[1] spread under the influence of tales made up
by those on the side of "Rabocheye Delo." To listen to them
—it is nothing more than an attack on personalities, nothing
but generalities and an exaggeration of trivialities because of
the slandering of personalities; nothing but the use of inadmissible methods etc. Actually the *principial* side predominates and
it predominates to a great extent. Attacks on personalities are
only by the way, and inevitable on account of the confused
and tense relationships which the young people have tried to
create. "Vade mecum" is a wail—simply a wail against economism, against the disgrace and shame of Social Democracy.
"I never thought that I was destined to live through such
disgrace," Plekhanov exclaims at the end of documents published by him. "We must get out of this chaotic and shameful
condition whatever happens. Woe to the Party who patiently
suffers such a muddle!" And against all the attacks on Plekhanov, first of all one must definitely establish that the whole
meaning of his pamphlet is a declaration of war against the
disgraceful principles of credism and fragmentarianism. It is a
cleavage in principle, while cleavage and a fight in the "Union"
is only a *side issue* of that difference of principles.

If the principial cleavage has associated itself with such a
fight (at the April 1900 II Congress of the "Union of the

[1] The pamphlet "Vade mecum" for the editorial board of the "Rabocheye Delo"
("the Workers' Cause") published by the Liberation of Labour Group in Geneva in
February, 1900, consisted of documents and material showing the anti-revolutionary
character of economism and with a long preface by Plekhanov. Against the economists'
"Credo," for instance, was Lenin's Protest of the Russian Social Democrats, written
by him when he was in exile.

Russian Social Democrats" abroad, matters *literally* reached the point of fighting, hysterics etc. etc. which is what caused Plekhanov's resignation [1])—if that is what has happened, then it is the fault of the young people. From the point of view of economism the young people waged a systematic, persistent and dishonest struggle against the Liberation of Labour Group throughout 1898. It was "dishonest" because they did not *openly* show their banner, because they blamed everything on to "Russia" (but saying nothing about the anti-economic, social democracy of Russia) because they made use of their connections and their practical resources to attack the Liberation of Labour Group and to represent their unwillingness to permit "disgraceful" ideas and "disgraceful" shallowness of thought as a refusal to allow any young forces to come to the fore in general. This struggle against the Liberation of Labour Group, this attack on it was effected in silence, on the sly, privately, by means of "private" letters and "private" conversations—or to put it bluntly: by means of *intrigues,* because the question of the rôle of the "Liberation of Labour Group" in Russian Social Democracy never was, never will be and never can be a *private* matter. The young people proclaimed "new" views against the old people, but the young hid those views so cunningly and so diplomatically, (proving thereby that for them the very question of views was a private matter), that the *old people* had to *expound* the disputes. "We sent the explanation of our disagreements with the young people to Petersburg," Plekhanov writes, (page XLVII Vade mecum). Thus as far back as 1898 "The Liberation of Labour Group" *proved* that its attitude towards the whole question consisted in the wavering of the young in the matter of principles, and who were capable of falling even to a complete denial of socialism. Already in 1898 the Liberation of Labour Group came forward with *an appeal* to Russian Social Democracy against a wavering of thought—but this appeal turned out to be a voice crying in the wilderness, for after the failures in the Summer of 1898,

[1] At this congress principial differences between the revolutionary wing ("The Liberation of Labour" Group) and the "economist" majority of the Union were further complicated by a row and fighting.

all the outstanding active Party workers were swept off the field of battle and in answer to the appeal only the voice of the "economists" was heard.

It is not surprising that after this, the Liberation of Labour Group should have left the editorial board; not surprising, that the open war against economism became more and more insistent and inevitable. But at this point there came to the aid of those who were of the "economic direction," people who were united with those economists by the old hatred for the Liberation of Labour Group. These people did not stop at an attempt to make allowances for "economism," without washing their linen in public, so as to allow economism to continue and with still greater comfort—to continue their tactics of private propaganda of their ideas under the flag of Social Democracy and under the cover of ambiguous announcements of the new editorial board, who wish to imitate that gentle calf which sucks the milk from two mothers.

The new editorial board announced in the very first number of the "Rabocheye Delo" that "it does not know about which young comrades P. B. Axelrod is speaking" in attacking the economists—it announced this in spite of the fact that the struggle with "the young" formed the whole history of the Union abroad for the last few years; it announced this even in spite of the fact that on the editorial board of the "Rabocheye Delo" there was a person that *adhered* to the "economic" direction (Mr. V. I-n) [V. P. Ivanshin]. To a man who stands outside this matter, who does not think deeply into the history of Russian Social Democracy and the Social Democratic Union abroad of the last few years, it may seem completely unintelligible and strange why this small and (*apparently*) casual remark made by the editors of the "Rabocheye Delo" (we do not know about what young comrades P. B. Axelrod is speaking) should be the spark that started a fire, and from which there flared up the most passionate polemics which ended by a split in the Union abroad and its collapse. Meanwhile there is nothing strange in this seemingly strange circumstance. The small remark made by the editors of the "Rabocheye Delo" in connection with their printing the articles by Mr. V. I-n very clearly showed *the radical difference between the two ways of understanding the immediate tasks and the vital demands of Russian Social Democracy.* The first can be expressed by the words laissez-faire, laissez-passer, with regard to "economism," those are the tactics of a conciliatory attitude towards it, tactics of covering the "extremes" of "economism"; tactics of protecting "economism" from a direct struggle against it, tactics of "free criticism" i.e. free criticism of Marxism on the part of all sorts of direct and disguised ideologues of the bourgeoisie. The other demanded a definite struggle against "economism," an open protest against the threatening belittlement and narrowing-down of Marxism, an irrevocable breach with bourgeois "criticism."

65. (128 R). TO HIS MOTHER

Paris, 24th August/7th September, 1900

Darling Mother,

I have received Manya's letter and postcard and was very glad to have news from home. I have been back some days from the trip on the Rhine. I do not intend to stay here long and shall probably remove somewhere else soon—where to, I do not know yet, but I will write when it is settled.

Manyasha complains about the brevity of my letters; I confess I am guilty, but I must say in self-defence that here willy-nilly one becomes "wrapped up" and with so many different diversions, it is difficult to make a selection and to dsecribe them in greater detail. I hope when I leave here—i.e. when I am somewhat removed from the rushing and fussing of the Exhibition and Exhibition atmosphere—I shall be in a condition and position to write more sensibly. Until then, please forgive me for my short letters.

I kiss you tenderly, my darling, and send greetings to all our people.

Your

V. U.

Manyasha does not mention your health. I hope this means

you are well? How are Mitya's affairs? When is Mark moving and when are you all going to Moscow? What is known about Manyasha's case? [1]

66. (129 R). TO HIS MOTHER

(Munich), 6th/19th September, 1900

Darling Mother,

Yesterday (no, the 16th, not yesterday) I received your letter of the 23rd August/5th September and I was very glad to have it. I also received the first letters from Manyasha and her postcard of the 24th August/6th September in which she says there has been another reminding letter from the office. I have *already sent* the address to Manyasha which should be given to the office.[2] I hope she has received it? It is most annoying that Mitya has been refused permission to enter the University. To lose another year—it's the very devil! Perhaps he will succeed yet with the help of one of those *dodges* about which you write. So Manyasha's position is also indefinite?

I had a letter from Anyuta yesterday and I hope to see her one of these days. We have had splendid trips together. I am thinking of beginning my water cure soon, so as to have more regular treatment. The weather here is very fine; the bad weather has gone and we shall be able to have some good walks. Darling Mother, I have enough clothes and money, so that for the present you do not need to send either one or the other. I hope not to have to write about money for some time and when I do need to, I shall try to reckon it out beforehand.

Yesterday I also had a letter from Nadya; she says she is "well settled" and has a large number of lessons—seven hours a day!

I embrace you warmly, my darling, and send greetings to

---

[1] Lenin's sister Manyasha was arrested in the autumn, 1899, and exiled to Nizhny-Novgorod. Later she moved to Paris. She remained for a year under police surveillance in Samara.

[2] The transport office, through which books were sent to Lenin.

all our people. I wish I could soon see a possibility of settling down for the Winter and of making better arrangements for myself.

Your

V. U.

Oh! I almost forgot to add: on the 17th September that is on the 4th (our date in Russia) I received Braun's "Arkhiv" which I had left behind. It came here very quickly. Many thanks to Manyasha.

67. (11 P¹). TO A. A. YAKUBOVA, AN ACTIVE SOCIAL DEMOCRAT IN LONDON

[München], 26th October, [1900]

I received your letter of the 24th October yesterday and as requested I answer it at once.

I cannot forward the letter at present hidden in something else to the address I have, but only as a "chemical" letter. I have however no time to copy the letter by this method. Yesterday I wrote to the addressee telling him the gist of the letter, and I hope to be able to send him the whole of it in the near future. Or perhaps you will copy it chemically into an unbound book—then I will forward it at once.

I will send the address to my sister [A. I. Elizarova]: she was not in Paris in September, so I doubt if they were there at the same time. I hope you have written a few lines to her to the address I gave you?

And now to business.

Your letter gives me a curious impression. If I were to exclude all the information about addressing and forwarding letters there remain nothing but reproaches; bare reproaches without any explanations or reasons. These reproaches are almost cutting ("Are you convinced you have done this for the benefit of the Russian Workers' Movement or for the benefit of Plekhanov?") but I do not intend to exchange cutting remarks with you.

You rebuke me for having dissuaded you. You quote my

words inaccurately. I remember distinctly expressing myself not at all categorically: "We find it difficult at the present moment to give advice," I wrote; i.e. I was simply stating our decision, this being conditional upon a further elucidation of the matter. What the elucidation was to be—is perfectly clear from my letter: it was essential for us to understand fully whether a "change of opinion" had actually taken place in the "Rabochaya Mysl" ["Workers' Thought"] (as we were told and had the right to conclude from the fact that you had turned to Plekhanov with a proposal to participate), and what that change was.

You do not say a word about this important question. Long ago you knew that we look upon the "Rabochaya Mysl" as a paper having a particular viewpoint from which we most seriously diverge. Both I and the addressee [A. N. Potresov] of your bulky letter plainly refused to participate in such a paper and it is obvious that, since we took up this attitude, we could not but advise others to do the same.

But the information about the change of opinion in the "Rabochaya Mysl" places us in a difficulty. An *actual* change would alter the matter fundamentally. Therefore it is natural that *before anything else* in my letter I should wish to ascertain all the details about this change, but you do not say a word about it.

However, perhaps you think an answer to my question is contained in your letter to Potresov? Perhaps that is so, if your approaching Plekhanov in the name of the editorial board of the "Rabochaya Mysl" and your letter to the friend can be considered as an authentic expression of editorial views. If *yes*, then I am inclined to conclude there has been no change of opinion at all. If I am mistaken—please explain where I am wrong. The other day a supporter of Plekhanov wrote to me about this change in the "Rabochaya Mysl," but, being in correspondence with you, I cannot believe these "rumours" if they are not confirmed by information from you.

I had better say again, (even at the risk of incurring fresh reproaches), that being in complete agreement with my friend (to whom you write) I support his words: "We shall have to fight with you"—if there is no such change of opinion. If there is, then we must elucidate in detail what exactly this change is.

You have written to the friend:—"fight if you are not ashamed." Of course, he will answer you himself, but I too would like to send my retort. We are not at all ashamed to fight, if matters have reached such a pitch that differences have affected the most fundamental questions, if an atmosphere has arisen of mutual misunderstanding, mutual mistrust and of the most complete divergence; (I am not talking *only* about "Rabochaya Mysl"; I mean everything I saw and heard, *not so much* here, as at home) and if on such grounds a number of splits has already arisen. Then to remove this ghastly atmosphere we can and must welcome even a terrible thunderstorm, and not only polemics in literature.

Besides, there is no need to be particularly afraid of the struggle: it will probably cause annoyance to a few people, but it will clear the air, define relations exactly, show what differences of opinion are essential and which are of secondary importance; it will show which people are following another path and where the Party comrades are who differ from us in certain particulars.

You say there were mistakes in the "Rabochaya Mysl." Of course, we all make mistakes, but how can one without a struggle separate these mistakes of individuals from that *direction* which is seen distinctly in the "Rabochaya Mysl" and which reaches a culmination in the Credo? There cannot be any critical examination even without a struggle, and without a critical examination there cannot be any advance, there cannot be any *firm unity*. And those who are beginning to struggle at the present moment are by no means *destroying* unity. There is no unity, it has already been destroyed, destroyed all along the line. Russian Marxism and Russian Social Democracy are ruined temples and an open, direct struggle is an essential condition for the *re-establishment* of unity.

Yes, a *re-establishment!* Such unity, when we hide economic documents from comrades as though they were a secret disease, when we take offence because of the publication of views propagated under the flag of Social Democracy, such unity is not worth a brass farthing! Such "unity" is pure cant! It leads only to an aggravation of the disease into a malignant condition. But I do not doubt for a single moment that open, direct and honest struggle will cure the disease and create a truly united, vigorous and powerful Social Democracy.

Perhaps it is out of place for me to use the expression "struggle" so often when writing *to you*, but I think our old friendship demands above all *complete frankness*.

Greetings
Petrov

P.S. In about a fortnight's time I shall have another address: Herrn Philipp Roegner, Zigarenhandlung, Neue Gasse, Nüremberg.

(Only for letters and always in two envelopes.)

(Please do not write initials in the letters, for goodness only knows whether the post here is entirely reliable.)

68. (12 P[1]). TO V. P. NOGIN (IN LONDON)

[München], 2nd November, 1900

Please excuse me, my dear Novoselov, [V. P. Nogin] for being so disgracefully late in answering your letter of the 17th October. Minor business here kept preventing me, and also I was waiting for an answer from Aleksey [Martov]. But it was essential to wait until I had the reply, in order to settle the question of our editorial announcement [about the appearance of "Iskra"]. Aleksey decided not to make it widely known for the present. Therefore, in sending you one copy, I would *emphasise* that you keep it secret, do not show it to *anyone* (excepting to that close friend of yours [S. V. Andropov] who has full powers from the Petersburg group [of the "Workers' Banner"] and about whom you write) and definitely do not give it into anyone else's hands. We have decided not to spread this matter abroad, until it has been made known in Russia, and since Aleksey is delaying it somewhat it is also particularly important for us to see that it does not circulate here. Relying on your close participation in our work, I decided to make an exception and to acquaint you with the announcement. Kindly notice, when you read it, that the intention is to publish both a newspaper and a *journal* (or a *miscellany*), but because of certain special considerations[1] connected with the plan of the publication of the journal, the announcement is silent about the latter. Certain passages of the announcement must therefore be taken as referring *not to the newspaper alone*.

Please write what impression the announcement has made on you and your friend.

What type of "agitational journal" are the members of the "Rabocheye Znamya" ["Workers' Banner"] group intending to publish? (You wrote about them, didn't you? What are its characteristics? And who are the collaborators?)

About getting the publication across the frontier into Russia: I think that can always be easily arranged. We have links with certain groups, who look after the transport and also one member of our group has recently received a promise (a reliable one, judging from everything) that they will be able to get anyone we like over into Russia without a passport. I think it is easy to arrange.

As for a Russian passport—the situation is worse. So far there is nothing yet and the "prospect" is still very indefinite. Perhaps that too will be settled before the Spring.

I shall probably stay here for a fairly long time and our correspondence can therefore continue without any inconvenience.

You ask: what kind of work should we like you to undertake? It seems to me that the following work will be particularly important for us (by the Spring or Autumn, when you are thinking of moving): (1) carrying literature across the frontier, (2) distribution throughout Russia, (3) the organisation of workers' circles for the distribution of the newspaper and the delivery of information etc. etc., i.e. the organisa-

---

[1] The reasons were conspiratorial. "Zarya" ("Dawn") was a scientific journal printed in Stuttgart, its printer, Dietz, was afraid of police interference, if its connection with the illegal "Iskra," then printed in Leipzig, became known.

tion of distributing the paper and the organisation of close and regular links between it and the separate committees and groups. We place great hopes on your collaboration—especially in the matter of direct links with the workers in various places. Would such work be agreeable to you? Have you any objection to travelling? It would probably need continuous moving about.

Is that Petersburg group from which your friend has received powers, in existence now? If so, then could he give an address for personal calls in Petersburg and a password so as to pass our announcement on to them? Have they any links with workers in general and with the St. Petersburg Workers' Organisation in particular?

I greet you warmly and hope you will spend your quarantine abroad as quickly and as easily as possible.

Your

Petroff

P.S. Am I writing the address correctly? Let me know if you have received this letter.

69. (131 R). TO I. ULIANOVA

[Munich], 24th October/6th November, 1900

I received your letter, Manyasha, and many thanks for it.

The books came the other day and I was horrified when I opened the last case. In it were medical books belonging to a certain Anna Fedulova (from Barnaul in Siberia) who studied in Lausanne and Geneva from 1893-1899. What carelessness and what a disgrace! I have no idea who she is and I hear her name for the first time in my life. How on earth could her books get here? How could they be sent to Moscow and to another person's address? Why did not someone enquire about them during the months they were in Moscow?

Try if you can to find out what has happened. I paid about 40 roubles (!) for all the books, which means I have overpaid about 30 roubles for somebody else's books through the fault of some muddle-headed creatures.

I shall write both to Siberia and Switzerland asking them to try to trace this person. Meanwhile I have had the books put into the barn.

I have received a letter from Lirochka [A. Yakubova] who sends Mother and you a thousand warm messages. I shall probably not be able to see her.

My own books have arrived in perfect order—thank you for them. I repeat my address:

Herrn Franz Modráček
Smečky 27, Prague
Austria

The weather was bad here until today, when it is lovely, sunny and warm. We must see what the Winters are like!

I am living here as before, studying languages a little, exchanging Russian for German lessons with a Czech (more conversation than lessons) and visiting the library.

Please kiss darling Mother for me. Is she quite well and how is Mark? Do not forget to get the Chinese Traveller's [A. P. Sklyarenko, working in Manchuria] address for me.

I send you my greetings

Your

V. U.

70. (73 P[1]). TO P. B. AXELROD IN ZÜRICH

[*München*], *8th November,* [*1900*]

My dear P. B.

I have received your letter of the 5th and the article [on the death of B. Liebknecht]. Many thanks for it. The alterations must have cost you no little trouble and still more unpleasantness, because it must have been extremely uninteresting work to condense such a theme. It is all the more valuable for us that you undertook to do it. Forgive us for not sending you the articles: our "secretary" [I. G. Smidovich] is burdened unfortunately with serious family responsibilities, and therefore the correspondence is progressing very slowly. I am sending you an article [by Martov] "New Friends of the Russian Proletariat" which we want to print in No. 1, as a serial. Please let me know your opinion—you may mark the article in pencil—and then be so good as to forward it to G. V. [Plekhanov].

With regard to the Parisians,[1] we have decided on those tactics which you advise: on the one hand "not to arm"; on the other, "to restrain ourselves." They are, of course, displeased with the restraint and recently we had to offer such resistance to their expression of displeasure, that we were afraid of a "cooling off" (afraid is hardly the word, for we decided to resist them, even if it were to lead to a definite break). Yesterday I received the reply of the secretary of the group formed by them in Paris; judging by the answer, our resistance had no harmful consequences and "everything is satisfactory." Let us hope that it will be so in the future. It is quite right that we shall probably have to think about the statutes and other pleasant and interesting matters, which you mention, but you did splendidly to fix a term of six months for this. It would be premature, until the venture is "in full swing"; we quite agree with you about this.

But now with regard to beginning to act openly here—I cannot agree with you. You say that "legality has already been lost," but I cannot even begin to think that. In my opinion it has not been lost for the present, and this present may last another few months, during which much will become clear. (Brother [A. N. Potresov] is already in Russia; so far everything is all right. The traveller [Y. Y. Martov][2] is also travelling quite safely so far.) Even with a complete and final loss of legality there may be weighty considerations against coming out into the open (for instance, considerations about travelling back home). Therefore until the appearance of the

---

[1] In organising "Iskra" and "Zarya," Lenin tried to attract all those elements of Russian Social Democracy capable of literary work. The Parisians were D. Ryasanov, Yu. Steklov (Nakhamkis), E. Gurevich, with whom Lenin had some difficulties over drawing them in as "Iskra" collaborators. The Parisians formed the small, principally indeterminate group "Struggle."

[2] Martov, then under police surveillance in Poltava, was making links with organisations, mainly in Sth. Russia.

first numbers and until such time when we shall all meet (with Aleksey [Martov] and brother), I at all events will continue in hiding. If the venture is destined to be successful then this decision may be altered—but my former optimism about this condition has been thoroughly shaken by the "prose of life."

With regard to the journal ["Zarya"],[1] it will probably soon be clear whether we can run it here or go to other countries to seek a haven. As soon as it is settled, I will let you know.

It is very inconvenient for me to write to America, for after all, I do not know anyone there and nobody knows me—I will have to have recourse to your intermediaries in any case: so would it not be better if you were to write direct and send the announcement [about the appearance of "Iskra"] saying that it is from the Russian group, that your relations with this group are such and such; that the pamphlet "May Days in Kharkov" is being set up in type on the same printing press and that when this is finished, a newspaper will be set up in type, that the announcement says nothing about the journal (or the "Miscellany") on account of conspiratorial and technical considerations; that such and such articles are being prepared for No. 1 (or that they are ready) G. V.'s, yours, Kautsky's ("Erinnerungen" ["Reminiscences"]—an interesting little thing, which V. I. is now translating) and others? I think that all the aims you wrote to me about will be much more directly and better achieved by your letter, and your sending the announcement to America will (I believe) no longer be threatened by undesirable publicity, especially the sending of one copy for the secretary of the society to read at their meeting.[2]

---

[1] Axelrod and Plekhanov were against "Iskra" and "Zarya" being published in Germany. They considered Switzerland more suitable. Lenin and Potresov favoured Germany. After the September, 1900, meetings near Geneva with Plekhanov, Axelrod and Zasulich, Lenin and Potresov saw it was more in the interest of the cause that the headquarters of these publications should not be in the same town as Plekhanov. Lenin and Potresov won their point. "Iskra" was founded in München where Lenin, Potresov, Zasulich and later Martov and Krupskaya settled.

[2] The society in question was the "American Socialist Society." Its Secretary was S. Ingerman, who in the 80's had been a member of the "Liberation of Labour" Group. He emigrated to America where he was at the head of the "Liberation of Labour Group" supporters from whom he procured funds for the group's activities and later for "Iskra." In 1903 he became a Menshevik.

I send you greetings,

Your

Petroff

P.S. I have received the pillow and book.[1]

71. (79 p[1]). TO P. B. AXELROD IN ZÜRICH

[*München*], *24th December,* [*1900*]

My dear P. B.

Yesterday I returned from a business trip [2] and received your letter. The newspaper must be ready today: as soon as I receive it, I shall send it to you, if you yourself do not move.

Brother [A. N. Potresov] is arriving tonight.

Aleksey [Y. Y. Martov] will not be free from hindrances and will not move before the 20th December (old style).

I could not send any proofs—I could not get any myself and had to go there to rearrange the 8th page. It was most annoying, but your article [on International Social Democracy] had to be cut into two and the second half left over for the next number: otherwise, the necessary material would not have fitted in because of setting it up (for technical considerations) in Borgese and not Petit type.

And so there is nothing from [N. V.] Vassiliev? From Adler? You do not write about Adler.

The journal is progressing: G. V. [Plekhanov] has sent an article about Struve ["A Criticism of our Critics"]—in all, 6 articles have been sent.

I send you my greetings and I hope sincerely that you will soon get rid of the influenza which is raging everywhere this year.

Your

Petroff

P.S. I have just read in Gurevich's letter that you have received an article about Austria. That is splendid. Have you

---

[1] An English illustrated journal "Family Pictures" in which either some secret correspondence or articles for "Iskra" had been sent.

[2] To Leipzig, where "Iskra" No. 1 was being printed.

a really good translator? If not, send us the article, we will
translate it here.

72. (135 R). TO HIS MOTHER

(München), 13th/26th December, 1900

Darling Mother,

You will probably receive this letter a few days before
Christmas. I send you my good wishes and I hope you will
spend it happily; perhaps Mitya will have arrived by then
and you will all foregather—at least those in Russia. Anya
and I also thought of being together, but it cannot be arranged.
It is "Weihnachten" here—there are Christmas trees everywhere and there is an unusual stir in the streets. I went to
Vienna the other day and enjoyed the trip after having sat
here for several weeks. But a Winter without snow is not
pleasant; it is not even Winter, but actually a rotten kind of
Autumn, very wet. It is a good thing it is not cold and I can
manage quite well without a Winter overcoat. All the same,
it is unpleasant without snow; I get sick of the slush, it is
boring and I remember with pleasure our real Russian Winter
—the sledges and the clear frosty air. I am spending my first
Winter abroad, a Winter which is not like Winter and I cannot
say I am pleased, though sometimes there are occasional fine
days like those we have in a fine late Autumn. My life goes on
as usual and fairly lonely . . . and unfortunately pretty sense-
less. I hope to begin my studies more systematically, but
somehow I cannot manage it. Probably it will be better when
the Spring comes and I shall then get "into my stride." Having
wandered about Russia and Europe after sitting in Shushenskoye I long for some peaceful bookwork and only the strange-
ness of living abroad prevents me from settling down to it
properly.

Are you quite well, my darling? Do you miss Anyuta very
much? What is the state of Manya's case? By the way, I forgot
to tell her, I have received Pushkin. Many thanks. I have also
had her letter of the 6th/19th December. I have not answered

before, because my trip [to Leipzig] prevented it and I was very busy.

I embrace you tenderly, my darling, and send much love to all at home.

Your

V. U.

1901

73. (14 p¹). TO V. P. NOGIN IN LONDON

[München], 24th January, 1901

My dear Comrade,

I have received your letter about the passports. I have written to my friend (here) from whom I expect help in this respect, and am now awaiting an answer. I think I shall manage to get a foreign passport (for entry into Russia) (a Bulgarian or a German one), but I have no hope of getting a Russian passport, not even a blank one, i.e., a blank passport book. Of course I may succeed in this, but I would advise you to take immediate steps to procure a foreign passport,—or else you will risk remaining without one at all. If a Russian passport can be obtained, then it is easier to secure one in Russia.

If one is not to mention the "Rabocheye Znamya" in the note, then could you think of some other way of saying it? For instance, "from a member of the 'Rabocheye Znamya' group, who worked in St. Petersburg in 1897," or something of the sort. I think it would be better to show in some way through whom the article has been received, but if you are of a different opinion, then presumably we shall print it without any such statement.[1]

I have been given the surname of that Petersburg man who (in the provinces, and a fairly distant one) proposed publishing a translation of Kautsky. I am afraid of entrusting the post with the surname. However, I will give it you in this way. Write Aleksey's [Martov] name, patronymic (in the Russian way) and surname; and mark all the 23 letters with numbers

---

[1] An article by H. M. Hyndman, "Socialism, Trade Unionism and Political Action," intended for "Rabocheye Znamya" No. 3, but which was not printed.

in their right order. Then the surname of that Petersburg man will be made up of the letters: 6, 22, 11, 22 (instead of that, read the next letter of the alphabet) 5, 10 and 13.[1]

We will write and ask those organisations abroad with which we have links about the sale of "Revolutions and Counter Revolutions."

The only trouble now is the transport which eats up so much money because the work is new. Therefore I cannot give you a definite answer about financial help for the fabrication of passports until it is clear exactly how much money is required and how great the chances are that all the rest which is necessary apart from money is available.

Aleksey paid over some money to a certain influential organisation in the Spring (sic!) for the purchase (which they promised) of blank passport books, but has so far not received anything.

Would you agree to take upon yourself in the near future the permanent function of transport—i.e., to live near the frontier, to travel, to have dealings with smugglers etc.? Do you know German or any language other than Russian?

Sincere greetings,

Your

Petroff

I am sending the newspaper.[2] Please do not show it to *anyone* excepting to your friend and let me know your opinion. No. 2 is being printed.

Write to me at this address: Herrn Georg Rittmeyer, Kaiserstrasse 53, I, München (without any "please forward," if the letter is in Russian).

74. (80 P[1]). TO G. V. PLEKHANOV IN GENEVA

[München], 30th January, 1901

I have just received your letter, my dear G. V. on my return

---

[1] The man's name works out to M. B. Smirnov, a Social Democrat; member of the S.P.B. "Rabocheye Znamya" group.

[2] No. 1 "Iskra"; not to be shown for conspiratorial reasons before the first number reached Russia. The first batch of "Iskra" sent over the frontier near Memel in January, 1901, was seized. News of this failure did not reach München till much later.

from a "final" conversation with Judas [P. B. Struve].[1] The matter is settled and I am terribly displeased with the way it has been settled. I hasten to write to you, so as not to lose the freshness of my impressions.

Judas did not argue about the "democratic opposition": he is no romantic and you cannot intimidate him by words. But with regard to point No. 7 (the utilisation of material for "Iskra," material which is sent to the "Sovremennoye Obozreniye") he very cleverly duped all our people, who all (P. B. y compris) took his side, against me. You see, Judas expected "Iskra" to be more popular, more of "a workers' paper"; he thinks that our free use of material sent to the "Sovremennoye Obozreniye" might create competition. . . . He insists that the material should be used for "Iskra" only with the consent of a representative of the "Sovr. Oboz." and the consent can be waived only when it is impossible to get into touch with this representative—apparently a very rare condition—for Judas says quite simply that he assumes there will be either the most regular correspondence or that a representative will be found abroad (not more than 12 hours away from München). He would like to publish *monthly*, 5 sheets at a time—i.e., about 200 thousand letters [of the alphabet], exactly as many as there are on 2 sheets of "Iskra." It is difficult to doubt that he will be able to *supply* sufficient material, for he is a man who is well provided for, writes much, and has good connections. The position is clear: competition is directed not so much against "Zarya" as against "Iskra": the same predominance of political

[1] Negotiations with P. Struve began as far back as April, 1900, in Pskov. At the Pskov conference Lenin, Potresov and Martov discussed with Struve and Tugan-Baranovsky the mutual publication of a revolutionary journal abroad. These negotiations were continued in München in Dec., 1900, Lenin, Potresov and Zasulich on the one hand, Struve and his wife on the other. Struve suggested a third political organ on the outside page of which there would be no mention of anything Social Democratic.

The last meeting, which Lenin mentions in this letter, took place in München in January. They discussed the question of the "Iskra" group publishing together with Struve, as representative of the "group of democratic opposition" a general political supplement to "Zarya" under the name "Sovremennoye Obozreniye" ("A Contemporary Survey"). Plekhanov wrote back advising agreement, after bargaining, and not a break.

In March a certain agreement was reached between the groups, but not realised.

material, the same newspaper character, namely a survey of current events, short articles (Judas with great intuition attaches enormous importance to the frequent publication of thin little books with short articles). We shall be loaded down with material of such type, we shall run messages for Judas who by his bossing in the "Sovremennoye Obozreniye" will make a magnificent "Liberal" career and will attempt to put into the shade not only the weighty "Zarya" but also "Iskra" (it is obvious, that he will be the master there, and the complete master; for he has the money and 99% of the material—we will very rarely be in a position to send anything there). We will do the running about, the fussing, the proof-reading, the transporting, while His Excellency Mr. Judas will be the editor-in-chief of the most influential journal (in the widest "social" sense); while a romantic consolation can be left to those right thinkers: let it be called a Supplement to the Social Democratic journal "Zarya"; let them be consoled by words, while I [Struve] grab the business into my hands. I ask you, surely such an illustrious hegemony over Social Democracy will seem to be pure cant? How will it be expressed except by the words: "Supplement to the Social Democratic journal 'Zarya'?" That it will crush us under material is certain, for we don't even have enough time to write for "Zarya" and "Iskra."

One of two things: either the "Sovremennoye Obozreniye" is a *supplement* to the *Journal* "Zarya" (as agreed)—and then it must appear not oftener than "Zarya," with *complete* freedom to utilise the material for "Iskra," or we are selling our birthright for a mess of pottage and are being led by the nose by Judas who feeds us with words.

If we are meant to succeed in getting a real hegemony, then it is to be solely with the aid of a political newspaper (supported by a scientific organ), and when we are informed with infuriating insolence that the political section of our newspaper must not compete with the political venture of those gentlemen, the Liberals, then our pathetic rôle becomes as clear as day.

I have taken a copy of this letter and append it to the Minutes of today's sitting as an announcement of my protest

and my own individual opinion, and I invite you also to raise
the banner of revolt. Better a breach, than this actual subordination to the programme of the Credo accompanied by
loud phrases against Credism.

If the majority will stand for it then I, of course, will submit,
but not before having washed my hands of it.

75. (140 R). TO HIS MOTHER

[*München*], *7th/20th February, 1901*

Darling Mother,

It seems a long time since I had any letter from you. I had
a note from Manyasha, dated 6th/19th, for which I thank her.
How are you? Are you freezing? Are you well?

It is cold again here and they have not had so much snow
for the last thirteen years. There have been delays in train
arrivals owing to snowdrifts, but it is evidently the last effort of
Winter. I am already used to it and am accustomed to the
Winter here, although next Winter if I have to stay, I shall
write for my padded coat. Without such a coat, you have
either to wear vests or two suits, as I do. At first it was not
very comfortable, but I am quite used to it now. Of course it
is not a Russian kind of cold; 10° is considered to be "terribly
cold."

The carnival ended here the other day. It was the first time
I had seen the last day of a carnival abroad—processions of
people in fancy dress moving along the streets, playing the
fool, and clouds of confetti (small bits of coloured paper)
thrown into your face, paper snakes etc. etc. They know how
to live in public, how to amuse themselves in the streets!

I am quite well, probably because I run about a good deal
and do not sit much. My life goes on as usual.

Nadya's term of exile is coming to an end soon—in our style
abroad March 24th, and March 11th in yours. I shall send a
petition one of these days for a passport to be issued to her.

Will you ask Manyasha to send by Nadya, a small box of
"my" pen nibs—just imagine, I could not find any here. The

Germans and Czechs are stupid people. There are no English nibs; only their "own manufacture"—awful rubbish!

What does Mitya write? When does he finish his exams?

How is Mark thinking of spending the Summer?

I embrace you warmly and wish you good health.

Greetings to all.

Your

V. U.

Do you go to the theatre? What is this new play by Chekhov, "The Three Sisters"? Have you seen it and what do you think of it? I read a criticism of it in the papers. They act brilliantly in the Arts Theatre, which is accessible to all. I still remember with pleasure my visits to it last year with that poor wretch Columbus [I. Kh. Lalayants]. Is he well? I always intend writing to him, but different things interfere.

76. (81 P[1]). TO P. B. AXELROD IN ZÜRICH

[*München*], *27th February, 1901*

My dear P. B.

I have received both your letters and have passed on to V. I. [Zasulich] your letter from Italy. I do not yet know the contents of that last letter, for I passed it on through Blumenfeld.[1] We are leaving tomorrow, together with the latter: he is going on, through Vienna, I via Vienna to Prague on personal business.[2] Forgive me for writing briefly but I have to see people and to pack.

A letter arrived from Dietz that he is *not* going to print the announcement (about union with the Liberals) because it is dangerous ("union," groups etc.) and he asks if a secret printing press would not be better for us?! We are staggered by the news from that daft idiot, Dietz. We have decided (provisionally) to leave "Zarya" *for the present* (for the present!) —and to print the rest in Geneva.

---

[1] An "Iskra" typesetter, sent by the group to Russia, where he was soon arrested.

[2] Lenin conducted his legal correspondence with his family through Prague. He visited Prague to procure a permit through his consulate for Krupskaya to come abroad.

I believe that diplomatic relations [about their collaboration in "Iskra"] have been resumed with the Parisians.

Molotov [Parvus] has already written an article about finance (for "Iskra" No. 3). He has promised a foreign survey.

We have still rather too little material for the No. 3 "Iskra."

Judas (the calf) [P. B. Struve] has not left yet. Thank goodness, he is clearing off at last, one day soon. "Everything is all right" with him.

From home: they keep writing about student disturbances. Brother [Martov] writes that he will soon be coming here.

The second number [of "Iskra"] has not yet reached Russia.

I send you greetings. I will certainly write in greater detail when I return (4-7 days) and when I get into my stride again.

Your
Petroff

77. (144 R). TO HIS MOTHER

Vienna, 19th February/14th March, 1901

I came here, darling Mother, to get the "paper" for Nadya. I found there was no Russian Consulate in Prague, but my petition that Nadya should have a foreign passport issued to her had to be certified. Vienna is an enormous, busy and beautiful city. After the provinces where I have been living, it is pleasant to have a look at such a city and there is much to see here. It is worth breaking a journey if any of you happen to be travelling this way. I have sent Nadya a small "Guide to Vienna" and I hope she will soon see you all—she ought not to be held up on account of her passport. Please ask Manyasha, when she happens to be in town, to buy Nadya a copy of Henshall's Telegraph (a Railway Guide)—2 marks (not worth sending such a book from here).

Among other places I visited the Museum of Fine Arts and even went to see a Viennese Operetta (!), but I did not like it very much. I also went to a lecture at one of the People's University Courses, but it was a dull one, so I soon left.

Greetings to all our people,
I kiss you, my darling,
                                              Your
                                                         V. U.

Probably Anyuta's letter, yours, and Manya's are waiting for me at home. I repeat my address: Herrn Franz Modràček, Vršovice bei Prag, Austria.

78. (82 p¹). TO P. B. AXELROD IN ZÜRICH

[*München*], *20th March, 1901*

My dear P. B.

I have received all your letters and given the Aunt [V. Zasulich] the news from her old friend [Dobrodzhanu-Herea]. You were unnecessarily worried about the addresses and about thinking that something had changed. I still live in the same place and you should write to the same address:

Herrn Georg Rittmeyer, Kaiserstrasse 53/0, München. And inside: für Meyer.

I am not expecting my wife here yet: her term of exile [in Ufa] ends only on Sunday and then she must go and see someone, so that she can hardly be here before the second half of April. And when she does arrive, you can still send letters to Rittmeyer, for he will always pass them on to me and I, in turn, will let you know my change of address in good time.

There is some unpleasantness over "Zarya." That capricious gentleman, Dietz, has definitely rejected your editorial article, having taken fright at the references to "Iskra," having sniffed out the smell of "groups" etc. and having put it down to the fact that both Bebel and Zinger (shareholders in his limited company) are nervous etc. etc. To our great regret we were forced to refuse your article[1] and to print instead a few words "to the readers." The new censorship is terribly unpleasant! And the cover too has suffered: they have even crossed out the words "in collaboration with a few Russian Social Demo-

---

[1] J. H. W. Dietz (1834-1922) the German publisher of "Zarya" was nervous that the police might discover the links between the German Social Democrats and the "Iskra" group, and therefore with active revolutionaries in Russia.

crats." When shall we be rid of the tutelage of such rotten comrades?

Also a pleasant affair with the calf (Judas) [P. B. Struve]: a letter arrived from his friend (about a supposed source of money = a gold bug [D. N. Zhukovsky]), it was an angry letter saying: "I am sending 200 roubles (two hundred!) for the *'Sovremennoye Obozreniye'* and please bear in mind that it is *not* for you, but for this publication." We are all indignant and have decided: (1) not to print the announcement about coalition, (2) to send an ultimatum to the calf and the friend, saying that we must either have a sound financing of our scheme or we refuse to do anything, (3) to finish printing the Witte note ["Autocracy and the Zemstvo"].

Now, is it not true that we have again been duped by Judas??

There is one consolation: No. 2 of "Iskra" has safely reached Russia. It is meeting with success, correspondence is prolific. The devil knows what is happening in Russia: demonstrations in St. Petersburg, Moscow, Kharkov, Kazan, martial law in Moscow (they have arrested my youngest sister [Manyasha] among others) and even my brother-in-law [Mark Elizarov] who has never taken part in anything!) bloodshed, the prisons are overcrowded etc. etc.

One of these days we are expecting our brother [Martov], who has set out (at last!) and our mutual friend [Blumenfeld] who has carried out successfully (so far) everything that was asked of him.

We are printing the May leaflet and will then begin on No. 3 "Iskra" and perhaps No. 4 at the same time—there is a mass of material.

"Zarya" ["Dawn"] will be coming out on Saturday, they say, and will be sent to you direct from Stuttgart.

Our cash position is very bad. For the present, therefore, we have definitely to refrain from spending money on a man (you intended we should use as a transport worker).

Sincere greetings,

Your

Meyer

79. (17 p[1]). TO F. I. DAN IN BERLIN

[München], 22nd March, 1901

Many thanks for the letter of the 2nd March sent to Ritt-meyer. We are very glad that correspondence has at last been established between us (about which I wrote to you on the 15th *July* last!). Please continue it regularly so that we shall always know that, in every important matter, letters will reach you. The address to which you last wrote is one of the best—use it.

Collect some money. At present we are almost reduced to penury and the receipt of a large sum is a matter of life or death. We shall send "Zarya" ["Dawn"] one of these days. So do your utmost with regard to finance. You can send the money through a bank, by cheque in a registered letter addressed to Dr. Med. Karl Lehman (the third letter is the German letter H) Kabelbergerstrasse 20-A. Take note of the address: it is good for money, letters and books.

How is the doctor's group? [1] Last Summer their represent-ative's behaviour amounted to a breach (he made idiotic de-mands on us)—but afterwards one of his group re-established links with our ["Iskra"] representative in Berlin. See that you find out: are they willing to help or not? Send an address for personal delivery of the trunk [2] and another reliable one for letters and books.

Your

Old Man

What about the Finnish routes [3]? We do not know anything and have not had a single letter from you about it. Please re-peat. If those transporting the trunk have not received a letter from the organisation, then *on no account* should you be frank with them *on any subject.*

---

[1] Which group Lenin means here is not known.

[2] Such illegal literature as "Iskra" and "Zarya" was sent over to Russia in trunks and suitcases with double sides and bottoms.

[3] The S.P.B. "Union of the Struggle for the Liberation of Labour" had used this means of communication via Finland and Stockholm, organised by the Swedish Social Democrat Branting and the Norwegian S.D. Garder. The latter was arrested in 1900 and transport through Finland became disorganised.

80. (84 P¹). TO P. B. AXELROD IN ZÜRICH

[*München*], *25th April, 1901*

My dear P. B.

It seems a long time since I had a chat with you. I could not get down to it, and besides, Aleksey [Martov] wrote to you about all our affairs (I was ill with influenza for a week), but the need to have a talk with you is now so great I have decided not to put it off any longer. I would like to ask your opinion both about the Parisians and the Zürich people [E. Rollau and E. Skubik] and about matters in general.

Do you know that the Parisians have "disbanded" the group for assisting "Iskra" (long ago, about 2-3 weeks) and have refused (for a second time) to collaborate, giving as a reason that we had broken the organisational neutrality (sic! we had been unfair to the Union and had attacked it unnecessarily in "Zarya")? The author [D. B. Ryazanov] of "Notes on the Programme of the 'Rabocheye Delo'" wrote this, to us, making at the same time the most obvious hints that the "Rabocheye Delo" was being reformed (in leaflet No. 6), (we thought it was even too reformed!) and consequently . . . consequently . . . vivrons verrons—ended up this dear comrade. He has evidently got an eye (like certain "young forces" about which G. V. [Plekhanov] wrote) on a better little job on "Rabocheye Delo." We were so incensed by this caddish behaviour that we did not even answer them. We intend to swear at "Rabocheye Delo" in No. 4 "Iskra" for being weathercocks. (No. 3 will be ready, they promise, by the 1st May. We want to begin work at once on No. 4.)

Now I do not know whether I should take the slightest notice of these intriguers, or whether I should try again. They are undoubtedly talented, they wrote, supplied material (both of them, and Danevich [E. L. Gurevich] also), they cleverly collected money (a whole 350 francs: so much has never yet been collected for "Iskra" abroad) and, actually, in their eyes we are not without fault: we did not pay enough attention to them, we did not send them a single article for perusal and "comradely advice." We did not offer them any "section" (not even some foreign survey in "Iskra," or notes for the social chronicle on certain questions). Evidently in foreign relations it is impossible, absolutely *impossible* without something of the sort. Now the Berlin people[1] (Arseniev [A. N. Potresov] was there recently) also want a certain position: they say that it is good enough for a student simply to help "Iskra," while *we* or *Dvinskaya* [E. S. Ettinger], for instance, must have something, you know. . . . (Dvinskaya and her husband are leaving the Union in which, when the members were asked, only three—Grishin [Ts. Kopelson] y compris supported the conference. Long live comrade G.!).

It is simply too bad! We shall have to think out an organisation—without that es geht nicht.

I have had an idea, whether we might not try the following plan of organisation: the "Social Democrat"[2] organisation, the editorial board of "Zarya" and certain groups (the Berlin people, for instance, the Parisians *perhaps* etc.) or such and such people should form a League,[3] let us say. With a threefold literary administration: the Liberation of Labour Group would manage its own printing press, the "Zarya" its own, and an elected Literary Commission would be the closest collaborator, taking part in periodic general-editorial congresses and printing (under the signature of the Literary Commission) pamphlets etc. in the printing offices of the *"Social Democrat"* and *"Zarya"* —eventually, also in a third printing press, if such a one will be arranged by the *League* (there are certain ideas for this). The *supreme decision* on literary questions in the League would belong to a *conference consisting of three members:* from the "Liberation of Labour Group," the "Zarya" and the Literary

[1] Gradually, in the main towns of Western Europe, young Russian students and revolutionary emigrants formed groups to help "Iskra," and "Iskra" cells abroad. These did important work for the organisation, collected money, arranged places of refuge for those revolutionaries who escaped from Russia, helped in the "Iskra" transport, procured passports, provided addresses for correspondence, etc.

[2] The Revolutionary Organisation of the "Social Democrat" was founded by the Liberation of Labour Group in May, 1900, after the split at the II Congress of the Union of Russia S.D. abroad and after the Liberation Group and its supporters had left the Union.

[3] "The League Abroad of Russian Revolutionary Social Democracy" was formed in the Autumn of 1901 from the organisations of "Iskra," "Zarya" and "The Social Democrat."

Commission. The administration would be in common, elective.

This is the gist of my project ("Iskra" being a Russian publication, of course, does *not enter* the League). It is approved here in principle and the eldest sister [V. I. Zasulich] also approves of it. It seems to me that such a constitution (an Austrian one, as Aleksey calls it in fun) is not in any way dangerous to us, but something similar is definitely wanted, for otherwise the public is very displeased and can fall away. Thus we are fully guaranteed against any disturbances or tittle-tattle, keeping our printing press and editorships, while we give the public that essential liberty without which it will not agree to help.

Please write and say what your attitude is towards such an idea, and discuss it with G. V. (to whom I am not writing, for he must soon be here, and he will certainly drop in to see you on his way). I am not giving any details: these can soon be settled. If we all agree to this (i.e. the whole of the "Social Democrat"), then the chances are good that the Berlin people (who have a printing press and are panting for work with a definite "position") will join in and then we shall be able to put up against the Union a united League with wide activities.

There is no need to fear the elective administration, for it will be responsible only for the transport and for collecting money abroad, to be distributed in certain proportions among "The Social Democrat," "Zarya" and others. It will have nothing whatsoever to do with "Iskra." The League can be formally announced as an ally abroad of the *Russian organisation of "Iskra"* which we are already arranging.

There is also no need to fear any literary stupidities for: (1) the Literary Commission can be restricted by statute as to independent printing, (2) it prints under its own signature: "The Liberation of Labour Group," and "Zarya" are not mixed up with it, (3) our people can also be in it, (4) it is subordinate to a conference in which we have the majority.

I do not know, of course, if the Parisians will be satisfied: they are too proud and we cannot very well ask them. If you approve of the plan, perhaps you would undertake to write to them and throw out a bait. After all, when you were in Paris they told you about their sad plight—and you could suggest this way out for them. If you approve the idea, we will ask Koltsov to work out a draft of the "League" statutes.

And now about the Zürich-Letts, [Rollau, Skubik and others]. I do not know if you have heard that the transport arranged with their aid *has definitely fallen through:* 3,000 copies of "Iskra" (No. 1) have been *seized* by the police, who also arrested the smuggler. Then one of them wrote to us asking for more money for the journey. We replied that we could not give any more for that journey—we could not involve our organisation, but if he would undertake specially to smuggle 40 pounds of literature (as he promised in conversation with me), then he could come here on his way.

Not a word in reply. Do you happen to know whether they have taken offence, or what? How are things with them and what are their plans? If you see any of them, please have a talk with them and find out the facts of the case.

We are beginning to think of No. 2 "Zarya"—it is time. The Witte note will soon come to an end—in about 2-3 weeks (Dietz is taking an incredible time over it: so far only 9 sheets are ready). So far no material, except the article you already know by Nevzorov [Yu. M. Steklov] on "The Historical Preparation of Russian Social Democracy." We are hoping to have a leader by G. V. on recent events and also his article against Struve, also your article (from a note from the Editors) —isn't that so? Luxembourg has promised an article (a new introduction to her articles "Die sozialistische Krise in Frankreich," which articles we want to translate), and Kautsky has promised a short article on academicians and proletarians.

We have no foreign surveys. How are matters with the "Austrian" articles? Will they not send anything from America? From Switzerland? Danevich, they say, is ill. There is no one we can ask to write on Germany—excepting perhaps Parvus, who has promised (?) a foreign survey, but that is not the same thing.

For the fourth number of "Iskra" we intend to have an

article on the Terror (Aleksey's) and have already: "Autocracy and the Zemstvo" (a continuation), "Autocracy and Finance" (by Parvus), something for the social chronicle (there are further details about demonstrations) and for the workers' movement. We are thinking of bringing out No. 4 in one sheet (No. 3 has swollen to 2 sheets, 8 pages, (seven pages are ready) just as in No. 1—and even so, we have had to leave part out!) It is essential to do our utmost to speed up the appearance of "Iskra"—to see that it appears monthly.

Goodbye! Greetings to yourself and all our people. My wife sends the same.

Your

Petroff

P.S. Write to me to Rittmeyer's address. I must not forget: the eldest sister [V. Zasulich] asked me to say that 250 francs have been received. An account of them will be printed in No. 3 "Iskra." ("From America, through Axelrod.") I am sending ten copies of "Zarya" via Stuttgart—send them to Ingerman, Mokrievich [1] etc. The eldest sister [Zasulich] is writing an article for the Germans on the [student] demonstrations.

81. (146 R). TO M. I. ULIANOVA (THEN IN PRISON)

München, 6th/19th May, 1901

I have decided to write a few words to you, my dearest Manyasha, or else you may think I am a pig. Actually, it is extraordinary how often I forget my duty! It is true that Nadya and E. V. have arrived; we have made better arrangements for ourselves, we have our own flat and I am beginning to work more regularly, but even so there are still far too many interruptions.

And how are you? I hope you have settled down to a more regular régime, which is so important when one is in solitary confinement. I immediately wrote a letter to Mark and de-

---

[1] A revolutionary Narodnik of the 1870's, who was living in Bulgaria in the 90's.

scribed to him in great detail how best to establish such a régime: for mental work I particularly recommend translations, especially *reverse* ones—namely, first a written translation from a foreign language into Russian and then translate the Russian back into the foreign language. From my own experience I learnt that this was the most rational way of learning a language. In the physical realm, I strongly recommended to him, and I repeat the same to you, daily exercises and then a rub down. This is absolutely essential in solitary confinement.

From one of your letters forwarded here by Mother I see you have managed to begin some kind of work. As a result of this I hope you will occasionally forget your surroundings and that the time (which usually flies in prison if there are not particularly unfavourable circumstances) will pass almost unnoticed.

I also advise you to spread your studies systematically over the available books, so as to vary them. I remember very well that a change in reading or occupation, from translation to reading, from letter writing to gymnastics, from serious reading to fiction—helped very considerably. Sometimes depression, (moods change frequently in prison), is simply the result of fatigue through monotonous impressions or monotonous work. Sometimes it is only necessary to change the activity to return to normal and to control the nerves.

I remember that in the evening after a meal I used regularly to read fiction for relaxation, and I never enjoyed it more than when I was in prison. Above all, do not forget the daily compulsory physical exercises. Force yourself to make several dozen different movements (without stopping!). It is most important.

Well, goodbye for the present, I kiss you warmly and wish you cheerfulness and health,

Your,

Vlad. Ul.

82. (32 p¹). TO N. E. BAUMANN[1] IN MOSCOW

[München], 24th May, 1901

We have received your letter with the report for January, February, March and April. Thank you for the thoroughness and accuracy of the income and expenditure account. As to your activity in general, we are not clear what this activity is or what are its results. You wrote that you were being "torn to pieces" and that there was no one to replace you, but you have not yet fulfilled your promise to describe this activity. Is your work limited to delivering literature to those centres mentioned in your report? Or are you busy forming groups? If so, then where, what sort, what has been accomplished and what are these groups for; for local work, for sending to us for literature, or for something else?

We ask about this, because this question is very important. Our affairs are rather in a bad way. Our finances are altogether bad; Russia contributes hardly anything. The transport is, as usual, irregular and at random. All our tactics in such conditions should be *wholly* directed to seeing that (1) the money collected in Russia in the name of "Iskra" should be sent here with a minimum deduction for local expenses; and (2) that money is expended almost exclusively on *transport*, since we already have agents in Pskov and Poltava, who are functioning comparatively cheaply as receivers and are not a burden on the finances.

Think about this carefully. Our daily bread on which we only just manage to keep alive—is as usual only suitcases. We pay about 100 roubles for two, and the fortuitousness of the men we send leads to a mass of delays, inaccuracies, losses etc. The organising of sending suitcase people from Riga (possible, according to Raznotsvetov [I. S. Blumenfeld]) and according to Ernst [E. H. Rollau] is not moving a step forward. No news at all from Leopold.[2] Nothing has been organised in Finland, although I am assured by various people that that too is possi-

---

[1] N. E. Baumann (1873-1905), Social Democrat, first illegal "Iskra" agent. At the time of his letter he was in Moscow, organising the distribution of literature in the central industrial region.

[2] Evidently the name for a transport group linked with N. E. Baumann.

ble. Is it rational, in such a state of affairs, to spend 400 roubles in four months on the business of local receivers and intermediaries for passing on literature?

In our opinion, you should settle in the immediate vicinity of the frontier, so as to be able to take across at least 2-4 suitcases and 10-20 pounds of literature on your person each month.

83. (33 P[1]). TO L. M. KNIPOVICH, A SOCIAL DEMOCRAT, "ISKRA" WORKER IN EXILE IN ASTRAKHAN

[München, 28th May, 1901]

In what way are you thinking of organising "Iskra" in Russia? A secret printing press or a legal one? If the latter, then write at once, if you hold definite views. We are ready to grasp this plan with both hands; (a possible plan, as we were assured in the Caucasus) and it would not require much money. If you have any decent links with legal printing presses, then do not fail to discuss the matter with them and write to us: we have our own, very practical (and tested) plan.[1]

If the former, then note that our printed sheet (4 pages) contains as many as 100,000 letters [of the alphabet] (and this in a month!). Could a secret printing press manage this? Would there not be an excessive risk of destroying both money and men? Would it not be better to devote this money and energy to transport. without which one cannot possibly do anything in Russia?

[Unsigned]

84. (20 P[1]). TO THE "ISKRA" HELPERS GROUP IN BERLIN

[München], *5th June, 1901*

The Doctor must settle abroad, in Polangen, [Kurland Province] for instance, (in such places we have links with the non-

---

[1] Lenin's plan was to have "Iskra" set up in type abroad, to prepare the matrix-mould and then to send it to Russia for casting the stereotype and the printing off.

Russian side and we have also our own store), he must study
the local conditions, (he ought to be able to speak Lettish and
German, but perhaps he might manage without) and he should
try to find some respectable occupation, (I am assured that a
man can live there by having a private practice). He must get
on good terms with the minor local officials and accustom them
to his frequent crossing of the frontier. One does not need a
passport to cross the frontier there, but a "Grenzkarte" (valid
for 28 days). With such frequent crossings he might be able
gradually to carry across a few pounds of literature at a time.
(On his person or in a case, according to our method and for
which he will need a small medical instrument case.) It is particularly important for us that the literature should be taken
over regularly and often, even if it is only a little at a time. If a
man were to undertake to arrange this and to do the work
himself, that is, to carry it across *himself*, then we would give
him some money for the journey and for living there one or
two months until he settles down.

85. (35 P[1]). TO L. E. HALPERIN[1] IN BAKU

[München, after June 18th, 1901]

There was a letter sent to Persia recently, through Vienna,
so that it is too soon to assume failure. It may succeed. Inform
the addressee in Tabriz that he is to receive some books from
Berlin and that he should write to us when they arrive.

As for organising "Iskra" in the Caucasus, we have already
sent "X" [L. M. Knipovich] a *detailed enquiry* and have not
yet received a reply. It is essential for us to know what the
plan is: (a legal or illegal printing press) how near it is to
realisation; for how much printed material it is intended (can
"Iskra" be monthly?), how much money they need at once,

---

[1] A Social Democrat, exiled in Astrakhan, who became linked with the "Iskra"
organisation. In the Spring, 1901, when his exile was over, he worked in Baku as an
"Iskra" agent, where together with L. Krassin and R. Classon for 10 months he
worked at creating an illegal workers' organisation, creating a Caucasian Workers'
Union, organising the work of the party Baku printing press and the transport of
illegal "Iskra" literature via Persia and Batum.

and how much a month. Our cash position at present is very bad and we can make no promises while we have no detailed information. Send it at once.

Do your utmost to get money: we have already written about this through "X" to one of your acquaintances [R. E. Classon] and we also advise you to ask "Z. Z." [I. K. Lalayants] with whom one of the members of the "Iskra" group spoke about money at the beginning of last year (remind him of the conversation in one of the theatres of a capital city).

As for the Eastern shore of the Black Sea, do not fail to discover ways of communication, particularly French ships—we hope to find a way to them from here.

86. (151 R). TO HIS MOTHER

[*München*], *4th/17th July, 1901*

Darling Mother,

The other day I received your letter sent on by Anyuta. I am extremely glad to hear there is hope that our people will soon be released. Perhaps they will be convinced that they cannot make "a case" of it. But even if there is "a case," they will still have to release them soon, for nowadays in incomparably more important matters, they release people much sooner and long before "the case" is finished. I am glad Manyasha feels cheerful; this can be seen from the letter forwarded by Anyuta.

Anyuta wrote the other day that she was thinking of moving into the country. It would not be a bad idea, although I must say the towns abroad in the Summer are better, namely the streets are watered oftener etc., so that it is easier to spend a Summer in town here than in Russia. For instance, we can bathe every day in a good swimming bath at a comparatively low price and there are plenty of walks and it does not take long to get out of town. There is much less traffic in the streets than in a Russian town of similar size: because bicycles and electric trams completely push the cabs into the background. As for goods traffic—it is quite insignificant in the suburb where Nadya and

I are living. We are therefore very pleased with the place where we are living and are not thinking either of going into the country or of taking a villa.

I kiss you tenderly, my darling, and hope you are keeping well.

Much love to Mitya and especially to Mark and Manyasha,

Your

V. U.

87. (37 P¹). TO S. O. TSEDERBAUM¹ IN VILNA

[*München, 2nd half of July, 1901*]

We have just received a letter containing the plan of brother Pahomy [S. O. Tsederbaum], Yablochkov [V. P. Nogin] and Bruskov [S. V. Andropov]. We cannot conceal the fact that we not only cannot agree with a single part of the plan (although one could argue over the first part) but that we were simply astonished at it, especially by the second part: (1) all of us to come to Petersburg, (2) to arrange a regional organ of the Russian organisation of "Iskra." We are so astounded that we must excuse ourselves in advance, if in our further remarks a sharp word slips out.

It is incredible! After a whole year of desperate efforts, we are only just beginning to group a staff of leaders and organisers in Russia for an enormous and important task: (this staff is still terribly small, for apart from the three people mentioned, we have only another 2-3 men), while for the All-Russia organ we need scores of energetic collaborators (using this word *not only* in a literary sense) and here, suddenly, we are to pull down the whole structure again and return to the old amateur methods. I cannot imagine any more suicidal tactics for "Iskra." A regional organ like the existing "Yuzhny Rabochy" ["The Southern Worker"] means again spending a mass of money and using people on editing the technical side, on distribution etc. And what for? For the sake of five issues in eighteen months! And it will never achieve that even in eighteen months. "The

---

¹ S. O. Tsederbaum, Yu. Martov's brother, was an "Iskra" agent in Russia.

Southern Worker" had this advantage: it was being created by an established committee, i.e., a whole organisation standing at the peak of its development. So far there are only three of you. Just think, instead of fighting that narrow-mindedness which makes a Petersburg man forget about Moscow, a Muscovite about Petersburg, a Kiev man about everything except Kiev, instead of training people to conduct an All-Russia work (they have to be trained for years for this, if we want to form a political party, deserving of the name), instead of that, to encourage again local narrow-mindedness and develop some petty Social Democracy instead of an All-Russia one—that would be nothing but provincialism, it cannot be anything else. Experience has shown us how few men we have for running a really political organ, how few collaborators, reporters, people with political connections, how few practical technicians and men experienced in distribution.

There are too few of them for the whole of Russia, and now we are to disperse them and give up an All-Russia undertaking, which has begun and needs help from all sides, for the sake of establishing a new local undertaking. In the best circumstances, even if the most brilliant success were to follow the new plan, it would lead to the lowering of the type of Russian Social Democracy, to the lowering of its political significance, because no "local" political newspaper can exist, for in a local organ the general political section will always suffer. You write: a "mass" organ. We are utterly unable to understand what sort of an "animal" that is. Is it possible that Pahomy's brother has begun to think that one must descend lower, from leaders down to the masses, to write in a simpler way and closer to life? ? Is this really our aim: to go down to the masses and not to raise them, when they have begun to stir, to the state of an organised political movement? Are we really short of letters from factories and works and not of political accusations, political knowledge and political generalisations? And so, for widening and deepening our political generalisations, it is suggested that we should split up the general matter into local matters! Quite apart from the political abasement they will inevitably damage the cause technically by the plan of a regional organ. By *uniting* all the

forces round "Iskra" we can have a monthly newspaper with
real political material (it has already been proved by the first
year's experience), whereas with a regional organ, one cannot
even dream of producing four numbers a year. And if we were
not to jump about so hurriedly from one plan to another and
were not upset either by temporary setbacks or the slow development of an All-Russia undertaking, then it would be quite
possible to establish say within six months to a year a fortnightly
organ (about which we are persistently thinking). We presume,
of course, that Pahomy's brother, Yablochkov and Bruskov are
on the old path, i.e., encouraging both the direction and the
organisational plan of "Iskra." If, however, they have changed
their views on the matter, then, of course, it is a different question. Altogether we are positively bewildered why these people
should have lost all faith in this plan and so quickly (because
they cannot fail to see that the new plan is destroying the old).
Because of transport? But to get their own way they have so far
only tried *once* and this attempt did not lead to a complete crash
—while even after two or three *failures* we must not give up the
matter. Have not these people begun to sympathise more with
a publication in Russia and not abroad? But after all, they know
that *everything* has been done and as much as 1,000 roubles
spent, whereas so far there have been no results. It must be
admitted that any plan to publish no matter what regional or
local organ of the Russian organisation of "Iskra" is positively
wrong and harmful. The "Iskra" organisation exists for maintaining and developing the latter and for *uniting* thereby the
Parties, and not for *breaking* up the forces, of which there is
already more than enough without this organisation. As for all
of us coming to Petersburg, I will just say this, that such workers
of ours as P., [V. P. Nogin] B. [S. V. Andropov] and Pahomy's
brother are all too few and they must be taken care of. But the
danger of a general failure through living in one place is a
hundred times greater. If they find that one man is not enough
there, (they can see that for themselves), then let them send to
him the man who is being released in the Autumn (Pahomy's
brother) but not both. Also, in the interests of their safety and

their unifying work let them not forget the extreme desirability of periodically changing their place of residence. If one succeeded at last in winning over the Committee in Petersburg then, of course, one must compel it to tackle "Iskra" and get it published more frequently and to fight against all new small-scale undertakings.

These are a much more deadly enemy than "economism," for it is our deepest conviction that the deepest vital roots of "economism" lie in such amateur efforts. And there will never be a political movement (not only in words, but political in deeds, i.e. directly influencing the government and preparing a general storm) so long as we do not overcome this method and undermine any faith in it. If Petersburg bought up 400 copies of "The Southern Worker," then the "Socialist" group undertook to distribute 1000 copies of "Iskra." Let them arrange for the distribution of such a number of copies; let them arrange that it should contain a detailed Petersburg section (in case of need it may form a special supplement) and then that same task, which overshadowed for you all other tasks, the winning of Petersburg, will be achieved. We consider it necessary to remind you that all the "practicians" agree that "The Southern Worker" has not got the advantage over "Iskra" in accessibility to the workers; so that this argument also disappears. It is both clumsy and criminal to scatter forces and means; "Iskra" has no money, not a single Russian agent sends it any money and yet everyone is starting a new venture, demanding new means. All this points to a lack of system. One should be more patient, for by means of our plan we shall achieve what we set out to achieve, even if not quickly. We can see from the lamentable memory of the experience of the "Rabocheye Znamya" ["The Workers' Banner"] on what we can reckon when this suggested plan is realised. Our acquaintances tackled their plan so enthusiastically that Yablochkov went to Petersburg contrary to arrangement and left Odessa, when it was essential that our agents should be there. We demand that the new plan be abandoned. If our arguments seem unconvincing, let them postpone any new plans until our Congress, which we will call in case of need and at which the matter will somehow be settled.[1] As for popular literature, we intend to develop the publication of pamphlets. This letter expresses the opinions not only of our group, but also those of the Liberation of Labour Group.

88. (154 R). TO HIS MOTHER

[*München*], *19th October/1st November, 1901*

Darling Mother,

I received your letter to Nadya the other day enclosing one from Manyasha. We were terribly grieved to hear that our people's affairs were so sad! My dear, I do not even know what to advise you. Please do not worry too much. Probably the Public Prosecutor is attacking our people because he is making a last attempt to build up a case out of nothing and after the failure of such efforts, they will have to be released. It might help if you were to go to Petersburg, that is if your health will allow it, and to lodge a complaint about such an unheard of thing as the absence of interrogation for six months. This is such a definite and obviously illegal fact, that it would be best to complain about it. Petersburg would probably ask Moscow about it and induce it to throw off its provincial unceremoniousness (which is, after all, what happened when Mitya was in prison). Those are the reasons in favour of such a journey. But there are, of course, reasons for not taking such a journey. The result is doubtful and the worry for you would be great. Where you are now you can judge better than I whether you should take such a journey and you have probably discussed the question with your friends. You should also complain about the refusal to permit a meeting between Manyasha and Mitya,[2] for that is something monstrous.

As for Anyuta—of course I shall not write and tell her what

[1] A meeting of the editors of "Iskra" with its agents who were summoned abroad from time to time.

[2] Dmitri Lenin was not allowed to see his sister, Manyasha, in prison, because he had recently been implicated in a political affair.

you have said, so as not to worry her unduly. I hope to see her soon, perhaps in a few weeks' time [1] and I shall try to calm her a little.

Please, my darling, write when you have a free moment and tell me how you are and feel. Are you quite well and how do you think of spending the Autumn? Shall you go to Moscow or stay in Podolsk? When is M. V. [Zvorykina, Manyasha's school-friend] leaving? When you see Manyasha and Mark, give them warm greetings from us all. The Summer is over—the Summer is the worst time for sitting in prison—and probably when the interrogation is over they will see more clearly that their case is not serious.

I embrace you warmly, my darling, and I hope you will keep cheerful and well. Do you remember, when I was in prison you also thought the case was much more dangerous and serious than it turned out to be and, after all, there can be absolutely no comparison between Manyasha and Mark's case and mine! The fact that they are being kept so long in prison is probably because crowds of people have been arrested and they cannot yet make out a proper case—of course such an absurdity would be impossible in Petersburg.

Once again I kiss you,

Your

V. U.

P.S. Our life goes on as usual. El. Vas. is not very well—influenza is about. Nadya has settled down I think and is quite acclimatised.

89. (39 p[1]). TO I. G. SMIDOVICH IN KIEV

[München, 18th December, 1901]

We have received the news that Akim [L. I. Goldman] is printing "Vpered" ["Forward"].[2] We refuse to believe this and

---

[1] At the Congress of the "Union of Russian Social Democrats," "Iskra," "Zarya" and the "Struggle for the Liberation of Labour" groups called in Zürich on 4-5 October to invite all the Russian Social Democratic organisations abroad.

[2] The newspaper "Vpered" ("Forward"), the Organ of the Kiev Committee, organised by M. Uritsky, ideologically close to economism.

ask you to explain if there is not some misunderstanding. We refuse to believe that people, who have been collecting hundreds and thousands of roubles on behalf of "Iskra" should secretly desert us and join another undertaking; and, moreover, at a critical moment for us, when the transports are at a standstill, when the whole of the North and the Centre (yes, and the South too!) have buried us under complaints on account of the non-appearance of "Iskra" and when the whole salvation lay in producing "Iskra" again in Russia—that people should do this by deception, for Akim wrote to us that he was printing No. 10 and we were confident of this, while the "beauty" [V. N. Krokhmal] did not breathe a single word to us about his magnificent plans—such an action which breaks not only all the rules of the organisation but also certain simpler rules—we simply refuse to believe it.

If, however, this incredible news is true, then we *demand* an immediate interview to settle this unheard of corruption and on our part we earnestly ask Yakov [S. O. Tsederbaum] and Orsha [L. N. Radchenko] to scrape all and any money together and immediately realise their plan to come here.

1902

90. (159 R). TO HIS MOTHER

London, 25th April/8th May, 1902

Darling Mother,

I received a postcard from Manyasha today showing a view of the Volga and sending good wishes. Please thank her for it. I do not know whether you have been receiving my letters regularly lately? Apart from this postcard, I do not seem to have had anything from you for a long time.

Do you correspond with E. V. who is now in St. Petersburg and is apparently not very pleased with it? She is already beginning to think of her return journey.

I hope to see you soon,[1] my darling. If only the journey

---

[1] In the Summer of 1902 Lenin's mother visited him abroad and spent a fortnight with Lenin and Krupskaya in Loguivy, Côtes du Nord, Nth. France.

does not tire you too much; you must definitely choose day trains and stop the nights in hotels. Hotels are not expensive abroad and you can spend the night very well in them. But without such rest, and with the speed of trains over here and the short stops, it is quite impossible to travel for several days on end.

I shall wait with impatience for news of your departure. Perhaps you will send a telegram from Russia, or from abroad, when you are about to take a direct train to come here; that would be better.

I meant to ask you to bring certain of my underwear I left behind, but I do not think it is worth it really: what I left of my things may have come in useful for Mitya and he has probably taken them, but it is no use buying new things in Russia and bringing them here. If there are a few things left and if they are not of any use to anyone, then you might bring them with you (of course only a few things, so as not to burden you).

I advise you to choose express trains in Germany and Austria (you pay a small addition to the third class fare, but the saving in time is enormous). Draw up your time table at home after buying Henshall's Telegraph. Manyasha probably knows this guide.

I embrace you warmly, my darling, and send many greetings to all our people,

Your

V.

91. (104 p[1]). TO G. V. PLEKHANOV IN GENEVA

[*London, 14th May, 1902*]

I have received my article ["The Agrarian Programme of Russian Social Democracy"] with your remarks. You have a fine idea of tact with regard to your colleagues on the editorial board! You do not hesitate to choose the most contemptuous expressions, not to mention the "voting" on the suggestions, which you did not even take the trouble to formulate, and even about the "voting" about style. I should like to know what you would say if I were to answer your article on the programme in the same way? If your aim is to make mutual work impossible—then the way you have chosen will very rapidly help you to succeed. As for our personal, apart from our business, relations, you have finally spoilt them, or more exactly: you have achieved their complete cessation.

N. Lenin

92. (44 p[1]). TO F. V. LENGNIK IN SAMARA

[London, 23rd May, 1902]

And so your task now is to create out of yourself a Committee for the preparation of the Congress [1] to admit the Bund member [K. Portnoy] into this Committee (after having sized him up from all points of view—note this) to push your people on to as many Committees as possible, taking the utmost care of yourself and of your people until the Congress. All this is extremely important! Remember this! Be bolder in this, more ingenious and in other ways quieter and more cautious.

Be wise as serpents and as gentle as doves (with Committees: the Bund and Petersburg).

All yours

The Old Man

93. (106 p[1]). TO G. V. PLEKHANOV IN GENEVA

[Loguivy, Côtes du Nord, France], 2nd July, 1902

My dear G. V.

Forgive me for writing in such a hurry. I have come to Brittany for a rest (I am expecting my people here [Mother and Anyuta], but in Paris Berg [Martov] gave me his note and

---

[1] This refers to the re-establishment of the Organisation Committee for calling the II Party Congress, as the O.C. chosen at the Belostok Conference was arrested, except K. Portnoy, who was co-opted on to the new O.C.

I have received the article you sent under the signature Veteran [Plekhanov].

I quite agree with "Veteran." As the result of a remark about Leckert in "Iskra" I have had a small battle both with Berg and the Great Dmitrievna [Zasulich], both, as usual, are nervous and have begun talking about the inevitability of the terror and that we must express this (in one way or another). The remark in "Iskra" appeared therefore as a compromise: that was all I could gain.[1]

Now Berg himself is more definitely against terrorism, even of the Leckert type.

But the question is: is it convenient to print your article, signed Veteran? *Obviously, if you wish it, it will certainly appear* (and will be in time for the next number)—but would it not be better if you were to use it for a leader for No. 22, combining it (so to speak) with Berg's article "How to Fight"? I enclose this article in which, in my opinion, there are passages needing to be corrected, passages undesirably evasive on the subject of Leckert.

At the same time I enclose a note about the priest's[2] letter. What is your opinion?

And so my dear G. V. please answer as soon as you can and send these three things back to London, direct. But write to me, to this address.

I think it would be best to say what you say *in the editorial:* the subject will gain in importance (the *"objections" against* "Iskra" will be smoothed over) and the impression of unity will be increased. And it will be natural and easy for you to develop your article into a leader, which would thus replace the article on "How to Fight." In my opinion that would be the best way out.

Sincere greetings,

Your

Lenin

---

[1] Plekhanov's article dealt with Leckert's attempted assassination of the Governor-General of Vilna, who had ordered corporal punishment for the arrested participators in the May 1st demonstrations in Vilna, Kovno, Vitebsk. It was intended for "Iskra" No. 22, but was not printed. Instead, there appeared Plekhanov's leader in "Iskra" No. 22, "The Russian Working Class and Police Rods."

[2] A letter sent to "Iskra," in which the writer agreed with that part of the Party

94. (26 P[1]). TO CH—— [AN UNKNOWN ADDRESSEE]

[London], *2nd August, 1902*

I have received your letter, my dear Ch, and am answering you in a few words: I feel terribly out of sorts and am lolling about.

I have not seen a *single* letter on the point which you raised. And I think you have misunderstood: who could possibly think of "re-organising" workers' circles, groups and organisations instead of multiplying and strengthening them? You write that I did not point out how a strictly conspiratorial organisation can have dealings with the worker masses. That is hardly so, for on page 96 you quote a passage about the necessity *"of having the very largest number of,"* and with the most varied functions, "masses" (N.B.!) (masses!!) of other organisations (i.e. apart from the central organisation of professional revolutionaries[1]). But you are wrong to see an absolute contrast there where I establish only a gradation and point out the confines of the most extreme links of that gradation. Beginning with a handful of a very conspiratorial and solid nucleus of professional revolutionaries (the centre) and *ending* with the mass "organisations without members"—there is, after all, a whole chain of links. I am pointing out only the direction of the changing character of the links: the *more "mass" the organisation, the less must that organisation be formed* and conspiratorial—that is my thesis. But you want to take it to mean that there is no need for intermediaries between the masses and the revolutionaries!! Spare us! The intermediaries are the whole point. And if I point out the qualities of the extreme links and emphasise (yes, *emphasise*) the necessity for having the intermediary ones, then it is clear that these intermediary links will stand *between* the organisation of revolutionaries and the mass organisation, *in between* in type —i.e., they will be less narrow and conspiratorial than the centre —but more so than the "Union of Weavers" etc. For instance, in the "factory circle" (obviously we must try for every factory

programme published in "Iskra" No. 22, which demanded the separation of the Church from the State.

[1] This refers to Lenin's work, "What is to be done."

to have a circle of intermediaries) it is essential to find "a centre": on the one hand the whole, or almost the whole, factory must inevitably *know* some particular foreman and trust him and obey him. On the other hand, the circle must arrange the matter so that not *all* its members could be found out, and the one who has the most dealings with the masses could not be caught redhanded; in fact, could not be caught at all. Does all this not follow of itself from what has been said in Lenin's work?

It is perfectly clear that the ideal for a "factory circle" is, let us say, four or five worker-revolutionaries—the masses must not know them *all*. They might know one of them and he should be protected from detection. Let them say of him: "He is one of us, has brains *although he does not participate in the revolution.*" Only one would have dealings with the centre. They would start *several* circles (professional, educational, pedlars, spy, armed etc. etc.) and obviously the degree of conspiracy in the circle for catching spies or procuring arms will not be the same as in the circle for reading "Iskra," or in the circle for reading legal literature etc. etc. The degree of conspiracy will be in inverse proportion to the numbers of members of the circle and in direct proportion to the distance of the aims of the circle from the *direct* struggle.

I do not know if it is worth writing about this separately: if you think so, return this letter to me, I will think the matter over, together with your letter, as material. I hope to see the Petersburg comrade and discuss the matter in detail here.

I greet you warmly,

Your

Lenin

95. (27 P¹). TO V. A. NOSKOV IN ZÜRICH

[*London*], *4th August, 1902*

My dear B. N.

I have received both your letters and was very glad to learn and to see from them that the suspected misunderstandings are really proving to be *smoke* as I had already written to the chef [F. I. Shchekoldin]. (I wrote to him that I was convinced of this.)

Now you are complaining about our "agents." And I want to talk to you on this subject—I too am very sick about it. "Agents were collected far too quickly." . . . I know, I know it very well, I never forget this, but that is the tragedy (I promise you "tragedy" is not too strong a word!) of our position; that we *have to* act in such a way, that we are powerless to overcome the mass of irresponsibility which exists in our work. But try to understand our position and place yourself in such a position that you will say not, "*your* agents," but "*our* agents." You *can* put yourself into such a position and (in my opinion) you should do so—only then, and once and for all, can *any* possibility of misunderstanding be removed. Substitute the first person for the second, watch "our" agents yourself, help to find them, to dismiss and replace them, and then you will talk not about our agents being antipathetic (such words cannot fail to be misunderstood: they are taken as an expression of estrangement by all, and by members of our editorial board who have not had the opportunity of elucidating the question with you)—but then you will speak of the faults of *our common work*. It is this accumulation of faults which oppresses me, and the more there are, the worse it is for me. And the time is approaching (I feel) when the question will become uppermost: either Russia will put forward her own people and will provide those who can come to our aid and improve matters; or . . . And although I see and know that such people are coming forward, and their number is growing, this process moves so slowly and with such intervals, while the "creaking" of the machinery is tearing the nerves to such an extent, that . . . it is sometimes very hard to bear.

"Agents were collected far too quickly." Yes, but after all we are not creating "human material" for ourselves, but are taking, and cannot refuse, *what is given to us*. Without this we cannot live. A man goes to Russia—he says he wants to work for "Iskra." He is honest and is devoted to the cause. Well? Of course he goes and passes as an "agent," although not one of us has *ever* conferred such a title. . . . And what means have we of checking these "agents," controlling them, allocating them to certain places? Why, we cannot even get any letters out of them—and in *nine cases out of ten* (I am speaking from experience) all our suppositions here about the future activity of an agent go to the devil the day *after he crosses the frontier* and the agent works as the spirit moves him. Believe me, I am literally losing all faith in suppositions made here, in itineraries, plans etc., because I know in advance that it is useless. We are forced to struggle like swimmers against the tide, doing (for lack of better people) not our own job. After all, to appoint agents, look after them, *answer* for them, unite and control them at work—one has to be everywhere, fly about, see them actually at work. *A guild of practical organisers and leaders* is necessary for this to be done and that is just what we have not got; we have, of course, a few, but so few. . . . That is our trouble. When I look at our lack of organisation on the practical side—then I get to such a pitch of anger, that I lose all power of work and only one thing consoles me: the work is growing and obviously growing *in spite of* all this chaos, then it means the real cause is alive. It means it will stop fermenting and will become good wine.

Do you understand why one remark of an "Iskra" member: "Your agents are feeble"—is capable of reducing us almost to despair? "Then hurry up and replace the feeble ones"—is what we should like to say to you. Are we not saying repeatedly and even in books that "our whole trouble is that there is a crowd of people and yet *no real people*," while this lack of people is being thrust under our nose all the time? There is only one way out: a way out which is insistently essential and most urgent in the most literal sense of the word and not at all exaggerated —for time will not wait and our enemies are also growing such as "Osvobozhdeniye" and the Social Revolutionaries and all sorts of Social Democratic groups, beginning with the superficial "Zhizn" [group in Geneva] and ending with those intriguers, the "Struggle" group. The way out is that Russian "Iskra" members should at last get together and find *people* and take "Iskra" into their own hands, for truly our country is great and wide, but there is no order in it. They *must* find some people for there are people, but they must also be treasured more than the apple of one's eye, not only in the literal sense of the word, meaning protected from the police, but be kept for this urgent work and not allowed to become interested in other possibly useful, but untimely, tasks. When we are compelled, because of a lack of suitable people, to grab at the most "feeble," then surely it is not surprising we are unable to watch others calmly as they postpone our work to "later on."

If all the *present* "Iskra" people were to take "Iskra" into their own hands at once and see to the *independent* organisation of transport and distribution of material etc., then we should have a Central Committee controlling its agents in actual fact (for the Committee and not the editorial board must control the agents and be in charge of the whole of the practical side).

They say: "If there are no people, then how can we form a Central Committee?" We find people even if they are feeble. One strong individual among ten feeble ones is not much, but all the same the experience is not lost. People learn from practice: some go and others take their places and *once the work has been started*, the others will find it ten times easier to continue the work. If we were to form a Central Committee at once (not a formal one), it would be formal by tomorrow and would attract capable people from every local organisation ten times more energetically than at present. Only this "attraction" from local organisations is capable of organising the work in such a way that the local organisations would be served as they should be.

This is why I *envy* and deeply so, Semen Semenich ["Northern Workers' Union" or "The Northern Union of the R.S.D.L.P."] and I am agitated at every glance (yes, even a glance) at an outsider. And I cannot feel otherwise, because if the "Iskra" members will not say: "This is *our* business," if they will not say this aloud and refuse to take hold of the affair, grasping it with both hands and teeth and if they refrain from swearing at the others for their lack of tenacity, if the "Iskra" members do not do this, then it means they *want* to leave us with the "feeble ones" and that means the beginning of the end. (Once you said to me: "Swear at the 'Iskra' people"; and I replied: "It is not I, but you, who should do this, for only a man who participates practically in the work itself and who knows it inside out has the right to swear.")

It is time to stop this letter. I am extremely anxious that you and "the chef" should see our position as clearly as possible and say not "*you*" but "*we*." In any case it is essential that "the chef" should write to us often and write to us directly and bind us more closely to Semen Semenich and him to us.

As for your arrival, if you have to stay longer in Zürich, then that alters the matter. Why are you feeling depressed? Are you quite well? Do you not need a rest?

I am still not at all well and I cannot even think of a journey.

Write me your opinion about Zernova [M. M. Essen] and Sanin. I have heard a few rumours from various people about the latter and I have the impression that he is not a worker and is far too wild.

I greet you warmly,

Your

Lenin

96. (47 P¹). TO E. Y. LEVIN IN KHARKOV

[*London*], *22nd August*, [*1902*]

My dear Comrades,

We were extremely glad to receive your letter with the news about the opinions and plans of the remaining editorial board of the "Yuzhny Rabochy" ["The Southern Worker"].¹ We heartily agree to your suggestion that the closest relations and collaboration should be established between "The Southern

---

¹ In the Spring, 1902, the C.C. of the Union of Southern Committees and Organisations had collapsed; the Union had fallen to pieces, and the members of the editorial board of "The Southern Worker" changed. In July, 1902, "The Southern Worker" resolved to support "Iskra." This was the first step on the part of South Russian Social Democratic groups with "The Southern Worker" at the head to unite with the "Iskra" organisation.

Worker" and "Iskra." The most energetic measures should immediately be taken to consolidate these relations and to begin *united action* proceeding from our own unity. Firstly, we will make use of your suggestion to negotiate with Chernyshev.[1] Send us an address to which we can write to him. Will he not be coming abroad (as we heard) and will he not visit us? Secondly, please let us know who your official representative is. Send us at once a direct address for letters to be sent to you from abroad and *from Russia,* as well as an address for personal calls. We have already taken steps for members of the Russian "Iskra" organisation to see you and to discuss everything in detail. So as not to lose time unnecessarily, you must also write to us in greater detail about certain matters. What are the immediate practical plans of the editors of "The Southern Worker"? Have they made contact with the Southern Committees and formal relations with them? From your remarks that you intend to conduct the matter in the way in which it was conducted *before the formation* of the "Union of the Southern Committees and Organisations," we conclude that both the staff and the *direction* of the present editorial board of "The Southern Worker" are different from the staff and the direction of that editorial board which existed in the Spring during the conference. In what exactly does this divergence of directions consist? And what position do the Southern Committees occupy, i.e. which of them are on the side of the direction of the "Union of Southern Committees and Organisations" and which on your side? What is your opinion, is this divergence deep; will it prevent Party union and what measures are desirable for the speediest achievement of solidarity? How do those six provincial groups about which you wrote stand in relation to the Committees of the South (and to both directions, about which you spoke)? We would very much like you to help us to elucidate these questions fully, for it would greatly assist the rapprochement between your friends and those members of the Russian "Iskra" organisation who are working in the South.

[1] I. V. Chernyshev, a Social Democrat, wavered between "The Southern Worker" and "The Workers' Cause." In July, 1902, I. V. C. arrived in Berlin, and in October joined the Berlin "Iskra" group.

97. (161 R). TO HIS MOTHER

[*London*], *1st/14th September, 1902*

Darling Mother,

We were all delighted to have your telegram and your post-card which followed. Was the rest of the journey pleasant? Did it overtire you? Please write a few words about this after you have rested and settled down a little.

Anyuta's photographs (i.e. those sent by her) were received in time and in perfect condition.[1]

Our life goes on as usual. We are all well. The weather here is remarkably fine for the Autumn—probably a reward for the bad Summer. Nadya and I have several times set out to look for—and have found—real country districts near to town.

I embrace you warmly, my darling, and send much love to Manyasha and Anya.

Your

V.

98. (162 R). TO HIS MOTHER

[*London*], *14th/27th September, 1902*

Darling Mother,

It is a long time since we had any news of you. We have still not heard how you reached Samara and whether you have settled down. Manyasha is no longer living in the old flat, but I am writing to her address, for I do not know any other and I think the letter will be sent on to her new address. Where is Anyuta? What news have you of Mitya and Mark? How are you thinking of spending the Winter?

Are you well, my darling? Did the journey tire you very much?

Our life goes on as usual, but lately we have had a more worrying time. Now however my life is more "regular" and I try to spend more time in the library.

---

[1] Anyuta, fearing arrest at the frontier, posted the photographs which Lenin wanted.

The weather is amazingly fine: a reward for the poor Summer. Nadya and I have been to a number of places just outside town and have found some very pleasant spots. If you are having the same kind of weather, then you should take advantage of it somewhere in the country, for I should not think it was particularly pleasant in Samara itself.

I embrace you tenderly, my darling, and wish you good health.

Much love to all from me, Nadya and E. V.

Your

V.

99. (50 p¹). TO E. Y. LEVIN IN KHARKOV

[London, not before December 11th, 1902]

Lenin writing. Very glad about the success and energy of the Organisation Committee [of the II Party Congress]. Most important to do one's utmost immediately to bring the matter to an end, and that as quickly as possible. Try to replace as soon as possible the member from Petersburg [V. Krasnukha, arrested] (it would be good to have Ignat [P. A. Krasikov]) and write fully how they reacted in the various places (Committees) to the Organisation Committee. Will Ignat be seeing Fekla [the Editors of "Iskra"] soon? We must know exactly and soon.

We were intending more or less the following list of questions (set out in the order of discussion): (1) attitude towards Boris [the Bund]. (If only a federation, then separate at once and have separate sittings. Everyone should be prepared for this.) (2) The programme. (3) The Party organ (the newspaper, a new one or one of the existing ones. Insist on the importance of this preliminary question. (4) Organisation of the Party (fundamental principle: two central establishments, not subordinate one to the other. (a) a central organ—ideological leadership abroad? (b) a Central Committee—in Russia. The whole practical control. Regular and frequent meetings between them and certain rights of mutual participation or occasional mutual co-option. Most important to prepare in advance the ground for carrying this fundamental principle and its complete understanding by all. Then: the greatest possible centralisation, autonomy of the local committees in local matters—with the Central Committee's right of veto in exceptional cases. Regional organisations only with the agreement and confirmation of the Central Committee). (5) Various questions of tactics: terror, professional unions, legalisation of the workers' movement, strikes, demonstrations, risings, agrarian policy and work among the peasantry and the army, agitation in general; leaflets and pamphlets etc. etc. here, the order is not observed. (6) Relations with other Parties ("Osvobozhdeniye" ["Liberation"], the Socialist-Revolutionaries, Poles, Letts etc.). (7) Reports of delegates (*very important* that the reports should be from each Committee and as full as possible—they should be prepared *at once* and for safety copies should be sent to the Organisation Committee, for forwarding to us). Always try to characterise local Social Revolutionaries and estimate their strength and links in the reports. (8) Foreign groups and organisations ("Rabocheye Delo" ["The Workers' Cause"], "Borba" ["Struggle"] "Zhizn" ["Life"], "Svoboda" ["Freedom"]. To entrust the working out of a plan for uniting them to a Commission or to the Central Committee). (9) 1st May. (10) 1904 Congress in Amsterdam. (11) Internal organisation questions: finance, type of committee organisation, entrusting transport and distribution of literature etc. to the Central Committee. Part of this will probably have to be discussed in commissions.

I repeat, that this is only an approximate scheme and the order only relative to points 1-5 was discussed here. When it was discussed, I, as a member of the editorial board, wanted point 3 to be placed in one of the first places (i.e. in the 3rd), while a second member (Pahomy)—wanted it placed after point 5. I consider it important to decide point 3 first, so as immediately to attack all opponents on a fundamental and a wide question and to see clearly the whole picture of the Congress: (to separate on a serious pretext).

Please explain if you will have any comments and on which questions (re 5:—in detail).

Which pamphlet does Ignat want published? Is it the letter to Erema [A. A. Schneerson]?

Do not fail to obtain from *each* Committee (and group) an official and *written* answer as to whether they recognise the Organisation Committee. That must be done at once.

I advise you to publish the announcement about the Organisation Committee also in Russia (i.e. not only print it in "Iskra"): even hectograph it, but publish it.

We will send you the editorial board's questions and the list of our reports, when we will have discussed this with all members of the editorial board, who are now living in various countries.

Appoint immediately members of the Organisation Committee in the main centres (Kiev, Moscow, St. Petersburg) and give special addresses for personal calls to these members, so that all travellers will be at the complete disposal of the Organisation Committee. That is very, very important.

And finally, one more thing: the meeting between Ignat and Fekla should be arranged (1) after he has seen as many people as possible; (2) after you have received from everyone their official acknowledgement of the Organisation Committee; (3) after you have *officially announced also to the "Rabocheye Delo"* that they will have a fully empowered member on the Organisation Committee. Only under such conditions can Ignat's meeting with Fekla serve for further serious business. Let Ignat, therefore hurry with these preliminary measures and not forget that when he meets Fekla he must be armed with the widest and officially recognised powers.

100. (165 R). TO HIS MOTHER

[London], *13th/26th December, 1902*

Darling Mother,

Please forward the enclosed letter to Anyuta. I have not got her address; it has probably gone astray (I have not written to her yet). Perhaps she is not in Tomsk, but with you. I believe you were hoping to be all together for the holidays, including

Mitya. Tell me if this came off and whether you have met Mitya's wife.

We have absolutely no news. The cold weather is over. It feels like the Autumn to us and by way of an exception is dry, which is very pleasant. It will soon be Christmas, probably fairly dull: few meetings, the Reading Room will be closed and it will not be easy to get into the theatres, because everything is crowded out. However I expect to see several new acquaintances during this time.

I have lately been studying German newspapers more than usual: events in Germany[1] were interesting and I wanted to follow them from a new source. Things are evidently calming down there.

How are you getting on? Are the fierce frosts over? Any new people?

Well, I hope you will spend the holiday happily and wish you all good health.

Your

V. U.

101. (107 p[1]). TO G. V. PLEKHANOV IN GENEVA

[London], 14th December, 1902

My dear G. V.

We do not seem to have had any news from you for a long time, and meanwhile there is an accumulation of business and questions.

First of all about articles for "Iskra": for No. 30 (No. 29 is appearing tomorrow or the day after) we have Julius's [Martov's] article "Autumn Results." Another article seems to be essential. What about you? Please write and tell us if you are writing anything and when you intend to send it to us—also about the serial: the serial you suggested against the Tarasov

---

[1] In Germany throughout 1902 there was great resistance against the project of a customs' tariff, introduced by the Government. The German Social Democracy, with Bebel at the head, led an energetic fight against any increase in the price of bread.

"page" [1] would be splendid for No. 30. I shall expect an answer.

Next, about the pamphlet against the Socialist-Revolution-aries, L. G. [Deitch] told me and also wrote to you that it would be better if you were to do this, for apart from dogmatic criticism you might also draw a *historical parallel* with the 1870's. I quite agree with L. G. that such a parallel is very, very important; as for me, of course I cannot even think of it. I should be really very grateful if you would write it. I am not very keen on doing it and moreover, apart from current affairs, I have much work ahead of me. I have to prepare some lectures for Paris (Julius tells me that they want me to go there to give three or four lectures on the agrarian question) and so every-thing points to the fact that you ought to write the pamphlet—it is definitely needed against the Socialist-Revolutionaries, for they should be attacked from all sides. They harm us and seri-ously damage our cause. So write and tell us what you decide to do.

L. G.'s reply to "Revolutionary Russia" was printed in Num-ber 29: which means that you will receive it at the end of the week; besides, you have already seen it in proof.

Today I learnt you are to be in Brussels for the International Conference (probably at the end of December or the beginning of January) and that you are to read a paper there, I hope you will not fail to visit us here. We are so close and the journey would cost very little during the holidays. Your paper would be most useful here, for there are many *workers* here infected with anarchism (I was convinced of this when I read my paper about the Socialist-Revolutionaries, which did not interest the public). Probably you would influence them. But the main rea-son is that we have a number of matters which need to be dis-cussed, especially about affairs in Russia. An organisation com-mittee [for calling the II Party Congress] which has long been discussed, has been formed and it may play an *enormous* rôle. It would be extremely important if we were to answer together a number of questions which *they have already asked us* (the

---

[1] An article by K. Tarasov in "The Messenger of the Russian Revolution" on "The Evolution of Russian Socialist Thought."

questions refer to the measures to be taken for uniting the Party, to the agenda for the General Congress; what papers are going to be read *by us* etc., in fact, important questions and being at the moment of particular importance). Please write and say when exactly the Conference is to take place in Brussels, how many days it is to last and whether you will be able to come here. Also it might not perhaps be out of place to make use of the fact at the Conference that the Organisation Committee has been formed. Write quickly and we will ask them in Russia: there might be time to receive some statement from them or a letter to you, if there is any need for that.

Do you see the "Zhizn" people? How is the rapprochement with them progressing? What are the chances and how are the "Rabocheye Delo" people? You know, I think it would be a good idea for them to take part in our "Marxist circle" and if we were to begin (informally) to be more friendly with them. It would be pointless to quarrel with them at the present moment: by substituting the "Red Banner" for the "Rabocheye Delo" they have really accepted our plan for the allotment of "literary functions" and there is nothing harmful in the Martynov pamphlet ["The Workers and the Revolution," published by the Union of Russian Social Democrats.].

I greet you warmly,
                                        Your
                                                    Lenin

P.S. I am to blame for the Bulgarian. I repent. I did not write, because there were no commissions and I had no idea you were worrying.

1903

102. (59 p[1]). TO G. M. KRZHIZHANOVSKY IN SAMARA

[*London*], *27th January*, [*1903*]

The old man writing. I have read your angry letter of the 3rd January[1] and am replying at once. Re correspondence,

---

[1] Krzhizhanovsky's letter reproaches Lenin for lack of organisation in the O.C. for the II Congress, complains that Krasikov is unsuited to conduct the work of the O.C., disapproves of the transfer of the O.C. bureau to Kharkov.

dogs [the Baku "Iskra" group] etc. the secretary [N. K. Krupskaya] will send you a reply. I cannot make out who is to blame, but we must definitely be in constant communication, not less than twice a month, but so far it has not been like that and we have not known anything about you for long stretches on end. Do not forget, that when we do not receive any letters we cannot do anything, we do not know if the people are alive and are compelled, literally compelled, to consider them almost as non-existent. You have not replied to my question about Brut's [G. M. Krzhizhanovsky] move: evidently there is little hope of a good settlement until that move takes place. And now to business. In swearing at us you exaggerate our strength and influence: we have come to an agreement here about the Organisation Committee. We insisted at the Congress that you should be invited, and wrote to you. We could do nothing else, absolutely nothing else and refuse to be held responsible for anything. The root of the trouble is that Brut was not at the Organisation Committee and all that followed was done without him (as also without us).[1] We did not receive the unknown member (he is a slow coach and unintelligent, I knew him personally in Pskov, he is tied by his family and work and is no good for anything, and Pankrat [P. A. Krasikov] has already been cursed about him). We have not transferred the O.C. office. We have given absolutely no "power" to Pankrat. But when Pankrat turned out to be the only live man in the Organisation Committee, then the result could not be otherwise than power. You write: there are people, but we have not any, we do not know them or see them. We have lost our tempers to the point of neurasthenia because of this complete absence of men for the Organisation Committee, for which active, free and illegal men are needed. Pankrat alone has gone over to illegal work, he has set out, has begun to hurry begun to know everything—and has naturally assumed the rank of corporal. We did not interfere, obviously, for we could not interfere, nor did we want to interfere: there was not anyone else!!! Cannot you understand that at

---

[1] Krzhizhanovsky was not present at the November conference in Pskov, through a misunderstanding regarding time and place.

last? Pankrat is lazy and casual, but he is clever, sensible, knows his job, knows how to fight, one can get on with him. Now he is stuck (in Paris) for an unknown length of time and we are swearing at him, driving him to Russia, for otherwise the Organisation Committee becomes a mere cipher. "She" (Akim's [B. Gorev-Goldman] brother) will soon be leaving for Russia, we will try to introduce her into the Organisation Committee. She seems energetic. Pero [L. D. Trotsky] does not want to leave. No passports, no copies. If Brut moves to a lively place, close by, then we will help him to have the office of the Organisation Committee moved to where he is and everything may be settled. Otherwise everything will go (if it does go) according to the will of Allah, the will of Pankrat and her will, and we here are powerless to do anything.

The literature has been sent. Over 160 pounds have been taken across the frontier. We are printing the Organisation Committee's announcement in No. 32 which is coming out the day after tomorrow.

Uncle [L. M. Knipovich] is also still away (like Brut) and has not got anywhere; if he and Brut would settle somewhere even in Poltava, they could take over the control of the office.

I am very angry with Zarin [F. V. Lengnik]: he will not write sensibly, is apathetic, knows nothing about Kiev, has allowed a split to take place under his very nose. It is positively extraordinary to be so remote from local affairs!! And how are we to blame, that of two members of the Organisation Committee equally empowered, Zarin "sits silent," while at least Pankrat is showing signs of life? I think (I do not know for certain) that Zarin is a man of little initiative and also tied by legality and by the place where he lives. And now such men automatically stand aside. I swear on my honour that is neither our fault nor our wish.

103. (55 P[1]). TO THE KHARKOV COMMITTEE

London, 15th January, 1903

My dear Comrades,

Many thanks for the detailed letter about the position of affairs: such letters are very rarely written to us, although we need them terribly badly and should be receiving ten times as many, if we really want to create a living link between the editorial office abroad and local workers and to make "Iskra" a complete reflection of our workers' movement, both as a whole and in its separate parts. We therefore beg you to continue in the same spirit and to send us, if only occasionally, little word pictures of conversations with workers (what they talk about in the circle; what complaints; doubts; demands. The themes of discussion, etc. etc.).

The plan of your organisation is evidently approaching a rational organisation of revolutionaries, if one can speak of a "rational" organisation, when there is such a shortage of men and if we understand the plan clearly from your short description.

Tell us in great detail about the independents. Then more questions: are there any workers left in Kharkov of the Ivanovo-Voznesensk school and tradition [extreme "Economism"]? Are there any people who were at one time in that "economic" and anti-intelligentsia company, or are there only their successors? Why have you not mentioned "The Leaflet on the Workers' Banks" or why don't you send it us? We have seen here only the manuscript copy of No. 2 of that leaflet. What sort of people are bringing it out? Are they out-and-out economists or only green youths? Is it a purely workers' organisation or is it under the influence of intellectual-economists?

Are there any traces left of the "Kharkov Proletariat" people?

Is "Iskra" read in the workers' circles? With explanations of the articles? Which articles are read most eagerly and what sort of explanations are asked for?

Is there any propaganda conducted among the workers about conspiratorial methods and about taking up illegal revolutionary work on a large scale?

Try to make greater use of the Petersburg Zubatovshchina and send us any correspondence from workers.

Your

Lenin

104. (166 R). TO HIS MOTHER

London, 22nd January/4th February, 1903

Darling Mother,

I have not had a single letter for ages, either from you or from any one of our people. One of your letters has probably gone astray, for I cannot believe that no one has written to me all this time. I do not know whether Mitya has been to see you, how long he stayed, what his plans are or where he is now. Have you had any news from Anyuta? Has she gone to Port Arthur[1] and when? Are you well? Is the frost still persisting?

We have fine weather; the Winter is exceptionally good, mild and (so far) little rain or fog. It is true that E. V. is often ill; she is at present laid up, but nothing serious, so we manage to treat her with Russian prescriptions and home remedies. It would probably help her to go somewhere further South. Nadya and I are well. Our life goes on as usual, quietly and modestly. The other day for the first time this Winter, we went to a good concert and were very pleased with it, especially with Tchaikovsky's Symphonie Pathétique. Are there any good concerts in Samara? We have been once to the German Theatre. How we should like to go to the Moscow Art Theatre to see [Gorky's] "The Lower Depths"!

I kiss you warmly, my darling, and send you best wishes, especially for your health. Greetings to all our people. Perhaps

---

[1] Anyuta and Mark Elizarov travelled to Port Arthur from Tomsk.

you will forward this letter to Anyuta, for when shall I know what her address is?

Your

[V. U.]

Am I writing the correct address?

105. (108 p¹). TO YU. O. MARTOV IN PARIS[1]

[*London*], *5th February, 1903*

I am sending a copy of the Union letter [of the Russian Social Democrats Abroad to "The League Abroad," about the question of creating an outside-Russia section of the Organisation Committee] and our suggested answer. An answer has been sent to Plekhanov, telling him to wait for your letter from Paris. Please arrange immediately for a meeting with P. A. [Krasikov] and Boris [Noskov] and answer Plekhanov *as soon as possible* whether you agree with the answer or if you think any alterations are necessary. It would certainly be helpful if the answer to the Union letter were not held up; in the event of a vote being taken on the alterations, the delay would be considerable: perhaps the unimportant alterations could be left for the time being, but of course if there is a difference of opinion upon the more important facts, then we shall have to hold up the answer (I am writing also to Plekhanov about this) and we should all have to vote.

In my opinion (and V. I. [Zasulich] and L. G. [Deitch] agree with it) the most important fact is that (1) the section of the Organisation Committee abroad should be a section of the Russian Organisation Committee. I believe the "Unionites" are imagining there will be two independent sections: a Russian one, and a foreign one. We definitely cannot in any way accept such an idea. The Russian Organisation Committee must act carefully (in this respect its announcement is drawn up in a model way), but in all matters and references to it, it should

---

[1] From Nov., 1902, to Feb., 1903, Martov was visiting Paris, Berlin, Geneva, Zürich, organising and lecturing.

adopt an arch-important and arch-severe attitude, i.e. insisting that the Russian Organisation Committee is in control of everything and no one in the Party can do anything otherwise than by order of the Russian Organisation Committee.

By their letter the Unionites recognise (or almost, i.e. ¾, recognise) the Organisation Committee and the more they recognise it, the sterner and firmer must the Organisation Committee hold itself. From the beginning it is essential to assume the right tone and place oneself in such a position that the Party position should be clear: either recognition of the Organisation Committee and *subjection* to it, *or war*. Tertium non datur. And now there are many chances of receiving *general* recognition, without offending anyone, but not giving in to anyone *one iota*.

(2) The Organisation Committee should reduce the functions of *its* department abroad to a minimum. The section outside Russia only attends to matters *abroad* (in the sense of preparing unification) and *assists* the Russian section. In every other question, even the slightest bit outside these limits, the outside-Russia section of the Organisation Committee must ask the *opinion and decision of the Russian Organisation Committee*. I therefore strongly insist that the Russian Organisation Committee should write a letter *as soon as possible* to the Union, the League and the Bund, with a proposal to form *its own section for conducting such and such functions*. It is essential that the Russian Organisation Committee should point out the "limits of control" to its section outside Russia and I propose below a draft definition of these functions, in *three,* and only three, strictly limited points. I do urge you to discuss this project as quickly as possible with P. A. [Krasikov] and Boris and to confirm it (voting on the amendments). (We will send all this data to Yury ["The Southern Worker" Group] asking him to await the arrival of P. A. and Boris, who must speed up their arrival to their utmost.)

(Of course P. A. could write a letter from here to the League, the Union, and the Committee of the Bund abroad, but I think that this is highly undesirable, for some sort of faking and intriguing would be suspected. Better wait a week or two, but get the letter sent from Russia without fail.)

I also think that we ought to begin thinking about electing a member from among ourselves on to the Organisation Committee (outside-Russia section) and to do the voting in advance, for with the colleagues being scattered, it may take much time and would be unpleasant to make people wait because of it. I, for my part, record my vote for L. Gr. [Deitch].

I have positively no time to write to Plekhanov as well. Simply forward him *this letter at once and the reply to the Union*, while I will scribble him a few lines.

Greetings to you,

Lenin

106. (168 R). TO HIS MOTHER

[*London*], *16th/29th March, 1903*

Darling Mother,

I received your letter the other day. Many thanks for it. So Anyuta has been delayed in the Far East for longer than she thought. And I was thinking she was with you! It is probably not possible to set out at once on such a long journey. So Mitya has also not yet decided where he is going to live? Is Manyasha very unhappy, poor thing?

It is a good thing the weather is reasonably warm with you, for excessively cold Winters are very tiring. Do you feel well, my darling?

It is warm here. The other day we took E. V. [Krupskaya's mother] for a long walk—we took sandwiches instead of having dinner—and went for the whole Sunday "ins Grüne." (We find that willy-nilly we are doing things in a foreign way: we go for walks on a Sunday, although it is not very comfortable, because everywhere is crowded.) We had a splendid walk, the air intoxicated us all as though we were children, and afterwards I had to sleep it off just as I used to do after a day's shooting in Siberia. Indeed, so far as walks are concerned, we do not miss much; we are the only ones of the comrades here who are studying the country round London. We find various field paths; we know the nearest places and are thinking of going farther out. I feel well lately, work regularly and do not suffer from nerves. Nadya and E. V. are also well.

I kiss you warmly, my darling. Please write from time to time (or ask Manyasha to write) about your life and plans.

Your

V. Ulianov

THE PERIOD OF THE II PARTY CONGRESS AND THE SPLIT IN THE RUSSIAN SOCIAL DEMOCRATIC LABOUR PARTY

1903–1904

SUMMARY

1903

July 30-Aug. 23. II Party Congress of the R.S.D.L.P. held in Brussels in July and moves to London in Aug. The S.D. groups in Russia send a majority of delegates supporting "Iskra" views. Activities: (1) Party programme fixed (2) Organisation of Party (3) Resolutions re relations with Liberals (Plekhanov) and S.R.'s. (Axelrod). Party splits into Bolsheviks and Mensheviks. Differences of opinion on; (1) who should be considered to be a Party member (2) relations between Central Organ and Central Committee (3) the personnel of the Central Organ and Central Committee. Lenin is head of Central Organ and Martov is head of Central Committee. Lenin suggests that editorial board of "Iskra" be 3 and not 6 (Plekhanov, Lenin, Martov, Zasulich, Potresov and Axelrod). Martov, Potresov, Zasulich and Axelrod refuse to take part in No. 46 of "Iskra." Mensheviks struggle against Bolsheviks. Congress of "League of Russian Revolutionary Social Democrats" resolves to call Party workers to fight Bolsheviks and bureaucratic centralism. Representative of C.C. announces that the league, its congress and resolutions are illegal.

Plekhanov goes over to Mensheviks. Invites old "Iskra" staff and beginning with No. 52 "Iskra" has Menshevik character.

1904

Russo-Japanese war. Active struggle of Bolsheviks against Mensheviks.

July: C.C. of Party comes to an agreement with Mensheviks and co-opts a few Mensheviks. Congress in Switzerland of various Party leaders of Narodnik groups.

1903

Attends Party Congress as delegate of the Union of R.S.D. abroad. Active at II Party Congress in spirit of revolutionary Marxism. Insists on personal participation of Party members in Party activity, thus including in the Party only active revolutionary workers. Suggests a revolutionary Marxist control of Party and defends the Party programme.

Lenin is at head of the Bolsheviks.

Elected member of Central Committee of the Party Council and Editor of Central Organ "Iskra."

November: Answers Plekhanov's move by resigning from Editorship of Central Organ "Iskra" and from Party Council.

1904

Becomes member of Central Committee.

THE RUSSIAN REVOLUTIONARY MOVEMENT	LENIN'S LIFE
Aug.: Central Committee announces to Party (1) complete legality of editorial personnel of Central Organ (2) proposal to co-opt Lenin on to editorial board (3) undesirability of calling general Party Congress (4) proposal to call Conference to conciliate enemy fractions. Bolsheviks led by Lenin struggle against Central Committee because of co-optation of Mensheviks.	Lenin leaves Party Central Committee. Heads agitation for III Party Congress in view of Menshevik infraction of the will and decisions of the Party majority.
Oct.: Mensheviks advocate the support of the Liberals. Revolutionary elements of workers' movement support Lenin. Dec.: No. 1 of "Vpered" ("Forward") appears.	Founds the Bolshevik organ "Vpered" and is its Editor.

107. (110 P¹). TO G. M. KRZHIZHANOVSKY, IN KIEV
(Unposted.)

[Geneva, Between 10th-17th September, 1903]

My thanks to Smith [G. M. Krzhizhanovsky] for his long letter. Let him write to Egor [Martov] appealing for the last time to reason. Zarin [F. V. Lengnik, C.C. representative] should immediately go to Egor [abroad], after receiving full powers for conducting affairs in Egor's province.¹ Formulate all this more fully, strictly and accurately. You must act formally and prepare for a definite war with the Martovites. Whatever happens their attempt to push themselves on to committees² should immediately be met with determined resistance. We should be on the watch for this and prepare all the committees. The Egorites [Martovites] are continuing and *widening* the boycott, they are devilishly angry, they have imagined a heap of offences and insults and think they are saving the Party from tyrants, they shout about it right and

¹ Lengnik was to come abroad to negotiate with the Menshevik (Martovite) opposition, with a view to liquidating the threatened split which became apparent at the II Party Congress.

² The Menshevik opposition intended to send their men to Russia to win over the local committees.

left and confuse people. Their revolt has already taken away from us (I do not know for how long, but *perhaps for ever*) two of our largest sources of money [A. M. Kalmykova and ?]. Direct all your most desperate efforts to the procuring of money —that is the main thing.

And so, let Smith not look upon Egor as before. The friendship is at an end. Down with all softheartedness! Prepare the most decisive resistance, send Zarin at once, nominate candidates (in case of Smith's death [= arrest]), nominate *members to the Soviet*,[1] put everything on a more formal footing, and act energetically. We will manage the literary side. We have set great hopes on Vadim [V. A. Noskov].

---

108. (135 p¹). TO THE DON COMMITTEE [2]

[Geneva, October, 1903]

Comrades,

We have received your letter containing the resolution. We would ask you to reply to the following:

(1) Have you listened to the reports both of the Mensheviks and the Bolsheviks (one of your delegates [S. I. Gusev], as you no doubt know, was on the side of the Bolsheviks), or only of the Mensheviks?

(2) What do you mean by the word "departure"? Departure where to? Do you mean that someone has been removed from his work, or has himself given it up for some reason or other; and for what reason?

(3) What do you call "abnormal conditions at elections"?

(4) Who exactly in your opinion should be co-opted on to the Central Committee? and

(5) Who ought to be co-opted on to the editorial board of the Central Organ?

---

[1] Two representatives from the C.C. to the Soviet of the Party.

[2] This letter was sent in the name of the "Iskra" editorial board in reply to the following resolution adopted by the Don Committee: "Taking into account those abnormal conditions under which the elections to the C.C. and the C.O. took place, and expressing great regret at the consequent departure of many forces, the Don Committee suggests that the C.C. and the C.O. should co-opt these forces, which are valuable to the Party."

109. (113 P¹). TO THE CENTRAL COMMITTEE IN RUSSIA

[Sécheron, 14th November, 1903]

Their conditions[1]: (1) co-option of the 4 on to the editorial board, (2) co-option to the C.C., (3) recognition of the legality of the League,[2] (4) 2 votes in the Soviet. I would suggest to the Central Committee that the following conditions be proposed to them: (1) to co-opt 3 on to the editorial board; (2) status quo ante bellum in the League,[3] (3) 1 vote in the Soviet. Then I would suggest that they should confirm (but for the present not to tell the fighting side) the *ultimatum*.[4] (1) to co-opt 4 on to the editorial board; (2) to co-opt 2 on to the Central Committee by the vote of the Central Committee; (3) status quo ante bellum in the League; (4) 1 *vote* in the Soviet. On non-acceptance of the ultimatum:—war to the end. The additional condition: (5) cessation of all judgments, altercations and conversations on the subject of the dispute at the II Party Congress and after it.

For myself, I will say that I will leave the editorial board and can remain only on the Central Committee.[5] I will stop *at nothing* and will publish a pamphlet about the fight of historical scandalmongers or rejected ministers.[6]

[Unsigned]

---

[1] These conditions were made by the Mensheviks for liquidating the split in Potresov's letter to Plekhanov, sent in answer to Plekhanov's offer to begin negotiations for peace within the Party. This offer was made against Lenin's wish, and marks the beginning of Plekhanov's move over to the Mensheviks and his break with Lenin.

[2] At the time of the II Congress the League was in the hands of the Mensheviks abroad, and was their base in the struggle against the central institutions of the Party.

[3] Lenin was suggesting annulling all the illegal resolutions of the Menshevik majority at the II Congress of the League and the return of the League to its position in the Party before the II Congress of the League.

[4] Ultimatum—the conditions submitted in the name of the C.C. of the R.S.D.L.P.

[5] When Lenin saw that Plekhanov was siding with the Mensheviks, he officially resigned from the C.O. editorial board and the Party Soviet (as delegate from the C.O.) and left the editorial board on Nov. 6. By Nov. 25th, when Krzhizhanovsky arrived to negotiate with the Mensheviks, Lenin was co-opted on to the C.C.

[6] Lenin's pamphlet: "One step forward, two steps back."

110. (115 P[1]). TO THE CENTRAL COMMITTEE IN RUSSIA

[*Geneva, 10th December, 1903*]

Dear Friends,

A new political position is clearly manifest in "Iskra" No.
53.[1] It is clear that the five [Plekhanov, Martov, Axelrod,
Zasulich, Potresov][2] on the Central Organ want to run down
not only Lenin, (even to the slander about his throwing out
the Southern Workers from the Party, even to the low asper-
sions at Schweizer[3]), but also the Central Committee and all
the Bolsheviks. Plekhanov says quite frankly that the Central
Organ is not afraid of any Central Committee. There is an
attack on the Central Committee both here and in Russia (the
letter from St. Petersburg about Martyn's [V. N. Rozanov]
trip).

If we miss the opportunity and the right slogan for a fight,
then *complete* defeat is inevitable, (1) because of the desperate
struggle of the 5 in "Iskra," (2) because of the failure of our
men in Russia. *The only salvation—a Congress. Its slogan: war
with the disorganisers.* Only with this slogan will we be able to
catch out the Martovites, attract the wide masses and save the
situation. In my opinion, the only possible plan is this: not a
word *for the present* to anyone *about the Congress,* complete
secrecy. *To move all our forces into the Committees and Circuits.* To fight for peace, for the cessation of disorganisation, for
submission to the Central Committee. To do our utmost to
strengthen the Committees with our own men. To do our
utmost to catch out the Martovites and the Southern Workers
at disorganisation, with documents, resolutions against the disorganisers. Resolutions of Committees must fly to the Central
Organ. Then we must push people on to shaky Committees

---

[1] No. 53 contained an article, "Our Congress," written by Martov.

[2] The 5, the new editorial board of the C.O., which meant that Plekhanov had
co-opted Mensheviks, former members of the Old "Iskra" editorial board. Plekhanov
took this second step towards the Mensheviks after the "ultimatum" had been presented to the Mensheviks by the C.C. This meant that now the C.O. was completely
in Menshevik hands. The Mensheviks replied to the "ultimatum" by a refusal to negotiate further with the C.C.

[3] Plekhanov hints a comparison between Lenin and a petit-bourgeois leader in the
German Labour Movement of the 1860's who dictatorially controlled the "All-German
Labour Union" after Lassalle's death.

and win over Committees in the name of the slogan: i.e. against disorganisation—that is the *main* task. *A Congress is essential not later than January*, so get to work more energetically, we too will do our utmost. The aim of the Congress: to strengthen the Central Committee and the Soviet, and perhaps also the Central Organ, by means either of the three (in case we manage to drag Plekhanov away, which is doubtful) or of the six which I will join on an honourable peace for us. The worst would be *if the Central Organ were theirs, and the Central Committee and the Soviet ours.*

I repeat: either complete defeat (the Central Organ will hunt us down) *or immediate preparations for a Congress. It must be prepared secretly at first*, taking a month at the most, *then three weeks to collect the demands of half the Committees and to call a Congress*. Again and again I repeat: this is the only salvation.

111. (157 p[1]). to the editors of "iskra"

[Geneva], *12th December, 1903*

I, as representative of the Central Committee, received an enquiry from Comrade Martov if they could print the Central Committee negotiations with the Geneva opposition.[1] I presume that they may and would ask the comrades on the editorial board of the Central Organ to consider carefully and once again the question of goodwill and peace in the Party.

It is still not too late to ensure this peace, still not too late to keep from the public and enemies details of the split and the talk about the false lists, which will be made use of probably even by the "Moskov Skiye Vedomosti." I guarantee that the "Bolsheviks" will gladly consent to forget all this dirt, on condition that good peace is assured within the Party.

Everything depends on the editorial board of the Central Organ, which includes representatives of the former opposition which rejected the Central Committee's suggestion about peace of November 25th, 1903. I ask you, comrades, to note that the Central Committee has since then made two further con-

---

[1] About peace within the Party.

cessions of their own free will, by advising Comrade R. [L. E. Halperin, a Bolshevik] to send in his resignation and by trying to settle the matter with the League.[1]

Meanwhile the boycott of the Central Committee, agitation against it and disorganisation of practical work in Russia continue. They write from Russia that the opposition is creating "hell" there. We have the most reliable information that the Menshevik agents are systematically continuing their work of disorganisation by touring round the Committees. They have written to us from Petersburg about Martyn's [Rozanov's] trip there with a definite object. Matters have reached such a pitch, that the opposition is organising its own transport and is offering it to the Central Committee through Dan![2]

I consider it my duty to the Party to ask the editors of the Central Organ for the last time to compel the opposition to sign a peace on the basis of a sincere recognition by both parties of both centres and the cessation of mutual wrangling which renders any work together impossible.

112. (116 P[1]). TO G. M. KRZHIZHANOVSKY IN KIEV

[Geneva, 18th December, 1903]

My dear Friend,

We must thoroughly clear up a question upon which we evidently disagree and I do ask you to pass this letter on from me for discussion among all the members of the Central Committee (or the Executive Commission).[3] Where we differ is this: (1) You think that peace is possible with the Martovites (Boris [V. A. Noskov] even congratulates us on peace! This is both funny and sad!); (2) You think that an immediate Congress is a proof of our powerlessness. I am convinced that

[1] By recognising the new administration of the League, chosen by the Menshevik majority of the League Congress after the Congress's further session was declared illegal by a representative of the C.C. and after the Bolshevik part of the League had left the Congress.

[2] The Mensheviks suggested that, since they had transport facilities and could carry 1,200 lbs. a month, if the C.C. provided the literature, *half* of it would go to the C.C., and the other to "their own" committees.

[3] The Executive Commission of the C.C., consisting of G. Krzhizhanovsky, L. Krassin and F. Gusarov, was formed in October, 1903.

you are cruelly mistaken on both points. (1) The Martovites are moving towards war. At the Geneva meeting Martov shouted that they were strong. In the newspaper they attack us and basely misrepresent the question and cover up their cunning with wails about bureaucratism at your expense. Martov continues to shout right and left about the complete inadequacy of the Central Committee. In short, it is both childish and impossible to doubt that the Martovites are aiming at getting hold of the Central Committee through cunning, boycott and scandal. It is beyond our strength to struggle against them on these grounds, for the Central Committee is a powerful weapon and our defeat would be inevitable, especially in view of the arrests. By allowing time to pass, you are moving towards an absolute and complete defeat of the majority. You are swallowing in silence all the insults (of the League) abroad directed against the Central Committee[1] and you are asking for fresh ones. (2) The Congress will prove our strength; it will show that not only in words, but also in deeds, we will not allow a clique of scandalmongers abroad to dominate the movement. The Congress is needed particularly at this moment when we have the slogan—War on Disorganisation. It is only this slogan which justifies the Congress and completely justifies it in the eyes of the whole of Russia. By losing time you also lose the slogan, proving your impotent, passive submission to the Martovites. It is simply ludicrous to dream of fortifying the position by positive work in the face of persecution from the Central Committee and the boycotting and agitation from the Martovites. This would mean slow death in an inglorious struggle with intriguers, who would then say (and are already saying): "See how reliable this Central Committee is!" I repeat: do not flatter yourselves with illusions. Either you will prescribe peace for the Martovites at the Congress, or you will be thrown out ingloriously, or be replaced at the very first arrests. The Congress now has an aim: to end the impossible disorganisation, to clear away the League[2] which derides the Central Committee; to take the Council

---

[1] I.e., the behaviour of the Menshevik majority at the II Congress of the League.
[2] Because of Menshevik members, the League supported opposition to the C.C.

firmly into its own hands and to organise the Central Organ. But how to organise it? In the *worst* event by leaving even the five members, (or by reinstating the six): but this worst event is unbelievable, if we have a large majority. Then we shall either conquer the Martovites finally (Plekhanov is *already talking* of a new Vade mecum,[1] seeing that there is no peace, and he is threatening to attack both disputants. And that is just what we want!), or we say openly that we have no controlling Central Organ and will convert it into an instrument for discussion with independent signed articles by Bolsheviks and Mensheviks (or better still, to confine polemics to the Martovites' pamphlets and to fight in "Iskra" with the Government and the enemies of Social Democracy).

And so, do give up your naïve hope of working peacefully in such an impossible atmosphere. Concentrate your *main* forces on Circuits[2] and let the Deer [G. M. Krzhizhanovsky] go. Provide immediately for your Committees, then begin an attack on other people's Committees and then the Congress, the Congress . . . not later than January.

P.S. If Martov asks the Deer about publication,[3] let him be sure to transfer his vote to Kol [F. V. Lengnik] without fail, otherwise again there will be the devil of a scandal. Martov and Dan are outrageously impertinent to Kol at meetings.

P.P.S. Today, the 18th, another new villainy from the Martovites—a refusal to print my letter "Why I left the editorial board" in No. 54, on the pretext that Hans [G. M. Krzhizhanovsky] was against the idea of publishing documents (Liars! Hans was against, on condition of *peace!*) The refusal is accompanied by further insolence; for instance, the statement that the Central Committee is trying to get into its own hands the control of the Central Organ, that there were conversations in progress about the return of confidence in the Central Committee etc. Their tactics are clear: hypocritically to cover up the opposition of the Dans, Martyns [V. N. Rozanov] etc. to the

---

[1] Plekhanov's pamphlet "Vade mecum" for publication by the "Rabocheye Delo."
[2] Visiting local organisations.
[3] I.e., of the negotiations between the C.C. and the opposition.

Central Committee and surreptitiously to throw mud at the Central Committee through the medium of the newspaper. I refuse to leave No. 53 unanswered. Telegraph at once: (1) if you agree to my letter being printed in a paper other than "Iskra," wire: *Actien* 203, (2) if you agree to concentrating your forces at once towards the Congress, wire: *Actien* 204. If it is "yes" to both questions, then *Actien* 407. If it is "no" to both, then *Actien* 45.

The day after tomorrow I shall send you my letter about leaving the editorial board. If you do not agree to an immediate Congress and intend to suffer the Martov insults in silence, then I shall probably have to resign from the Central Committee also.

113. (137 P¹). TO N. E. VILONOV IN EKATERINOSLAV

[Geneva, 22nd December, 1903]

My dear Comrade!

I was very glad to receive your letter, because here, abroad, we hear far too seldom the outspoken and independent voices of those who are occupied with work on the spot. It is extremely important for a Social Democratic writer abroad to exchange opinions more frequently with leading workers who are active in Russia, and your story about how our dissensions are being reflected in the committees was most interesting to me. If the occasion arises, I may print your letter.

It is impossible to answer all your questions in one letter, because a detailed report about the Bolsheviks and Mensheviks would occupy an entire volume. My letter to the editors of "Iskra," ("Why I resigned from the editorial board"), has been printed as a separate leaflet. In it I state briefly the reasons for our separation, and try to show how wrongly the matter was presented in "Iskra" No. 53 (beginning with No. 53 there are four Menshevik representatives on the board, in addition to Plekhanov). I hope you will soon see this letter, (a small printed leaflet of eight pages). It has already been taken to Russia and it will probably not be difficult to distribute it.

I repeat, the matter is very briefly stated in that letter. It is not yet possible to give it in greater detail; not until the publication of the official reports of the II Party Congress and the II League Congress (it was announced in "Iskra" No. 53 that the reports of both Congresses would be published in full and very soon). I know that they are to come out in a volume of about 300 pages or more; nearly 300 pages are ready; the book will probably appear in a week's time, at most two. It is quite possible that I shall have to write another pamphlet ["One step forward, two steps back"] after the publication of all these reports.

Personally, I consider that the split has been caused first of all and most of all through discontent on account of the personnel of the centres (the Central Organ and the Central Committee). The Mensheviks wanted the establishment of the old six in the Central Organ, whereas the Congress elected only three of the six, finding them evidently more suitable for political leadership. In the same way the Mensheviks were defeated on the question of the Central Committee personnel, i.e., the Congress did not elect those men whom the Mensheviks wanted.

Because of this, the discontented Mensheviks have begun to exaggerate very minor differences, to boycott the centres, to canvass for supporters, and even to prepare a split in the Party. (There are persistent rumours here, and probably reliable ones, that they have already decided to found, and have begun to assemble, their newspaper under the name of "Kramola" [Revolt]. No doubt the feuilleton in "Iskra" No. 53 has been purposely set up in a type which does not exist in the Party printing press!)

Plekhanov has decided to co-opt them on to the editorial board to avoid a split and has written an article "What not to do" in "Iskra" No. 52. After No. 51 I left the editorial board, because I considered this transforming of the Congress under the influence of scandals abroad to be wrong. But of course I did not want personally to prevent peace, if peace was possible, and therefore (considering it was now possible for me to work in the "6") I left the editorial board, without, however, refusing to collaborate.

The Mensheviks (or the opposition) also want to push their own people by force on to the Central Committee. The Central Committee agreed for the sake of peace to take two—but the Mensheviks were still not satisfied and continue to spread evil rumours about the Central Committee, such as, that it was incompetent. In my opinion it is the most revolting infringement of discipline and Party duty. And besides, it is all only gossip, for the Central Committee was elected by the Congress from among people of whom the *majority* of the "Iskra" organisation approved and the "Iskra" organisation, of course, knew better than anyone who was suitable for this important rôle. The Central Committee, elected at the Congress, consisted of three people,—all three had long been members of the "Iskra" organisation, two of them [G. M. Krzhizhanovsky and F. V. Lengnik] were members of the Organisation Committee [for the II Congress]; the third [V. A. Noskov] was invited on to the Organisation Committee, but did not join, because he personally did not wish to, and moreover, he had worked on the Organisation Committee for a long time on general Party matters. This means, that the most reliable and tested people were chosen and I consider it very bad policy to shout about their incompetence, when the Mensheviks themselves are hindering the Central Committee in their work. All accusations against the Central Committee (about formalism, bureaucratism etc.) are nothing more than malicious invention, without any foundation whatsoever.

There is no need for me to say I fully share your opinion that it is indecent for people to shout against centralism and against the Congress, people who spoke otherwise before and are displeased on the one personal score that the Congress did not act as they wished. Instead of acknowledging their mistake these people are now disorganising the Party! I think Russian comrades must definitely rise up against any disorganisation and insist that the decisions of the Congress be fulfilled, so that petty disputes as to who should be on the Central Organ and the Central Committee do not interfere with the work. Disputes abroad among literary people and all sorts of other "Generals" (whom you too severely call "intriguers") will only then become innocuous to the Party when Russian committee leaders have become more independent and manage to insist firmly on the execution of that which their representatives resolve at the Party Congress.

With regard to the relation of the Central Organ to the Central Committee, you are quite right, that once and for all neither the one nor the other should be allowed to predominate. The Congress itself, in my opinion, must decide that question separately each time. The Council of the Party dominates by statute both the Central Organ and the Central Committee, and on the Council there are two members from the Central Organ and two from the Central Committee. A fifth however was elected by the Congress. Which means that the Congress itself decided which one this time should be given predominance. Stories that we apparently wanted to quash the Russian Central Committee by the Central Organ abroad are pure gossip, in which there is not a word of truth. When Plekhanov and I were on the editorial board, then we had *three* Russian Social Democrats on the Council [F. V. Lengnik, L. E. Halperin, V. A. Noskov] and *only two* who were abroad [Plekhanov, Lenin]. The Martovites now have the reverse! Just judge their speeches by this!

I greet you warmly and ask you to let me know, if you receive this letter and if you have read my letter to the editors in "Iskra" Nos. 52 and 53 and how matters stand in your Committee.

With comradely greetings,

Lenin

114. (118 p¹). TO THE CENTRAL COMMITTEE IN RUSSIA

[Geneva], 30th December, 1903

We have received your letter of the 10th December (old style). We are astounded and indignant at your silence on fighting questions and the irregularity of your correspondence. It is quite impossible to conduct affairs in this way! Find another Secretary, if the Bear [M. I. Ulianova] and the Deer

[G. M. Krzhizhanovsky] are not able to write each week. Just imagine, up till now we have had nothing detailed from the Deer [G. M. Krzhizhanovsky]! There is so far no answer (some twenty days) to our letter of the 10th December (new style). Such a disgraceful state of affairs must be stopped at all costs.

Next, we categorically insist that it is essential fully to elucidate our position in the struggle with the Martovites, to agree among ourselves and to adopt a quite definite line.

Why did you not send Boris [V. A. Noskov] here, as Hans [G. M. Krzhizhanovsky] wanted? After a stay here, Boris would not have written us absurd speeches about peace. Why has not Hans kept his promise to write to the Old Man [Lenin] in detail about Boris's mood? If you cannot send Boris, send Mitrofan [F. V. Gusarov] or the Animal [M. M. Essen] to clear the matter up.

I repeat again and again: Hans's fundamental mistake is that he trusted his last impression. No. 53 should bring him to his senses. The Martovites have taken the Central Organ to conduct their war, and now the war has spread all along the line: persecution in "Iskra," fighting at public lectures (the other day Martov was reading a paper in Paris about the split before an audience of 100 people and fought with Lebedev [S. I. Gusev]), and the most shameless agitation against the Central Committee. It would be unpardonably short-sighted to imagine that this will not spread to Russia. Matters have reached such a pitch that relations have been severed between the Central Organ and the Central Committee (the resolution of the Central Organ of December 22nd has been sent to you[1]), that printed *lies* have appeared in the Central Organ (No. 55 "Iskra"), that it had been agreed not to print the conversations.

Do think over the whole political situation, take a wider view, tear yourselves away from the petty everyday fussing over pennies and passports and without hiding your heads

---

[1] The editors of "Iskra" turned to the C.C. with a resolution of Dec. 22, protesting against publishing Lenin's letter "Why I left the editorial board of 'Iskra,'" and demanded that Lengnik should be substituted on the C.C. by another representative from abroad.

under your wings, make it clear to yourselves where you are going to and why you are delaying.

There are two tendencies in our Central Committee, if I am not mistaken, (or perhaps three? Which?). In my opinion they are: (1) to delay matters by not calling a Congress, to ignore as far as possible all attacks and insistent mud-throwing, and to strengthen the position in Russia. (2) To raise a host of resolutions against the Central Organ; to direct all the forces towards capturing shaky Committees and to prepare a Congress to take place in two, maximum three months' time. And so, I ask you, in what does your strengthening of positions consist? Only, that you are losing time in Russia while your enemy is gathering strength here, abroad—which is important; you are delaying a decision until your arrest is inevitable and will come fairly soon—it would be childish to ignore it.

And what will there be for us after your arrest? The Martovites have fresh and increased forces. We have broken ranks. They have a fortified Central Organ. We have a group of people badly transporting a C.O. which only swears at them. Isn't that the true way to defeat, isn't that only a disgraceful and stupid delay of inevitable defeat? You only shut your eyes to it, taking advantage of the fact that war abroad takes a long time to reach you. Our tactics literally boil down to: "after us (i.e. after the present members of the Central Committee) the deluge" i.e. deluge for the majority.

I think that even if a defeat is inevitable, then we will have to withdraw openly and honestly, and that is only possible at the Congress. But defeat is not at all inevitable, for the five are not united, Plekhanov is not with them, but *for peace* and by a Congress we can catch out both Plekhanov and them with their apparent differences of opinion. The only serious argument against the Congress is that it will inevitably legalise the split. And I answer: (1) even that is better than the present position, for then we can withdraw honestly and not be in the disgraceful position of being spat at; (2) the Martovites have allowed the moment for the split to slip by and it is improbable they will withdraw from the III Congress, for the present struggle and the in full publication[1] remove the possibility of a split. (3) Bargaining with them, if that is possible, is best of all at the Congress.

Discuss the matter sensibly and do hurry up and write back, giving the opinion of each (of each without fail) member of the Central Committee.

Do not bother me about leaflets[2]: I am not a machine and cannot work in the present disgraceful situation.

1904

115. (57 P[1]). TO I. V. BABUSHKIN IN PETERSBURG

[London], 16th January, [1904]

We have received from Geneva No. 16 of the "Rabochaya Mysl" [Workers' Thought] (evidently printed and written by "Svoboda" ["Freedom"] i.e. by Nadezhdin) and marked already as the organ of the "St. Petersburg Committee." There is an emendatory letter in it from the Vyshibalovtsy, a trifling correction, actually not a correction at all, but a *compliment* to "Svoboda." If they assert that they are on the side of "Zarya" and "Iskra," then it is an obvious deception, pure swindling: they want to gain time, so as to grow stronger. We therefore advise you insistently and earnestly to issue (and if you cannot issue, then send it here) a leaflet with a protest in the name of the Committee and altogether reject any reconciliatory moves and approaches, and begin a decisive war, a relentless war with the Vyshibalovtsy, accusing them of going over from social democracy to the revolutionary-socialistic "Svoboda." We welcome Novitzkaya's [I. V. Babushkin] energetic behaviour and once again ask you to continue in the same fighting spirit, without admitting the slightest wavering. War on the Vyshibalovtsy and to the devil with all conciliators, people with "indeterminate views"—idiots! Better small fish than a large beetle! Better two or three energetic and completely devoted men than a dozen dawdlers. Write as often as you can and *without delay*, give us some notion of your workers (and

---

[1] Of the negotiations between the C.C. and the Menshevik opposition.
[2] Lenin was asked to write some new leaflets.

describe them), so that in case of failure we should not run aground.

116. (121 P¹). TO THE CENTRAL COMMITTEE IN RUSSIA

[Geneva, 31st January, 1904]

The three meetings of the session of the Soviet of the Party ended yesterday. These meetings shed definite light on the whole political situation in the Party. Plekhanov is on the side of the Martovites, overriding us in anything at all important. Our resolution about condemning boycott etc. (boycott on *both sides*) was not put to the vote; the separation of permissible and non-permissible forms of struggle was accepted only in principle. But Plekhanov's resolution that it is desirable that the Central Committee should co-opt a *corresponding* (sic!) number from the Mensheviks was accepted. After that we take back our resolution and present a protest, in which we oppose this policy of settling precedence disputes in the Council. Three members of the Council (Martov, Axelrod and Plekhanov) answer that it is beneath their dignity to examine the protest. We announce that the only *honest* way out is a Congress. The Council dishes this. Three members pass resolutions which authorise (!) members of the editorial board to send round their own men independent of the Central Committee, and which empower the Central Committee to give the editorial board literature in such a quantity as necessary for distribution(!!). This means—to give them to be used for their own transport and their own distribution, for one "agent" after another travels from them and *refuses* to fulfil the commissions of the Central Committee. Besides, their transport is ready, (they offered to share it with us).

There is an article by Plekhanov in "Iskra" (No. 57) which calls our Central Committee *eccentric* (there are no Mensheviks on it) and invites it to co-opt some. How many, is not known; from private information, not less than *three* from a very short list (evidently from 5-6) and perhaps even insisting on some members resigning from the Central Committee.

Only the blind can fail to see now what the game is. The Council will bring pressure to bear on the Central Committee *by all and every means,* insisting on a complete concession to the Martovites. Either an immediate Congress, the immediate gathering in of resolutions about the Congress from 11-12 Committees [a sufficient quorum], and the immediate direction of all energy to agitation for a Congress, or, resignation of the whole of the Central Committee, for not a single member of the Central Committee will consent to a disgraceful and absurd rôle: to accept people who *foist themselves* and who will not rest until they take everything into their hands, who will drag every trifle before the Council to get their own way.

Kurz [F. V. Lengnik] and I insistently demand that the Central Committee *should immediately meet, whatever happens,* and that it should decide the matter, after, of course, taking into account our votes. We insistently repeat for the hundredth time: either an immediate Congress or resignation— we invite those who do not agree with us to come here to judge on the spot. Let them try in actual fact to agree with the Martovites and let them stop writing to us empty phrases about the advantages of peace.

We have no money. The Central Organ buries us under expenses and is obviously plunging us into bankruptcy, evidently reckoning on a financial crisis, in order to take extra measures which would reduce the Central Committee to nought.

We must have immediately 2-3 thousand roubles and without fail. Immediately and immediately: otherwise our *complete* crash in a month!

We repeat: think it over, *send delegates here* and look at the matter properly. Our last word: either a Congress or the resignation of the whole of the Central Committee. Reply at once, are you giving us your vote? If not, let us know *what is to happen if Kurz and I resign.* Do not fail to inform us.

117. (122 P[1]). TO G. M. KRZHIZHANOVSKY IN KIEV

TO HANS FROM THE OLD MAN

[Geneva, between 2nd-7th February, 1904]

My dear Friend,

Yesterday I saw the Animal [M. M. Essen] and it was only from him that I learnt about your affairs [in Russia, the C.C., and local committees]. I think you ought to make the Deer [G. M. Krzhizhanovsky] go away at once and change his skin. It is both stupid and ridiculous for him to wait for the blow to fall. The only way out is to change over to an illegal position and to move his place of residence more frequently. And really it is only to him that such a step seems difficult and hard: he must try to take it and then he will soon find that his new position will seem normal. (I absolutely cannot understand or share Konyaga's [L. E. Halperin] arguments against this.) Next—about the political situation: the whole thing is terribly muddled. Plekhanov has gone over to the Martovites and is making things difficult for us in the Soviet. The Soviet has expressed the wish that the Central Committee be increased in size (this is printed in "Iskra," Number 58). The Soviet has given the editorial board the right to send out agents and the right to receive literature for distribution.

The Martovites have evidently their own fighting fund and are waiting for a suitable moment to spring a coup d'état (such a moment as a financial crash—we have no money—or failure in Russia etc.). I do not doubt this, and Kurz and I insist that the Central Committee members who doubt this should come here to be convinced—otherwise it is both ludicrous and unworthy to have certain members pulling in one direction and others in another.

In my opinion it is essential (1) to raise a storm in the Committees against the Central Organ with the most militant resolutions, (2) to polemicise with the Central Organ by means of leaflets, (3) to receive in the Committees and to print on the spot resolutions about the Congress, (4) to set Schwarz

[V. V. Vorovsky], Vakar and others on to preparing pamphlets for the Central Committee.

Hans [G. M. Krzhizhanovsky] must be warned that he will certainly be put forward as a false witness against me. If he does not want this to happen, let him at once send a categorical written announcement: (1) that there was no agreement about the non-publication of negotiations, (2) that in the Council of November 29th, 1903, Hans did not promise to co-opt on to the Central Committee, (3) that Hans understood the Martovites were taking the Central Organ for the sake of peace and that contrary to expectations they started an attack in Number 53. We will print this announcement, *only* if we are provoked.

118. (123 p¹). TO THE CENTRAL COMMITTEE IN RUSSIA

Geneva, Second half of February, 1904

I have read the letters from Zemlyachka and Konyaga [L. E. Halperin]. Why he imagines that I had seen the uselessness of the Congress, Allah alone knows! On the contrary, I insist, as always, that it is the only honest way out and it would be shortsighted and cowardly to run away from such a solution. I continue to insist that Boris [V. A. Noskov], Mitrofan [F. V. Gusarov] and the Horse [L. B. Krassin], should be sent here without fail, because the people must see the situation for themselves, (especially the position which has arisen after the sittings of the Council), instead of wagging their tongues at a distance or hiding their heads under their wings and taking advantage of the fact that from here to the Central Committee you could gallop for three years and still not reach it.

There is nothing more stupid than the opinion, that the work connected with the calling of the Congress, agitation in Committees and the passing of well-considered and decisive (not sloppy!) resolutions *excludes* "positive" work or contradicts it. Such an opinion only shows an inability to understand the political situation, which has arisen in the Party.

The Party is actually rent asunder, the statutes are turned into a rag, the organisation is bespattered, only simple-hearted provincials could possibly fail to see this. But he who has understood this must see clearly that the Martovite pressure must be repulsed by similar pressure (and not by a disgusting mouthing about peace etc.). And all our strength ought to be used for such pressure. Let agents, helpers and subordinates occupy themselves exclusively with technical questions, transport and receipt of literature. It is arch-foolish to appoint the members of the Central Committee to do this. The Central Committee members must capture all Committees, mobilise a majority, travel round Russia, unite our people and begin pressure (in answer to the Martovite attack) against the Central Organ; pressure by resolutions: (1) demanding a Congress, (2) *asking* the editorial board of the Central Organ if it will submit to the Congress on the question of the personnel of the editorial board, (3) branding the new "Iskra" without any mincing of words, as Astrakhan, Tver and the Urals did the other day. These resolutions must be printed in Russia, we have said so hundreds of times.

I really think we have bureaucrats and formalists, and not revolutionaries, serving on the Central Committee. The Martovites are spitting in their faces, but they merely wipe their faces and moralise to me that it is useless trying to fight! Only bureaucrats can fail to see that the Central Committee is not a Central Committee and its efforts to be one are ludicrous. Either it will become an organisation of war against the Central Organ, war in deeds and not in words; war in Committees, or the Central Committee will be a worthless rag fit only for the dust-heap.

For Christ's sake do understand that centralism has been irrevocably torn by the Martovites. Give up idiotic formalities, capture the Committees, teach *them* to fight for the Party against circles abroad; write leaflets for them (that will not interfere with agitation for the Congress, but will help it). Use auxiliary forces for the technical side. Guide the attack against the Central Organ or give up once and for all absurd pretensions to "leadership" by constantly wiping away the spit.

Clair's [G. M. Krzhizhanovsky's] behaviour is disgraceful and it is worse still that Konyaga has encouraged him. Nothing angers me so much as our so-called "Central Committee."

Addio

The Old Man

119. (124 p[1]). TO THE CENTRAL COMMITTEE IN RUSSIA

[*Geneva*], *13th March, 1904*

Comrades,

I have received the information about the collective decision of the majority in the Central Committee against the idea of holding a Congress and about the desirability of putting an end to dissension. The three of us (Kurz [F. V. Lengnik], the Animal [M. M. Essen], and Lenin) have discussed this communication and we unanimously resolved that:

(1) Kurz and Lenin are *temporarily* to relinquish their duties as members of the Council (remaining members of the Central Committee), until the true character of our differences with the majority of the Central Committee have been cleared up, (we announced in the Council that we saw no other honest way out from the dissension excepting by having a Congress and we voted for a Congress). We emphasise that we are resigning temporarily and conditionally and in no way tender permanent resignations and that we are anxious for a friendly clearing-up of differences and misunderstandings.

(2) In view of (a) the necessity of finding abroad Council members from among the members of the Central Committee, (b) the necessity of personal negotiation with Russian members of the Central Committee, and (c) the need to have abroad a member of the Central Committee after the departure of Kurz, the Animal and Lenin, (Kurz and the Animal are going to Russia, while Lenin is to take leave for two full months[1]), (d) the need to see that affairs here which give rise to dissension are conducted by those Central Committee members, who disagree with us, for we are unable to struggle against dissension in any other way:—in view of all this we must insistently ask

---

[1] During which time Lenin finally prepared his pamphlet "One step forward, two steps back."

the Central Committee to send here immediately, and without fail, at least *one* of the Russian members. We ask you to let us know at once that you have received this letter and to send us an answer.

P.S. To avoid gossip and premature talk we have informed the Council of our resignation as follows:

(Copy)

TO THE PRESIDENT OF THE PARTY COUNCIL

14th March, 1904 [*Geneva*]

Dear Comrade,

We would inform you that in view of the departure of one of us and leave being taken by another, we are unfortunately temporarily compelled to resign as members of Council from the Central Committee. We have informed the Central Committee of this decision.

With Social Democratic greetings,

Kurz,
Lenin

120. (125 P[1]). TO G. M. KRZHIZHANOVSKY IN RUSSIA

[*Geneva, May, not earlier than the 26th, 1904*]

My dear Friend,

You will of course understand the whole affair through our agreement with Nil [V. A. Noskov].[1] For God's sake do not make hasty decisions and do not despair. First of all you must become familiar with the Council Minutes and my pamphlet. Do not be upset by your temporary removal from the affair. Better refrain from voting, but do not withdraw entirely [from the C.C.]. Believe me, you will still be very much needed and all your friends are counting on your speedy resurrection. A crowd of people in our Party are still at a loss and bewildered; they cannot get used to the new situation and feebly lose faith

---

[1] Noskov was sent as C.C. representative abroad and as second member of the Soviet from the C.C. instead of Lengnik. An agreement between Lenin and Noskov for mutual action abroad in the name of the C.C. was signed on May 26th.

in themselves and in the cause. Meanwhile, we here are seeing more clearly that we are benefitting by these postponements, the tittle-tattle is dying down of its own accord and the question of principles is definitely coming to the forefront, while the new "Iskra" is devilishly feeble.

Do not believe the stupid tales about our striving for a split. Store up some patience and you will soon see that our people are splendid and that we shall conquer by the strength of our convictions.

Answer me without fail. It would be splendid if you could be clever enough to come over here for a week—not on business, but simply for a rest and to meet me somewhere in the Alps. Do believe that you will be definitely wanted and although Konyaga [L. E. Halperin] has mistakenly dissuaded you from a certain plan of yours, it is only postponed and not lost! Gather your strength and we shall still do some fighting!

Your

Lenin

121 (163 P[1]). TO V. D. BONCH-BRUEVICH IN GENEVA

[*Switzerland*],[1] *26th July, 1904*

My dear Vladimir Dmitrievich!

Thank you for your letter of the 23rd July, 1904, about [C.C.] business. I am answering it in the right order.

With regard to general policy, I stand as before for armed peace, for withdrawing with protests (as we said with Nina Lvovna [M. M. Essen] in the presence of you and Martyn Nikolaevich [M. M. Lyadov]), in other words, for the old tactics. To protest against every infringement, to publish, to agitate without giving any cause for a coup d'état which they desire. As for the details about separate measures, you will be able to see that better for yourself, since you are on the spot.

It is Boris's [V. A. Noskov] fault that the Central Committee

---

[1] Lenin and Krupskaya were absent from Geneva from July to September.

agents were not given a paper, for he was the last to leave.[1]
I had already written to Martyn Nikolaevich that I advised
explaining to the editors of the Central Organ the stupidity of
insisting on such papers: Boris has been written to twice, *there
is news of his arrest;* are we to wait for an answer from Russia
in say six months' time?? Do protest, but de facto it will be
you who will do everything.

As for finances, I am afraid that we have undertaken the
library in vain; we cannot think of luxuries now, but how to
keep alive. Do you remember I told you this? And the 300
francs are lost!! Oh! do take care, for God's sake don't concentrate on the library, think of the *whole*.[2]

My greetings to Ignat [P. A. Krasikov]. How is he?

It is most worrying about Nina Lvovna. Write to me at once
if you hear anything.[3]

I think an answer to Plekhanov should be published (as a
pamphlet, not as a leaflet, together with a short foreword,[4])
that is if the Central Organ will not print it after all the protests. And *don't delay* over this or the interest will be lost.

I greet you warmly and send greetings to Vera Mikhailovna
[V. M. Velichkina][5] and to all friends.

Your N. Lenin

Write to me (and send newspapers) to Meiringen, Poste
Restante.

122. (139 P[1]). A LETTER TO THE CENTRAL COMMITTEE AGENTS
    AND TO COMMITTEE MEMBERS OF THE R.S.D.L.P. PARTY
    WHO SUPPORTED THE BOLSHEVIKS AT THE II PARTY CON-
    GRESS

[Swiss Mountains, 18th August, 1904]

Comrades!

The conflict within the Central Committee has developed

---

[1] An official paper from the C.C. representatives abroad (Lenin and Noskov)
authorising the collegium of the outside-Russia C.C. agents in Geneva to conduct
the affairs of the outside-Russia section of the C.C. in the absence of C.C. members.

[2] A Geneva Party library was organised in the outside-Russia C.C. section, and
was an autonomous organisation which paid for itself.

[3] M. Essen was arrested on the Russian frontier.

[4] An open letter from 37 Bolsheviks (of the Geneva Group) to Plekhanov.

[5] An active Social Democrat, "Iskra" worker, Bolshevik.

to such an extent that I consider it my moral duty to write about it to all Bolshevik adherents at the II Party Congress. I am compelled to take this step, both by the illegal actions of the four members of the Central Committee and by the fear of taking any step in the Party, which would again be in any way rash and harmful to the Party, without consulting fellow-thinkers, who are working locally, who know better the actual mood of the Party, and who in deeds and not only in words have declared war on the old parish-pump circles abroad in the name of the new, growing young Party.

It will be apparent from the four documents enclosed herewith what the conflict within the Central Committee is about: (1) The agreement of May 26th 1904 between three Central Committee members: Glebov [V. A. Noskov], Zverev [M. M. Essen] and Lenin. (2) My letter of the same date to the Central Committee members. (3) The decision adopted by all the Central Committee members, excepting one. (4) My protest against the legality of that decision.

I would ask all comrades, who share the same opinion in the present Party struggle, to read carefully through these informative documents and to express their frank and final opinion on them. For my part I will refrain from any public appearance in the Press on these questions, I will refrain at any rate for a certain time, until I learn the opinion of those who are working in Russia, or until circumstances compel me to take such a step. I will limit myself to a few questions to the Party, if the members of our organisations find that we still have a Party: (1) Can a party, worthy of the name of a Workers' Party, allow the existence of a Central Committee, which was elected by the Bolsheviks and which declares the policy of the Bolsheviks as a "group" policy? (2) Have people, who in March said one thing in their declaration and in July something different, a moral right to our trust? (3) [omitted]. (4) people, who take advantage of the arrest of two Bolshevik Central Committee members, to trample on the interests of the Bolsheviks? (5) people, who in the name of a struggle with group politics talk about a conference with the group of Mensheviks and ignore the Bolsheviks? (6) people,

who are afraid of their actions being judged by the Congress
and who therefore dare to intimidate the Party by a split, who
dare to forbid Party members to use their elementary right
to agitate for a Congress? (7) people, who show such an in-
fantile lack of understanding of our Party crisis, that they can
seriously try to prove the "legality" of the Central Organ and
decree the "*height*" of that Central Organ? (8) people, who
consciously and contrary to the will of the Party, try to push
out of the Central Committee the consistent supporters of the
Bolsheviks?

I will end by a request to answer me these questions and to
see that you let all active Party members know about this
letter and the position of affairs. For the present I do not see
the necessity to publish this letter.

Central Committee member,
Lenin

123. (175 R). TO HIS MOTHER

[*Geneva*], 15th/28th August, 1904

Darling Mother,

I have not written to you for some time because I was not
sure of the address. Today we received letters from El. V.
and Manyasha. Thank her for her trouble over the translations. Nadya will write to her in detail about this. I have received Hobson's book on Imperialism [1] and have begun to
translate it—a little at a time, because I am still having a
Summer holiday. I walk, I bathe and do nothing in particular. I have had a splendid rest this Summer!

And how are you all? Is the Summer villa in Sablino
pleasant? Are you resting as you should? What are your plans
for the future? And are you well, Mother? How do Anyuta
and Manyasha feel after prison? Tell me about this, for
Manyasha writes only about the translation.

I embrace you warmly, darling Mother, and send my love
to all,

Your
V. Ulianov

---

[1] Lenin's M.S. of this has not been traced, nor was a translation published.

Am I using the right address? Write in good time about your change of address. My address: Rue de la Colline, 3, Geneva, but you must write *on the envelope* "Personal" for V. I. Ulianov.

124. (166 p¹). TO G. O. LEITEISEN IN PARIS

[Geneva], 26th September, 1904

Dear Comrade,

I was very pleasantly surprised by Sergei Petrovich's [P. A. Krasikov] and Martyn Nikolayevich's [M. N. Lyadov] news about your political position at the present time. There is no need for me to tell you how painful it was for me when the good relations, which had always existed between us, ceased.[1] In view of the above information, I think we ought not to pay any attention to the past. We can probably re-establish the old relations solely on the basis of the positive tasks of the present and future. If I am mistaken in this, you will, of course, correct me, but I consider it my duty, after the conversation with Martyn Nikolayevich, to make the first attempt to understand our relations.

Yours truly,

N. Lenin

125. (144 p¹). TO THE SIBERIAN COMMITTEE

Geneva, 30th October, 1904

Honoured Comrades!

I should like to send an answer through your intermediacy to Comrade Simonov [V. A. Gutovsky],[2] who was here as President of the Siberian Union and who left me a letter before his departure, (I was not in Geneva at the time), which con-

---

[1] At the II Congress of the League, when Leiteisen, being absent, gave his vote to M. Vecheslov, who voted for the Mensheviks. Leiteisen offered no explanation of his position.

[2] V. A. Gutovsky was sent to investigate the differences within the Party between the Bolsheviks and the Mensheviks. He took up a conciliatory attitude.

tained an exposition of his conciliatory point of view. I should like to discuss this letter; its contents you probably know from Comrade Simonov. Comrade Simonov's point of view amounts to this: of course they, (the Mensheviks) are anarchists and disorganisers, but, after all, one cannot do anything with them; a truce with them is essential (Simonov emphasises the point that he, in contrast to those other conciliators, is speaking of a truce and not of peace) so as to escape, no matter by what means, from an unbearable position, to strengthen our forces for a further struggle against the Mensheviks.

It was most instructive for me to learn from the letter that Comrade Simonov was a *sincere* adherent of conciliation. Among the conciliators there is such an amount of hypocrisy, that it is a change to read the arguments (though incorrect) of a man who says what he thinks. Now his arguments are absolutely incorrect. He understands that it is impossible to be reconciled with lies, confusion and tittle-tattle, but what sense is there in talk of a truce? After all, the Mensheviks will take advantage of that truce merely to strengthen their position. Factional polemics have not ceased, (the hypocritical Central Committee hypocritically promised its cessation in its last letter to Committees, a letter which you too have probably already received), they have assumed particularly vile forms, which even Kautsky condemned, and he stood for the Mensheviks. Even K. Kautsky announced in his letter to "Iskra" that veiled polemics are worse than any other, for the question becomes tangled, hints remain obscure, straight answers are impossible. Take "Iskra" as an example—in the leader of Number 75, whose subject is remote from our differences of opinion, you will observe that senile embittered swearing against the Ivanov advisers, ignoramuses etc. etc. has been introduced quite irrelevantly. From the point of view of our turncoats from the Central Committee this is perhaps not considered to be factional polemics! I am not talking of the arguments used by the leader writer (evidently Plekhanov): Marx was *soft* towards the Proudhonists. Can anyone imagine a more false use of historic facts and historic great names? What would Marx have said

if the confusion of the difference between Marxism and Proudhonism had been hidden by the slogan of softness? (And
is not the new "Iskra" thoroughly busy in confusing the difference between the "Rabocheye Delo" and the "Iskra" cause?).
What would Marx have said if the printed admission of the
correctness of Proudhonism over Marxism were hidden by
softness? (And is not Plekhanov being a sly fox now in print,
pretending that he acknowledges the Mensheviks as being correct in principle?) Why, by this one comparison alone Plekhanov gives himself away and reveals that the relationship
between the Bolsheviks and the Mensheviks is comparable to
the relationship between Marxism and Proudhonism, to that
relationship of the revolutionary and opportunist wing which
also figures in that ever-memorable article "What not to do."
Look at the decisions of the Party Council (Number 73 and
the Supplement to 73 and 74) and you will see that the cessation of a secret Menshevik organisation proclaimed in the
above-mentioned letter from the Central Committee to the
Committees means nothing else but that the three members
of the Central Committee have gone over to the secret organisation of the Mensheviks. In *that* sense the secret organisation has actually disappeared . . . for now all three of our so-
called central institutions have become a secret organisation (to
struggle against the Party): not only the Central Organ and
the Soviet, but also the Central Committee. In the name of
struggle ("or principle") against formalism and bureaucratism,
they declare war against the "headings," announcing that the
publications of the Bolsheviks are non-party. They falsify the
Congress by counting the votes wrongly ($16 \times 4 = 61$, for the
number sixty-one includes five Soviet members, but in half of
the organisations the Soviet figures as an organisation with two
votes!!) and by concealing from the Party the resolutions of
the Committees (what sort of Congresses were held at Nizhny,
Saratov, Nikolaev and the Caucasus was not revealed: see the
resolutions in our pamphlets "Towards the Party" and "The
Fight for the Congress.") They introduce petty wrangling into
the Soviet by impossibly misinterpreting the affair about the

representation at the Amsterdam Congress.[1] They dared to
print about the "deception" of the Northern Committee,[2] when
that incident had not only not been investigated (although the
Central Committee as far back as July had resolved to investigate it), but when the comrade [P. Krasikov] who had been
accused by some slanderer or other *has not been questioned*
even up to now (this comrade was abroad for three months, i.e.
August, September and October, and saw Glebov, a Central
Committee member, who had adopted the resolution about the
investigation and had not even bothered to present the accusation to the accused himself!!) They encourage disorganisation
in the name of the Council by making the "peripheries" attack
the Bolshevik Committees and tell unheard of lies about Petersburg and Odessa. They condemn what they call the "abuse"
of the same comrades voting on a number of different Committees, when simultaneously three Council members, Plekhanov, Martov and Axelrod, vote *against* the Congress *three*
times: once as members of the editorial board, once in the
Council and once in the League! They take upon themselves
the full power of the Council by proclaiming that the mandates
are invalid. Is not that a falsification of the Congress? And how
can Comrade Simonov possibly advise a truce with regard to
such tactics??

Take the report to the Amsterdam Congress, which has just
been published in Russian. The Mensheviks speak in the name
of the Party and obviously against its wishes, and hide in a
veiled way the same lie about the old "Iskra" which Martynov
and Company always preached and which today is presented
by Balalaikin-Trotsky. Or perhaps Comrade Simonov wants a
truce with that Balalaikin also (his pamphlet ["Our Political
Tasks"] was published by "Iskra," as was frankly announced
in that paper). Perhaps here too he believes in the cessation of

---

[1] Not being able to be present, Lenin sent his substitutes at the beginning of
August and before his conflict with the C.C. in the second half of August, but nevertheless Lenin was accused of infringing Party discipline, and of wanting to represent
the C.C. at the Congress when he was already antagonistic to the C.C.

[2] It had voted for a Congress, but immediately took it back, informing the Central
Committee that they had been misled by a person who had said that the C.C. considered a Congress essential. Krasikov wrote to Lenin that this was a lie.

factional polemics, as promised by the Central Committee?

No, the opinion that a truce is permissible with hypocrisy and disorganisation is unworthy of a Social Democrat and is utterly wrong. It is faintheartedness to believe that nothing can be done with those literary men, even though they may be famous, and that so far as they are concerned there are only tactics left as formulated by Galerka [M. S. Olminsky] ("Down with Bonapartism") in the words "you curse and bow." The Bolsheviks reply to the transformation of all central institutions of the Party into a secret organisation for fighting against the Party and to the Council's falsification of the Congress by a further and inevitable step towards consolidation. Despising hypocrisy, they come into the open with a programme of struggle (see the resolution of the twenty-two approved by the Caucasus Union and by the Committees of St. Petersburg, Riga, Moscow, Odessa, Ekaterinoslav and Nikolaevsk). Of course the Central Organ has concealed this resolution from the Party, although it received it two months ago. The Southern Committees have already accepted the resolution about the consolidating of the Bolshevik Committees and the creation of an Organisation Committee for the struggle against this mockery of the Party. There can be no doubt whatsoever that such an organisation of the Bolsheviks will be created one of these days and will act openly. In spite of the lying tales of the Central Committee's turncoats, the adherents of the Bolsheviks are growing in numbers in Russia and young literary forces, who have shied off from the muddled and hypocritical "Iskra," are beginning to trail from all quarters towards the Bolshevik printing press, which has just been started (the publishing firm of Bonch-Bruevich and Lenin abroad), with a view to supporting, transforming and developing it.

No, Comrade Simonov lost heart unnecessarily. It was quite unnecessary for him to decide in a hurry that it was wrong, but nothing could be done. Something can be done! The more they ridicule the Congress (Balalaikin-Trotsky writing under the protection of "Iskra" announced that the Congress was *a reactionary attempt* to strengthen the "Iskra" plans. Ryazanov is more sincere and honest when he called the Congress a "collection"). The more rudely they mock the Party and the workers in Russia, the more relentless becomes the resistance against them; the more firmly do the Bolsheviks come together, uniting all men of principle and veering away from the unnatural and rotten political union of Plekhanov, Martynov and Trotsky. It is such a union which we find now in the new "Iskra" and in Number 5 of "Zarya" (a reprint of Martynov's article as appeared). Whoever sees a little beyond the end of his own nose and refuses to cling to the policy of passing interests and coalitions, which last only an hour, will understand that such a union which gives birth only to confusion and petty bickering is doomed to die and that the adherents of the *direction* of the old "Iskra," men, who know how to separate that direction from the circle of foreigners however well known, must be and will be the gravediggers of such a union.

I should be glad, Comrades, if you would tell me that you have received this letter and also whether you have managed to pass it on to Comrade Simonov.

With comradely greetings,
N. Lenin

126. (146 p[1]). TO A. M. STOPANI IN BAKU

(Organiser of the Bolshevik Committee in Baku)

[Geneva, 10th November, 1904]

My dear Comrade,

I was exceedingly glad to receive your letter. Please write regularly each week, even if it is only a few lines, and do not fail to see that all addresses are working properly and that there are reserve addresses for letters and visits. It is simply disgraceful that the Bolshevik adherents are so scattered! Without regular communications it is quite impossible to have any kind of common work. And we have received nothing from you for over half a year.

I am completely and utterly in agreement with all you say about the need for the Bolsheviks to unite, for the Bolshevik Committees to be linked together and for the need to prepare for a united congress which will know how to insist upon the will of the Russian workers being fulfilled. The closest relations between all is essential for this, otherwise we wander apart and one knows absolutely nothing about general affairs.

The Central Committee has wholly fused with the Mensheviks and has *in fact* entered its secret organisation, whose aim is to struggle against the Congress, no matter what happens. The new decisions of the Council simply falsify both the counting of votes and the will of the Committees (see Numbers 73 and 74 of "Iskra"—have you seen them?) We must be prepared for their convening a Congress without any reason and for the fact that they will not stop at the infringement of the statutes, nor at further mockery of the Party. They laugh at us openly: "let us see where your strength is now," they jeer, and we would be children if we were to stop at faith in the Congress without immediately getting ready to meet strength with strength. To do this we must: (1) unite at once all the Committees of the Bolsheviks and create a Bureau of the Bolshevik Committees (a beginning has already been made by Odessa and Nikolaev and Ekaterinoslav for fighting Bonapartism in the Central Institutions; (2) to make every effort to support and extend the publications of the Bolsheviks begun here by Bonch-Bruevich and myself—Bonch-Bruevich is only an editor. A group of Russian literary men has undertaken to do this and we must at once begin to collect and despatch all sorts of material: correspondence, pamphlets, notes etc. especially from the workers and about the workers' movement. Without fail, without fail! (If you do not begin from henceforth to send a report each week, we shall have to sever relations with you.)

With regard to the Bureau, this is what has already been done: the Committee of Odessa and Nikolaev and Ekaterinoslav have adopted the following resolution: . . . The Twenty-Two answered in this way. . . .

Do try to go to Tiflis soon to tell them about this. Let them join in as quickly as they can. Presumably the Bureau could be completed by members from the Caucasus. And so, let all the Caucasus Committees immediately express their opinions about the Bureau: i.e., let them write to us and to *Petersburg* (or Riga?) (the address . . . Code . . .), saying whether they approve of the Bureau or whether they want an alteration in, or an addition to the number of candidates. For God's sake, do see that this matter, which is of the first importance, is attended to sensibly and quickly.

Certain Comrades are demanding conferences of the Bolshevik Committees in Russia. We here think it would be expensive, it would delay matters, and without much result. But we must do our utmost to hurry. There is no need to meet to elect a Bureau; it is better to agree to this in writing, or by one or two Comrades travelling round. When the Bureau is established and Ekaterinoslav + Odessa + Nikolaev + St. Petersburg + Moscow + Riga + the Caucasus join it, then the Bureau will begin to function at once as the representative of organised Bolsheviks.

And so, for God's sake, do hurry and answer me as soon as you can.

I greet you warmly,

Your

N. Lenin

127. (148 p[1]). TO RAHMETOV [A. A. BOGDANOV], R. S. ZEMLYACHKA, PAPA [M. M. LITVINOV] IN RUSSIA

[Paris], 3rd December, 1904

My dear Friend,

I have received news of Martyn Nikolayevich's arrival (I have not seen him myself) and have concluded that our affairs are not at all satisfactory. Again there is some divergence between the Bolsheviks in Russia and those abroad. I know (from three years' experience) that such divergence is devilishly harmful to the cause. This is where I see the divergence: (1) they are delaying Rahmetov's arrival; (2) they are shifting the centre of gravity from the Organ here to the Congress, to the

Russian Organisation Committee etc. (3) they allow, or even support, some sort of an arrangement between the Central Committee and the Bolshevik literary group and almost the idiotic undertakings of the Russian Organ. If my information about this is correct, I must say that the most bitter enemy of the Bolsheviks could not have invented anything worse. That they are delaying Rahmetov's departure is simply unpardonable folly, amounting to treachery, for gossip grows terribly and we risk losing the necessary size here because of childishly stupid plans to effect something at once in Russia. It is still more unpardonable that they are delaying the Bolshevik Organ abroad (for which there is only insufficient money). The whole point is in that Organ; without it we are moving towards certain and inglorious death. Whatever happens, at the price of no matter what, we must get some money, if only a couple of thousand and begin at once, for we are cutting our own throats. *Only the most hopeless fools can place* all their hopes on the Congress, for it is clear that the Council will prevent any Congress being called. For God's sake, do understand me correctly: I am not suggesting that we should give up agitating for the Congress, to renounce that slogan, but I do say that only children can stop at that and be blind to the fact that the whole point is in *strength.* Let resolutions about the Congress come pouring in as before, (for some reason or other Martyn Nikolayevich's tour did not yield a single confirmation of the resolution, that is a very great pity), *but that is not the point,* how can people fail to see that? The Organisation Committee or a Bolshevik Bureau is essential, but without an Organ it would be a pathetic cipher, mere comedy, a bubble which would burst at the first defeat. Whatever happens, we must have an Organ and money. Send money here, murder anyone you like, but produce the money. The Organisation Committee or the Bolshevik Bureau must give us full power for an Organ (quickly, quickly) and must make a tour of the Committees, but if the Organisation Committee were to think *first* of starting "positive work" and *to put off* the Organ *for the meantime,* then such an idiotic Organisation Committee would be the death of us. Finally, it is simply treachery to publish anything in Russia and to come to any sort of terms with those rotten people on the Central Committee. It is quite clear that the Central Committee wants to separate and break up the Bolsheviks in Russia and abroad; it is an old plan of theirs and only the most feeble-minded dolts could have been caught on that little bait. It is madness to start an Organ in Russia with the help of the Central Committee, pure folly or treachery, this is proved and will be proved by the objective logic of events, because the organisers of the Organ or of a popular paper will inevitably find themselves fooled by all sorts of disgusting vermin, such as the Central Committee. I prophesy this and I wash my hands in advance of such people.

I repeat: the first consideration must be the Organ, the Organ and again the Organ, money for the Organ; to spend money on anything else now would be the height of folly. Rahmetov should be brought here at once without delay. The Committees should be visited first of all for correspondence (it is both unforgivable and shameful, that until now we have no correspondence! ! It is simply a disgrace and death to the cause! !). And the whole agitation for the Congress must be only a *secondary* work. All the Bolshevik Committees must immediately *and in actual fact* sever all connection with the Central Committee, transferring all links to the Organisation Committee or the Bolshevik Bureau; that Organisation Committee *must immediately* send out a printed notification of its formation, which must be published immediately and without fail.

If we do not stop this incipient divergence among the Bolsheviks, if we do not come to some agreement about it, both in writing and (*chiefly*) by an interview with Rahmetov, then all of us here will simply wash our hands of *the whole business*. If you want to work together; then you must keep in step and agree, act according to agreement (and not contrary to it) or without agreement. It is both disgraceful and scandalous that you set out to get some money for the Organ, yet here you are busy with the devil knows what kind of dirty business!

One of these days I shall come out in print against the Central

Committee and still more energetically. If we don't break with the Central Committee and with the Council, then we shall only be worthy of being spat at.

I await an answer and Rahmetov's arrival.

N. Lenin

128. (167 P[1]). TO N. K. KRUPSKAYA IN GENEVA

[Paris], 3rd December, 1904

Today I posted a business letter to Bonch. I forgot to add an important point: to print 3,000 copies of Leiteisen's dictionary; it is essential to know this for calculating the price. Tell Bonch this at once.

I am sending you the announcement of the Union Committee and the Caucasus representative of the Central Committee[1] received by Raissa today. I think it is *essential* to reprint this immediately as a *leaflet* in your printing press; do this at once and without fail. You can add to the leaflet the Nikolaev and other resolutions [for the convening of a Congress], but the leaflet must be quite short, two to four pages (maximum) without any headings and with only a reference below as to who published it.

I have just received your letter. I do not understand what is wrong with Lyadov's and Rahmetov's [A. A. Bogdanov], "Plan," but there is something wrong there. I shall try to come *soon* and to hurry Lunacharsky's arrival.

I have been warming the appended pages without any result. Perhaps you will try other reagents.

Quite unexpectedly I have a free evening. I enclose a letter [No. 148] and advise you to send it *at once* to all three and as though personally from me, without calling the Soviets: let it shake them up thoroughly and later we can find out whether the news was exaggerated: the fact is, a divergence is beginning and it is necessary to forestall and attack it from the outset. I strongly advise you to send this letter to all three *at once* and

---

[1] A document about the conflict of the Baku Committee with the Caucasus Union Committee and the Caucasian representative of the C.C.

from me personally. I will talk it over with the Destroyer [Lunacharsky] tomorrow and he will probably be on my side; also Vasily Vasilievich [M. S. Olminsky] and Schwartz [V. V. Vorovsky], but the text had better be from me personally. I wanted to write to Martyn Nikolayevich [M. N. Lyadov] and swear at him, but I think there is no point in doing so; when I come I shall discuss it. So far he is quite harmless here. But the Russian trouble which has started slightly paralyses my letter. You were wrong not to insist on Martyn Nikolayevich writing to me in Paris *at once*—it was very wrong, for it was essential.

I have re-read the letter to Rahmetov: possibly a few angry words could be omitted, but I advise that this arch-cutting letter be sent at once and from me personally.

I went to see Leiteisen. He read out to me Plekhanov's letter to him and in which, of course, Lenin is thoroughly cursed. Plekhanov writes "Trotsky's pamphlet ["Our Political Tasks"] is as rotten as himself." He asks Leiteisen to follow him (Plekhanov), and not the Mensheviks, he complains about the "tragedy" of his life, that after twenty years he has no comrade who believes in him; he asks for comradely trust and not submission to an authority, and says that he is seriously thinking of resigning. For the present this is strictly "entre nous."

Deitch has written recently to Leiteisen, asking him to help by sending some money and complains that he has none. Zasulich has also written to Efron swearing at Galerka [M. S. Olminsky], having mistaken Galerka for Sergei Petrovich!! [P. A. Krasikov].

I hope to leave here on Monday, that is the day after tomorrow: to lecture in Zürich on Tuesday and Wednesday; on Thursday in Berne and to be back home on Friday. But it will probably take a few days longer. Write to me at Zürich through Argunin (in two envelopes—the inner one to be stronger and take more care with it).

Has there been a letter from Lausanne, asking me to go there? Have they given any address?

Your

N. Lenin

P.S. It is essential that *all* our Committees should be written to at once, telling them to send us a *formal* order to reprint *openly* for everyone to read the letter to the editors about the Zemstvo. This might be useful. Do this without making any excuses. Get hold of the letter itself, reprint it and send it round in envelopes to the Bolshevik Committees.

129. (149 P[1]). TO R. S. ZEMLYACHKA IN RUSSIA

Geneva, 10th December, 1904

I have just returned from a lecture tour and have received your letter No. 1. I have spoken with the Nymph [M. N. Lyadov]. Have you received my scolding letter (sent both to Papa [M. M. Litvinov] and Sysoika [A. A. Bogdanov])? I, of course, accept the general decision with regard to the personnel of the Organisation Committee. In my opinion it is essential not to drag the Ryadovoy [A. A. Bogdanov] into the business, but to send him out here at once. Next, it is necessary to organise a special group (or to increase the numbers in the Organisation Committee) for repeated tours of the Committees and for maintaining links between them. Our links with the Committees and with Russia are still extremely inadequate and we must do our utmost to develop the correspondence as well as a simple comradely exchange of letters. Why do you not link us up with the Northern Committee? With the Moscow printers (most important!)? With Ryahovsky? With Tula? With Nizhny? Do this at once. Next, why do not the Committees send *us* reaffirmed resolutions about the Congress? It is essential. I am very much afraid you are far too optimistic about the Congress and about the Central Committee. You will see from the pamphlet "The Council against the Party" (it has already appeared), that they are ready to adopt any measures, for the devil knows what tricks they are up to, out of a wish to quash the Congress. I think it is definitely a mistake that the Organisation Committee does not bring out a printed notice. In the first place, the notice is essential in order to contrast our open method of action with the secret organisation of the Mensheviks. Otherwise the Central Committee will certainly trap you, will take advantage of the ultimata of Sysoika and will divulge your "secret" organisation: that will be a disgrace for the Bolsheviks, and it will be you who will be wholly to blame for this disgrace. In the second place, the printed notice is essential in order to inform the mass of Party workers about this new centre. You will never achieve this by any letters, not even approximately. In the third place, the announcement about the consolidation of the Bolshevik Committees will have an enormous moral significance for calming and encouraging the downhearted Bolsheviks (especially here abroad). It would be the greatest political mistake to neglect this. I therefore insist again and again that the Bolshevik Bureau (or the Organisation Committee of the Bolshevik Committees) should issue immediately after the Northern Conference a printed announcement with a reference to the consent and *direct* instruction of the Committees of Odessa, Ekaterinoslav, Nikolaev, the four Caucasian Committees, Riga, St. Petersburg, Moscow, Tver, the Northern, etc. (Perhaps Tula and Nizhny-Novgorod) i.e., 12-14 Committees. This will not only not harm the cause of the struggle for a Congress, but will help it enormously. Answer at once, if you agree or not. With regard to the Zemstvo campaign, I emphatically recommend the immediate and open publication in Russia of my pamphlet and letter to the editors of "Iskra" (without any stupid heading: "For Party members"). Perhaps I shall write another small pamphlet, but it is essential to reprint the polemics with "Iskra." Finally, something particularly important and urgent: may I sign the manifesto from here about the new Organ with the name of the Organisation Committee of the Bolshevik Committees (or better the Bureau of Bolshevik Committees)? May I act here in the name of the Bureau? May I call the Bureau the publisher of the new Organ and the organiser of the editorial group? That is most essential and urgent. Answer at once, after seeing Ryadovoy, to whom you will say and repeat that he must come at once, immediately and without any postponement, if he does not want to ruin himself and to do terrible harm to the cause. The gossip everywhere abroad is incredible: I myself heard it at lectures in Paris,

Zürich, etc. A final warning: either to rush here at once or to ruin oneself and to throw back our cause for a year. I do not undertake to present, nor will I present any ultimata to anyone, for that will provoke only derision and laughter; there is no need to stage comedies. Our position will be ten times cleaner and better if we come forward openly with the Bolshevik Bureau and openly stand for the Congress, and not with some stupid little conversations back stage, which in the best event will only serve to delay the cause and produce fresh intrigues on the part of the Glebovs, Konyagas, Nikitiches and other worms. All the Bolsheviks here are struggling, suffering, and panting for an Organ and demand it everywhere. It cannot be published without the direct authority of the Bureau, but it must be published. We are doing all we can about the money and hope to get some: you too must get some. For God's sake, send us quickly an authorisation to publish in the name of the Bureau and print a leaflet about it in Russia.

130. (151 P[1]). TO A. I. ERAMASOV, SOCIAL DEMOCRAT, IN RUSSIA

[Geneva, 1st half of December, 1904]

My dear Friend,

Your help was most valuable to us all in general and to me in particular. If I have never turned to you with a special request before, it was because there was no urgency, but I was certain that you would support us as far as you possibly could. At the present time a moment of urgency is approaching, and the moment is so serious, that I could not even anticipate anything of the sort before. Our cause is threatened with ruin, if we do not hold out *with the help of extraordinary resources* for at least six months. And to hold out, without curtailing the work, we need 2,000 roubles a month, minimum. That is why I turn to you with a most insistent request to help us out of our difficulty and to get us this support. Please let us know as soon as possible, if you can fulfil our request.

[Unsigned]

131. (152 P[1]). TO M. M. ESSEN IN RUSSIA

[Geneva], 24th December, 1904

I have long been intending to write to you, but was prevented by our many activities. Our spirits have been raised and we are all terribly busy now. An announcement about the publication of our newspaper "Vpered" ["Forward"] came out yesterday. All the Bolsheviks are rejoicing and are encouraged, as never before. At last we have broken up the cursed dissension and are working harmoniously with those who want to work and not to create scandals! A good group of literary collaborators has been got together; there are fresh forces, little money, but soon we must receive some. The Central Committee who betrayed us has lost all credit; has co-opted (basely and in secret) some Mensheviks [V. Krohmal, V. Rozanov, R. Halberstadt], and is busy fighting against the Congress. The Bolshevik Committees are joining together; they have already chosen a Bureau and now the Organ will completely unite them. Hurrah! Do not lose heart, we are all reviving now and will revive. Thus or otherwise, a little sooner, or a little later, we definitely hope to see you too. Write me a line about your health and above all be cheerful; remember that you and I are not so old yet—everything is still ahead.

Your

Lenin

132. (153 P[1]). TO R. S. ZEMLYACHKA IN RUSSIA

Geneva, 26th December, 1904

My dear Friend,

I have received your authorisation. One of these days I am coming out in print about your affair.[1] A few days ago I also received the report of the Northern Conference. Hurrah! You have worked splendidly and you (together with Papa [M. M. Litvinov] the Mouse [P. I. Kulyabko] and others) can be congratulated on an enormous success. Such a conference is a

---

[1] In "Iskra," No. 77, Zemlyachka was accused of disorganising the Party.

most difficult business under Russian conditions and it has evidently succeeded splendidly. Its importance is enormous: our announcement about our newspaper "Vpered" comes just at the right time. The announcement has already appeared. The first number will come out at the beginning of January, new style. Now our task is as follows:

(1) To come out in Russia as soon as possible with a printed leaflet about the Bureau of the Bolshevik Committees. For God's sake, do not put this off for a single week. The devil know's how important it is!

(2) To travel once more round the Committees in the South (*and the Volga*) and to stress the importance of supporting "Vpered" in any and every way.

There will be transport so long as we have Papa. Let him take the most energetic measures for handing over his inheritance in case of failure.

Tell Rahmetov [A. A. Bogdanov] to hurry up and leave the dangerous places and to go to his appointed place.[1] Quickly!

When we have money we shall send many people.

We are going to publish something ["It is Time to End"] about the Petersburg disgrace (the stopping of the demonstration by the Mensheviks) in No. 1 of "Vpered." Hurry up with the public announcement about the Bureau and definitely with the enumeration of all the 13 Committees. Hurry! Hurry! Hurry! Then we shall also get some money.

Warm greetings to all friends,

Your

Lenin

133. (154 P[1]). TO THE MONK [A. T. ERAMASOV] IN RUSSIA, FROM
LENIN—PERSONAL

Geneva, End of December, 1904

My dear Comrade,

I was very glad to hear that we can now set up more regular communications with you. It would be a good thing if you

---

[1] Abroad, to work on "Vpered."

took advantage of this and were to write a few lines yourself about your mood and your immediate plans. For until now all information about you as come through intermediaries which always somewhat complicates mutual relations.

Our Party matters, as you have probably heard, have been progressing disgracefully all the year. The Mensheviks finally ruined the II Congress, created a new "Iskra" (have you seen it? What is your attitude towards it?) and now, when an enormous majority of the Committees that have expressed themselves at all, have definitely risen up against this new "Iskra," the Mensheviks have ruined also the III Congress. It has become all too clear to the Mensheviks that the Party will not be reconciled with their Organ of gossip and petty wrangling of the return to "Rabocheye Delo" principles, of the famous theory of the organisation-process.

Now the position has become clear, the Bolshevik Committees have united (4 in the Caucasus, Odessa, Ekaterinoslav, Nikolaev, Petersburg, Moscow, Riga, Tver, the North and Nizhny-Novgorod). I have begun publishing a newspaper here, called "Vpered" (with fresh literary forces). (The announcement has appeared; No. 1 will come out in the beginning of January, new style.) Let us know what you think of it and whether we can count on your support, which would be most important for us.

THE PERIOD OF THE REVOLUTION
1905–1907

SUMMARY

1905

Jan.: Strike of Putilov workers. Workers led by Father Gapon shot down in S.P.B. General Party Conference of Narodnik groups (National Socialists) but Social Democrats refuse to participate.

Feb.: Most C.C. members arrested at house of Leonid Andreyev, the author. "Vpered" is Bolshevik organ from Dec. 22, 1904-May 5, 1905.

May: III Congress of R.S.D.L.P. first Bolshevik Congress ((1) revision of Party statutes, (2) the abolition of Council, (3) concentration of power in Central Committee to whom editing of Central Organ "The Proletariat" (May 14-Nov. 12) is entrusted. "Iskra" no longer Central Organ). Tactical resolutions: organisation of armed rising and participation in revolutionary government. Support of peasant movement to confiscate land.

Oct.: All-Russia political strike begins. Oct. 13-Dec. 3: Work of S.P.B. Council of Workers' Deputies. Formation of Executive Committee of the Social Revolutionary Democrats. The S.R.D. paper "Izvestia" is published. After Oct. 17, legal S.D. papers: (1) "Novaya Zhizn" (Bolsheviks in S.P.B. with Lenin's collaboration); (2) "Borba" (Bolsheviks in Moscow); (3) "Nachalo" (Mensheviks in S.P.B., Parvus and Trotsky); (4) "Moscow Newspaper" (Menshevik).

1905

Works for convening III Party Congress. Edits "Vpered" and contributes articles. Actively participates in III Congress (in London). Tries to consolidate the Bolshevik Party. Editor of "The Proletariat" and head of Central Party Committee.

Aug.-Sept.: Agitates for boycott of Bulygin Duma (consisting of bourgeoisie and landowners' representatives) and for a rising to overthrow autocracy. Propaganda for arming the working classes.

Oct. 19: S.R.D. proclaim freedom of the Press.

Oct. 29: S.R.D. introduce 8-hour day.

Nov.: Czarism recovers from panic and begins policy of open counter-revolution. Trotsky at head of S.R.D.

Returns to Russia after 5 years abroad. Edits "Novaya Zhizn" and writes for "Borba"; wide propaganda of S.R.D. slogans among workers. Struggles against Party neutrality of workers' organisations. Advocates boycott of Witte's Duma. Works for armed rising. Visits Moscow.

Dec.: Manifesto of S.R.D. to refuse payment of Government taxes and to remove savings from Savings Banks. Arrest of S.R.D. Suppression of armed rising in Moscow. Government crushes revolution in Siberia, Caucasus and Baltic Provinces.

Dec. 29-Jan. 14, 1906. I Congress of Party of Social Revolutionaries. Negotiations for reuniting both factions.

Leads Tammerfors Conference of Bolsheviks. Careful study of December uprising.

1906
Struggle against Cadets (liberal bourgeoisie and Mensheviks).

April-May: IV Unity Congress of the R.S.D.L.P. in Stockholm. Mensheviks secure majority at Congress. Bolsheviks keep their political and organisational independence.

April 27: First State Duma summoned.

May: First Soviet of S.R. Party.

July: Dissolution of First Duma. Dictatorship of Stolypin. Armed risings in Navy at Sveborg and Kronstadt. Mutiny suppressed.

Aug.: Appearance of illegal Bolshevik paper "The Proletariat."

Oct.: II Soviet of S.R. Party.

Nov.: S.D. Helsingfors Conference (on the initiative of the Bolsheviks); an All-Russia Conference at Tammerfors: (1) re the election campaign to the II Duma. The Bolsheviks oppose bloc with the Cadets; (2) decision to convene Party Congress not later than March 15, 1907; (3) discussion re All-Russia Labour Congress.

1906
Jan.: Lenin visits Moscow on Party work.

March: Escapes arrest. Leads Bolshevik faction at IV Unity Congress and makes reports and speeches. Writes "Report on Unity Congress." Returns to Russia, contributes articles to Bolshevik papers and conducts work of Bolshevik section of the S.D. Party.

Fights the slogan: Support the Duma.

Connected with organisers of risings in Navy. Edits and publishes "The Proletariat."

Actively opposes Labour Congress bloc with Cadets and Mensheviks.

THE RUSSIAN REVOLUTIONARY MOVEMENT

1907

Jan.-Feb.: Elections to the II Duma (34 S.R. deputies, 35 S.D. deputies).

June 26: Dissolution of II Duma. Triumph of counter-revolution. III All-Russia Party Congress. President: Lenin (Bogdanov, Kamenev support boycott of elections to III Duma; others advocate participation in Duma in interests of revolution).

Dec.: Central Committee decides to transfer its activities and "The Proletariat" abroad.

LENIN'S LIFE

1907

Controls work of Bolshevik S.D. deputies.

May 13-June 1: Takes part in V Congress of the R.S.D.L.P. in London (336 delegates = 105 Bolshevik, 97 Menshevik, 57 Bund).

Returns to Russia. Edits and introduces translated letters of Marx to Kugelmann and Sorge.

Aug.: Attends Stuttgart Congress of II International. Becomes member of International Socialist Bureau. Publishes a collection of articles "Twelve Years," which is confiscated.

Leaves Finland to evade police. Goes abroad to Geneva via Stockholm and Berlin.

Second period of exile begins, 1907-1917.

1905

134. (173 p[1]). TO R. S. ZEMLYACHKA IN PETERSBURG

[Geneva, Beginning of January, 1905]

I received your angry letter[1] and hasten to answer it. You took unnecessary offence. If I was cursing, then believe me I did so out of kindness and provisionally, namely *if* Lyadov's information was correct. We deeply value your tremendous achievement in winning over fifteen Committees and in organising three [regional] Conferences [of Bolshevik Committees] and surely you saw this in our last letter about the Northern Conference [No. 153]. We have not taken and do not take a single step without you. The young woman who has gone to Petersburg promised to use her personal links to procure money, but we wrote to Lisa [Lalayants?] on your account and not without you in our mind (the word "personal" was

---

[1] Lenin had accused the members of the Bureau of Bolshevik Committees (Bogdanov, Zemlyachka and Litvinov) of the discrepancy between their activity in Russia and the plan of an immediate publication of a Bolshevik Organ.

used solely as protection against enemies). We will explain to Lisa at once the misunderstanding about letters and she can of course go to the devil!

Many thanks to the Committees for sending the addresses. Please send some more. We have sent Gusev off and Lyadov will set out as soon as we have money. Lyadov has slightly misrepresented the question about the Organ in Russia and I ask you to forgive me for having lost my temper a little and for having offended you.

I will not argue any more about the Bureau coming out in the open to fight. A fortnight is only a trifle of course.[1] Believe me, I definitely intend to take into account opinion in Russia and I ask you seriously to do one thing: for Christ's sake keep me more frequently informed about Russian opinion. If I am guilty of falling under the influence of the Bolsheviks abroad, then I am innocently guilty, for Russia writes devilishly little and seldom. I submit completely (and I swear I do this willingly) to the resolutions of the Northern Conference [re elections of the Bureau of Bolshevik Committees]. Do try to get some money and write that you are no longer angry.

All yours
Lenin

135. (174 P^1). TO A. A. BOGDANOV IN PETERSBURG

Geneva, 10th January, 1905

My dear Friend!

At last we have begun "Vpered" ["Forward" No. 1, 4 January, 1905], and I want to tell you about it in detail. Number 2 is to come out the day after tomorrow. We are thinking of publishing it weekly. We shall have sufficient contributors; everybody's mood is excellent, also their energy to work (with the exception of Vasily Vasilievich [M. S. Olmin-

---

[1] In letter No. 148, p. 216, Lenin insisted on a complete break with the C.C. and on the Bureau of Bolshevik Committees acting as an O.C. for convening III Congress. The Northern Conference resolved to ask the C.C. if it was ready to convene a congress immediately, and gave it a fortnight in which to reply. Failing this, the Bureau of Bolshevik Committees elected at the Northern Conference was to act as the Organisation Committee.

sky], who is slightly depressed). We feel certain it will go
well, so long as we do not go bankrupt—440 francs (150
roubles) are essential for each number and we have only 1,200
francs in all. It is devilishly necessary to have some help during
the first few months, for if it does not appear regularly, then
the whole Bolshevik position will suffer a gigantic and irrep-
arable blow. Do not forget this and try to collect some money
(*especially from Gorky*).

Further, it is particularly important to tell Rahmetov [A. A.
Bogdanov] to do his utmost to organise literary collaboration
from Russia. The success of such a weekly newspaper depends
principally upon the energetic work of Russian writers and
Social Democrats. Write to Rahmetov and tell him to mobilise
for this work the *Finn* [A. Yu. Finn-Enotayevsky], *Kollontay*
(articles about *Finland* are urgently needed), *Rumyantsev* and
Andrew Sokolov [S. Vol'sky], particularly the last named and
without fail. I know from long experience that in such matters
Russians are diabolically, unpardonably and incredibly slow. It
is therefore necessary to act as follows: firstly, by personal
example, and secondly, not to rely on promises, but to make
certain of getting the finished articles. Let Rahmetov order
short articles and correspondence and have them sent to him;
then let him send them to us and not give the writers any peace
until they have submitted their work to him. (I would also
add *Suvorov* and *Luntz*, but of course Rahmetov knows many
others).

Urgently needed are: (1) short articles on Russian life
6/18,000 letters [of the alphabet]; (2) comments on the same
subject 2/6,000 letters [of the alphabet]; (3) correspondence
on all subjects and of varied length, (4) quotations and copies
of most interesting passages from local Russian and specialist
Russian publications; (5) notes on newspaper and periodical
articles in Russian publications. Young workers and especially
students are quite capable of attending to the last three points
and it is therefore necessary to draw their attention to this, to
further this work, to stir up the public by giving concrete examples of what is necessary, by showing how any trifle should
be utilised and by explaining that we people abroad are

devilishly hard up for raw material from Russia (we can polish it up in a literary sense!). It must be made clear to them that it is extremely foolish to be shy because of literary defects, that they must learn to express themselves simply and to correspond with the newspaper abroad, if they want it to be their own newspaper. In view of all this, I would consider it absolutely essential to distribute "Vpered" addresses to each student circle, to each workers' group (abroad there are many, and there will be still more). I assure you, that among our Committee members there is an idiotic prejudice against widely distributing addresses to the young people on the periphery. Fight this prejudice with all your strength, distribute addresses and insist on *direct* relations with the editors of "Vpered," without which the paper will not flourish. We are in great need of correspondence from workers and there is too little of it. Dozens and hundreds of workers should be writing simply and directly to "Vpered."

We must all strive for the workers to give their private addresses for "Vpered" to be sent to them in an envelope. The workers will not be afraid. The police will not be able to intercept even a tenth part of the envelopes. The small size of "Vpered" (4 pages) and its frequent appearance makes the question of envelope distribution a most important one for the paper. We must make it our aim to increase the number of worker subscribers to "Vpered," to develop the habit of sending money direct abroad (after all a rouble [2/-] is not much!) and also their address. If this is taken well in hand it would be possible, I swear, to revolutionise the distribution of illegal literature in Russia. Do not forget, that in the best circumstances the delivery takes four months. And that for a weekly newspaper! Whereas, when sent in envelopes, probably 50% to 75% would travel through the post as quickly as an ordinary letter.

Next: the authors—they must be made to write regular weekly or fortnightly articles, otherwise we shall say: "we do not think you are reliable, and are severing our connection with you." The usual excuse will be: "We do not know what to write about: we are afraid that our articles will be written in vain and they probably have enough material." It is with such foolish excuses that Rahmetov will have to contend. The main subjects: a survey of internal affairs in Russia (those which in larger periodicals come under the survey of domestic policy and the social chronicle), and smaller articles and notes on Russian technical publications, statistical, military, medical, prison, church, etc. etc. We always need material for these two sections and it is only Russians and solely Russians who can conduct these two sections properly. *The centre of gravity lies there—fresh facts, fresh impressions and special material, inaccessible abroad is what is wanted, and not discussions or evaluations from the Social Democratic point of view.* Such articles and notes will never be useless, because they will always be used. The responsibility of organising this matter lies directly with Rahmetov and he must find for us at least five good, sensible, not lazy or unreliable collaborators, who will each have direct dealings with the editors. Complete agreement about the details of the work can be achieved only through direct dealings with a collaborator. We must attract people by the argument, that nowhere else will they be able to appear in print so quickly as in a weekly newspaper.

In conclusion, a few words about our slogan. After the article "It is time to end" (No. 1 "Vpered") the slogan should be clear enough, but the public is so dull-witted that Rahmetov will have to explain and do his utmost to push it into their heads. There is a *complete split* at present for we have exhausted all our means. The *Third Congress* is against the will of the Central Committee and the Soviet, which are not part of it. We have broken completely with the Central Committee; we have announced that we have our own Bureau. Mensheviks and the new "Iskra" men are being excluded from everywhere. We have done everything to get on together and now we have to declare openly and clearly that we are compelled to work apart. Any trust or childish faith would cause only immense harm.

We implore you, for God's sake, to issue as quickly as possible an open and curt announcement about the Bureau. It is essential: (1) to express complete solidarity with "It is time to end," and to repeat its call, (2) to announce that "Vpered" is the Organ of the Bolshevik Committees and that the Bureau is working harmoniously with them and is in complete agreement with them, (3) that the Central Committee and the Soviet have deceived the Party in the most shameful way and have ruined the Congress, (4) there is now no other way out excepting by a Congress of the Committees *without* the Central Committee or the Soviet, and (5) that the Bureau undertakes to help the Committees in their positive work, (6) that people have completely lost confidence in the Central Organ through their wavering and lies.

Believe me, we value Zemlyachka highly, but she is wrong in regard to Papa [Litvinov] and you must correct this mistake.[1] Any links with the Central Committee must be severed as soon as possible all along the line; the fact that the Bureau is the Organisation Committee and that it is summoning the Third Congress must be printed at once.

136. (176 P[1]). TO S. I. GUSEV IN PETERSBURG

[Geneva], 15th February, 1905

My dear Friend,

Many thanks for your letters. Do not fail to continue in the same spirit; but there is just this I would like to add: (1) never stop at summarising the letters or information handed over to you, but do not fail to forward them *in toto* (except your own letters); (2) do not fail to link us up directly with new forces, with young people and fresh groups. Do not forget that the strength of revolutionary organisation lies in the number of its links. We must judge the efficiency and results of our friends through the number of new Russian links created. So far not one of the Petersburg people (shame on them!) has

---

[1] At the Conference of Northern Committees Litvinov insisted that the foremost question for discussion should be the attitude of the Bolsheviks towards the Mensheviks and the C.C., and whether it was possible for local committees to submit to Central Organisations of the Party which obviously did not represent the will of the Party and disobeyed the instructions of the II Party Congress.

Zemlyachka however insisted on a discussion of Party slogans, and Litvinov's question was not fully discussed.

given us a single new link (neither Serafima, [S. N. Afanasiev]
nor Sysoika [A. A. Bogdanov], nor Zemlyachka, nor Nikolai
Ivanovich [I. K. Lalayants]. It is a scandal, it is murder, it is
ruin! For God's sake, learn from the Mensheviks. In "Iskra"
(No. 85) there is a wealth of correspondence [re 9th Janu-
ary]. You have read "Vpered" to young people, haven't you?
Then why have you not linked us up with any of these young
people?? Remember you have only to fail and we run aground,
until you find for us *ten* new, young and loyal friends of
"Vpered" who know how to work, who know how to establish
links and who will manage to correspond without you. Remember this!! A professional revolutionary must create in each
place dozens of new links, entrust the whole work into their
own hands under his supervision, teach them and pull them up,
not by lecturing, but by work. Then he has to go to another
place and after a month or two return to check up the work
of the young substitutes. I assure you that there is among us
some kind of idiotic, philistine, lazy fear of young people. I
implore you: fight this fear with all your strength.

Your
Lenin

137. (178 P[1]). TO S. I. GUSEV IN PETERSBURG, MEMBER OF THE
BUREAU OF BOLSHEVIK COMMITTEES

[Geneva, the beginning of March, 1905]

My dear Friend,

Very many thanks for your letters. You are simply saving
us from foreign impressions. Do continue this. For God's sake,
get hold of letters from the workers themselves. Why do they
not write?? It is a positive disgrace! Your detailed account of
the agitation in the Committee at the election to the Shidlovsky
Commission was magnificent. We shall print it.[1]

---

[1] On 29 Jan./11 Feb., 1905, the Government organised a special commission "to
elucidate the reasons of the workers' discontent in St. Petersburg and the suburbs,
and to find means to eliminate it," under the presidency of Senator Shidlovsky and
with the participation of worker representatives.

The industrial workers were to elect electors and these elected deputies to the
Shidlovsky Commission. The Bolshevik Petersburg Committee managed to utilise the

Another question: have you accepted the six selected workers for the Committee? Answer without fail. We strongly advise you to accept workers on to the Committee, at any rate half. Without this you will not strengthen yourselves against the Mensheviks, who will send strong reinforcements from here.

No one writes from the Bureau about the Congress. This makes us anxious, for the Nymph's [M. N. Lyadov] optimism (and partly your own), that the Central Committee consent to the Congress is a plus, inspires us with gigantic fears. It is as clear as daylight to us that the Central Committee wanted to fool you. You must be a pessimist so far as the Central Committee is concerned. For God's sake do not trust it! Take advantage of the moment to force Menshevik Committees and especially weak Committees to appear.[1] It is extremely important to exert pressure on Kiev, Rostov and Kharkov. We *know* that in these three centres there are "Vpered" supporters, both among the *workers* and the intelligentsia. Whatever happens, they must send delegates to the Congress with a consultative vote. Write to the Nymph and the Demon [R. S. Zemlyachka] about all this. The same applies to the Moscow printers. It is a great pity that the Bureau did not publish our decision to invite Workers' Organisations to the Congress: that was a *terrible* mistake. Put it right at once and without fail.

I would strongly advise an agitation among the three hundred organised [Bolshevik] workers in St. Petersburg that they should send *at their own expense* one or two delegates to the Congress with a consultative vote. That will probably flatter the workers and they will take up the matter enthusiastically. Do not forget that the Mensheviks will do their utmost to discredit the Congress to the workers by saying that there were no workers. This must be taken into account and we must not fail to pay serious attention to the workers being represented. The St. Petersburg workers will surely be able to collect 300 roubles for two worker delegates (or perhaps some Mæcenas

elections for their own ends. The demands of the workers, such as the release of arrested fellow-workers, freedom of meetings and speech for discussing the demands of the workers, etc., were refused by Shidlovsky. On March 5th the Commission was dissolved and the worker-electors arrested.

[1] This refers to the participation of the Committees in the III Party Congress.

will present this amount for such a purpose). The collecting
of 5 kopeks a head will create a stir and everyone will know
about it. It is extremely important. Do not fail to read this to
your Committee and at the organising and agitators' meetings.
Are all our organisers and agitators talking to the workers about
direct links with "Vpered"?

Greetings to you.

Your

Lenin

P.S. Both leaflets of the Bureau (No. 1 about the rising and
No. 2 about the attitude to the Liberals) are splendid and we
are publishing them in full in "Vpered." If only you would
continue in the same spirit!! By the way, why has the group
of writers announced itself as belonging to the organisation
of the St. Petersburg Committee? This is not expedient and
for the following reason: the group of writers attached to the
Committee has *no mandate* at the Congress. If it were *separate*,
not a Committee, but an *all-Russia* group of writers belonging
to the Russian Social Democratic Revolutionary Party, it would
have the right to send (*with the Bureau's permission*) a delegate with a consultative vote. Do arrange this! We will not
print that it is a group attached to the Petersburg Committee.
(1) Let the Petersburg Committee strike it off the list, (2) let
it become for a time a separate group, (3) let it send a petition (here is bureaucracy for you!) for its delegate to be admitted to the Congress with a consultative vote, (4) let the
Bureau decide the question. Surely ten writers can find 200
roubles for a delegate?? And surely there could be a delegate
(Rumyantsev, for instance or somebody else) who would be
useful at the Congress. Tell the Bureau about this or better
still do it yourself *without any reports*.

138. (181 P[1]). TO S. I. GUSEV IN PETERSBURG

[Geneva], *4th April, 1905*

My dear Friend,

You yourself wrote that they were beginning to follow and watch you. Also I have gathered from Petersburg people, who have recently arrived from the scene of action, information which completely confirms this fact. There can be no doubt about it whatsoever. I know from my own experience and from the experience of masses of comrades that possibly the most difficult thing for a revolutionary to do is to leave a dangerous place *in time*. Always, and just when it is essential to leave the work in a given place, it becomes particularly interesting and *particularly important;* this always seems to be the case to the person who is working. Therefore I consider it my duty to insist in the most emphatic manner that you should leave Petersburg for a time. It is absolutely necessary. No excuses whatever, no considerations for the work must delay that step. The damage from inevitable failure would be enormous, whereas the damage through leaving would be insignificant and only apparent. Appoint some young assistants for the time being, say a month or two, to take the higher positions and rest assured that the whole cause will gain considerably through this temporary loss. The young people will gain experience in doing more responsible work and any mistakes they make can soon be remedied. Whereas your ruin would entirely spoil the most important opportunities of arranging the main work for us. Once again I insistently advise you to go *at once* to the provinces for a month. There is a tremendous amount of work to be done everywhere and a guiding hand is needed. If you want (and it is essential that you should want) to leave, then it can always be arranged.

I am not writing about the agreement of March 12th, 1905.[1] There is no need to swear about that. Evidently it could not be helped. The question now is to prepare energetically for

---

[1] The agreement between the Bureau of Bolshevik Committees (in the person of Gusev and Rumyantsev) and the C.C. (L. Krassin) about creating an O.C. and about convening a Congress.

the Congress and to increase the number of delegates. As for money, do not be extravagant, save it: it will be wanted more than ever after the Congress.

139. (185 P¹). TO THE INTERNATIONAL SOCIALIST BUREAU IN BRUSSELS

[Translated from the French]

Geneva, 8th July, 1905

Dear Comrades,

Your letter of the 6th July somewhat surprised us. You should have heard by now that Citizen Plekhanov is no longer the representative of the Russian Social Democratic Party in the International Socialist Bureau.

In "Iskra" (No. 101) Citizen Plekhanov published the following letter which we translate literally and which, it would seem, he ought to have brought to the notice of the Bureau:

> "Comrades,
>
> The decisions of the Conference (of those who split from the Party¹) which have dealt a death blow to the central institutions of our Party compel me to resign from the editorship of the Central Organ and from being the fifth Council member of the Soviet (elected by the second *legal* Congress).
>
> G. Plekhanov
>
> P.S. I take this opportunity of asking in print that section of the Party, which acknowledges the decisions of the III Congress as binding, whether it wishes me to continue to represent the Russian Social Democratic Party— now alas! split—at the International Socialist Bureau. I can remain as the representative of the Russian Social

---

¹ The Geneva Conference of Mensheviks and adhering delegates from certain committees elected at the III Party Congress took place in Geneva at the same time as the III Congress in London. A number of resolutions were adopted, expressing the tactics of the Mensheviks at the given moment of the revolution, and an O.C. was elected, a practical controlling centre that split from the Party of the Menshevik faction.

Democratic Workers' Party only if *both* factions wish this."

Montreux, 29th May, 1905

To the announcement of Citizen Plekhanov, the editors of "The Proletariat," the Central Organ of the Party, answered him by the following statement printed in issue No. 5, of June 30th, 1905.

"With regard to Comrade Plekhanov's postscript, we wish to announce that the question of his representing the Party on the International Bureau has been handed over for decision to the Central Committee of the Party."

The question has not yet been decided and consequently Citizen Plekhanov cannot at present sign any documents coming from the International Bureau as a representative of the Party.

In view of this we would draw your attention, comrades, to the fact that it is awkward for us to have any dealings with the Bureau through a comrade who announces *publicly* that he cannot represent the Party, until it definitely empowers him to do so. We repeat our request that the International Secretariat should send, until the question of representation is decided, all that concerns us (letters, documents, manifestos, money, etc.) to the address of the Central Committee of the Party (V. Ulianov, Rue Colline 3, Geneva).

Please, accept, dear comrades, the assurance of our fraternal feelings.

140. (195 P¹). TO THE CENTRAL COMMITTEE

[Geneva], 14th August, 1905

My dear Friends,

I have just read in "Iskra" (No. 107) the official report of the meeting of the 12th July, 1905, between the Central Committee and the Organisation Commission.¹ It is most disappointing that so far we have not received the reports which you promised; nor any letters. Really, you cannot conduct

---

¹ On the question of Party union between the Bolsheviks and Mensheviks.

matters in this way. I knew nothing either about the idea of publishing an open letter or about the idea of meeting for discussion, or about the plan for concessions. Now, is it right to behave like this towards a member of the Collegium? Just think of the position into which you have placed me: it is an impossible position, for here abroad I have to answer openly to everyone—surely when you think about it calmly you can realise that for yourselves.

Your answer to the Organisation Commission raises a number of questions. I cannot understand anything—perhaps you are being sly? Have you forgotten the direct resolution of the III Congress about the need for a new Congress to confirm the conditions for union? How can you talk seriously about co-optation on to the Central Committee when there are two competitive Organs? How can one leave unanswered the permitted existence of two Central Organs i.e. a complete infringement both of the statutes and the decisions of the III Congress? How could one not present an ultimatum to the Mensheviks on the question of organisation: (1) Congresses instead of plebiscites as the supreme Party Organ, (2) definite subordination of Party literature to the Party, (3) direct election to the Central Committee, (4) subordination of the Mensheviks (without inverted commas) to the Bolsheviks etc.??

Is it possible that you are not warned by the disappointing experience with "the agreement" about transport which was at once broken by The Suit [V. L. Kopp, a Menshevik] and which caused a tremendous amount of fresh anger?? Nothing can harm the work of future unity so much as a fictitious agreement which satisfies no one and which leaves room for struggle: such an agreement will only *inevitably* lead to a new break and will multiply resentment tenfold!

Or are you being cunning? Are you hoping to fool the Organisation Commission or to force the Russian Mensheviks to quarrel with the Mensheviks abroad? Have you not had enough experience on that score to prove the futility of such efforts?

I repeat most seriously: you are placing me in an *impossible* position. I am not exaggerating. I ask you most insistently to answer me: (1) Shall we have a Congress on the 1st September, as we had decided, or have you altered this decision? (2) If you have changed your minds, then how, when and where will your congress (of Central Committee members) take place and what measures are you thinking of adopting, so that I could give my vote and (what is still *more important*) learn your *present* intentions? A meeting is devilishly important for a thousand and one matters. We have no money. The Germans are not giving us any, for some reason or other. If you do not send 3,000 roubles, we will crash. Almost all the official reports [of the III Party Congress] have been set up in type, we need 1,500 roubles for their publication. The cash box is as empty as it has *never* been before.

What is this resolution of the Orlov-Bryansk Committee? [1] ("Iskra" No. 106). There must be some muddle. For God's sake let me know what you know about it. Cannot someone be sent there, Lubich [I. A. Sammer] for instance, from Voronezh?

[Unsigned]

141. (188 P[1]). TO M. A. REISNER, A BOLSHEVIK, IN BERLIN

[*Geneva*], *4th October, 1905*

Dear Mihail Andreyevich,

I am very grateful to you for your letter which, even more than Felix Aleksandrovich's [V. V. Vorovsky's] information about a conversation with you, tells me about the plans and tactics of our so-called Cadets. Your news that the Liberals, Witte and others, are deadly afraid of active boycott is most valuable. I have just received news from Russia that there has been an Inter-Party Social-Democratic Conference, (both parts of the R.S.D.L.P., the Bund, probably the Letts etc.[2]). The

---

[1] That it is unable to decide whether to take the side of the Bolsheviks or the Mensheviks in the disputes.

[2] The Conference took place at the beginning of September, 1905. Representatives from the Central Organisations of the Bund, the Lettish S.D.L.P., the Revolutionary Ukrainian Party, the S.D. of Poland and Latvia, the C.C. of the R.S.D.L.P. and the O.C. of the Mensheviks. In spite of Menshevik protests the Conference resolved to boycott the State Duma.

tactics of active boycott [of the Bulygin State Duma] were definitely accepted.

Your plan is not clear to me: (1) Is there really some slight hope that the Cadets will refuse to vote in the State Duma? I do not think there is the slightest hope. (2) Would it not be better for us to conclude an agreement with the Radicals; to demand a million roubles from them for arming the Petersburg workers rather than insist on elections to the Constituent Assembly? What point would there be in such elections before a struggle with Trepov, or without a struggle with Trepov?

Of course this ought to be discussed in greater detail. I place my hopes, first on the interview which you will have in Berlin with one of my friends and secondly on our meeting you here, and about which Felix [V. V. Vorovsky] has written.

With good wishes for success in the fight for active boycott. I am at your service.

142. (197 P¹). TO THE CENTRAL COMMITTEE

[Geneva], 5th October, 1905

My dear Friends,

I have just received Reinert's [A. A. Bogdanov] new letter. I have carefully thought over his proposal, have talked it over with Delta [E. D. Stassov] and have revised my negative answer in the letter of 3rd October, 1905.[1]

I shall be able to send back Orlovsky [V. V. Vorovsky, a member of "The Proletariat" editorial collegium] in a week's time. They might then manage somehow without me for a fortnight or so, and I would write a few articles in advance; I might even be able to write something on my journey. But all the same, your plan still seems to me impossibly irrational. Judging by all the news with which the foreign newspapers are full, there is now terrible anger in Finland. They speak quite openly about a number of outbreaks which are being prepared, about the preparation of a rising. Large numbers of troops are

---

[1] In his letter of Oct. 3, 1905, Lenin refused to come to a general meeting of the C.C. in Finland, as he could not leave the newspaper "The Proletariat."

being sent there. The coastal and naval police have been strengthened fourfold. After the "John Grafton" affair,[1] attention is specially paid to vessels that approach the shores. Arms have been found in many places and weapons are searched for very thoroughly. It is considered quite possible that hostile encounters will be deliberately provoked so as to have armed interference.

In such conditions it would be quite an unnecessary risk to organise a general meeting there. That would be a hopeless thing to do. It would be sufficient to have one trifling accident (the probability of such a thing happening in Finland is particularly high) and there will be a complete crash both of the Central Committee and the Central Organ, for everything here would also collapse. One should look straight at things: that would mean wholly to hand over the Party for the Menshevik leaders to tear it to pieces. I am convinced that after thinking the question over, you will agree we have no right to do this.

I would ask you to judge whether the plan could not be altered in this way: that we should all meet in Stockholm. In comparison with the present plan this would mean only slight inconvenience for you and an enormous advantage. The inconvenience is a half-day delay (reckoning from Abo near where the meeting was proposed to be held) or a maximum of one day. In all, two, perhaps even four days. That is nothing. The advantage: an increase in safety. There can then be absolutely no crash. Which means, that we are not risking the fate of either the Central Organ or the whole Central Committee, we are doing nothing stupid or desperate. Some of you can come quite legally: it will be impossible to arrest you. Others will get false passports (Delta says that the Finns easily arrange frontier crossings without passports). In case of failure this will then be: (1) a single failure and not a complete crash, and (2) absolutely without any traps, for by conducting the matter legally the police will not be able to fish out anything of any serious import. We are then guaranteed two or three days of a completely safe meeting; we shall be able to

[1] S.S. "John Grafton" carrying arms for the Bolsheviks blew up near the Finnish coast on 26 Aug./8 Sept., 1905.

have all the documents (I will bring them, and you will send yours by post etc.) and it will be possible for us to draw up any protocols we like, proclamations etc., and finally, we would then be able to test if it were possible for me to travel oftener to Stockholm in order to work there for you, and on the leaflets etc. (I believe the Mensheviks did something of the sort in the South).

I would ask you to think over this plan very carefully. If you approve, send a telegram addressed to Kroupsky, 3, Rue David Dufour, Geneva, signed Boleslav and giving only a number, meaning the date when I am to be in Stockholm (30 would mean I must be there on 30th September; or 2 or 3 meaning I must be there by the 2nd or 3rd October etc.).[1]

I greet you warmly,

N. Lenin

143. (198 P[1]). TO THE CENTRAL COMMITTEE

[Geneva], 25th October, 1905

My dear Friends,

I have just received your letter about my appointment to the International Bureau (I am sorry that Orlovsky was not appointed, but we will discuss this when we meet) and about the meeting in Odessa [Berlin]. The meeting [of C.C. members] must certainly be arranged as quickly as possible. I would suggest Warsaw [Königsberg] instead of Odessa.[2] All the conditions are the same, but it is nearer, and more unexpected for the police. In this last place you could finish everything in *four* days, in the best conditions (a legal passport) and I advise you to begin working for it energetically at once. In the worst conditions, the time limit is not great, and if possible it would be a good thing to increase the number of participants. If you choose an unusual town (Königsberg—22 hours from Petersburg) then the meeting could be fixed at a café, hotel or public house, in advance, from a guidebook.

---

[1] The general meeting of C.C. members did not take place in Stockholm in September.

[2] For conspiratorial reasons Berlin was called Odessa, and Königsberg, Warsaw.

I am writing to the International Bureau today about the Conference [of the International Socialist Bureau] and its date; as soon as I receive their reply I will forward it to you. I ask you most urgently to hurry with the meeting, irrespective even of the Conference with the International Bureau.

Were any Minutes kept of the Inter-Party Conference? [1] If yes, then send them to us without fail.

(Unsigned)

144. (199 P[1]). TO THE CENTRAL COMMITTEE

Geneva, 27th October, 1905

Please write to me at once if you leave it to me to invite Plekhanov on to our editorial committee (seven members) and on to the editorial board of "Novaya Zhizn" ["New Life"].[2] Telegraph (signed Boleslav, address: Krupskaya): yes or no. I will make another attempt to approach him, although there is not much hope.

1907

145. (176 R). TO HIS MOTHER

Stirsudden, Finland, 27th June/10th July, 1907

Darling Mother,

I have not written to you for a long time. Anyuta has probably told you about our plan for taking a rest. I have returned feeling terribly tired. I am quite rested now.[3]

I am having a wonderful rest: bathing, walks, no people, nothing to do. No people and nothing to do is the best thing for me. I hope to stay here another fortnight and then to return to work. Nadya and Elis. Vas. are well and are also having a wonderful rest.

---

[1] The September Conference mentioned in letter No. 188 P[1].

[2] The first legal Bolshevik newspaper prepared by the C.C. in Petersburg came out on 27 Oct./9 Nov., 1905. The editorial committee included the editors and collaborators of "The Proletariat" who were abroad (i.e., Lenin, Olminsky, Vorovsky, Lunacharsky) and 3 literary men in S.P.B. (Bogdanov, Bazarov, Rumyantsev). Plekhanov "refused the invitation."

[3] Lenin was resting in L. M. Knipovich's villa in Finland after the IV Party Congress.

How are you all living? Are you well? Have you seen Anyuta? And where is she? Is she with you or with Mark? Write to me when you can or ask Mitya to send me a few lines.

I embrace you warmly,

Your,

V.

Much love to Mitya and his wife.

146. (177 R). TO HIS MOTHER

[Kuokkala, Finland], *15th/28th October*, *1907*

Darling Mother,

I do not seem to have written to you for a long time. I believe my last letter was sent from my summer "Mon Repos."[1] We are now settled like a happy family in our old place for the Winter. I hope it will not be as cold as it was last year, but we shall know how to manage better and dig ourselves in comfortably. I am quite pleased both with the house and all our arrangements. Manyasha has been staying with us and is still here, but she is thinking of leaving, now that the Winter has come; the first snow fell today and the weather has turned cold.

How are you? Will it be pleasant in the country when the real frosts begin? Please give Mitya my warm greetings. I am sorry it was impossible to see him this Autumn for we should have had some splendid shooting together. It was a magnificent Autumn. When does he take his leave and for how long? Where is he going to?[2]

We have had two letters from Anyuta. She is evidently pleased with her trip abroad: a very interesting itinerary, and at present it is probably particularly nice in the South.

We are living among a group of good friends [A. Bogdanov, I. Dubrovinsky, N. Rozhkov, G. Leiteisen]. There are books and work. We walk along the seashore. I think Manyasha felt well here and she worked a lot—she was translating.

[1] See No. 176 R.
[2] Lenin's brother Dymitry was then a doctor in the Moscow Province.

THE PERIOD OF REACTION
1908–1910

SUMMARY

1908

S.R. Party crushed. Demoralisation sets in. Weakening of workers' movement; professional and cultural organisations close down; publications banned; cuts in pay and increase in hours. Philosophic disagreements among Bolsheviks.

Aug.: Geneva. Plenum of C.C. (Mensheviks suggest re-organisation of C.C. by turning it into an Information Bureau. This is rejected by Bolsheviks). Bureau of C.C. abroad is formed. Trotsky publishes "Pravda."

Dec.-Jan.: Paris. All-Russia Conference: (creation of the Five for Russia—small personnel of the C.C. with full plenary rights. Resolution against striving to liquidate existing organisation of the S.D. Party and on the need to use Duma in the interests of revolutionary agitation: negative attitude to S.D. faction activities in Duma).

1909

Reaction in Russia.

March: Publication of "Vekhi" ("Signposts") articles written by Struve, Berdyaev, Bulgakov—the expression of reactionary mystical mood of the Liberal bourgeoisie.

May: V Soviet of the Party; Bolsheviks split into (*a*) "Vpered" group (Bogdanov, Lunacharsky, Gorky and Alexinsky $=$ Otzovists and Ultimatists; (*b*) Lenin's group (Zinoviev and Kamenev). Mensheviks split into (*a*) Liquidators ("The Voice of Social Democracy"); (*b*) Plekhanovites. Trotsky's "Pravda" forms a separate group. "Vpered" group founds a Party School on Capri.

1908

Struggles against Liquidators (Mensheviks). Lives in Geneva.

Feb.: Writes articles for Granat's Encyclopædia on "Agrarian question in Russia at the end of 19th century."

Aug.: Trip to London. Opposes Bogdanov, Lunacharsky and Bazarov in advocating Empirio-Criticism.

Oct.: Attends meeting of International Socialist Bureau in Brussels.

Attends Conference in Paris, opposes Liquidators of the Right (Mensheviks) and Liquidators of the Left. (Otzovists $=$ those in favour of Bolshevik members being withdrawn from Duma.) Editor of "The Proletariat." Prepares book against the criticism of the philosophic foundations of Marxism on the part of the Empirio-Critics.

1909

Writes against "Vekhi." Book on "Materialism and Empirio-Criticism" published.

Nov.: Attends International Socialist Bureau Meeting in Brussels.

Dec.: Lectures to Party School on Capri.

1910

Reaction in Russia continues. Police persecute local Narodnik cells, workers' professional unions, etc.

Jan. 15-Feb. 5: Unity Plenum of the C.C. of the R.S.D.L.P., consisting of (1) Bogdanovite Bolsheviks, (2) Leninite Bolsheviks, (3) Plekhanovites, (4) Liquidators, (5) Trotskyites, (6) Bundites. Activities to create a united Party (1) Publication of Bolshevik "The Proletariat" and Menshevik "Voice of Social Democracy"; (2) New organisation of C.C. = new collegium, "The Seven"; (3) "The Social Democrat" is the central Organ of the Party, its supplement "The Discussional Leaflet." (4) Resolution re the need to unite the scattered illegal S.D. groups and Party workers' cells, to utilise all illegal organisations for the revival of a mass movement and to turn these organisations into centres of S.D. work. Agreement with Trotsky. Kamenev joins "Pravda" editorial board. "Nasha Zarya" ("Our Dawn") appears.

Moscow arrest of newly-formed Seven of the C.C.

Dec. 16: No. 1 of "Zvezda" (Marxist newspaper "The Star") appears.

1910

In Paris, working in C.C. Plenum, and has a consultative vote.

Joins editorial board of "Social Democrat."

Aug. 28-Sept. 3: Attends Copenhagen Congress of II International. Member of the Co-operative Commission.

Nov.: Founds the "Rabochaya Gazeta" ("Workers' Gazette").

1908

147. (178 R). TO M. I. ULIANOVA

[Geneva] 1/14th January, 1908

My address is: Vl. Oulianoff, 17 Rue des deux Ponts, (Chez Küpper) Genève.

Darling Manyasha,

I am sending you "Obrazovaniye"[1] which I have brought here by mistake. I do not think I have any more debts so far as books are concerned. If I have, please let me know.

[1] A popular literary, scientific and political journal in which Marxists collaborated.

For several days now we have been stuck in this damned Geneva.[1] A sordid hole, but it cannot be helped. We will adapt ourselves. How are you living? Are you freezing? Is Mother well? Kiss her, please, from me and give Anyuta my love, also Mitya if he has not left yet.

Yesterday I wrote to Lev Borisovich [Kamenev, a Bolshevik] about a short article and asked him to get me the protocols of the III Duma (the official publication of the shorthand reports, as well as announcements, questions and proposed legislation in the Duma).

These can be obtained only through personal links. Please try to find someone who would agree to do this for me and send them all to me, without missing any. I would also ask you to send me *all* the professional periodicals still appearing in Russia (St. Petersburg and also Moscow), buy them at once. For your expenses, take about 50 roubles from Eliz. Vas. from the sum which should be received from the publisher on the 4th January, and please send me any new publications of the Mensheviks (if they are publishing anything) etc. I have subscribed to "Tovarishch" ("Nash Vek")[2] as from the 1st of January and I will also keep in touch with the new books. If L. B. is too busy or too lazy to write, please find out from him the answer (to my questions) and let me know what it is. By the way, I need an answer about Granat (History of Russia); has an agreement been made with him about my article ["The Agrarian Question in Russia towards the end of the 19th Century"] or has the matter fallen through? Let L. B. find this out and tell you.

I greet you warmly,

Your

V. Ulianov

Tournez la page, s'il vous plait.
Have you despatched Nadya's and my documents? If not,

---

[1] At the end of Nov. or early in Dec., 1908, Lenin, hiding from the police, was forced to leave Finland. He arrived in Geneva on Jan. 7th. This, his second emigration, lasted till April, 1917.
[2] An Organ of the Left Cadets.

please send them by registered post as soon as you can. I must have those papers to receive a permis d'établissement.

148. (200 P[1]). TO G. A. ALEXINSKY IN ITALY [1]

[*Geneva*], *7th January, 1908*

My dear Peter,

Nadezhda Konstantinovna and I arrived in Geneva today.[2] We have not yet decided finally where we shall settle: Alexander Alexandrovich [Bogdanov] is very much against Geneva and we are reconnoitring in various places.

But we must understand fully the position here. Please write at once: (1) whether you know of a suitable person who could be in charge of the printing press and the posting [of "The Proletariat"]. (2) What do you think of the Doctor for this? (3) What special points must be taken into consideration about the printing press? Must it have an owner, if it belongs to the Central Organ of the Bolshevik section of the Stockholm Congress? Why do you consider only the Menshevik printing press as the property of the Central Committee? (4) Do you think a weekly newspaper possible, and on what circulation could one reckon? 300—500—1000?

We received your letter sent to Berlin in the midst of panic caused by the arrest of the 17 [3] and therefore destroyed it before having read it sufficiently carefully.

Answer to the following address. . . . How are you? When do you think you will be able to return here? Have you recovered at all in health in the interval?

I send you greetings,

(Unsigned)

---

[1] In Jan., 1908, Alexinsky was still a Bolshevik, a month later Lenin noticed his wavering in the Party.

[2] After the London Party Congress Lenin lived in Finland, near Petrograd. But when arrests of Bolsheviks began, it was decided to transfer "The Proletariat" abroad with Lenin, Bogdanov and Dubrovinsky in charge.

[3] Some State Bank money in transit was expropriated in Tiflis on 23 June, 1907. The perpetrators managed to escape. The Russian Government published the numbers of the notes. People changing these notes abroad in Berlin, München, Stockholm, Geneva, were arrested. In connection with this, other arrests were made among the Social Democrats abroad.

149. (202 P¹). TO A. M. GORKY AND M. F. ANDREYEVA
IN CAPRI, ITALY

[*Geneva*], *15th January, 1908*

My dear A. M. and M. F.,

I received your express letter today. It is amazingly tempting, damn it, to come to you to Capri! You have described it so well, that I swear I will certainly come, and I will try to bring my wife with me. Only I do not yet know when. I cannot cease work on "The Proletariat"; it must be *organised* and the work set going whatever happens. It will take a month or two, at least. But it must be done. But by the Spring we shall come to drink white Capri wine, to look at Naples and to talk with you. By the way, I have begun learning Italian and, like a student, immediately fell upon the "Expresso" instead of "Espresso" which Maria Fedorovna had written on the address! I searched for it in my dictionary!

You have written about "The Proletariat" at your own risk. Now you will not wriggle away from us so easily! I have at once a whole heap of instructions for M. F.:—

(1) To find at once the secretary of the union of steamship employees and workers (there must be such a union!) on steamers that have relations with Russia.

(2) To find out from him exactly *from where to where* the steamers ply; *how often*. He is to arrange a *weekly transport* for us without fail. How much will that cost? He must find us a reliable man (are Italians reliable?). Must they have an address in Russia (let us say Odessa) for delivery of the newspaper or could they *temporarily* keep a small supply with some Italian innkeeper in Odessa? That is *most important* for us.

(3) If M. F. cannot arrange all this herself, find out, explain, check up etc. then let her not fail to link us up with this secretary direct. We will then arrange matters with him by letter.

We must hurry with this matter: in 2-3 weeks' time we hope to publish here the first number of "The Proletariat" and to send it off immediately.

Well—goodbye—till we meet on Capri! A. M., see that you keep well!

Your

V. Ulianov

150. (180 R). TO M. I. ULIANOVA

[Geneva], 25th January/7th February, 1908

Darling Manyasha,

I have received your letter of the 20th January/2nd February, the young literary man's [L. Kamenev] letter about the same thing and today I received "Rech."[1] Very, very many thanks for the last, it was really a most interesting little article.

I answered the young literary man about Webb and sent him a form of authorisation. In any case I repeat:

(1) I do not know the number of copies in the 1st edition.

(2) Struve was then responsible for the editing; it was he who edited the first volume;

(3) E. Smirnov (Gurevich) translated the second volume. I received 20 roubles a sheet for the translation of the first volume and 10 roubles a sheet for editing the second. Let the young literary man do some bargaining,—in extreme need coming down to half, but the number of copies must be stated in the agreement.

Yesterday I also received a letter from a colleague about Granat. Matters are being settled for me there quite satisfactorily.

As for our marriage certificate [see Letter 147] and palm-greasing in Krasnoyarsk, my advice is not to bother too much, not to give any large tips at all; we can evidently manage without.

In a month's time, *or possibly sooner*, we intend to settle down here in a flat of our own.

---

[1] "Rech" ("Speech") a political, literary and economic newspaper in S.P.B. 1906-17, the C.C. Organ of the Cadets.

Re the volume of collected articles in memory of Marx, from all appearances I too will not take any part in it: it is impossible to write such a thing in a hurry.[1]

It is amazing how slow our people are to recover! It is simply awful. This year the influenza must be a particularly vicious variety or our weather is bad. Write and tell me about Mother's health.

I have not yet settled down here—e.g. I have not yet joined my "club"[2] where it is easy to read periodicals and get hold of new books. I shall try (as soon as I join—probably in a day or two) to find what I can in the way of a translation for you. Do you receive "Neue Zeit"? In the No. 1 supplement to that periodical there is an article by Kautsky: "Nationalism and Internationalism." I have not seen it yet. Would that be any good for translation? I read Kautsky's "Socialism and Colonial Policy" (a new pamphlet of 80 pages), I think it is legal. Have a talk with Zerno,[3] it would be a good thing to translate it. I am surprised I have not seen any announcements of the translation of Parvus [A. L. Helfand][4] ("Kolonial-politik und Zusammenbruch"). Has not anyone any initiative? Ask Zerno. I might get into touch with the author abroad.

I greet you warmly and kiss Mother,

Your

V. U.

P.S. We have not received the "Selected Works" ["An Anthology of Russian Poetry"] by Bonch-Bruevich. Of the professional journals—I have received "Gudok" and "The Textile Industry." Please go on sending me *all* such journals.

---

[1] Lenin did contribute an article: "Marxism and Revisionism."

[2] A Geneva library attached to the "Société de Lecture" club.

[3] A publishing firm started in 1906; most of its publications were confiscated.

[4] Parvus, a Russian émigré, worked in the left wing of the German S.D. Led a bitter campaign together with R. Luxembourg against Bernstein and opportunism in the Party. Author of a number of Marxist works. Collaborated in "Iskra" and "Zarya." Became a Menshevik. During the war period he became a Social Chauvinist.

151. (203 P[1]). TO F. A. ROTSTEIN IN LONDON

[*Geneva*], *29th January, 1908*

My dear Comrade,

In Finland, about two and a half to three months ago, I received your letter with a reminder of the debt[1] and I have passed it on to the Central Committee. The present "devastation of Finland" forced me to leave for Geneva and the move caused much loss of time and worry. Today a comrade here informs me that you are insistently reminding us of our debt and the Englishman even threatens to publish the fact in the newspapers (!) etc.

I am writing at once to Russia that the debt must be paid. But, you must know, it is extremely difficult to do so now! The trouble in Finland, the arrest of many comrades, the seizure of papers, the necessity to keep moving the printing presses, and the need to send many comrades abroad, all this has caused an accumulation of quite unexpected expenses. The financial position of the Party is all the more distressing, since in these last two years all have lost the habit of working "underground" and have been spoilt by legal or semi-legal work. Secret organisations have now to be started again almost anew. This costs masses of money and all the intelligentsia and petit-bourgeois elements are forsaking the Party! The falling away of the intelligentsia is enormous. There remain pure proletarians without any possibility of open money collections.

Consequently it should be explained to the Englishman and he should be made to realise that the conditions at the time of the II Duma, when the loan was made, were quite different, that the Party will of course pay its debts, but that it is impossible and unthinkable to demand it *now*, for that would be sheer usury etc. etc.

The Englishman must be convinced. It is doubtful if he will be able to receive the money. A scandal would not lead anywhere.

[1] During the V London Party Congress (13 May-1 June, 1907) an Englishman, Joseph Felts, lent the Russian S.D.'s a sum of money. This debt was paid by the Party in 1923.

I seem to remember that the signatories were separate members of sections and are not the sections separately responsible?

I send you greetings,

Your

N. Lenin

P.S. Not knowing your address, I wrote to Quelch asking him to collect some literature. *I am extremely grateful to him:* I am afraid he cannot always understand my terrible English! My address is: Vl. Oulianoff, 17, Rue des deux Ponts, Geneva.

152. (208 P[1]). TO A. M. GORKY, CAPRI, ITALY

[*Geneva*], *13th February, 1908*

My dear Al. M.,

I think some of the questions you raise about our differences of opinion are simply the result of a misunderstanding. Of course I was not dreaming of "persecuting the intelligentsia" as the stupid little Syndicalists do, or to deny its necessity for the workers' movement. You and I *cannot* have any divergence of opinion on any of these questions: I am firmly convinced of this and since for the moment we cannot meet, it is essential to begin working together straight away. It will be through working together that we shall most easily agree.

Your plan to write short articles for "The Proletariat" (an announcement has been sent to you) gives me much satisfaction. But, of course, if you are busy writing at present, do not tear yourself away from your work.

I wanted to write to you about Trotsky in my last letter, but I forgot. We (that is the editors of "The Proletariat" here: Al. Al. [Bogdanov], the Monk [I. F. Dubrovinsky], a very good colleague among the Russian Bolsheviks, and I) decided at once to invite him to join "The Proletariat." We wrote him a letter and suggested a subject. We were in full agreement when we signed the letter "The Editors of 'The Proletariat,'" for we wanted the matter to be on a joint basis (I, for example, had done battle with Trotsky, having fought desperately with him between 1903 and 1905, when he was a Menshevik). I do not know whether he took offence at the joint letter, but he sent a letter not written by him, but "on the instruction of Comrade Trotsky" in which the Editors of "The Proletariat" were informed that he refused to write for the paper as he was "busy."

In my opinion that is posing. And he was also posing at the London Congress. I do not know whether he will join up with the Bolsheviks. . . .

The Mensheviks here have issued an announcement about the monthly "The Voice of Social Democracy" under the signatures of Plekhanov, Axelrod, Dan, Martov, Martynov. I will get a copy and send it to you. The conflict may become more acute. And Trotsky wants to stand "above the fighting factions."

As for materialism being considered as a world philosophy I do not think I agree in substance with you, not so much about the materialistic understanding of history (our Empirios[1] do not deny this), but about philosophic materialism. I definitely dispute that the Anglo-Saxons and the Germans owe their bourgeoisdom to materialism and the Latin peoples their anarchism. Materialism as a philosophy is driven everywhere and by them all into the background. The "Neue Zeit," a most reserved and sound paper, is indifferent to philosophy and never has been an advocate of philosophic materialism, but latterly it has printed the Empirio-Critics without a single exception. It is untrue, untrue, that dead petit-bourgeoisdom could be produced out of the materialism which Marx and Engels taught. All the petit-bourgeois currents in social democracy rage above all against philosophic materialism and tend towards Kant, Neo-Kantianism and critical philosophy. No, that philosophy which Engels founded in "Anti-Düring" does not admit petit-bourgeoisdom even on the doorstep. Plekhanov harms this philosophy by linking this struggle with factional struggle, but not a single Russian Social Democrat ought to confuse the present Plekhanov with the old Plekhanov.

[1] I.e., Empirio-Critics and Empirio-Monists (Bogdanov, Bazarov, Lunacharsky).

Al. Al. has just left me. I will tell him again and again about the Congress.[1] If you insist—it can be arranged for a few days and in the near future.

I greet you warmly,

Lenin

153. (209 P[1]). TO A. M. GORKY, CAPRI, ITALY

Geneva, 25th February, 1908

My dear A. M.,

I did not answer your letter at once for, strange though it may at first seem, we have had a fairly difficult fight with Al. Al. [Bogdanov] on the editorial board with regard to your article. Hm. . . . Hm. . . . I did not speak *in that place* nor on that subject which you imagine!

This is how it was:—

The book "Studies of the Philosophy of Marxism" [publ. by Zerno, 1908] very seriously sharpened the old differences among the Bolsheviks on questions of philosophy. I do not consider myself sufficiently competent in those subjects to hurry to appear in print. But I always carefully followed our *Party* debates on philosophy—beginning with Plekhanov's struggle against Mikhailovsky and Co. at the end of the "80's" and up to 1895, then his conflict with the Kantians in 1898 and the following years (here I not only followed, but beginning with 1900 partly participated as a member of the "Zarya" editorial board), and finally his conflict with the Empirio-Critics and Co.

I followed Bogdanov's writings on philosophy, beginning with his book about "The Historical View on Nature," which book I studied when I was in Siberia [1899]. For Bogdanov, this position was only a transition to other philosophic views. I made his personal acquaintance in 1904 and we immediately exchanged our writings: I presented my "Steps" ["One Step

---

[1] Gorky proposed to meet Lenin and the Bolshevik writers of the Bogdanov group abroad for a discussion of the noticed differences of opinion. This did not take place.

forward, Two Steps back," Geneva, 1904], and he, one of his philosophic books which at that time he had just written. And I wrote to him at once (in the Spring or early Summer of 1904) from Geneva to Paris that he thoroughly disproves to me the correctness of his views and proves the correctness of Plekhanov's views.

When Plekhanov and I were working together we discussed Bogdanov many times. Plekhanov would explain to me the mistakenness of Bogdanov's views, but considered it as not in any way a serious deviation. I remember perfectly that in the Summer of 1903 Plekhanov and I, as editors of "Zarya," were talking in Geneva with a delegate from the publishers of "Studies of the Realistic Viewpoint" [1] and we *agreed* to collaborate:—I on the Agrarian question and Plekhanov *on philosophy against Mach*. Plekhanov put his attack against Mach as the *condition* on which he would collaborate—which condition was fully accepted by the delegate from the publishers of "The Studies." Plekhanov then looked upon Bogdanov as an ally in the conflict with revisionism, but as an ally who was erring in so far as he followed Ostwald and later on, Mach.

In the Summer and Autumn of 1904 we finally agreed with Bogdanov, as Bolsheviks, and formed a silent bloc which silently set aside philosophy as a neutral region. This lasted all through the revolution and allowed us to introduce mutually into the revolution those tactics of revolutionary social democracy (of Bolshevism) which I am deeply convinced were the only right ones.

I had no opportunity to study much philosophy during the fever of the revolution. In the beginning of 1906 and when in prison Bogdanov wrote another book—I believe it was Part III of his "Empirio-Monism." He presented me with a copy in the Summer of 1906 and I sat down to a careful study of it. On reading it through I lost my temper and was unusually furious: it became clearer than ever to me that he was moving along an arch-mistaken way, not a Marxist way. I wrote then

[1] A Marxist Miscellany directed against the Narodniks and Revisionists, published in 1904 in S.P.B.

"a declaration of love" to him, a short letter on philosophy to the length of three exercise books. In it I explained to him that I was a *rank Marxist* in philosophy, but that it was his clear, popular and excellently written works which had finally convinced me that he was wrong in substance and that Plekhanov was right. I showed the little exercise books to a few friends (Lunacharsky among them) and I thought of having them printed under the title "Notes on Philosophy by a rank Marxist" but I did not do so. I regret now that I did not print them at once. The other day I wrote to Petersburg, asking that these exercise books should be found and sent to me.

And now "The Studies of the Philosophy of Marxism" have appeared. I have read all the articles with the exception of the one by Suvorov (I am reading it at present) and every article made me simply furious. No, that is not Marxism! Our Empirio-Critics, Empirio-Monists and Empirio-Symbolists are simply sinking into a bog. They assure the reader that "faith" in the reality of the external world is "mysticism" (Bazarov); in the most disgraceful fashion they confuse materialism and Kantianism (Bazarov and Bogdanov), they propound the difference between Agnosticism (Empirio-Criticism) and Idealism (Empirio-Monism)—they teach the workers "religious atheism" and the "adoration" of the higher human potentialities (Lunacharsky)—they proclaim the teaching of Engels on Dialectics (Berman) to be mysticism; they have taken from some abominable source some French "Positivists"—the devil knows what kind of agnostics or metaphysicians with a symbolical theory of knowledge (Yushkevich)! No, that is too much! Of course we, the rank Marxists, are people who are not well read in philosophy, but why should we be so insulted as to be offered such a work as being the philosophy of Marxism? I would rather be hanged and quartered before agreeing to collaborate in a work which propagates such ideas.

I was very drawn to the idea of "Notes on Philosophy by a rank Marxist" and I began to write them,[1] but of course I

---

[1] Lenin began work on his "Materialism and Empirio-Criticism."

expressed my impressions to Al. Al. directly and rudely while I was reading these studies.

And you will ask, what has your article got to do with all this? Just this: during the time when this divergence of opinion among the Bolsheviks was threatening to become particularly acute, you manifestly begin to express views of a certain tendency in your work for "The Proletariat." Of course I do not know how and what you would have developed. Besides, I consider that an artist can draw much that is useful to him from any philosophy. Finally, I fully and completely agree that in questions of literary creation, all books can be useful and that by extracting the particular point of view both from your artistic experience and from a philosophy, *even idealistic philosophy*, you may come to conclusions which may be enormously helpful to the Workers' Party. All that is quite true; none the less "The Proletariat" must remain absolutely neutral throughout all our differences in philosophy and give readers no shadow of cause for connecting the Bolsheviks as a direction, as a tactical line of the revolutionary wing of Russian Social Democrats, with Empirio-Criticism or Empirio-Monism.

When after reading your article I told A. A. that I was against it being published, he became darker than a cloud. There is a cloud of divergence hanging over us. Yesterday we had a special meeting of our three editors to discuss the question and we were suddenly helped by a stupid statement in the "Neue Zeit." An unknown translator had published in Number 20 Bogdanov's article about Mach ["Ernst Mach and the Revolution"] and blurted out in the preface that the differences of opinion between Plekhanov and Bogdanov tended among the Russian Social Democrats to become a *factional difference* between the Bolsheviks and the Mensheviks. By dint of this statement the male or female idiot who wrote the preface united us. We agreed at once that it was absolutely essential to announce our neutrality in the very next number of "The Proletariat." This completely coincided with my mood after the publication of the "Studies." We drew up the announcement, confirmed it unanimously and tomorrow it is to appear in No. 21 of "The Proletariat" a copy of which will be sent to you.[1]

With regard to your article, we have decided to postpone printing it by explaining the whole position to you in three letters, one from each of the editors of "The Proletariat" and by speeding up Bogdanov's and my trip to you.

This means, that you will receive a letter from Al. Al. and the third editor [I. F. Dubrovinsky] about whom I have written to you once before.

I consider it essential to give you my frank opinion: I think it is inevitable that there will be a conflict among the Bolsheviks on the subject of philosophy, but I think it would be stupid to split on that account. We have formed a bloc for pursuing a definite policy in the Workers' Party. We have pursued this policy and so far are pursuing it *without any disagreements* (our only disagreement was on the subject of the boycott of the Third Duma[2]) but: (1) it never came to the hint of a split, and (2) it did not correspond with the differences between the Materialists and Machists, for the Machist Bazarov, for instance, was like me against the boycott and he wrote a long article about it in "The Proletariat."

I think it would be unpardonable folly to interfere with the carrying out of the policy of Revolutionary Social Democracy in the Workers' Party for the sake of arguments on Materialism or Machism. We must quarrel over philosophy in such a way that "The Proletariat" and the Bolsheviks as a faction *of the Party would not be affected by it*. And that is quite possible.

I think you ought to assist with this, and you can help by working in "The Proletariat" on neutral (that is unconnected with philosophy) questions of literary criticism, journalism, and artistic creation etc. As for your article—if you want to prevent a split and help to localise a new quarrel—you should alter it: anything even indirectly connected with the Bogdanov philosophy should be printed elsewhere. Thank God, you

---

[1] It was announced that this philosophic argument was not a factional dispute. In both factions, Bolshevik and Menshevik, there were adherents of both philosophic positions.

[2] Lenin was against a boycott of the III Duma. Bogdanov was in favour of a boycott.

have somewhere else where you can write, apart from "The Proletariat." Everything unconnected with Bogdanov's philosophy—and the *greater* part of your article is not connected with it—should be developed in a series of articles for "The Proletariat."

I think that any other action on your part, namely a refusal to alter the article or a refusal to collaborate in "The Proletariat," would inevitably lead to a sharpening of the conflict among the Bolsheviks, would cause a difficulty by localising a new quarrel and would weaken the daily and practically and politically essential work of the Revolutionary Social Democrats in Russia.

That is my opinion. I have told you all I think and I shall wait for your reply.

We wanted to leave here and travel to you today, but we found we had to postpone it for a week, perhaps even for two or three weeks.

I greet you warmly,

Your

N. Lenin

154. (183 R). TO A. I. ELIZAROVA

[*Geneva*], 26th February/10th March, 1908

Darling Anyuta,

I have received your letter of the 21st February/5th March. It is really terrible that you have got into a damp flat and have all fallen ill. And what an anxiety that Manyasha has caught typhoid fever! Lidya Mikhailovna (Knipovich) writes every day and tells me that her temperature is not high. But I am afraid of attributing much consoling importance to this news: after all, there are serious cases of typhoid with low temperatures.

And how is Mother's health? If you are too busy, ask L. M. (since she does write to me) to add a few words about this.

It is really quite unnecessary for Mark to have left such a large sum from his own money, for my publisher is paying me quite enough.[1] It is natural you should spend this money to make Manyasha and Mother more comfortable or to help them to move to a better place. Why should they not come here?

I sent Manyasha a book to translate (a German novel). Have you received it (from Leipzig)?[2] I also wrote to her about a book by Anatole France (La Vie de Jeanne d'Arc) and one by Sinclair (G. A. Alexinsky suggests it should be translated).

I send you greetings and ask you to kiss Mother for me.

Nadya has gone out on business. She asked me to send you her love.

Your

V. Ulianov

155. (212 P[1]). TO A. M. GORKY IN CAPRI, ITALY

[Geneva], 24th March, 1908

My dear A. M.

I have received your letter about my quarrel with the Machists. I quite understand and respect your feelings and I must tell you the Petersburg friends are sending me the same opinions, but I am deeply convinced that you are all mistaken.

You must and you will understand, that once a Party man has become convinced a certain theory is decidedly wrong and harmful, then he is bound to oppose it. I would not have murmured about it, were I not absolutely convinced (which daily increases in me as I come to discover the sources of the wisdom of Bazarov, Bogdanov and Co.) that their book ["Studies of the Philosophy of Marxism"] is foolish, harmful and philistine from beginning to end, from root to branch, to Mach and Avenarius. Plekhanov is quite right in opposing them on principle, only he does not know how to or he does not want to, or he is too lazy to say so *concretely* and in detail, simply and without any excessive frightening of the public by

---

[1] The second edition of Lenin's "Development of Capitalism in Russia" came out in March, 1908.

[2] Lenin was in Leipzig on his way from Finland and Sweden to Geneva in 1908.

using philosophic subtleties. And whatever happens, I shall say this *in my own way*.

How can there be any "reconciliation," dear A. M.? Why, it is even ridiculous to mention it! A fight is *absolutely* inevitable. And Party people should do their utmost not to confuse matters, or postpone, or wriggle away, but should see that the practically essential Party work does not suffer. *You* must see to this and nine-tenths of the Russian Bolsheviks will help you and will thank you.

How can this be done? By neutrality? No, there cannot and *will not be* any neutrality in such a question. If it can be mentioned, then it should be in a specific sense: this quarrel ought to be separated from the faction. So far you have written as one who is outside the faction; continue to do so. It is only in this way that the faction will not be involved, will not be compelled if not today, then tomorrow, to decide, *to vote*, i.e., to make the quarrel chronic, protracted and endless.

This is why I am *against* introducing any kind of philosophy into the journal.[1] I know I am being cursed because of this opinion and they want to shut my mouth before I have had time to open it! But do think it over calmly.

The journal with philosophy No. 1 contains three articles by Bazarov, Bogdanov and Lunacharsky against Plekhanov, and one article by me, where I say that the "Studies of the Philosophy of Marxism" are Berdyaevism and Popovism.

No. 2—contains three times three articles by Bazarov, Bogdanov and Lunacharsky against Plekhanov and Lenin, written in a tense style. Also an article by me, where I prove that the "Studies of the Philosophy of Marxism" are Popovism.

No. 3—wailing and cursing!

I can write six or twelve articles against "The Studies of the Philosophy of Marxism" and an article against each author and each facet of their different views. But is it to drag on like this and for how long? Will not this constant bickering and tension make a split inevitable? Will it not unite the faction by the decision: make up your mind, understand what it is all about and end this discussion by taking a vote.

[1] A Bolshevik journal Gorky proposed, but which was not published.

Think this over carefully, if you are afraid of a split. Would the practical workers undertake to distribute a book containing such an attack? Would not another way be better? Write as you used to do before, without obviously taking sides. Quarrel outside and the faction can *temporarily* wait. If it is possible to mitigate the inevitable anger, then I believe it can be done only in this way.

You say that the Mensheviks will benefit by the fight. You are mistaken, A. M., deeply mistaken. They will win, only if the Bolshevik faction does not separate itself from the philosophy of the three Bolsheviks. *Then* they would definitely win. But if the philosophic quarrel is conducted outside the faction, then the Mensheviks would be finally brought down to politics and that would mean their death.

I say: separate the quarrel from the faction. It is of course rather difficult and painful to create this separation as between strong people. Time is needed. Thoughtful comrades are needed. And here practical people will help. Here you must help. Here is psychology for you and books put into your hands. I think you could help in this and a great deal if, of course, on reading my book against the "Studies" you do not fall into a rage against me, as I fell into a rage against them.

Think carefully about the journal and answer me quickly. I am a little doubtful whether it would be any good for us [Bogdanov and Lenin] to come to see you *now*. What is the use of unnecessarily straining one's nerves? A long journey . . . ending in an inevitable quarrel. Would it not be better to decide more simply the question of the journal, without any long discussions or formal and unnecessary meetings? I put these questions to you simply to get your advice.

Best wishes to M. F.

I will certainly come to Capri and will try to bring my wife, but I should like to do this independently of a philosophic quarrel.

I greet you warmly,

Yours,

Lenin

P.S. I enclose some *important* information about spying at your place.

156. (214 P[1]). TO A. M. GORKY, CAPRI, ITALY

Geneva, 16th April, 1908

My dear A. M.

I received your letter today and I hasten to answer it. It would be both harmful and useless for me to come to you: I cannot and will not talk with people [1] who have begun to advocate combining scientific socialism with religion. The time for exercise books is over.[2] We must not argue, it is stupid to strain the nerves unnecessarily. Philosophy must be *separated* from Party (factional) affairs. The decision of the Bolshevik centre also compels us to do this.[3]

I have already sent to press a most formal declaration of war [an article against the philosophy of Bogdanov, Bazarov, and others: "Marxism and Revisionism"]. Diplomacy is out of place here. Of course I do not mean diplomacy in a bad sense, but in a good one.

Good diplomacy on your part, my dear A. M. (if you have not also begun to believe in a God) must consist in separating our mutual (that is including me) *affairs* from philosophy.

A discussion about other matters, apart from philosophy, is not urgent now: it would be unnatural. But, if these other matters are not philosophic, and if "The Proletariat," for instance, necessitates a conversation with you, I could come to see you. (I do not know if I should be able to find the money: I have difficulties at present). But I repeat, I should come only on condition that I do not talk about philosophy or about religion.

But I am definitely thinking of coming to see you when I am free, after I have finished my work, to have a talk with you.

I greet you warmly.

Your

Lenin

P.S. Good wishes to M. F. [Andreyeva]. She does not stand for God, does she?

---

[1] Bogdanov and Lunacharsky were both there, and Gorky invited Lenin to come and discuss the projected Bolshevik journal.

[2] See Letter 153.

[3] The C.C. of the Bolshevik faction (Lenin, Zinoviev, Bogdanov, Dubrovinsky, Rozhkov, Kamenev and others), elected in May, 1907.

157. (185 R). TO HIS MOTHER

[*Geneva*], *7th/20th June, 1908*

Darling Mother,

I do not seem to have written to you for a long time. I believe the last time was a postcard from London.[1] I arrived from there feeling quite ill with "catarrh" of the kidneys. I have recovered, am eating as I should; I always feel hungry after a diet. I have begun work.

Our life goes on as usual. The weather is most unsettled, at one time stifling heat, then storms, then rain and cold, as it is today. The Summer will not settle down to be Summer.

How are you living in the country? I hope Manyasha has quite recovered. We shall expect her here.

Greetings to Mitya,

I embrace you tenderly, my darling,

        Your

         V. Ulianov

P.S. I am sorry that the Moscow philosopher, the publisher [P. G. Dauge], has refused to publish my book. If possible, I would ask you to write to one of our Moscow literary friends and perhaps they may find a publisher. I have no such links now.

They say Anyuta has finished reading the proofs of my agrarian book [Part 2, Vol. 2, "The Agrarian Question"]. So far I have not had a single copy! And for many reasons it is *most important* for me to have two or three copies, even unbound. Of course I quite understand that in every way it would be most awkward, rash, inconvenient to ask for them direct. But if it could be done somehow privately, or if Anyuta has even one copy—I would ask her to send it to me, if only for a short time. I need it just now very badly.

Greetings from us all,

        Your

         V. Ul.

---

[1] Where Lenin worked on his book "Materialism and Empirio-Criticism," in the British Museum Reading Room.

158. (189 R). TO HIS MOTHER

[The letter has not been preserved.]

P.S. Today I received an amusing serial story about the inhabitants of Mars—based on "Mars and its Canals," a new English book by Lowell. This Lowell is an astronomer, who has been working in a special observatory and, I believe, the best one in the world (America).

It is a scholarly work. It proves that Mars is inhabited, that the canals are engineering marvels, that the people on it are 2-2/3rds. larger than the people here; moreover, they have trunks instead of noses and are covered with feathers or animal skins, with four or six legs. Well, well, our author [A. Bogdanov (A. A. Malinovsky)] has cheated us a bit by not describing the Mars beauties *in full*, probably on the recipe that: "a deception that raises us up is dearer to us than a host of base truths." . . .

"The Last," a new tale by Gorky, has just been published.

159. (190 R). TO A. I. ELIZAROVA

[*Geneva*], *14th/27th October, 1908*

Darling Anyuta,

I am very surprised at your long silence. Probably the move to Moscow was a great bother and you had no time for letters.

Please send me an address to which I can forward the manuscript of my book ["Materialism and Empirio-Criticism"]. It is ready. There are 24 printed sheets (40 thousand letters of the alphabet), i.e., about 400 pages. In about a fortnight's time I shall finish the revision and post it: I should like to have a reliable address to which it could be sent.

The question of a publisher is evidently a difficult one: today I received news that Granat has bought the "History" of the Mensheviks, which means the Mensheviks there have got the upper hand.[1] It is clear that he will now refuse to publish

---

[1] The "History" = The "Social Movement in Russia at the beginning of the 20th Century," edited by Martov, Maslov and Potresov. Granat did not publish this work; the negotiations did not materialise.

my book. Bear in mind that I am no longer interested in the money, i.e., I am agreeable to concessions and to postponement of payment until there is a profit on the book—in a word, the publisher will have absolutely no risks. As for the censorship, I will also agree to *anything*, for everything I have written is quite legal and only certain expressions are unsuitable. (Ergo, make an agreement, if you have the slightest chance, on *any* conditions.)

160. (192 R). TO HIS MOTHER

[*Geneva*], *4th/17th November, 1908*

Darling Mother,

Manyasha has gone to Lausanne today to see Dr. Mermod, a famous specialist in ear diseases. He made an appointment by letter; you have to wait your turn with these local celebrities, but from all accounts he is a sensible doctor. Four years ago I underwent a minor operation in his clinic; they do splendid work. I hope therefore he will be able to help Manya; her ear troubles her considerably and interferes with her work. She has taken a room in our house and on the floor above us; they have put a stove in her room, so it is warm and comfortable. She has dinner and supper with us. She was in trouble over Latin. It appears Latin is compulsory and the examination could be taken only on the 19th November. There were only ten days to that day. I tried to persuade her to risk it by cramming the grammar, for she knows French well. But it seems she could not work intensively, her ear prevented it; besides, the time was so short, that her chances would have been poor. So she gave up Latin; she consoles herself with the fact that we shall probably move to Paris, and she will come too. Latin is not compulsory in Paris. As for our removal, it is almost decided, but we cannot move before another month. Presumably we shall have plenty of trouble with the removal. We hope that a large city will cheer us up a little; we are sick of sitting in this provincial backwater. It is more expensive in Paris, true; the climate probably no worse than in Geneva.

Here the climate is usually damp and the fogs are unpleasant. We must find out what to do with our bicycles. It is a pity to leave them here—they are splendid for recreation and exercise, but the duty would be fairly high. However, I hope to arrange this. Please tell Anyuta that the philosophical manuscript has already been sent to the acquaintance [V. A. Levitsky] who lived in the small town where we met before I left for Krasnoyarsk [Ufa] in 1900. I hope he has received it and delivered it to you; if not, you must find out; he lives not far from you. I do ask you to send me a few words as soon as you receive the manuscript. I wrote to two friends [L. Kamenev and ?] in Petersburg asking them to help to arrange for the publication. I told them to get into touch with Anyuta if anything were to happen through our mutual friend [Bonch-Bruevich] working on "Znaniye." I scarcely expect anything from "Znaniye" itself; "the Boss" [the manager, K. P. Pyatnitsky] who gave a half promise to Anyuta is a sly fox and, having smelt the air on Capri, where Gorky lives, he will probably refuse.[1] We shall have to look elsewhere. I have written that I am prepared to make any concessions.

I embrace you tenderly, my darling, and wish you good health.

Your,

V. Ul.

161. (195 R). TO A. I. ELIZAROVA

[Paris], 6th/19th December, 1908

Darling Anyuta,

I received your letter today forwarded from Geneva and a postcard sent to Manya. So everything is settled and signed? That is excellent. I wrote to you about the corrections in the letter which has gone astray. I will repeat what I then said: I agree to my remarks [in "Materialism and Empirio-Criticism"] about Bazarov and Bogdanov being toned down; with

---

[1] After the August plenum of the C.C. the Otzovists and Ultimatists began to take steps to organise a Party school on Capri, which was an attempt on the part of Bogdanov, Alexinsky and Lunacharsky to create their own factional organisation as a counterbalance to the Bolshevik centre.

regard to Yushkevich [Social Democrat, Menshevik] and Valentinov [Menshevik, an orthodox Machist] it is not worth altering what I said. So far as "Fideism" etc. is concerned, I agree only on compulsion, i.e., if the publisher issues an ultimatum. As for the proofs, I do not intend to correct them here and make the publishers wait for them. That is probably impossible. I would ask you to send the galley as soon as it has been printed (meaning the first uncorrected offprint as well as sending the sheets as they are printed) so that in case of need I may be able to send a telegram to let you know about the misprints etc. "Cauwelart" will have to be corrected to "Couwelart," although he is probably Flemish and the devil only knows whether in that language it should be "Cau . . ." or "Cou . . ."[1]

I sent you from Geneva and to the right address a letter containing corrections and additions. Did you receive it?

We are just moving from the hotel to our new flat: Mr. Vl. Oulianoff, 24 Rue Beaunier, Paris (XIVme), au deuxième au-dessus de l'entresol. We have found a very good flat, grand and expensive (840 francs, plus a tax of about 60 francs, plus about the same to the concierge). According to Moscow standards it is cheap (four rooms, kitchen plus cupboards, larders, water, gas), but it is expensive for Paris. It has plenty of space and will, we hope, be comfortable. We bought some furniture yesterday for Manyasha, and our furniture has been brought from Geneva. The flat is almost on the edge of Paris, on the South side, near to the Park "Montsouris." It is as quiet as in the provinces, very far from the centre, but they will soon bring the metro, the underground electric railway, two yards away from us. There are however all sorts of ways of getting about. So far we are pleased with Paris.

I greet you warmly. All our people send greetings,
Kiss Mother for me,

Your

V. Ul.

Leave what I say about Purishkevich. I agree to qualify the

---

[1] Couwelart, F. von, a professor of psychology in Freiburg.

swearing, also the indecent expressions. "I invented God"—
will have to be altered to: "I have invented for myself" . . .
well, shall we say mildly, "religious conceptions," or to something of the sort.

1909

162. (202 R). TO A. I. ELIZAROVA

[Paris], 25th February/19th March, 1909

Darling Anyuta,

I arrived in Paris last night (after a magnificent rest in Nice)
and read your letter of the 16th.

I am sending you the corrections to the printed sheets 10
and 11, made up into pages. Only two are important. The
title of Bogdanov's book is "Empirio-Monism" and not
"Empirio-Criticism." It is *essential* to rectify this misprint in
the list of errata if it is too late to correct it. (I do not know
whether you received my postcard from Nice—I sent you two
postcards from there. On one of them I pointed out this misprint.) The second—page 170, line 9, from above, the word
"this" is not necessary in the quotation from Plekhanov.

As for passing on the proof reading, you are, of course, right
to make all arrangements for this, because it must be incredibly
difficult to combine such tedious and laborious work with
looking after Mother. I can only marvel how the last proofs
were so exemplary, when you have to work in such trying
circumstances. The most important thing for me is the speedy
publication of the book ["Materialism and Empirio-Criticism"]. There has already been too much delay. If only it
could appear by the 15th March (old style)! If it doesn't, it
will be too bad! With regard to the fine for a breach of contract, I do not really know if it can be exacted. I doubt it. And
besides, is it worth spoiling one's relations with the publishers?
No, it is not.

Have you stopped sending me any proofs during the last
few days on account of my being away? I hope this *is* the

reason, and not a delay at the printers. Please send them all now.

I see from Mitya's letter that Mother's health is improving. At last! I kiss Mother and send you all much love.

Your,
V. U.

P.S. Please do not tone down the passages against Bogdanov and Lunacharsky's "Popovshchina." Our relations with them are *completely* severed. It is not worth while modifying the passages.

P.P.S. A thousand thanks to "The Writer" for agreeing to help. He seems to be a real Marxist and not "a Marxist for an hour" as certain others. Present him at once with a copy of my book. I enclose corrections to sheets 10 and 11 made up into pages.

163. (211 R). TO A. I. ELIZAROVA

[*Paris*], *13th/26th May, 1909*

Darling Anyuta,

I received your letter a few days after posting a letter to Mother in Alupka.

I have received the book and find it has been well produced. There are no less misprints at the end of the book than at the beginning and the proof reader's ignorance of languages is obvious! (e.g. the English "a new name for old ways of thinking" has been ridiculously mutilated, but that is an inevitable and unimportant fault). On the whole I am pleased with the publication. Everybody complains about the price—and rightly so. In future we shall have to include in the agreement, not only the number of copies, but also the price. But I was forced by the publisher and in any case would have agreed to *any* conditions, so long as the work was published.

The publisher has not sent any money yet. I am beginning to feel anxious lest he swindles me.[1] I have written to Peres.[2]

---

[1] Lenin was paid in full.
[2] A Bolshevik in Moscow connected with the book trade.

Do please also write to the publisher: three or four weeks have passed, but he promised to write in a week's time. (You must take a bill of exchange for the remaining sum.) I ask you please to send me five hundred roubles from the deposit account (Credit Lyonnais, Agence Z, Avenue d'Orleans, 19, Mr. Oulianoff. Current account No. 6420), for I cannot depend on the publisher.

Our affairs at present are in a sorry state. There will probably be a split[1]; in about a month to six weeks' time, I hope to give you detailed information about this. Meanwhile one cannot go further than surmise. . . .

Manyasha is cramming hard: she is well and will probably pass her examination. What she will do after that, I do not know. I think she wants to return home.

We have not yet decided when and where we shall go to the seaside.[2] But we shall definitely go away in the Summer.

I kiss Mother warmly and send you my greetings,

Your
V. Ul.

164. (212 R). TO D. I. ULIANOV

[Paris, (June-beginning of July/1909]

My dear Mitya,

Manyasha has already written to you about her illness. I also want to consult you. The doctors find she has inflammation of the outgrowth of the blind intestine (appendicitis—is not that right?). I consulted a very good local surgeon. He confirmed: appendicitis. He advises an operation. They all say it is not dangerous and that the cure is definite.

The surgeon (Dr. Dubouchez) is greatly praised by all. He recently performed the same operation on the wife of a friend of ours—excellently; a teaspoonful of blood; she began to get up after eight days. The hospital is a good one.

---

[1] At a meeting of the editors of "The Proletariat" on the 4-13th July, 1909, there was a definite differentiation from the Ultimatists and Otzovists, from Bogdanov and his group.

[2] Lenin, Krupskaya, his mother-in-law and Manyasha spent the Summer of 1909 in Bonbon, a village near Paris.

The attack is not acute at the moment. *No* raised temperature. The pain is very acute. I ask you to reply *at once*. I am in favour of an operation, but I am nervous of deciding without your advice. *Answer at once.*

The operation will undoubtedly be well done here. The doctor does not advise travelling before the operation.

I am not writing to Mother, for I am afraid of unduly alarming her. There is no danger whatsoever—Manyasha is not even in bed all the time—I am also not writing to Anyuta, for Mother might read the letter.

Please write to Mark and—through him (if that can be done so as not to frighten Mother)—to Anyuta. But perhaps it would be better not to write at all to the Crimea for they will all get a fright.

And so I await your answer; they advise hurrying with the operation here. Do you advise the same?

I greet you warmly,

Your

V. Ul.

165. (214 R). TO HIS MOTHER

Bonbon, Département Seine et Loire, 11th/24th August, 1909

Darling Mother,

Yesterday I received your letter and I am answering it by the first post. You are worrying unnecessarily about Manyasha; she is recovering satisfactorily. It is true she cannot walk much yet: she still feels some pain in the leg (the right one). We asked the doctors both in Paris and here in the country whether this indicated anything serious. They all said no, it did not. They feel that the recovery is normal, only somewhat slower than usual. They advised her to wear a bandage so that there would be less shaking when she moved. She walked about five or six versts yesterday, slept splendidly afterwards and feels all right; altogether she looks *incomparably* better, her appetite and sleep are good and she looks quite well. In short, I am writing *absolutely frankly* to you, everything is progressing splendidly, only slowly. This can

probably be explained by her severe exhaustion during the
Winter. We are having a good rest. We have already spent
three weeks here and are thinking of staying another two,
perhaps three. I cannot say yet whether Manyasha will be able
to go to Russia in a month's time or not. She has improved
vastly in health during the three weeks. I keep advising her
to drink more milk and to eat youghourt. She prepares it for
herself, but in my opinion she does not eat enough and she and
I constantly squabble about this. Our rooms are good. The
pension is good and inexpensive (ten francs a day for the four
of us). Nadya and I often go for bicycle rides.

I embrace you, my darling, and wish you good health,

Your

V. U.

P.S. What news have you from Mark? Has he quite recovered after his operation? Greetings to him from us all.

1910

166. (221 R). TO M. I. ULIANOVA

[*Paris, the beginning of 1910*]

Darling Manyasha,

I received your postcard, thanks for the news. As for the
bicycle, I thought I should soon receive compensation, but the
matter has been protracted. I am having a law-suit about
it. I hope to win the case. I was riding from Juvisy and a
motor car crashed into my bicycle. (I managed to jump off
in time.) The crowd helped me by giving me the number of
the car and witnesses came forward. I recognised the owner
of the car (a Viscount—the devil take him!) and I have brought
an action against him (through a lawyer). In any case I should
not be riding about now: it is cold (but it is a fine Winter,
delightful for walks).

I enclose the exact title of two books on the subject of agriculture, which I urgently need. Have you managed to find
someone who can get hold of them?

I send you warm greetings.

Kiss Mother for me. Is she freezing in your flat?

Your

V. U.

(1) "A Survey of the Activities of the Main Department of Agriculture for the Years 1907 and 1908," S.P.B., 1909 and

(2) "A Survey of the Activities of Local Land Commissions (1907-1908)."

(I am not sure whether these are one and the same book. If there *are* two books, then the second is more important for me.)

(3) "The Annual of the Main Department of Agriculture," S.P.B., 1908.

167. (223 R). TO M. I. ULIANOVA

[Paris], 17th/30th or 18th/31st January, 1910

Darling Manyasha,

A few days ago I received your letter and kept meaning to answer it, but lately I have been busy with an urgent matter [the meeting of the C.C. plenum of the R.S.D.L.P.] and I could not snatch a free hour. I have also received the Historian's letter and will answer him—(tell him this when you have an opportunity). But now (at this moment) I cannot sit down to it.

I have had a letter from Mitya and was most surprised to hear about his accident.[1] He writes that he is on the mend and will soon be learning to walk again. Write to me please and tell me how he progresses. Has he lost his job or are they keeping it open for him and will they wait until he recovers? Will he be able, when he recovers, to travel round his district as before?

You write nothing about Anyuta. I too have heard nothing from her for a long time. Does she like being in a new town [Saratov]? How is Mother's health at present? Has she recovered from influenza?

We have had (and it is still continuing) a flood in Paris

---

[1] Dymitry broke his leg and collar-bone.

such as has not been seen for a long time. You probably know about it from the newspapers. Twice I went as far as the Seine (the trams are running on a shortened route; the metro and electric railways have stopped). "Venice in Paris" is really very strange. Masses of people are unemployed. Probably when the water subsides, there will be all sorts of calamities: earth subsidences etc.

Our life goes on quietly. Nadya runs to all the schools where they are teaching French and is getting on with it very persistently.

My bicycle law-suit has ended in my favour. I have received the Moscow town statistics; many thanks.

Kiss Mother warmly for me,
    Much love from us all,

                                        Your

                                        V. U.

Forgive me for writing scrappily. Have been called away.

168. (224 R). TO A. I. ELIZAROVA

Paris, 19th January/1st February, 1910

Darling Anyuta,

We have had a very "stormy" time lately, but it has ended in an attempt at peace with the Mensheviks. Yes, yes, strange though it may seem; the factional Organ has been closed down and we are trying hard to move towards union.[1] We shall see whether we shall succeed. I freed myself recently from very urgent matters in view of these changes.

Paris is a rotten hole in many respects. . . . I have still not been able to adapt myself to Paris (a year since settling here) but all the same, I feel that only special circumstances will drive me back to Geneva.

---

[1] At the C.C. plenum meetings of the R.S.D.L.P. in Paris (Jan. 15-5 Feb., 1910).

169. (223 P[1]). TO PLEKHANOV IN SAN REMO, ITALY

[Paris], 29th March, 1910

My dear and much respected Comrade,

I fully share your thoughts expressed in Number 11 of "The Diary [of a S.D.]" on the need for a close and sincere union between all true Social Democratic elements in the struggle against Liquidators and Otzovism.[1]

I should very much like to talk to you about the recently arisen position of affairs in the Party. If you too think it is necessary, and if your health allows it, will you write (or wire) a few words to me, saying when you can arrange a meeting in San Remo. I am ready to come to you for this purpose.

With comradely greetings,

N. Lenin

Vl. Oulianoff,
    4, rue Marie Rose,
       Paris XIV.

170. (224 P[1]). TO N. E. VILONOV IN DAVOS

[Paris], 7th April, 1910

My dear Comrade,

I am sending you the resolution of our local Plekhanovites, or more exactly the Mensheviks.[2] If it is true that you in Davos have a predominance of Party people among the Mensheviks, then it would be most important if they would immediately speak up and in one way or another come out in the open. Presumably the Bolsheviks must be very careful in approaching the Mensheviks with such advice, for even among the Plekhanovites there is no more terrible, terrifying and intolerable accusation than that of helping the Bolsheviks, or of working for the Bolsheviks etc.

[1] Lenin refers to Plekhanov's article, "The Last Plenary Meeting of our Central Committee."

[2] In the interests of abolishing factions the resolution demanded the closing down of "The Voice of Social Democracy" as an Organ of a definite political line.

In the present muddled state there are, I believe, only two ways out: either back to our Bolshevik faction, or a *definite battle* with the Plekhanovites against the voters for the Party. The second is more desirable, but does not depend on us. While it is possible, we will do all that we can for the second way out. Only after exhausting all the possibilities, all the means for the second way out, will we return to the first. I am very glad that an acquaintance with pragmatism has begun to put you off Machism. All these "newest" philosophic bounders are now being translated in Russia: Petzold and Co., the pragmatists etc. That is good: when the Russian public and the Russian workers in particular see the works of these teachers of Bogdanov and Co., they will very rapidly turn away from the masters as well as from the pupils.

To consider truth as the instrument of knowledge means to go over to the side of agnosticism—i.e., to forsake materialism. In this and in all fundamentals the pragmatists, Machists, Empirio-Monists—are berries from the same field.

I greet you warmly and send you good wishes for a thorough and speedy recovery.

Your

N. Lenin

171. (225 P[1]). TO M. M. ZOLINA, N. VILONOV'S WIFE, IN DAVOS, SWITZERLAND

Paris, 30th April, 1910

My dear Comrade,

Thank you for letting me know about Mikhail's [N. E. Vilonov's] position. I immediately took steps for a subsidy to be granted to him. This is how the matter stands: it is hopeless to pass the matter through the Central Committee's Bureau abroad, for we are now in the minority there. There was an opportunity of communicating with Russia and I sent a message to the Russian Central Committee that they should grant a subsidy for Mikhail. I hope to have a favourable reply in about a fortnight. *In any case* it would be essential to see that

Mikhail continues his treatment and remains meanwhile in Davos until he recovers completely.

I greet you,

Your

N. Lenin

My address: Mr. Vl. Oulianoff,
4, Rue Marie Rose,
Paris XIV.

172. (231 R). TO HIS MOTHER

[Paris], *5th/18th June*, *1910*

Darling Mother,

We send you, Anyuta and Mitya, greetings from a Sunday walk. Nadya and I are on bicycles. The Medon forest is beautiful and quite near—45 minutes from Paris. I have received Anyuta's letter and answered it.

I kiss you both for myself and for Nadya,

Your

V. U.

173. (232 R). TO M. I. ULIANOVA

[Pornic], *15th/28th July*, *1910*

Darling Manyasha,

I am writing to you from Pornic.[1] It is almost a week since E. V., Nadya and I settled here. We are having a wonderful rest. We bathe, etc. How are your affairs? How is Mother's health? How are the Copenhagen and Stockholm questions? Write Pornic (Loire inférieure) Rue Mon Désir, K, Les Roses, Mr. Oulianoff.

Greetings to all,

Your,

V. U.

I wrote a week ago from Paris to Mother at Mikhnevo. Has the letter been received?

---

[1] Where Lenin spent a fortnight with Krupskaya and her mother.

174. (233 R). P. C. TO HIS MOTHER

[*Naples*], *19th July/1st August, 1910*

Darling Mother,

I send much love from Naples. I arrived here by steamer from Marseilles; cheap and pleasant. It was like travelling down the Volga. I am going from here to Capri for a short time.

I hug you,

Love to all,

Your

V. U.

175. (234 R). TO HIS MOTHER

[*Copenhagen*], *22nd August/4th September, 1910*

Darling Mother,

I send you and Anyuta much love from Copenhagen. The Congress ended yesterday.[1] I am at last in correspondence with Manyasha: on the 4th September (old style), i.e. 17th September (our style here) I am expecting you on the landing stage at Stockholm. A comrade will find two rooms for me for the week 17th-24th September. Manyasha has my address here. Write to me Hr. Ulianof, Poste Restante, Stockholm.

I kiss you. We shall soon meet.

I shall stay here until the 15/9/1910.

Your

V. U.

176. (230 P[1]). TO G. L. SHKLOVSKY IN BERNE

[*Paris*], *14th October, 1910*

My dear Comrade,

Many thanks for your letter and news about the Plekhanov agitation. All such information is most valuable to us for it

---

[1] The Copenhagen VIII Congress of the II International.

allows us to apprise correctly the mood of the Social Democrats abroad. I am thinking of going to Switzerland to lecture (in Geneva, Lausanne, Berne, Zürich). I do not know if the trip will pay for itself.[1]

As for the Plekhanov bloc, I think you are quite right that we must be on the side of the bloc. Since 1909 I have been standing *completely* for a rapprochement with the Plekhanovites. And now still more so. Only with the Plekhanovites can we and must we build the Party—it is high time for us to give up hoping to agree with the Vperedovites and the Liquidators. It is a mistake to think that the Plekhanovites are weak, cyphers, (as it is sometimes said) etc. That is an impression abroad. I am deeply convinced that the Menshevik workers in Russia are nine-tenths Plekhanovites. The whole history of Menshevism in the Revolution vouches for the fact that Plekhanovism is the best product (and therefore the most vital) from the proletarian source of the Mensheviks.

In Copenhagen [at the International Socialist Congress, 28 Aug.-3 Sept.] Plekhanov and I spoke about the publication of a popular newspaper. It is essential. (Trotsky has openly moved towards the Liquidators, to the support of the "Golos" people to breaking the Party bloc of the Bolsheviks and Plekhanovites). Plekhanov and I fully agree that we cannot do anything about Trotsky. We will either organise a popular newspaper together with the Central Organ or *separately* from the group of Bolsheviks. Plekhanov promised to collaborate. We shall need money—we have just a little. I hope I shall have every assistance from you. We are struggling hard to have a journal in Russia (like "Vozrozhdeniye" and "Zhizn"). There is no link, no secretary, no one through whom we could arrange this—our people keep failing us. It is terrible! But the journal is absolutely necessary.[2]

---

[1] Lenin lectured in Switzerland in the second half of November, 1910.

[2] "Vozrozhdeniye" ("Resurrection") was a legal Menshevik-Liquidator journal published in Moscow, 1908-10. When it was banned in 1910, the Liquidators began publishing "Zhizn" ("Life"). Lenin wanted a legal Bolshevik journal. As a result, a social, economic and philosophic monthly journal, "Mysl" ("Thought") began to appear in Dec., 1910.

I send you greetings.

Your

Lenin

177. (235 R). TO MARK ELIZAROV

[Paris], 20th December/3rd January, 1910/1911

My dear M. T.

Many thanks for your letter. One feels quite cut off here, so that your tales, impressions and observations "From the Volga" (how I miss the Volga!) are real balsam. Your observations are most interesting, especially as they have been collected as a result of various business meetings and travel, without any preconceived aim. Your letter in the Summer also gave me great joy and I feel very guilty for not having been able to sit down and answer it on account of my travels between the sea and Paris, from Paris to Copenhagen and Stockholm.

As for my journey to Italy, it will evidently not come off (either now or in the near future). My finances (about which, by the way, Anya asked me) will not permit it. I have not found a publisher [for "The Agrarian Question in the first Russian Revolution"]. I have sent an article to the "Sovremenny Mir"[1] but evidently there are difficulties there too; I have had no reply for several weeks. I shall have to put off long distance journeys until better times. But Italy is no distance from here: surely you will come to Paris, if you decide to go to Italy. And it must be a true saying that whoever has been to Paris once will be drawn a second time.

It would really be better for Manyasha to rest a little longer in Saratov and not to be in a hurry to leave; it would be better in every way.

Our life goes on as usual. Nothing very exciting. Times have lately been particularly full of squabbles, so I beg you to excuse me for the irregularity of my correspondence: I have

---

[1] The leading literary Mensheviks contributed to this journal. During the period of rapprochement with the Plekhanovites, the Bolsheviks also collaborated.

not answered Anyuta, who told me about the unsuccessful negotiations with Lvovich [a publisher]. I have not written to Mother for a long time. Almost all the family is with you now, so please give them my apologies. Much love to Anya, Manyasha and a kiss to Mother.

I greet you warmly,

Your

V. U.

Mother told me in Stockholm about your struggle with the principal. Once funds have gone up, this means an improvement. Congratulations! You will get rid of unpleasantness! A happy New Year! A happy New Year *to all*.

Yesterday I received No. 1 "Zvezda"[1] from Russia and today No. 1 "Mysl."[2] That is what makes me happy! I hope you too have seen them. It is very consoling.

[1] A Bolshevik legal newspaper in Petersburg (29 Dec., 1910-18 Oct., 1912) to which Lenin contributed an article "Differences of Opinion in the European Labour Movement."

[2] A Bolshevik legal monthly published in Moscow. The editing was wholly in the hands of the Bolshevik centre abroad (Lenin, Zinoviev, Kamenev). Only 5 numbers appeared. No. 5 (April, 1911) was confiscated. No. 1 contained Lenin's article "On the Statistics of Strikes in Russia."

THE PERIOD OF THE DEVELOPMENT OF THE WORKERS' MOVEMENT

1911–1914

SUMMARY

1911

Growth of Imperialistic tendencies among the Liberal bourgeoisie.

June 10-17: Meeting of C.C. members in Paris resolves to re-organise Bureau of C.C. abroad and to convene an All-Party Conference for creating a new C.C.

Final split in Central Party's organisations.

Summer: Party School in Paris, Long-jumeau.

Nov. 5: Stolypin killed.

Dec. 27: Conference of Bolshevik groups abroad. Paris.

1912

Renewed activity in the Workers' movement.

Jan.: Prague Conference of Party Workers. Bolsheviks sever their connection with the Mensheviks and become an autonomous political party. Decision to take part in elections to IV Duma.

March: Paris Conference of the Opposition: Plekhanovites, "Vpered" groups, Trotskyites, Bundites and representatives of "The Social Democrat" decide not to acknowledge Prague Conference resolutions.

April: Workers shot down at Lena gold-fields.

Wave of political workers' strikes.

1911

May: Breaks off relations with the Bureau of the Central Committee abroad which was controlled by the Liquidators and had opposed the convening of the Plenum. Calls a conference of Central Committee members.

Lectures at Party School on political economy, Marx, the Agrarian question and the Theory and Practice of Socialism.

Sept. 23-24: Attends meeting of International Socialist Bureau, Zürich.

Dec.: Reports at Conference on Internal Party situation and attacks Liquidators.

1912

Active at Prague Conference as head of C.C. of Party. Elected representative in International Socialist Bureau. Becomes the recognised leader of the proletariat.

THE RUSSIAN REVOLUTIONARY MOVEMENT	LENIN'S LIFE
April 22: "Pravda" No. 1 appears, S.P.B. (Legal Bolshevik organ). June 23: Law of State Insurance of Workers passed.	Contributes frequent articles to "Pravda."
Aug.: Vienna Congress of "Vpered" group. Trotskyites and Mensheviks.	July: Moves from Paris to Galicia to be nearer to Russia and to have greater influence on the revolutionary movement there. Writes a pamphlet on "The present situation in the R.S.D.L.P." Writes articles against Mensheviks and defends the Party policy.
13 S.D.'s elected to IV Duma (6 Bolsheviks). "Luch" ("The Ray") newspaper published. "Pravda" banned.	Controls activities of Bolshevik deputies.

1913	**1913**
Growth of Workers' movement continues. Increased strikes. Dec. 28-Jan. 1: Cracow meeting of C.C. of the R.S.D.L.P. (Lenin, Zinoviev, Krupskaya, Stalin, Malinovsky, Badayev, Petrovsky, Lobov, Medvedev, Troyanovsky, Rozmirovich).	Active participation in work of C.C., constant relations with worker deputies in IV Duma. Writes for "Pravda" and "Prosveshcheniye" ("Enlightenment").
	May: Moves from Cracow to Poronin in Galicia.
Split among "Vpered" group.	June-Aug.: Lectures in Switzerland on the national question.
July: Private meeting of C.C. members held in Poronin, Galicia, (Lenin, Zinoviev, Kamenev, Krupskaya, Malinovsky).	Aug. 5: Speaks on internal Party situation at Berne, Conference of the Organisations of the R.S.D.L.P. abroad.
Aug. 25: No. 1 "Nash Put" ("Our Path") appears in Moscow. Sept.: Arrival of the 6 Bolshevik Duma deputies in Poronin, Galicia. Sept. 25-Oct. 1: Meeting of Bolsheviks in village Dunaets, Galicia. Oct. 1: Meeting of C.C.	Oct. 13: Lenin conducts Summer Conference of C.C. and Party Workers in Poronin. Nov.: In Cracow.

Nov. 1: Meeting of C.C.

1914
The revolutionary movement increases. Political strikes and demonstrations more frequent.

Summer: Strikes in central textile region, Baku and S.P.B.
June: International Socialist Bureau convenes a unifying Conference in Brussels of all sections of Russian Social Democracy. The Bolshevik delegates on Lenin's instructions present an ultimatum that the C.C. be acknowledged as the sole controlling Party centre and to abolish the Menshevik centre. The Conference is a failure.
July: "Pravda" is banned.
Aug.: Outbreak of European Great War.

1914
In Galicia.
Struggles for Bolshevik Party with the leaders of the II International. Contributions to "Pravda" and "Prosveshcheniye."

1911

178. (236 R). TO HIS MOTHER

[Paris], 6th/19th January, 1911

Darling Mother,

I have just received your letter. Nadya thanks you very much and sends you her love. As for me, I am hurrying to put right the misunderstanding which I have evidently unwittingly caused. Please do not send me any money. I do not need any at present. I wrote that I could neither place my book nor article—this was in one of my last letters. In the last letter I wrote that they had said my article was to be accepted. I have written to Gorky about the book ["The Agrarian Question in the first Russian Revolution"] and am hoping to have a favourable reply. In any case my position is not any worse *now*; I am not in need. And I beg you, my darling, not to send anything and not to economise out of your pension. If things become difficult I shall write frankly, but that is not the case now. It is not easy to find a publisher, but I will keep on looking for one—besides I *continue* to receive the same salary[1] about which I spoke to you in Stockholm. So please do not worry.

Nadya has written twice to Manyasha and is writing again today. Is Manyasha receiving these [chemical] letters?

I am very glad that Mitya sends good news about his transfer.

With much love from us all to Mark and Anyuta.

We are all well. Our life goes on as usual.

Yesterday I gave a lecture here on Tolstoy—perhaps I shall tour Switzerland with the same lecture.[2]

The weather is not so bad here. Dry cold (our flat is very warm), quite nice for walking.

I embrace you, my darling, and wish you good health,

Your
V. U.

P.S. Tania's Mother has fallen ill in Moscow.[3]

179. (240 R). TO HIS MOTHER

[*Lucerne*], *10th/23rd September, 1911*

Darling Mother,

I am writing from Lucerne, having found myself unexpectedly in Switzerland [on the occasion of the meeting of the International Socialist Bureau in Zürich]. I am on a lecture tour.[4]

I climbed Pilatus yesterday (2,122 metres). So far the weather is wonderful and I am having wonderful walks.

I kiss you warmly and send much love to all.

Your
V. U.

---

[1] The Party salary which Lenin received when he had no other sources of income.
[2] Lenin did not lecture in Switzerland on Tolstoy.
[3] This refers to the arrest of Sofia Smidovich, an active Bolshevik.
[4] Lenin lectured on "Stolypin and the Revolution" in Zürich (26 Sept.), in Geneva (2 October) and in Paris (31 Oct.).

180. (6 P²). TO A. M. GORKY, CAPRI, ITALY

[Paris], 15th September, 1911

My dear A. M.

It must be nearly two months since I last wrote to you—at the beginning of the school[1] (which is now over and the people attending it have left). There was no reply, so I wondered whether the "conversations" had been protracted or whether something had altered radically.[2] Leshchenko [a Bolshevik] was here the other day and told us about Capri and I was very glad to hear that it was all due to the postponement of your meeting after the Fair.[3] Leshchenko said the plans on Capri were the same as before: a large periodical and a large newspaper and also a farthing newspaper.

Yes, this appears to be the right moment. The Liquidators are buying the Kiev farthing newspaper (so they say in Petersburg, from where we heard this morning) and they are transferring it to Petersburg. It is most important to organise resistance against this.

So far we have only been able to get hold of some money to renew the "Zvezda." I count upon your help. Please send an article. It is particularly important to have your support at the beginning, for it will not be easy to restart an interrupted publication.

Have you received and have you read [L. B.] Kamenev's pamphlet ["Two Parties" with a preface by Lenin]? I hope it will dispel certain prejudices which you evidently hold against the author.

We are in a thorough mess so far as Party matters are concerned, but all the same we are nearer to a solution. Plekhanov is wriggling: he is always like that before a solution. It is like

---

[1] The Party school at Longjumeau, near Paris, was organised by the Bolshevik centre in the Summer of 1911 for workers who had come from Russia. Lenin lectured on political economy, the agrarian question, on the theory and practice of socialism.

[2] Gorky's conversations in connection with the plan to publish a journal in Russia and a daily newspaper in which Lenin was to collaborate. These plans were not realised.

[3] Evidently the June meeting of the members of the C.C. of the R.S.D.L.P. in Paris (10-17 June, 1911).

a disease. Martov has sent Kautsky and Zetkin a typescript translation of his pamphlet ["Saviours or Destroyers"], which has greatly helped us: both Kautsky and Zetkin cursed our pamphlet, the former calling it "revolting" and the latter calling it "dirty." [1]

Well, best wishes to you. Write for the "Zvezda." Write me a few lines, if you are not too lazy. Greetings to Marie Fedorovna [Andreyeva].

Your

Lenin

181. (31 P[2]). TO A. NEMETS [2] IN PRAGUE

Paris, 1st November, 1911

Dear Comrade,

I should be much obliged if you would assist me with your advice and help in the following matter: several sections of our Party intend to convene a Conference (abroad of course).[3] The number of Conference members will be from twenty to twenty-five. Would it be possible to organise the Conference in Prague? (It would last about a week.)

It is very important for us to organise the affair arch-conspiratorially. No one, not a single organisation, must get to hear of it (the Conference is to be *Social-Democratic* and consequently legal, according to European laws, but most of the delegates do not possess *passports* and cannot give their real names).

I would ask you, dear comrade, if you think it is possible, to help us and to let us know as soon as you can the address of a comrade in Paris, who (in the event of an answer in the affirmative) could arrange this matter practically. It would be best if the comrade understood Russian:—but if that is impossible, we could make ourselves understood in German.

---

[1] Martov's pamphlet which appeared in Paris in the Summer of 1911 was devoted to the inter-Party strife. Kamenev's pamphlet was an answer to it.

[2] One of the 3 representatives from the Czech Social Democracy in the International Socialist Bureau. Editor of the C.O. of the Czech Social-Democratic Party.

[3] The All-Russia Conference of the R.S.D.L.P. in Prague, 18-30 January, 1912.

I hope, dear comrade, you will forgive my troubling you with this request. I thank you in advance.

With Party greetings,

N. Lenin

1912

182. (241 R). TO HIS MOTHER

[Paris], 23rd or 24th February/8th or 9th March, 1912

Darling Mother,

The other day we received another gift from you—fish, caviare and dried sturgeon. Many thanks. We are now eating these delicacies and while enjoying them we think of the Volga. This year you have spoilt us with home products!

How are you living? Judging by the newspapers you have frost and snow. It is almost Spring here. About a week ago I cleaned up my bicycle and went out to the Bois de Verrières (Manyasha has been there) and I brought back with me some willow catkins. I went again today with Nadya—the cherry blossom is already out. The weather is Springlike, but unreliable; much rain.

Where are you going to in the Summer? E. V. [Krupskaya's mother] is thinking of going to Russia, but I do not think it will come off. We are thinking of sending her to friends in Arcachon, in the South of France.

Is everyone well? I kiss you warmly, my darling.

Much love to Anyuta, Manyasha and Mark, also to Mitya.

Your,

V. U.

P.S. Nadya and E. V. send much love.

183. (243 R). TO A. I. ELIZAROVA

Paris, 11th/24th March, 1912

I have been sitting at home lately working on a translation [?] and I have seen little of what is going on in Paris. Besides, there is so much squabbling going on among our people and such mud slinging as has not happened for a long time, if it ever was as it is now. All the groups and sub-groups are up in arms against the last Conference and its organisers, so that matters literally reached fighting pitch at the local meetings.[1] In short, there is so little of interest, never mind anything good, that it is not worth writing.

184. (244 R). TO HIS MOTHER

[Paris], 25th March/7th April, 1912

Darling Mother,

You will probably receive this round about April 11th (old style). I can congratulate both you and Manyasha on your Namesday. I kiss you and send you my best wishes.

What is the Spring like on the Volga? Are you all well? Each day I have grown used to looking at the Saratov weather report in the "Rech" and I see it is still cold where you are.

I believe Spring is early here this year. The other day I again went a bicycle ride into the forest. All the fruit trees in the gardens are in white blossom (as though milk had been poured over them), the perfume was wonderful. How delightful Spring is! It is a pity I was alone. Nadya has caught cold and has lost her voice.

We are planning to go to Fontenay for the Summer—near Paris, and we are thinking of settling there for a whole year.[2] Life is expensive in Paris—our rent was raised—besides, a suburb will probably be healthier and quieter. One of these days I shall cycle out and look for a place.

We have waited for a long letter from Manyasha—it has not come. I am sending her a prospectus—all I could find. Are Mark and Anya well? What news of Mitya?

[1] This refers to the campaign between the Liquidators and the others against the All-Russia Conference of the R.S.D.L.P. in Prague, in January, 1912. The Central Party apparatus was re-established at the conference. It was also decided to have a daily paper ("Pravda") instead of the weekly "Zvezda." "Pravda" appeared in April, 1912.

[2] This did not take place. Lenin moved to Cracow.

Once again, I kiss you warmly. Much love to all,

Your
V. U.

185. (32 P²). TO K. HUYSMANS IN BRUSSELS

[Paris, End of March, 1912]

Dear Comrade Huysmans,

Thank you for sending the Paris "resolution."[1] As I have already told you, the Conference of the R.S.D.L.P. has condemned the Liquidators and various groups abroad who brought disorganisation into our Party and who do not represent anything in Russia. On the one hand, in Paris, at the present time, it was such groups who voted for the above-mentioned resolution. In conformity with a long established custom, all those who have been condemned have the right to swear at their judges for twenty-four hours. Those who signed the resolution made excessive use of that right and perhaps even abused it.

On the other hand, there were other groups who were *invited* to the Conference, but who did not want to take part in it. Now they are "protesting" and are trying to convene another Conference and are calling the gods to witness that they stand for unity. That is a very original way of showing unity! Let us see whether they will create anything serious in Russia. Just as it is easy to vote for the resolutions of protest in Paris, so it is difficult to achieve anything in Russia, and of course the right to talk in the name of Russia neither belongs to Paris nor to Vienna etc.

In any case, those who signed the Paris resolution are in too great a hurry when they begin to speak of a "split." In order to determine the existence of a split, it is necessary to prove that there are at least two Central Committees *in Russia*. So far there are not two.

---

[1] A resolution of protest against the all-Russia Conference of the R.S.D.L.P. in Prague (Jan., 1912) adopted by the Social Democrats of various directions in Paris on 12 March, 1912.

As for Citizen Plekhanov, the Central Committee told him about the resolution of the Conference more than a month ago. He has not deigned to answer. I am also completely ignorant as to whether at the present moment Citizen Plekhanov has full powers as a member of the International Socialist Bureau (and from *which* Central Committee).

If, dear comrade, you will have better luck than I have had, i.e. if you receive an answer from Citizen Plekhanov, then I hope you will be good enough to inform me of this.

Fraternal greetings,

Your

N. Lenin

186. (9 P²). TO A. M. GORKY ON CAPRI, ITALY

Cracow, Austria, 1st August, 1912
(Krakau, Oesterreich
(Zwierzyniec 218 Wl. Ulyanow)

My dear A. M.

I have received your letter and a letter from the Siberians. My address is Cracow and not Paris—see above.[1]

I do not quite understand from which Party you are thinking of chasing me. Is it perhaps from the Social Revolutionary?

No, joking apart, you have adopted a bad manner which is both bourgeois and petty to wriggle away: "you are all wranglers." Just look at the new Social Revolutionary literature: "Pochin" ["Initiative," a Social-Revolutionary publication]. "News of the Regional Organisation Abroad" [published by S.R. organisation abroad] compare it with "Revolutionary Thought" [S.R. Organ in London], with "Revolutionary Russia" [C.O. of the Union of Social Revolutionaries] also with Ropshin [B. Savinkov, novelist] etc. Remember "Signposts" [a Miscellany about the Russian Intelligentsia]. Remember Milyukov's and Gredeskul's (who has recently dis-

---

[1] Lenin arrived in Cracow from Paris on 2 July, 1912, and stayed there until August, 1914, the outbreak of the war.

covered that a second revolution in Russia is not necessary) polemics (quasi-polemics) with them etc. etc.

Compare *all* these in toto; the whole sum of ideological currents between 1908 and 1912 among the Social Revolutionaries, the Trudoviki, the Bezzaglavtsy,[1] and the Cadets with that which the Social Democrats had and have (some day, someone—a historian probably, will certainly do this work). You will see that *all*, literally all those outside the Social Democrats have decided the very same, literally and identically the same questions, on account of which our small groups separated from the Party in favour of Liquidatorism and Otzovism.

The bourgeois, the Liberals, the Social Revolutionaries, who are not *serious* with regard to thorny problems and trail after others, are diplomatic and are satisfied with eclecticism, love to shout about the wrangling among the Social Democrats. The difference between the Social Democrats and all of them is that the wrangling has invested the Social Democrats in their group struggle with *deep* and clear ideological roots, while their wrangling is externally smoothed over, but inwardly is empty, petty and mean. I would never for the world exchange the acute conflict of ideas among the Social Democrats for the sleek emptiness and poverty of the Social Revolutionaries and Co.

Warm greetings,

Your

Lenin

P.S. Greetings to M. F.

P.P.S. And in Russia there is revolutionary enthusiasm, not any sort of enthusiasm, but a revolutionary one! And after all, we have been able to organise a daily "Pravda"—by the way, thanks to that same (January) Conference against which some fools barked! [2]

---

[1] The Bezzaglavtsy were the collaborators in the weekly journal "Bez Zaglaviya" ("Without a Title") published in Petersburg which tried to create a group of adherents of "Critical Socialism" and occupying a position near to the Left Cadets.

[2] The All-Russia Party Conference in Prague, January, 1912.

187. (10 P²). TO A. M. GORKY ON CAPRI

[Cracow, August/September, 1912]

My dear A. M.

If you admit that "our wrangling has been caused by an ir-reconcilable difference in ideological roots"—which the Social Revolutionaries also have (and which the Cadets also have— "Signposts"—you did not add this, but there is no doubt about it) and that a reformist (good word!) party is being formed, then you simply *cannot* say both to the Liquidator and to his enemy: "Both of you are wranglers."

It is the function of those, who have understood the ideological roots of the wrangle and who are not participating in it, to help the masses to *discover* those roots and not to justify the masses for examining disputes as being a "personal general matter."

"We leaders have not written one single clear book or single large pamphlet. . . ." That is not true. We wrote as we could, neither less clearly nor less sensibly than before. And we wrote much. There were cases when we wrote against people without *any* "wrangling" against the "Signposts" [in the newspaper "Novy Den" ("New Day") No. 15], against Chernov [Kamenev's article "On the Duties of a Democrat"], against Rozhkov [article signed by Lenin in "Zvezda" No. 32] etc. Do you see each issue of "The Neva Star"? . . . "The result of this is: there are very many good young people in Russia among the workers, but they are so incensed against people abroad. . . ." In actual fact that is true, but it is not the result of the fault of the leaders, but of the severance, or more exactly the disseverance, of Russia and the émigré centres. The dissevered must be linked up again; it is cheap enough and popular to swear at the leaders, but futile . . . "which dissuades the workers from participating in the Conference. . . ."

Which Conference? The one which is now being called by the Liquidators? So we are dissuading them, are we? Is there not some misunderstanding here? [1]

---

[1] The August bloc organised by Trotsky against the Bolsheviks. The bloc consisted of Trotskyists, Mensheviks, "Vpered" people, the Bund, etc., who formed the Conference

I read that Amfiteatrov wrote in a Warsaw newspaper ["Warsaw Latest News" No. 2], advocating the boycott of the IV Duma. Perhaps you have this article? Please send it and I will return it.

Things are brewing in the Baltic Fleet! A special delegate sent by a meeting of sailors and Social Democrats came to see me in Paris (this is between you and me). No organisation— I simply want to weep!! If you have any links with officers, you ought to do your utmost to organise something. The sailors are in a fighting mood, but again they might perish in vain.

Your articles in the "Demands of Life" are not successful. By the way, it is a strange journal: Liquidatorial, Trudovist, Signpostian! However, it is just exactly a "classless reformist party."

You ask why I am in Austria. The Central Committee has established a Bureau here (this is between you and me), the frontier is near and we shall make use of it; we are nearer to Petersburg; newspapers reach us from there within three days; it is much easier to write articles for the papers in Russia and collaboration is being arranged. There is less wrangling here, which is an advantage. There is no good library, which is a disadvantage. It is hard to be without books.

I send you warm greetings,

Your

Lenin

188. (248 R). TO A. I. ELIZAROVA

[*Cracow, Autumn, 1912*]

Darling Anyuta,

I was very glad to have your short note. Your hand must have been fearfully painful, for the handwriting is still shaky!

Life is better for us here than in Paris. Our nerves are resting; more literary work—less wrangling. I hope it will be easier for us to see each other—that is, if war does not break out and I do not believe it will.

of R.S.D.L.P. organisations, 12/25 Aug., 1912, in Vienna as a counterbalance to the All-Russia Party Conference in Prague in January, 1912.

Occasionally I have news from Gorky, who is less unfriendly towards us than before.

How are Mark and Mitya?

Please kiss Mother warmly for me.

Wonderful Autumn weather here and we are taking long walks. Material conditions are so far bearable, but are very unreliable—in case of need, I shall write to you.

I send you warm greetings and apologise for the hurry.

Your
V. Ulianov

P.S. E. V. and Nadya ask me to send their love and kisses. Both are well.

189. (28 P²). TO V. A. KARPINSKY IN GENEVA

[Cracow, 8th October, 1912]

My dear K.

I have not been following the last World Congresses. I have heard, but only *heard*, that the Socialists are participating and also about its opportunist character.[1]

I will not undertake to express any definite opinion on the subject without reading the reports of at least one Congress. It is a complicated question. Undoubtedly the general growth of opportunism and the balancing of its forces with the revolutionary social democracy in the main countries of the Labour movement (Germany) will also be felt here. Let Bebel use his diplomacy with the opportunists: *if* that is necessary (???) But that does not suit us. That is all I can say at present.

Greetings to Comrade Olga [S. N. Ravich] and to all friends —Gorin included. How is he? What news have you? What are your relations with Plekhanov? Do you converse?

Kamenev will go to Switzerland in the Autumn to lecture (he is here now—on his way to Paris). I may also go in the Winter.[2]

Greetings,

Your
Lenin

[1] International Peace Congress, 24-28 September, 1912, in Geneva.
[2] Lenin did not go to Switzerland in the Autumn.

190. (37 P²). TO THE EDITOR OF THE NEWSPAPER "PRAVDA"
["TRUTH"] IN PETERSBURG

[*Cracow, 2nd November, 1912*]

Dear Colleague,

I read in "Pravda" and "Luch" ["The Ray"] today about the results of the elections for the Workers' Curia in Petersburg.[1] I cannot help expressing to you my congratulations on the leader [by I. V. Stalin] in No. 146. At the moment of defeat, sustained not at the hand of Social Democrats, (from the analysis of figures it is clear that it was not the Social Democrats who let down the Liquidators), the editors immediately adopted the correct, firm and dignified attitude of pointing out the significance of the principal position of the protest towards "suppression." Do not misunderstand what I say. Do not think that it is prompted by anything else except the wish to share opinions, which is only natural for a permanent collaborator. It was a difficult time. The struggle was hard. Almost everything possible was done, but the cleavage made itself felt and non-party members voted for the Opportunists. The principal, persistent work of a united whole (a united editorial board, for instance, or united collaborators) is all the more insistently intent on counteracting any falling to pieces.

It is most important not to break off the work of studying the elections begun by "Pravda," but to continue it; to collect and publish the votes of all the candidates (you have only nine and thirteen); to collect and publish details of the enquiry about how Non-Party members voted, how the Putilov men voted (seven and two Liquidators), Semyannikovtsy (two and one Liquidator) and so on, by factories. Only "Pravda" can execute this important work successfully.

Greetings and best wishes,

Your

Lenin

[1] Elections of worker electors to the State Duma from the Petersburg Province 17 Oct., 1912.

191. (249 R). TO M. I. ULIANOVA

[*Cracow, End of November, 1912*] [1]

Darling Manyasha,

Very many thanks for your photographs and letters. At last! How are you feeling now?

It does not surprise me that you have chosen the North.[2] I too would probably have chosen it. All the same I hope they will not send you into exile too far away—there are some bad places there. Please write as soon as you arrive.

The last few days have been very rushed and I have therefore not been able to answer you at once.

There is much talk about war here as can also be seen in the newspapers. If war breaks out I shall probably have to go to Vienna (or perhaps to the town where we last met [Stockholm]) but I do not believe there will be a war.

I kiss you warmly, my darling. E. V. and Nadya also.

Your
V. U.

P.S. Write and tell me whether you receive "Neue Zeit."

192. (40 P²). TO I. V. STALIN IN PETERSBURG
FOR VASILIEV [STALIN] [3]

Cracow, 6th December, 1912

My dear Friend,

With regard to the 9th January it is most important to think out and prepare the matter in advance. The leaflet announcing the meetings and calling for a one day strike and demonstrations must be prepared in advance (this must be decided on the spot, for it will be easier to judge from there). The mistake of the 15th November must be remedied, of course against

---

[1] Written soon after Manyasha's release from prison, Oct., 1912.
[2] At the request of relations she was exiled to the Vologda, instead of to the Astrakhan Province.
[3] This letter, written in between the lines "chemically" by Krupskaya, was intercepted by the police.

the Opportunists. The slogans of the pamphlet must be the three revolutionary ones (a republic, an eight hour working day and the confiscation of land), with special emphasis on the 300 year disgrace of the Romanov dynasty. If there is not a full or the fullest conviction of the possibility of having this pamphlet in Petersburg, it must be prepared here beforehand in good time and sent across. The insolence of the Liquidators concerning the question of Jagello is unparalleled. If we have all six members in the Workers' Curia we cannot silently submit to some Siberians or other. The six members must come out with the acutest protest and if they are being majorised they should publish a protest in "Truth" ["Pravda"] and announce that they appeal to the lower classes, to the workers' organisations. The Liquidators want to inflate their majority and to bring about a split with the Polish Social Democracy. Surely the representatives of the workers of six workers' provinces will not submit to Skobelev and Co. or to some casual Siberian [I. N. Mankov]? Write oftener and in greater detail. The articles in "Luch" [No. 53] against strikes are the depth of baseness. We must attack them vigorously and illegally. Write and let me know on which of the proposed plans of attack you have decided.

Send back the document, you cannot very well keep it. The owner may be in Petersburg.

[Printed from a copy made by N. K. Krupskaya.]

193. (41 p²). TO M. A. SAVELIEV, A BOLSHEVIK, THEN EDITOR OF "PROSVESHCHENIYE" AND MEMBER OF THE "PRAVDA" EDITORIAL BOARD IN PETERSBURG

[*Cracow, 11th December, 1912*]

My dear Friend,

There were some articles left [in the office of] the weekly ["Zvezda"] which now might be suitable for you. They must be found whatever happens. Such articles as Fry's [Lenin's] "From the Practice of English Liberal Politicians" also his "Two Utopias" (Cadets and the Narodniks) Skopin's [G. E.

Zinoviev's] "Marx and Freilingrath" and several others. We ask you to find them as quickly as possible, to read through them and to send us your opinion. We await your letter with impatience! Has the money been received and when is the last date for sending in the manuscript? Greetings. . . .

We enclose a questionnaire for the six deputies chosen from the Workers' Curia. It must be handed to them and you should see that they give answers immediately to the questions. One or two of them have already promised to do this. None of them will refuse, if the importance of this is explained to them. But do not let it be put "officially" in the faction, which would only result in a fuss and wrangling. Let them do it themselves and quickly. Best of all, they ought not to confine themselves to dry answers to the questions but, guided by the questionnaire in general, they should each give a connected account about his own province. Ask somebody to help them. Invite them all to collaborate. What news is there in the paper? Why are not your announcements appearing? Have you written to the Viennese [N. I. Bukharin or A. Troyanovsky]?

Questionnaire: Elections for the Workers' Curia.

1. How many people had full powers?

2. How great a part did the workers take in the election of those who had full powers? If you can, state the approximate average number or the percentage of those who attended the elections of the workers. Was there any conscious boycott? If so, where and by whom? In your opinion, what were the reasons for the insufficient attendance of workers at the election?

3. Were there any meetings before the election of the people with full powers? Where? And by whom and how were the meetings conducted?

4. Were there any election platforms at factories and works? At which exactly? How did the workers react to these platforms? Were there any orders given to the elected? Which exactly?

5. How were the candidates for full powers selected? Were

there any dual Social Democratic candidatures? Were there any candidates from other parties? (Monarchists and Non-Party?)

6. Were there any preliminary meetings of the men with full powers before the elections of the electors? By permission or not? What was discussed at these meetings?

7. How were the lists of electors compiled? Were there any suggestions from Social Democratic groups and organisations? Was there one or were there two lists?

8. Describe the main discussions at the meeting of the men with full powers before the election of the electors. The speeches of the Right and Non-Party members. The clashes between Social Democrats of various tendencies.

9. Was a deputy for the Duma chosen at the meeting of the men with full powers?

10. Were any instructions given to the electors?

11. What element predominated among the men with full powers? Young? Old? Party members? Nondescript? Have you read the workers' newspapers? How is their distribution of workers' newspapers organised? Were there any participators of the professional movement etc. among them? How many Bolsheviks, Mensheviks, Liquidators and non-faction?

12. Were there any arguments or disagreements among the electors?

13. Did the Right make any attempt in the Government district meeting to elect deputies who were not wanted by the workers?

14. Were there any worker electors at the preliminary conferences with oppositional electors? What was discussed at these conferences? How did the workers behave? The Cadets? The Progressists? The peasants?

15. Describe all the cases you know where pressure has been brought to bear by the administration and police at the workers' election: arrests, explanations, omission from the lists, sudden fixing of elections etc.

16. Is there any organisation link left between the men with full powers and the electors?

17. Was the deputy given any instructions and what kind exactly?

18. What are you (deputy): a Bolshevik, Liquidator or Non-Factional?

19. Add any information you may consider necessary.

It would be best if you gave the material not in the form of dry answers to the questions, but if, guided by the above questions, you described quite simply, as best you can, all that you saw at the elections. It is most important to collect this information. Of course we shall print only that which you consider should be printed, after the material has been revised, and before printing it we shall refer it to you. Do not postpone this.

Do not put this question "officially" before the faction. It would only lead to fuss and bother. Do it yourself first of all among the six deputies from the Workers' Curia.

194. (25 P²). TO G. L. SHKLOVSKY IN BERNE

[Cracow, Beginning of December, 1912]

I believe your letter is the first to contain the proposal of a "report" about Basle!!¹ Rather late in the day. Evidently something was lacking (or was there a surplus of something?) in Basle. I think there was not sufficient organisation among the delegates. And that is extremely disappointing. Kamenev was, of course, up to his eyes in work, but what about the other four?² Surely it was obvious that one ought to have written *daily* for "Pravda"? Surely, it was not difficult to distribute the work? Not a single letter went to "Pravda" from the place, whereas the Liquidators sent several to "Luch."

Now isn't that disgraceful? Of course, as long as we go to sleep and the Liquidators work, their cause will progress. Is anything being done about collecting money for "Pravda"? I do not see that this is being done; whereas the Liquidators have reports in "Luch" about their collectors of funds abroad. But "Pravda" is very, very greatly in need of money.

¹ The report of the C.C. delegates of the R.S.D.L.P. at the Basle Socialist Congress, 24 Oct./11 Nov.-25 Oct./12 Nov., 1912.
² Troyanovsky, G. Shklovsky, E. F. Rozmirovich, M. F. Vladimirsky.

None of the delegates (excepting Kamenev) wrote here about Basle. You ought to have distributed the work and written twice a day. Instead, you were all silent. Evidently you were displeased about something. With what? Allah only knows! I am *very* pleased with the Basle results, for those idiots, the Liquidators, allowed themselves to be caught out on the initiative group! ! [1] Those swine could not have been better trapped, but our own delegates' inactivity and their refusal to speak, which I do not understand, has upset me. Did you speak to the German delegates? (After all, four or five of you could speak German). Who? With whom? And about what? We have heard nothing except from Kamenev. Agitation among the Germans is *very* important.

You write that affairs both in the Press and in the section are not particularly satisfactory. Matters are also unsatisfactory with regard to "Prosveshcheniye." No money. A serious crisis. Help is needed.

"Pravda's" circulation is about 23,000. "Luch" has about 8/9,000. So far it is wicked to complain. But "Pravda" had 60,000 in April and May; the circulation dropped to 20,000 in the Summer. It is increasing *very* slowly. *It cannot be done without assistance.* Matters in the section are better than they have ever been. . . . The group of six workers is on our side,[2] and it has *never* been like this before. For the first time they have won over the South. Out of 12—6 and 6. Mankov is a Menshevik, Rusanov—unknown. One can fight. Here are exact details of our progress: deputies from the Workers' Curia:

Into the IInd Duma: 12 Mensheviks, 11 Bolsheviks = 47%
  ”   ” IIIrd Duma: 4 Mensheviks, 4 Bolsheviks = 50%
  ”   ” IVth Duma: 3 Mensheviks, 6 Bolsheviks = 66%
(this is from the Minutes of the London Congress [of the R.S.D.L.P. 1907], page 451).

If you know of anyone, anywhere, who is depressed, let him

[1] The 6 C.C. representatives left the sub-section of the R.S.D.L.P. at the Basle Congress, refusing to confirm the mandate of the representative of the Petersburg "initiative" group (Gorbunov), as a hostile organisation conducting strife in the Party.

[2] Six State Duma deputies, Social Democrat Bolsheviks: A. Badayev, R. Malinovsky, M. Muranov, G. Petrovsky, F. Samoilov, N. Shagov.

think of these statistics and be ashamed of his depression. For the first time among our people in the Duma, there is an outstanding worker leader (Malinovsky). He will read a declaration. He is not another Alexinsky. And the results will be *great* —though they may not be so at once. We began by having no one in the IIIrd Duma!

Thanks to the transfer of the Bureau here, it has done more in the way of illegal work than before. We are moving forward, even though it is slow. We are publishing more illegal material than the others. We have no money. If we are given financial assistance—we shall publish another workers' paper etc.

The only way of helping illegal work from abroad is by journeys. Next, the help of new links is most important: (a) through letters, (b) through opportunities, (c) passports, (d) etc. etc. *There is too little* of this. There is a hundred times less done abroad than could be done. The most important thing to be done at the moment is to help to rescue "Pravda," but it is not being properly supported. One man from Vienna [Bukharin?] is doing his best. But nothing is being done in the other towns! No one corresponds regularly. No one collects any money. No one collects interesting local books or pamphlets to send them here for the compilation of interesting articles. Comrades, you should give more thought to this! For instance, who of the Social Democrats in Nüremberg, in Switzerland, has bothered? What has been done?

I send you my greetings,

Lenin

P.S. Please forward this letter to Yury [A. Bekzadian] so that he can send it on to Antonov in Paris and from there to Vienna. So far we have not discovered whether Plekhanov spoke at the October meeting of the Bureau about uniting with the Socialist Revolutionaries (compare Martov in "Luch" No. 37).[1] Surely you have tried to find out about this from Rubano-

[1] Plekhanov announced at the International Socialist Bureau in Basle, 28, 29 Oct., 1912, that the time was not far distant when Russian Social Democrats would be united, not only among themselves, but also with the Socialist Revolutionaries.

vich, or the German, or Huysmans, or from somebody else?

195. (13 P²). TO A. M. GORKY ON CAPRI, ITALY

Cracow, 23rd December, 1912

My dear Al. M.

I do not seem to have had any news from you for some time. How are you? Are you well?

Today I received No. 187 of "Pravda" with a subscription notice for 1913. This newspaper is in difficulties: after the Summer fall in the circulation, the increase is *very* slow and there is still a deficit. They have even temporarily stopped payment to two constant collaborators and have thus made our position extremely difficult. We intend to develop an increased agitation among the workers to get them to subscribe, so as to consolidate the position of the newspaper with their money and to enlarge it; otherwise, when the Duma opens, there will be no room left for articles.

I hope you too will take part in the agitation for increased subscribers, so as to help the newspaper to get on its feet again. How? If you have a tale or something suitable, then an announcement about it would be good propaganda. If not, send a promise to contribute one in the near future, namely in 1913. And finally, simply a few lines of a *letter to workers* from you about the importance of *actively* supporting a workers' newspaper (by subscriptions, distribution and collections), would also be excellent propaganda.[1]

Please write one or the other and send it direct to the Editors of "Pravda" (Yamskaya 2, St. Petersburg) or to me here: Ulyanow, 47, (Lubomirskiego, Krakau).

There will probably not be a war and we shall stay here for the time being, taking "advantage of" the Poles' desperate hatred of Tzarism.[2]

---

[1] "Pravda" No. 1 (205) Jan. 1, 1913, printed an extract from Gorky's "Great Love."

[2] "Taking advantage":—Cracow was the centre for Polish emigrants fleeing from Tsarist persecution. There were about four thousand émigrés in Cracow. The Cracow administration did not put any obstacles to Lenin's constant visits from Russia.

The Liquidators are now leading an attack *against* revolutionary strikes! That is where they have got to! There is talk of having a strike and a demonstration on the 9th January.[1]

For the first time during three Dumas, i.e. the IInd, IIIrd and IVth, all six worker deputies from the main provinces are on the side of the Party. It is difficult, but all the same, the work is progressing.

Did you see Ropshin's "defence" in the "Zavety" in the name of "The Freedom of Thought and Criticism" in answer to Nathanson and Co's letter to the Editor?[2] Surely that is worse than any liquidatorism—a muddled, cowardly, wobbling renegadeness, but none the less systematic.

We are swimming "against the current." . . . We have now to fight against a large number of also-revolutionaries for revolution among the masses. . . . Undoubtedly there is a revolutionary spirit among the masses, the workers, but a new democratic intelligentsia (among the workers) with a revolutionary ideology is growing slowly, lagging behind and has not yet caught up.

Warmest greetings,
    Write me a line,

Your

Lenin

P.S. Greetings to M. F. She has become quite silent. . . .

1913

196. (14 P²). TO A. M. GORKY ON CAPRI, ITALY

[*Cracow, 8th/10th March, 1913*]

My dear A. M.

I read through the Manifesto today.[3]

The literary amnesty seems to be complete. You will have

---

[1] For conspiratorial reasons, Lenin is purposely speaking vaguely, the Party was preparing actively for Jan. 9th, 1913.

[2] Ropshin's novel, "That, which did not happen," resulted in a number of protesting letters sent from the S.R. Left.

[3] The manifesto about amnesty on the occasion of the tercentenary of the ruling house of Romanov.

to try to return—*after first finding out, of course, whether you will not have to suffer on account of "The School"* etc.[1] They will probably not be able to trap you for this.

I hope you do not think it is impossible to accept the amnesty? It would be a wrong view! A revolutionary at this time will do more good from within Russia and our deputies are even signing a "solemn promise."

There is no question, however, of your signing such a "promise," but of your taking advantage of the amnesty. Send me your opinion and views. I suppose you will drop in to see me if you decide to move: after all, we are on your way!

The change to wander about Russia (new Russia) will give a revolutionary writer the chance to hit out a hundred times more strongly against the Romanovs and Co.

Have you received my last letter? I have not heard from you for some time. Are you well?

Yours

Lenin

P.S. Have you received N. K.'s [Krupskaya's] letter containing information?

197. (259 R). TO M. I. ULIANOVA

(In exile in Vologda, N. Russia)

[Poronin, 29th or 30th April/12th or 13th May, 1913]

Darling Manyasha,

I think I am in your debt (and certainly in Mark Tim's). At last I can sit down to write to you. We moved here the other day (partly because of Nadya's illness (goitre) which greatly worries me). We shall spend the Summer here in the mountains in the village Poronin which is 7 kilometres from Zakopane, close to the Tatra Mountains about 6-8 hours in the train from Cracow, travelling South—Cracow is a main railway

---

[1] The S.D. propagandist-agitational school for workers, organised on Capri in 1909 with M. Gorky's close co-operation.

LETTER 197. APRIL 29, 1913

junction between Russia and the West, slightly farther from Russia—but that cannot be helped.

We have rented a villa (enormous—far too big) for the whole Summer until October 1st (new style) and we moved into it after much fuss. I feel Nadya's illness has become worse as a result of the removal. I may have to take her to Berne to be cured. . . .

The country is magnificent here. The air is excellent—altitude about 700 metres. No comparison with such a low lying and rather damp place like Cracow. We have a number of newspapers and are able to work.

The people are Polish peasants "gurali" (mountain folk) with whom I talk in an incredibly broken language of which I know five words and the rest are Russian words which I alter. Nadya speaks very little and reads Polish.

The village—almost a Russian type. Thatched roofs and poverty. The women and children—barefoot. The men go about wearing the "gurali" costume—white cloth trousers and white cloth half cloaks, half jackets. This place is not a health spa (but Zakopane is) and it is therefore very quiet. I hope Nadya will get well in this peaceful mountain air.

We have begun living a country life—we get up early and go to bed almost at the same time as the cocks and hens. Each day we go to the post and to the railway station.

Do you see "Pravda" [Bolshevik daily] and "Prosveshcheniye" [Bolshevik journal] regularly? We rejoiced over the Jubilee Number [No. 92-296] and the victory in the Union of the Metal Workers over the Liquidators.[1]

How are you? Shall you keep your lessons during the Summer? Are you getting enough books?

Greetings to all Polish friends and wishes that they will help in every way. . . .

E. V. and Nadya kiss you and send much love. I too.

Your V. U.

P.S. Address: Herrn Ulyanow, Oesterreich Poronin (Galizien) Austria.

---

[1] The Bolsheviks gained 13 places out of 15.

Please forward this letter to Mother, if you do not expect her to come to you soon.

198. (15 P²). TO A. M. GORKY ON CAPRI, ITALY

Poronin, Beginning of May, 1913

My dear A. M.

How are your article and story for the May number of "Prosveshcheniye" ["Enlightenment"] progressing? They write to me saying it may be possible to publish *10/15,000* copies (see what strides we are making!) if it contains something from you. Write and tell me if it will.[1] "Pravda" will then reprint it and thus there will be a total of 40,000 readers. Yes . . . "Prosveshcheniye" ought to do well; otherwise, the devil take it, there is not a single sustained journal for workers, for Social Democrats, for revolutionary democracy—nothing but wishy washy, mouldy ones.

How is your health? Have you been resting and will you continue to rest in the Summer? I do feel it is essential for you to have a *thorough* rest.

I am in trouble. My wife is ill with goitre. Nerves! And my nerves also are playing tricks with me. We have come to this village Poronin near to Zakopane, for the Summer. (My address: Herrn. Wl. Ulyanow, Poronin, Galicia, Austria.)

Beautiful country. Healthy, about 2,100 feet above sea level. And what about you? Will you make a little journey here? There will be some interesting workers here from Russia. Zakopane (about six miles away) is a famous health resort.

Have you seen Demyan Bedny's "Fables" [S.P.B. 1913]? If not, I will send them to you. If you have seen them, send me a line and let me know what you think of them. Do you receive "Pravda" and "Luch" ["The Ray"] regularly? In spite of everything, our cause is moving forward and the Workers' Party is becoming a *revolutionary* social democratic one against Liberal renegades and Liquidators. One day we shall have a

---

[1] The May number had no Gorky contributions. The June number printed Gorky's story: "The Theft."

holiday in our street! We are now rejoicing about the triumph of the [Bolshevik] workers in Petersburg over the Liquidators at the elections of the management of the new Union of Metal Workers.

And "your" Lunacharsky is a fine fellow! Oh, a very fine fellow! So he says Maeterlinck is a "scientific mystic"! [1] Or are Lunacharsky and Bogdanov no longer "yours"?

Joking apart, *do keep well*. Send me a line. *Rest more*.

Your

Lenin

Ulyanow, Poronin, Galicia, Austria.

P.S. What did you think of the jubilee number of "Pravda" [April 23, 1913]?

199. (3 p²). TO G. V. PLEKHANOV IN GENEVA

Cracow, May-June, 1913

Dear George Valentinovich,

On the instruction of six Social Democrat deputies I write to you to suggest that you come to Zakopane for a few weeks in the Summer to give a few lectures on whatever questions concerning Marxism and the Social Democratic movement you care to select.[2] We have heard today from Petersburg that four deputies, who are supporting the Liquidators or are wavering, may also come (Buryanov, Tulyakov, Haustov and *perhaps* Mankov). As Mensheviks, they naturally attribute special importance to your participation.

As for us, we should consider it very useful if Party members holding various opinions were to participate. It would strengthen our links with workers and consolidate Party work.

In view of the conspiratory nature of the affair we have decided not to let a single group abroad know about this plan

---

[1] Lunacharsky's feuilleton "Fear and Hope" in "Kievskaya Mysl," No. 357, Dec., 1912.

[2] The C.C. of the R.S.D.L.P. proposed to have a school for the Bolshevik members of the State Duma and certain other Party workers during the Summer. This did not materialise. But in Sept., 1913, there was a meeting in Poronin of the C.C. of the R.S.D.L.P. with Party workers and the Bolshevik deputies.

of organising the lectures—especially as the deputies are no doubt threatened with serious persecution.

Poronin, where it is proposed to hold the lectures, is seven miles by rail from Zakopane—one of the best mountain health centres in Galicia. So far as the financial side is concerned, (travelling expenses) we shall be able to arrange that by correspondence.

Please send me a line if you agree to the proposal.

I am at your services,

N. Lenin

My address: Herrn Wl. Ulyanow,
           Poronin (Galizien)
           Austriche.

200. (262 R). TO HIS MOTHER

[*Berne*], *Saturday, 13th/26th July, 1913*

Darling Mother,

At last on Wednesday (after two weeks' preparation) they operated on Nadya in the Clinic. The operation evidently went off successfully, for yesterday she already looked fairly well and began to drink with pleasure. The operation was apparently rather difficult; for about three hours they tortured her without an anæsthetic, but she bore it heroically. On Thursday she was very ill—a high temperature and delirium—and I was thoroughly alarmed. Yesterday, however, things were obviously better, no temperature, the pulse better, etc. Kocher is a remarkable surgeon and people suffering from goitre ought to go to him: he has many Russian patients, especially Jews.

I am already thinking about our return journey: we intend leaving on August 4th (if Kocher does not detain her—which sometimes happens). We shall stay the night in Zürich, Munich, and Vienna, and then home. I shall have time to receive one more letter from you, after which you must write to Poronin. If I have to stay here I shall write again.

The closing down of the newspaper to which I contributed[1] places me in a critical position. I shall assiduously look for publishers and translations; it will be very difficult now to find literary work.

I embrace you warmly, my darling, and send much love to Manyasha and Anya. Nadya sends her love.

Your

V. U.

201. (49 P[2]). TO THE EDITORS OF THE NEWSPAPER "PRAVDA"
IN PETERSBURG

Cracow, Between the 18th and 26th October, 1913

Dear Colleagues,

In welcoming the excellent beginning made in the struggle of the six deputies, that the will of the majority of workers should be respected, and the magnificent campaign started by your paper ["Za Pravdu" ("For Truth")][2] I would ask you also to take note of the following:

If the seven deputies insolently announce themselves as being a Social Democratic faction (as they did at the end of their article in No. 60), then the six must without fail announce calmly, curtly and firmly: "We, the Social Democratic Workers' Faction—for we conform to the will of the majority of conscious workers and see that it is carried out—we represent the Bolsheviks. The seven non-Party deputies did not refute a single fact or a single figure from the mass of facts and figures quoted in our newspaper and proving this truth. This is our address, refer to us, comrade workers, and do not think that we shall insult you by thinking you capable of believing the theory that the seven deputies stand above the Party, above the will of the

[1] "Pravda" was banned on the 5/18 July, 1913. But it reappeared again on 13/26 July under the new name "Rabochaya Pravda" ("Workers' Truth").

[2] The 6 deputy Bolsheviks demanded the 7 to acknowledge equality in the decision over all questions in the S.D. Duma faction. The 7 refused. This letter throws light on the last stage of the open conflict between the 6 and the 7. Lenin insisted on equality of both halves in the S.D. faction, and then advocated a complete break with the 7. In November the 6 formed a separate "Russian Social Democratic Duma faction."

majority of workers. Even seventy-seven deputies cannot stand above that will. And we are strictly fulfilling it."

Such a short announcement is essential [in No. 20 "Za Pravdu"]. Next, you must present a formal acknowledgment also to the Convent of the Seigneurs (i.e. to the Duma). *Then* very rapidly, at once, the seven deputies will grow humble and even more rapidly they will *agree* to equality (a written acknowledgment by *all* of them). There cannot be any other way out, *either* for them, *or* anyone else.

Once the work has begun, it must not be given up. The six deputies have made an *excellent* beginning and their victory is *assured*. If they continue in the *right* way, a second victory is inevitable in a week's time.

Best wishes and greetings,

V. I.

202. (265 R). TO M. I. ULIANOVA

[Cracow, Autumn or Winter, 1913]

Darling Manyasha,

I received your letter a few days after having posted a letter to you from Nadya and me.

You made me feel ashamed of my silence. I really am guilty —the delay has been particularly long because of the removal and influenza. E. V. is ill—she has had 'flu very badly; she is now *on the mend*.

New German literature? I have just finished reading four volumes of the Marx-Engels correspondence. I want to write about it in "Prosveshcheniye"[1]—much of it is interesting. It is a pity those devilish Germans have published it at such a high price—40 marks! I have not yet read Beer's new book "The History of Socialism in England" but I shall soon read it.

There recently appeared Cunow's book on the origin of religion. I would send it to you (buy it), but I am afraid it would

---

[1] Lenin's unfinished article: "The Marx-Engels Correspondence."

never reach you. If you get "Neue Zeit" there is a survey of all that is interesting. I do not see any new bourgeois literature. If you like, I will send you a list of new German books (small edition of Hinrich, a bookseller in Leipzig—I receive it each month).

I greet you warmly. Kiss Mother for me and for Nadya.

Your

V. U.

P.S. We have not had news from Anya for a long time. I am reading Octave Mirbeau's "Dingo." I think it is bad.

203. (19 p²). TO A. M. GORKY ON CAPRI, ITALY

[Cracow, Beginning of November, 1913]

My dear Alexsey Maximych,

I am sending you today under registered cover the beginning of a novel which is appearing in "Prosveshcheniye." We think you will approve of it. If, however, contrary to our expectation you disapprove of it, then *wire* to "Prosveshcheniye"—"Postpone Voitinsky" or: "Reject Voitinsky's novel." [1]

Your news that a Bolshevik, although a former Bolshevik, was treating you by a new method, has made me really very anxious. God preserve us from "comrade" doctors in general and Bolshevik doctors in particular! But seriously, in ninety-nine cases out of a hundred, "comrade" doctors are asses, as a brilliant doctor once told me. I assure you that one should be treated only by first-class foreign specialists (except in unimportant cases). It is terrible to allow a Bolshevik to try his experiments on you. I can understand being under the control of Neapolitan professors, if these professors are really men who know. . . . If you travel in the Winter, you should visit the first-class doctors in Switzerland and Vienna, it would be unpardonable if you did not do this. How is your health now?

Your

Lenin

---

[1] Gorky rejected it.

P.S. Our work is progressing quite well in Petersburg, the workers are uniting in a Party way in all the legal societies, including insurance companies. Some interesting and sensible young fellows came to see us here.

Address: Wl. Ulyanow, 51, Ulica Lubomirskiego, Cracow, Galicia.

1914

204. (57 P²). TO ISAAC A. HOURWICH IN WASHINGTON

Cracow, 27th February, 1914

Dear Colleague,

Long ago I received your book "Immigration and Labour [1912]" and I began to search for your address so as to thank you, but it was not easy to find. Only yesterday I heard what it was and I hasten to express my gratitude to you for having sent the book. I have already written something about it, basing a short article on it in our Social Democratic paper "Pravda" and I mean to write still more about it. In my opinion your book gives a great deal of valuable material for the study of capitalism and is at the same time a transference as it were of the best methods of our rural district statistics on to *Western* soil.

The comrade who sent me your address (Mr. John Ellert) [N. N. Nakoryakov] tells me that you can be influential in helping us to receive information from the Statistical Bureau in Washington. Let me therefore ask you a favour—of course, only if it does not inconvenience you too much and does not disturb you in your work:

In Paris I studied the American agricultural statistics (Vol. V. Agriculture. Census 1900)—I found much that was interesting, but now living in Cracow I cannot get hold of these publications. When Kagan, the editor of the Socialist Jewish newspaper ["Vorwärts"] in New York, was here twelve months ago, he promised to send them, but evidently he has forgotten. They say that with influence the American Statistical Bureau will send its publications gratis, even abroad. If that is true, will you exert your influence? (I could send the library of the

Statistical Bureau my own books on "The Development of Capitalism" and on "The Agrarian Question.") I particularly need "Agriculture, Vol. V. Census 1900" and also the Census of 1910. (If this has not been published yet, then the preliminary bulletin.)

If this is impossible, will you kindly send a postcard to Mr. John Ellert (C/o "Novy Mir," 140 East 4th Street, New York). I will send him the money for posting the most important publications to me.

Once again I thank you for the book and apologise for troubling you.

With Social Democratic greetings,

N. Lenin (V. Ulianov)

Address: Wl. Ulyanow,
          51, Ulica Lubomirskiego, Cracow, Galicia, Austria.

205. (270 R). TO M. I. ULIANOVA IN VOLOGDA

[Cracow], 9th/22nd April, 1914

Darling Manyasha,

I have received news that you are annoyed at my long silence. I am guilty where letter writing is concerned—it is very difficult in our position (especially yours and mine) to carry on a correspondence as one would wish. . . .

Yesterday we received Mother's letter written to me and Nadya. Kiss Mother warmly for me. Perhaps circumstances will be better for you in the Summer than in the Winter.

I had news recently of the exiles in Olonetsk where they are collecting information about their social status: the majority of them are workers. New men (post revolutionary), two Liquidators in the district to 150 people—few Left Narodniks. Evidently the exiles are changing rapidly—it would be interesting to collect data about this and to publish them occasionally in "Prosveshcheniye." Nadya has written to you and is thinking of writing again.

In about a fortnight we shall again go to Poronin. There

are mountains there and I hope Nadya's goitre trouble will soon disappear. Mountain air cures this disease. The weather here is magnificent at present; I often go for bicycle rides.

No matter how dead alive this town is, I am happier here than in Paris. The intrigues among the Russian colony there were incredible and our nerves went absolutely to pieces and all to no purpose; work is difficult in Paris. The Bibliothèque Nationale is badly arranged and we often thought of Geneva where it had been easier to work; the library was convenient and there life was less nervous and disorganised. Of all places in my wanderings I would choose London or Geneva if they were not both so far away. Geneva is particularly good both in general culture and real comfort of living. Here, of course, one cannot even speak of culture; it is almost like Russia—the library is bad and "arch-uncomfortable," but I rarely go to it. Autumn is magnificent in the Tatra (the mountains near which we live in Poronin) at any rate last year after a rainy Summer, the Autumn was beautiful. Are you not finishing in the Autumn? Sometimes I dream that we shall meet in the Autumn. If it is fine this Autumn, we shall probably stay in the country.

I greet you warmly,

Your

V. U.

206. (59 P²). TO N. N. NAKORYAKOV (MR. J. ELLERT) IN
NEW YORK

[Poronin], 18th May, 1914

My dear Comrade Nazar,

Many thanks for the bulletin of the Thirteenth Census and for Vol. V. of the Twelfth Census (1900).

Each day I fully expected to receive a similar volume (Agriculture) of the Thirteenth Census (of 1900), but it has not arrived. Probably the Bureau has sent it to you, for Hourwich wrote to me, saying that this volume had been published. Send me a line please, saying whether you have this volume (Agri-

LENIN IN GALICIA, 1914

culture, Census 1910) or whether you can get hold of it and send it: I will at once send you the money for the postage.

Please notice my new address: Poronin, (Galicia).

Congratulations on the excellent May Day in Russia; 250,000 in Petersburg alone! ! The 1st May issue of "The Path of Truth" was confiscated, but I heard from the "Novy Mir" [a Socialist newspaper in N. Y.] that you often have copies confiscated. Altogether, news from Russia witnesses to the growth of revolutionary feeling not only among the workers.

On the 15th May Sima [S. Mikhailova, an active Ural Bolshevik] is leaving Cracow to take up a job for the Summer in a village between Cracow and Poronin. She is very glad to have found a job.

Nadezhda Konstantinovna sends greetings.

I sincerely hope you will rest this Summer and get really well.

Your

V. I.

P.S. Recently we had news from the organisation in the Urals: affairs are quite satisfactory there. The flame is alive and growing!

207. (53 p²). TO S. G. SHAUMYAN IN BAKU

[Poronin], 19th May, 1914

My dear Suren,

I received your letter of the 17th April. I hope you will answer me after reading the end of the article on the self-determination of nations in "Prosveshcheniye" ["Enlightenment"] (I am writing it now).

You *must* give "Selbstanzeige" or an exposition of your pamphlet against A. H. N. in "Prosveshcheniye." I suggest the following plan:

In order to struggle against the stupidity of the cultural-national autonomists, the Russian Social Democratic workers' faction must introduce into the Duma the project of a law about the equality of nations and about the defence of the rights of national minorities.

Let us draw up such a project.[1] The general position of equality, the division of the country into autonomous and self-governing territorial units according to nationality (the local population determines the boundaries and the State parliament confirms it), the limits of government of autonomous districts and regions, as well as the self-governing local units; the illegality of any departure from the equality of nations in the decisions of autonomous districts, zemstvos etc.; general school councils democratically elected etc., freedom and equality of languages, the choice of languages by municipal institutions and so forth. The protection of minorities: the right to a proportional share of expenses for school buildings (gratis) for non-Russian national students, for non-Russian national teachers. Expenses for non-Russian national departments of museums, libraries, theatres etc.—the right of each citizen to seek redress (before a court) of any departure from equality with regard to any infringements of the rights of national minorities (a five year census of the population in the mixed population districts and a ten year one for the whole country) etc.

It seems to me that in this way we shall be able to explain in a popular manner the stupidity of cultural national autonomy and finally to quash the adherents of such idiocy.

The Marxists of all or most of the nationalities within Russia might work out this project.

Write at once, if you agree to help. Do write oftener and not less than once a week. It is inexcusable not to answer at once. Remember this, especially now! !

Greetings

From

V. I.

---

[1] Lenin's project is now in the Marx-Engels Institute, No. 18183.

THE WAR PERIOD

1914–1917

SUMMARY

THE RUSSIAN REVOLUTIONARY MOVEMENT	LENIN'S LIFE

THE RUSSIAN REVOLUTIONARY MOVEMENT

March: Berne II Conference of R.S.D. L.P. organisations abroad. Resolutions passed on Lenin's initiative: defence of the Fatherland pronounced a false slogan; the correct slogan is to turn the Imperialist war into civil war; recognised need to have a III International.

May-June: Russian Army defeat in Galicia.
July: Poland lost.
July 2: Vorkonferenz in Berne decides to call the proletariat to united action for peace.

Sept. 5-8: Zimmerwald Conference. Delegates from Russia from the C.C. and the O.C. of the R.S.D.L.P.; the C.C. of the S.R. Party; the Bund; the Lettish S.D.; the Editorial Board of "Nashe Slovo" and "Zhizn." Formation of the International Socialist Commission.
Nov.: Defeat of Russian Army. Rasputin's influence in Russia.

1916

Struggle against Social Chauvinism and the imperialist war continues. Economic life of Russia becomes dislocated. Dissatisfaction grows among workers.
Feb.: Berne Conference: report on socialist activities in the belligerent countries against the War.

April: Kienthal II International Socialist Conference Left Opposition led by Lenin, Luxembourg and Radek suggests that the Conference should adopt most extreme

LENIN'S LIFE

Lenin and Zinoviev publish "Socialism and War" pamphlet defining their attitude towards the War.
Lenin represents the Left Wing.

1916

Speaks at Conference on the need to wage an illegal war for the social revolution. Maintains that after the War a proletarian revolution against the existing capitalist order is inevitable.

Lectures in Berne and Zürich on the need to revise the Agrarian programme of the R.S.D.L.P. Municipalisation must be replaced by nationalisation. He discusses the nearest tasks of social democracy in Russia.

Attends the Kienthal Conference.

In Zürich writes "Imperialism, the highest stage of Capitalism."

measures to liquidate the War: (1) a general strike, (2) sabotage, and (3) armed rising.

Bureau of the Zimmerwald Conference adopts the slogan "Convert the Imperialist War into Civil War."

Growing disorder in economic life of Russia. Police repression causes discontent among workers. Local strikes more frequent. Struggle among S.D.'s between Oborontsy and Porazhentsy in Russian and International Workers' Movement.

Dec.: Rasputin murdered.

Spreads the ideas of revolutionary internationalism among Swiss workers.

1917

Jan.-Feb.: Final disorganisation of Russian Government activity. Growing discontent among workers.

Feb. 23: Disorders in S.P.B. caused by food crisis. Attempt to dissolve the Duma.

Feb. 27: Troops go over to the side of the rising masses. Organisation of the Petrograd Soviet of Worker and Soldier Deputies. Power passes into the hands of the IV Duma and the Petrograd Soviet of Worker and Soldier Deputies.

March 2: Nicholas II abdicates. Collapse of monarchy in Russia. Formation of Provisional Government (Liberal bourgeois elements).

1917

During February revolution Lenin is in Switzerland and begins negotiations to be allowed to return to Russia.

208. (62 P²). TO M. V. KOBETSKY, AN ACTIVE COMMUNIST ÉMIGRÉ IN COPENHAGEN

[Poronin, 4th/6th August, 1914]

My dear Comrade,

Our trip has not come off.[1] I do not know whether you received the letter. If you did, then send a reply so as to check up if the post is regular. You will probably find you are an

---

[1] To the meeting of the International Socialist Bureau in Brussels.

exception now, and a rare exception, as an inhabitant in a neutral country and, therefore, if only the postal service functions properly, you must without fail keep us informed and send us news papers which will not be accessible here. Of course I mean only the most important news (especially about Russia). Let me know whether you will have (or already have) good links with Stockholm. Can you forward letters? Can you give an address for receiving money from Russia?

Greetings,

Your,

V. I.

209. (147 P²). TO VICTOR ADLER IN VIENNA

[Zürich], 5th September, 1914

Honoured Comrade,

I have arrived safely in Zürich with the whole family.[1] They asked to see the permit only at Innsbruck and Feldkirche; thus your help was very useful to me. Passports are required for entry into Switzerland, but I was allowed to enter without a passport when I named Greilich.

Best wishes and the utmost gratitude.

With Party greetings,

Lenin. (V. Ulianov)

210. (63 P²). TO V. A. KARPINSKY IN GENEVA

[Berne], 6th September, [1914]

My dear Comrade,

Yesterday I arrived quite safely with the whole family after a short imprisonment in Austria. Zinoviev will also be arriving.

---

[1] At the outbreak of the War Lenin was in Poronin, Galicia. On 25 July/7 Aug., the Austrian authorities searched his rooms. Lenin's MS. on the agrarian question was confiscated, the statistical tables being mistaken for a cypher. On the following day Lenin was arrested. After two weeks' imprisonment, Russian and Polish Social Democrats, aided by the Austrian Socialist, V. Adler, and the Austrian Parliamentary deputy, Diamand, procured his release. Lenin was permitted to leave Austria for Switzerland. Lenin arrived in Berne on 23 Aug./5 Sept., 1914, together with Krupskaya and her mother.

We thought of settling in Geneva, where all our old sym-
pathies draw us, but here we have begun to hesitate in favour
of Berne. They say the new French emigration from Paris,
Brussels etc. has made a bee line for Geneva. Have not prices
risen excessively, especially rents? Also, we can settle down only
temporarily. Shall we be able to find furnished rooms (two
small ones) with the use of kitchen, and on monthly terms?

Another question: if it is not too much trouble—please go
to the Société de Lecture (Grand' Rue 11) and borrow their
regulations. I must see if any changes have been made. It is this
particular society which draws me to Geneva; although here
too it is expensive. . . . But the printing press? Is there a
Russian one? Is it possible to publish a leaflet etc.? In Russian?
With special precautions, or as before? (Against the war of
course and against the new type of nationalists—from Haase to
Vandervelde and Hyde—they have all acted basely.)

I shall be much obliged if you answer my questions quickly.

Are there any other Bolshevik comrades in Geneva? Are
there any Bolsheviks travelling to Russia?

Greetings from us to you, to Comrade Olga [S. N. Ravich]
and to all friends.

Your,

N. Lenin

211. (64 p²). TO V. A. KARPINSKY IN GENEVA

[Berne, after the 27th September, 1914]

My dear K.,

I have received your postcard and I hasten to answer. Wait
a bit: we will tell you what can and must be done with regard
to what you (and we) wish. By the way, don't forget that the
law here is very strict now. Have you spoken about this with
your friends in Lausanne? [1] Do not fail to do so.

---

[1] The Lausanne Section of Bolsheviks: N. Bukharin, F. Il'in, N. Lukina, M.
Movshovich, Mira Movshovich, L. and E. Rivlin.

We are staying in Berne, address: Donnerbühlweg 11 a. Uljanow.

I do not know yet about the lecture. I shall have to think it over and discuss it in greater detail. On how many people can you count? [1]

Warm greetings from us all.

Your,

L.

P.S. "La Critique" and my "Anti-Critique" might form a better subject for the talk. However, two words: we cannot formalistically defend the base Chauvinism of the Germans. There were bad resolutions and others not so bad. There were announcements of both kinds. But there is a limit to everything. *And it has been exceeded.* We cannot, we must not, put up with it. We must not diplomatise. We must rise up against this disgraceful Chauvinism and with all our strength.

212. (65 P²). TO V. A. KARPINSKY IN GENEVA

[*Berne, before the 11th October, 1914, when Lenin
arrived in Lausanne*]

My dear Karpinsky,

I take this opportunity of having a frank chat with you.

There is *every* ground for expecting that the Swiss police and military authorities (at the first sign from the Russian, French Ambassadors etc.) will hold a court-martial or will insist on our expulsion for having infringed neutrality etc. Do not therefore write anything openly in letters. If you have anything to communicate, then use chemicals when you write. (The sign for chemicals is that the date of the letter is underlined.)

We have decided to publish the enclosed manifesto instead [2] of the rather unreadable theses. When you acknowledge its receipt, call the manifesto "The Development of Capitalism."

---

[1] Lenin lectured in Geneva on Oct. 15, 1914, on "The European War and Socialism."

[2] The manifesto of the C.C. of the R.S.D.L.P. about the War: "War and Russian Social Democracy," printed in No. 33 "Social Democrat," Nov. 1, 1914.

It ought to be published. But we advise you to do this only on condition that you use (and are *able* to use) the utmost precaution.

No one must know *where* and by whom it has been published. All rough drafts should be burnt. The publication ought to be kept *only* at the house of an influential Swiss citizen, a deputy or somebody like that.

If this is impossible, do *not* publish it.

If you cannot print it, then have it duplicated (also taking the maximum precaution). Reply: "I have received 'The Development of Capitalism' (so many copies) and will reprint so many copies."

If you cannot publish it either printed or duplicated, write at once. We shall think of something else. Reply more fully.

(If you manage to publish it, send us three-quarters of the issue *when an opportunity occurs* and we will find a place where it can be stored.)

I await your reply,

Your,

Lenin

P.S. We shall find the money for publication, only write beforehand, saying how much you need, because there is *very* little money. Could not the 170 francs from the Committee of Organisations Abroad[1] be used for this purpose?

213. (66 p²). TO V. A. KARPINSKY IN GENEVA

[Berne, before the 11th October, 1914]

My dear Friend,

I have received your letter about the conversation with Sig regarding the publications.[2] Excellent! Take what you need from the 170 francs (as little as possible of course, because we are hoping to publish a small miscellany) and publish the *manifesto*[3] (*not* theses,[4] but the *manifesto*) taking the utmost pre-

---

[1] The centre of R.S.D.L.P. organisations abroad.

[2] It was proposed that the Bolshevik publications should be stored at his house.

[3] See Letter 212.

[4] "Theses on the War"—the resolution of a group of Social Democrats, adopted on Sept. 6-7, 1914, by the Bolshevik Conference in Berne.

caution; do not publish many copies (2/300) and *hide* the stock *without fail* at the Swiss deputy's house.

If you have not the text of the manifesto, but only the theses, then get the manifesto in Lausanne.

I await a reply,

Your,

Lenin

P.S. We shall send the published material to Paris and to Russia; 100 for abroad and 200 for Russia. We can come to an arrangement by correspondence as to how to send them and to what addresses.

214. (67 P²). TO V. A. KARPINSKY IN GENEVA

[*Lausanne, 11th October, 1914*]

My dear Friend,

I spoke here today at a lecture by Plekhanov against his Chauvinism. I intend to lecture here on Tuesday on "The Proletariat and the War." I should like to lecture in Geneva (on the European War and European Socialism) on Wednesday. Please arrange this, after discussing the matter as secretly as possible, i.e. so that no permission will be necessary. (Of course it is also desirable that there should be as many people present as possible.) You will know best how to do this: to combine the maximum number of people with the minimum amount of police publicity and interference (or police threats). I lectured in Berne before members of groups and friends, recommended by the members, (120/130 people), without any bills being posted up etc. Is not that the best way of arranging it?

Reply to me at once c/o Mr. Ryvline, Villa Rougemont, Chailly-sur-Lausanne. I am lecturing here in Lausanne on Tuesday and your reply must be here by Tuesday afternoon. We will meet and discuss our affairs in greater detail. And so, if a permit is necessary for Geneva, think it over carefully as to whether it would or would not be better to have a secret meeting. Of course it is you who must make the decision. If I can manage Wednesday, then I shall arrive on Wednesday morning (arrange the lecture for Wednesday evening).

Greetings,

Your

Lenin

215. (68 P²). TO V. A. KARPINSKY IN GENEVA

[Berne, 17th October, 1914]

My dear K.,

Just while I was in Geneva, good news came from Russia, also the text of the reply of the Russian Social Democrats to Vandervelde.[1] We have therefore decided to issue a newspaper "The Social Democrat," instead of the separate manifesto.

Today this decision will, so to speak, be ratified.

And so, please take all steps, and as soon as possible, to discover some Frenchman, i.e. a Swiss subject, who will be the responsible editor, and to determine the approximate expenses. We propose that the paper shall be of two pages and about the size of the Paris "Golos" ["The Voice"].[2] How often it is to appear is not definitely decided, probably not oftener than two or three times a month. Not a large printing, for on account of our views we cannot reckon on the general reader (500 copies?); the price about 10 centimes. All this is still only hypothetical, but you must know this when you talk to the compositors.

What do you think its price should be?

How much time is required for the publication of such an issue (the setting up in type etc.)? Next: what kind of type? Have you only large type or is there a smaller type? How many thousand letters [of the alphabet] will fit into two pages, the size of "Golos" (1) in large type and (2) in small type?

---

[1] Vandervelde sent a telegram to the Social Democrat deputies of the IV State Duma, calling upon them in the name of Socialism to support the Russian Government in its struggle against Prussian junkerism.

[2] A daily Internationalist paper of the Left Wing of the Mensheviks which appeared in Paris, 13 Sept., 1914-17 Jan., 1915.

There is no need to disperse the print of the manifesto; we will include it in the newspaper. By Monday we shall send you some slight alterations to the manifesto and the altered signature (for after having heard from Russia, we are acting more officially).

A thousand greetings,

Your,

Lenin

P.S. Please notice whether my letters to you are arriving punctually (without any delay).

216. (69 p²). TO A. G. SHLYAPNIKOV IN STOCKHOLM

[*Berne*], *17th October, 1914*

My dear Friend,

I have read through the reply to Vandervelde and I append my thoughts on the subject of this reply.

It would be most desirable, if in the case of a summoning of the Duma (*is it true* that it will be summoned in a month's time?), our faction were united and announced a consistent policy. Reply without delay:

1. Will the Duma be summoned?

2. Are your links good with the Duma faction and how many days does it take for you to get into touch with them?

21st October, 1914

I continue my interrupted letter. My criticism of the reply is of course a private matter, intended *solely for friends* and with the object of establishing complete mutual understanding. The Central Organ ["The Social Democrat" No. 33] will appear in a day or two and we shall send it to you.

With regard to the International, do not be an optimist and beware of the intrigues of Liquidators and Opportunists. Although it is true that Martov is moving more towards the Left, yet he stands alone. But what will happen tomorrow? Tomorrow he will roll down towards the general plan: to shut the workers' mouths (and dull their minds and consciences) by an elastic resolution in the spirit of Kautsky, who justifies all and everything. Kautsky is the most hypocritical, revolting and harmful of all! Internationalism consists, kindly note, in the workers of each country shooting at the workers in another country under the pretext of "Defense of the Fatherland"! ! !

Let them intrigue—it is no more than a petty intrigue to be thinking at such a universally historic moment of diplomatising with Opportunism and of creating a "German" International Socialist Bureau! We must take a firm line and at once. The Petersburg workers have better feelings—hatred towards those who have betrayed German Social Democracy. We must encourage and consolidate this feeling and turn it into a firm decision to fight international Opportunism. Until now the authority was German Social Democracy—now it is a model of *what not to do!*

You are needed in Stockholm. See that correspondence with Russia is better organised. Forward my letters to the man who gave you a note in pencil (is that possible?). We must come to an understanding with him [L. B. Kamenev] and in greater detail. It is most important. We are beginning to issue the Central Organ.

Write oftener,   Your
                                                                      Lenin

217. (71 P²). TO V. A. KARPINSKY IN GENEVA

[Berne, 23rd October, 1914]

My dear V. K.,

The printers have held up the matter terribly! The manifesto was promised for Monday and today it is Friday. Terrible!

Surely it will not always be like this? ?

With regard to the address which ought to be printed on the newspaper: is it worth having a box number? (1) Would not that make you go there unnecessarily? (2) And the authorities would still know who owned the box number. Think it over;

would it not be better to give the address of the Bibliothèque Russe, for the Editors of the Central Organ?

Let us think this over.

Nicolet, [Swiss Social Democrat] they say, is *incapable* of looking after or passing on money etc. I have sent a number of articles; send the proofs in sections, as they come out. Then there will be no need to lose *two* days (which is far too long) in sending what is ready (one day is sufficient, if it is sent *express*).

We are waiting impatiently for the proofs.

On Monday I am lecturing in Montreux, on Tuesday [27 Oct. 1914] in Zürich. I shall not go to Geneva.

Greetings and best wishes,

Your,

Lenin

P.S. I have just received your letter. We will temporarily postpone the question of Jaures and Franck. We shall have to wait a little. It would be rather awkward simply to swear at them; and there is no reason to praise them. We have decided to say nothing for a time. And what about the proofs? ? ? Will they always take so long? The last number of the Central Organ was in December 1913—No. 32. So now the next must be No. 33.

218. (72 P²). TO A. G. SHLYAPNIKOV IN STOCKHOLM

Berne, 27th October, 1914

My dear Friend,

I have just received your second letter and I am sitting down to talk to you.

Many thanks for the letter about the Petersburg events.[1] It will make excellent correspondence in the Central Organ. An issue of the C.O. is appearing in a few days' time and we shall send you a copy. You can expect it. You can also expect

---

[1] Demonstrations on the Viborg side, Petersburg, in the first days of mobilisation in 1914.

the next issue. You will have to stay at present in Stockholm until the transport is *completely* organised *via* Stockholm, i.e. (1) of letters and (2) people and (3) literature. To do this you must systematically prepare and test a good intermediary in Stockholm. Is Comrade Skovno suitable for this? She would be suitable, because she is a Bolshevik. She would not be a turncoat. But is she businesslike and accurate?

If Comrade Kollontay is on our side, then I am sincerely glad; also I am glad that Martov in Paris is (on the whole) running the newspaper "Golos" very well, but I am seriously afraid that Martov (and those with him) will go over to the Kautsky-Trul'stra side. I hate Kautsky and at the moment I despise him more than anyone: a beastly, rotten, smug hypocrite. Oh no,—they say—nothing has happened, no principles have been violated; everyone was right in protecting the Fatherland; internationalism (kindly note) consists in the workers of all countries shooting at each other in the name of the "Defence of the Fatherland."

Rosa Luxembourg was right; she saw long ago that Kautsky, the servile theoretician, was cringing to the majority of the Party, to Opportunism. There is nothing in the world at present more harmful and dangerous for the *ideological* independence of the proletariat than this filthy, smug and disgusting hypocrisy of Kautsky. He wants to hush everything up and smear everything over and by sophistry and pseudo-learned rhetoric lull the awakened consciences of the workers. If Kautsky succeeds in doing this, he will become the principal representative of the bourgeois rottenness in the workers' movement and Trul'stra will be on his side. Oh! that Opportunist Trul'stra is nimbler than our kind little old man, Kautsky. How Trul'stra manœuvred to push honest people and Marxists out of the Dutch party (Horter, Pannekuk and Weinkoop). Never shall I forget how Roland Holst came to see me in Paris and said of Trul'stra: "Ein hundsgemeiner Kerl" ["a dirty dog"] "gredin" in French. I am sorry you have been casting pearls before him.[1] . . . Trul'stra plus those swine Opportunists in the Central Committee of the German Social Democrats are conducting a dirty

[1] Re Shlyapinov's meeting with Trul'stra in Stockholm, 23 Oct., 1914.

little intrigue to cover everything over. Keep your eyes open! Do not become an unwilling victim of the intrigue! Do not accidentally help these worst enemies of the Workers' Movement who, at a critical time, are defending Chauvinism "theoretically" and are using a wretched kind of diplomacy. The only one who spoke the truth to the workers, even if in half tones and occasionally not quite aptly, was Pannekuk, whose article ["The Crash of the International"] we sent to you (send a translation of it to the Russians). His remark that "if the 'leaders' of the International, which was killed by the Opportunists and Kautsky, were to meet and begin sticking the pieces together, it would not be of the slightest importance"—is the only Socialistic remark which has been uttered. And that is *the truth*. Bitter, but nevertheless true. But the workers need the truth now more than ever, the whole truth and not filthy diplomacy, nor the game of sticking pieces together, nor the covering up of evil by elastic resolutions.

It is quite clear to me that Kautsky, Trul'stra plus Vandervelde (possibly plus X, Y, Z, or even minus X, Y and Z, which is unimportant) are busy intriguing with this object in view. The transfer of the International Bureau to Holland is a similar kind of intrigue by these same rascals.

I will stand apart from them and from it all. I would also advise our representative in the International Socialist Bureau to do so (Litvinov, 76 High Street, Hampstead, London, N.W.), and I advise you to do the same.

"Do not follow the council of the ungodly." Do not believe Trul'stra, etc, etc, etc, etc, etc, but present them with a short ultimatum: here is our Central Committee's manifesto about the War (the theses revised; we will send it in printed form in a few days' time); do you want to print it in your language? No? Then, goodbye! We are evidently on different paths.

If Kollontay is on our side, let her help to push the manifesto in other languages. Get to know Hëglund, a young Swedish Social Democrat and leader of "the opposition." Read our manifesto to him (mention me: we met in Copenhagen). Try to find some ideological common ground (he is only a simple, sentimental anti-militarist; these people should be told: either you support the slogan of Civil War or you remain with the Opportunists and Chauvinists).

Our main task in Russia today is to organise an ideological repulse against the Opportunists of the International and Kautsky. That is the heart of the matter. Will Martov go over to them? I am afraid he will.

Warm greetings,

Your,

Lenin

219. (73 P²). TO A. G. SHLYAPNIKOV IN STOCKHOLM

[Berne, 31st October, 1914]

My dear Friend,

In about two or three days' time, you will receive our Central Organ ["The Social Democrat" No. 33] and then I hope there will be complete agreement in our views. Honestly, I am a little afraid that some of the steps you are taking could be interpreted as though you were acting without our legal representative in the International Socialist Bureau, Mr. Litvinov, 76 High Street, Hampstead, London, N.W. Of course such an interpretation would be a mischievous misinterpretation, but all the same, do be more careful.

Trul'stra has deceived you or led you into temptation. He is an arch-Opportunist and an agent of the intrigues of the basest centre of the most base Opportunists, the German Social Democrat intriguers (with Kautsky at their head basely defending the Opportunists) and their most base Central Committee. We shall not agree to any conferences, nor join in any steps on the initiative of such scoundrels. We shall stand aside; let them disgrace themselves and, having disgraced themselves once, they will again disgrace themselves. The French have already rejected their intrigues and without the French, only a dirty farce of filthy scoundrels is possible!

Larin [a Menshevik Liquidator] is evidently deceiving you mercilessly. If he expresses confidence in the German Central

Committee, then I understand that Trul'stra has "written this down." Of course! Faith in the foulest Opportunists! For God's sake, put right what can be put right and do not show the slightest confidence either directly or indirectly in any of the Opportunists, neither the French, nor the German. Pannekuk was right: the Second International is definitely dead. The Opportunists have killed it (and not "Parliamentarisation" as that clumsy Pannekuk called it). The patching up of differences is only a miserable intrigue and *we* must not take *any* part in it, neither directly, nor indirectly.

We shall try soon to send you a couple of leaflets. Do not go away. Be patient for a time. Arrange everything about which I wrote to you. Wait until the Central Organ is in Russia. Wait also until we reach a *complete* agreement with our Russian colleagues (and with Kamenev and others) after they have received the Central Organ. Before this is done, it is useless for you to think of leaving. It would be premature for us to move. By the way, find out if it is possible to print Social Democratic material in Sweden (similar to our Central Organ).

Poor Gorky! What a pity he has disgraced himself by signing that foul little paper of those dirty Russian Liberals.[1] Meshkovsky and Plekhanov, etc. (Maslov and Smirnov among them) have joined him.

Do not fail to get hold of and to re-read (or ask for it to be translated for you) Kautsky's "Way to Power" and see what he wrote in it about the revolution of our time!!

And how treacherous he has been in renouncing all this now!

Our task at present is a merciless war against Chauvinism (which hides behind chatter about the "Defence of the Fatherland," etc.) and especially against the Socialistic Chauvinism of Plekhanov, Hyde, Kautsky (the worst of all, the hypocrite) and Co. By defending the revolution (a bourgeois one in Russia and a socialistic one in the West) we also advocate it at the war. Our slogan is civil war. It is sheer sophistry to say that this slogan is unsuitable etc., etc. We cannot "make" it,

---

[1] M. Gorky signed an appeal "From writers and artists" protesting against German atrocities, printed in "Russkiye Vedomosti," 23 Sept., 1914.

but we advocate it and are working in that direction. In each country the first thing to be done is to struggle against Chauvinism in that country and to arouse hatred against one's own Government, to appeal (repeatedly, insistently, frequently, incessantly) for solidarity among the workers of the fighting countries and to conduct *mutual* civil war against the bourgeoisie.

No one would venture to *vouch* when and to what extent this preaching will be justified in practice: that is *not* the point (only low sophists renounce revolutionary agitation on the grounds that it is uncertain when a revolution would take place). The point lies in such a *line* of work. *Only* such work is socialistic and not chauvinistic and it *alone* will yield socialistic fruit, revolutionary fruit.

The slogan of peace is now inappropriate and mistaken (especially after the treachery of almost all the leaders up to and including Hyde, Plekhanov, Vandervelde and Kautsky). In actual fact, it would be a petit-bourgeois wailing. But we —even on military ground—must remain revolutionaries. And we must conduct propaganda for class warfare among the soldiers.

With warm greetings. Write oftener.

Your

Lenin

220. (272 R). TO A. I. ELIZAROVA

[*Berne*], *1st/14th November, 1914*

Darling Anyuta,

I have received your letter, also one from Mark, and a postcard from Mother. Many, many thanks! I am not hard up for money at the moment. My imprisonment was quite short, only twelve days, and I very soon received special privileges; altogether the "sitting" was quite easy, conditions and treatment good.[1] I have been able to look round a bit

---

[1] Lenin was accused of spying for Russia. He was in prison from the 8th to 19th August.

and have fixed myself up here. We are living in two furnished rooms, very good ones, we dine in a restaurant close by. Nadya feels well; E. V. also, although she has grown very old. I am finishing my article for Granat's Encyclopædia (about Marx) and am sending it to him one of these days; only I had to leave the major part (almost all) of my books in Galicia. . . . I am nervous about what may happen to them.[1]

It is very sad to watch the growth of Chauvinism in the various countries and such treacherous acts, as those of the German (and not only German) Marxists or pseudo-Marxists. . . . It is quite understandable why the Liberals are again praising Plekhanov: he has fully deserved this shameful punishment.[2] Tell me as soon as you can how matters stand about the journal ["Vozrozhdeniye"]. Is there any possibility of restarting it and when? Does the post take any responsibility for registered manuscripts? I embrace you warmly and kiss Mother. I wish you good health. Greetings from all to all.

Your

V. Ulianov

We saw the shameful and shameless number [9] of the "Sovremenny Mir."[3] A disgrace! A disgrace!

221. (74 P²). TO A. G. SHLYAPNIKOV IN STOCKHOLM

[Berne], 14th November, 1914

My dear Friend,

I was very glad to hear from you that the Central Organ had been received and that it would go where it ought to.

With regard to your speech at the Congress of the Swedish Social Democrats [23 Nov. 1914], I can give you only this advice: either not to speak at all, or to say that you welcome the fraternal party of Swedish workers and you wish it all success *in the spirit of revolutionary international social democracy.*

---

[1] Many of Lenin's books were confiscated and later handed over to the General Staff in Warsaw.

[2] From the beginning of the War Plekhanov became a nationalist.

[3] Containing an ultra-Chauvinist article by N. Iordansky.

If you cannot say *this*, then it is not worth saying anything at all. But if you can, then of course it would be better to add that the Russian workers (a) have expressed their view through the Social Democratic faction, which did *not* vote for the budget; (b) that they are issuing *illegal* proclamations in Petersburg, Riga, Moscow and the Caucasus; (c) that their Party Organ, the Central Committee and the Central Organ have come out against international Opportunism.

Is that "correct"? H'm. . . . Of course Branting will not like this, but it is not our business to please the Opportunists. If you are allowed ten to twelve minutes and *freedom* of speech, then you ought to say something *against German* (and other) Opportunism; without, of course, offending by a single word either the Swedish Social Democrats or their "young people" etc. I would advise you *not* to mention the re-establishment of the International either directly or indirectly. I send you an article [Pannekuk: "The Crash of the International"] (a very good one!) on this subject (translate it and send it over to Russia). We will be silent on the subject of the re-establishment of the International and will stand aside. We must wait. The German *Left* is stirring [1]; if they have a split, then perhaps the International will be saved from rotting.

You are mistaken in thinking that the bourgeoisie do not want to hear about the slogan of peace. Today I read the English "Economist" [No. 3716, "The Opening of Parliament" article]. The *clever* bourgeois of a leading country are *for* peace (of course for the sake of *strengthening* capitalism), but we must not allow ourselves to be mixed up with the petit-bourgeois, the sentimental Liberals etc. A bayonet period has begun! And that is a fact which means that we must fight *with the same kind of weapon*.

The slogan of peace will be caught up if not tomorrow then the day after tomorrow by the *German* bourgeoisie and especially by the *Opportunists*. We must stand for the slogan of a *revolutionary proletariat* capable of *fighting* for its *own* aims and

---

[1] The formation of a Left International wing of the German S.D. Party, with Karl Liebknecht and R. Luxembourg at the head, which formed the kernel of the "Spartak" union.

that means civil war. It is also a *very* concrete slogan and only through it are the main tendencies clearly revealed: for the proletariat or for the bourgeoisie.

With regard to the debt to the Swedes[1]; neither I nor Nadezhda Konstantinovna remember anything at all about it, but it is possible I may not have known about it, or else have forgotten. It would therefore be helpful to send an amiable letter of thanks and suggest that the debt be wiped out. I think you can manage this quite easily; for instance, in the name of the Petersburg Committee plus *several* Social Democratic deputies who empowered you in Petersburg. I think that would be the best way.

And with regard to the loan, I think you should act in a similar way. I do not advise you to put forward a letter from me (factional difficulties would follow!!). If you insist, then I will send you a letter, but my advice is that this is not necessary. Really, they would be more inclined to give it to you without me. Refer to Petrovsky (if necessary, get a letter from him). I feel sure that would be better.

I greet you warmly and send you my best wishes.

Your
N. Lenin

P.S. If Kollontay translates the Central Committee manifesto into German (in No. 33 of the Central Organ), perhaps you will send us a copy.

P.P.S. With regard to the question of the peace slogan: an interesting article ["English Radicalism and the War"] by Bernstein in the last number of "Neue Zeit" [No. 6, 13 Nov. 1914] shows that in England, where the bourgeoisie are the freest and most enlightened etc., there is a movement *for* peace from the point of view of arch-Opportunism. Namely, peace guarantees "social peace" i.e. the *submission* of the proletariat to the bourgeoisie, the calming of the proletariat, the *continuance* of the existence of capitalism. Bernstein does not develop this. But evidently there are many such peacemakers among

---

[1] The Swedish S.D. Party lent 3,000 kroner to the R.S.D.L.P. during the London Congress of the R.S.D.L.P. in 1907.

the Liberal and Radical bourgeoisie of all countries. Add to this: (a) that *all* Chauvinists are also for peace (only on *what* terms?), but in a censored Press we shall *not be allowed* to speak about our terms; (b) that the German and Russian *Imperial Courts* (secretly today, half openly tomorrow) also want a separate peace one with another; (c) that all sentimental bourgeois and ordinary people want peace from an "anti-revolutionary," common, serf point of view.

The question arises: objectively, who will benefit by this peace slogan? It will certainly not help the propaganda of the ideas of the revolutionary proletariat. Nor will it help the idea *of making use* of the war for accelerating the crash of capitalism.

Add to this the victory of the Opportunist Chauvinists in almost all countries. It is only such people that the peace slogan *will help*.

222. (159 p²). TO THE SECRETARY OF THE GRANAT PUBLISHING
HOUSE IN MOSCOW

[Berne], 17th November, [1914]

Dear Colleague,

I sent to you yesterday, and by registered post, an article for the Encyclopædia on Marx and Marxism. It is not for me to judge how far I have succeeded in solving the difficult task of fitting the exposition into the framework of 75,000 letters [of the alphabet], or thereabouts. I should like to say that much of the material had to be considerably condensed: (75,000 was the ultimatum) and I had to select only the most *essential* points in the various movements (of course giving predominance to those which supported Marx). It was difficult to make up my mind to reject many *quotations* from Marx. I think quotations are very important in an encyclopædia (especially those relating to the most disputed questions of Marxism, of which the foremost are philosophy and the agrarian question). The readers of the Encyclopædia should be able to refer to *all* the most important pronouncements of Marx, otherwise the aim of the Encyclopædia would not be achieved; or so it seemed to me. Also, I do not know whether you will be satisfied with it from the censorship point of view: if not, we might be able to agree to the *alteration* of certain passages to comply with the censorship. For my part, I could not decide to alter, for the sake of the censorship, a number of quotations and positions of Marxism, unless it was insisted upon by the editors.

I hope you will immediately acknowledge the receipt of my article if only by a postcard. Please send me the money for the article as soon as possible to M. T. Elizarov's address. My address is: Herrn Wladimir Ulyanow, Distelweg 11, Berne.

Please accept my assurance that I am always at your service.

V. Il'in

P.S. As the result of the War, my library is now stuck in Galicia and I have not been able to find certain quotations in the *Russian* translations of Marx's works. If you think it essential, perhaps you can entrust this to someone in Moscow. By the way, I should be glad if you could send me the proofs of my article and tell me if partial alterations are permissible in proof-reading. If you cannot send the proofs, I hope you will not refuse to send me an off-print.

223. (76 p²). TO A. G. SHLYAPNIKOV IN STOCKHOLM

[Berne], *28th November, 1914*

My dear Friend,

I received a telegram today from Branting that "the newspapers confirm the arrest of five deputies" [of the R.S.D.L. faction of the State Duma]. I am afraid there can be no doubt about the arrest!

It is a terrible thing. The Government has evidently decided to avenge itself on the Russian Social Democratic Labour faction and will not stop at anything. We must expect the worst falsification of documents, pretexts and the setting of traps; false evidence, cases in camera, closed Courts etc., etc.

I think that without using such means, the Government would not have been able to get a conviction. Can you try to discover the names of the arrested people?

Is Kamenev safe?

In any case, the work of our Party has become a hundred times more difficult. And yet we will carry it forward!

"Pravda" has educated thousands of conscious workers from among whom in spite of all difficulties a group of leaders will again be found—a Russian Central Committee of the Party. It is now particularly important that you should stay in (or *near*) Stockholm and that you should concentrate on the establishment of links with Petersburg.

(Write and tell us whether you have received the money that was on loan. In my last letter I enclosed a note about this for you. If you have not received any money and you cannot find any, we shall probably be able to send you a little; write in greater detail.)

The newspaper "Otkliki" ["Re-echoes," the Bund Organ] has been promised in Zürich since last December (the Liquidators plus Trotsky probably). In Paris a daily Social Revolutionary paper "Mysl" has begun to appear [2/15 Nov. 1914] (arch-base phrasemongering, with leanings towards the Left). There is an abundance of newspapers, full of phrases from the intelligentsia, revolutionary today and what tomorrow? (Tomorrow they will make peace with Kautsky, Plekhanov and the patriotic, Chauvinistic Liquidator intelligentsia in Russia). They never had anything in common with the *workers'* class in Russia and have nothing now. You cannot trust them an inch.

I greet you warmly and hope you are cheerful.

Times are hard, but we shall succeed!

Your

Lenin

224. (273 R). TO M. I. ULIANOVA

[Berne], 9th/22nd December, 1914

Darling Manyasha,

Today I received your letter of the 14th/27th November and am very glad to get it. You wrote to the address of our old flat. Our present address is Distelweg 11.

You ask whether there is a bureau of information here about Russian prisoners; I will try to find out; also about the prisoner [Aaron Rosenfeldt, the brother of a Party member] you are enquiring about. On account of the approaching holidays you will probably not hear this at once, but in any case I shall try.

We are living here quite comfortably; quietly and peacefully in sleepy Berne. The libraries are good and I am well supplied in the way of books. It is pleasant to do some reading —after a period of daily newspaper work. Nadya has found a pedagogic library here and is writing a work on pedagogy.

I wrote to Anyuta and asked whether it would be possible to find a publisher for a book on agriculture: I could write it here. *If* the occasion arises, please find out for me.

Why have you not written anything about yourself—how is your health? Have you work? What sort and where? Is it bearable?

Write when you can,
I greet you warmly,
Your
V. Ulianov

Nadya and El. Vas. send much love. If you have an opportunity, find out (if it is not a nuisance) whether Granat has received my article on Marx. It would be good to have work for the Encyclopædia: but that is probably not easy to arrange unless there is a chance of getting to know the secretary of the editorial board.

225. (80 p²). TO ANASTASIA KOLLONTAY [1] IN CHRISTIANIA

[Berne, the end of December, 1914]

Dear and honoured Comrade,

I am very grateful to you for sending the leaflet [2] (for the moment I can hand it over only to local members of the editorial board of "Rabotnitsa." They have sent a letter to Zetkin (evidently the contents tallied with yours)). Also I thank you for offering to send me information about England for the Central Organ. I am in correspondence with a comrade in London, Mr. Litvinov, who represents the Central Committee of our Party in the International Socialist Bureau, but presumably the more links we have with representatives of the Left of the International the better. I quite agree with you that such representatives should keep closer together and meet each other; but before realising this aim I will take advantage of your pleasant letter to continue our correspondence.

Evidently you do not quite agree with the slogan of civil war and you give it an almost subordinate (perhaps a conditional) position behind the slogan of peace. And you emphasize that "we must bring forward a slogan which will *unite all*."

I tell you frankly, that at present I am afraid of such wholesale unifying, which in my opinion is most dangerous and most destructive to the proletariat. Has not Kautsky already composed an arch-unifying theory in "Neue Zeit"? [3] . . .

226. (81 p²). TO A. M. KOLLONTAY IN CHRISTIANIA

[Berne, the end of December, 1914]

Dear Comrade,

I have received your letter and the English enclosure. [4]

---

[1] An active participator in organising the Left Internationalist elements among the Social Democrats in the Scandinavian countries.

[2] An appeal to women by the members of the Stockholm Group of the R.S.D.L.P.

[3] See Kautsky's articles: "Die Internationalität und der Krieg," "Sozialdemokratie im Kriege," in "Neue Zeit," Oct.-Nov., 1914.

[4] Questions of the English Independent Labour Party to the Socialist Parties on the attitude of their centres to the war.

Many thanks.

I send you both little articles about which you write. Let me know whether you will translate and forward them and what happens to them.

They say there was a leader in the "Hamburger Echo" about our "treachery to the International." And it says that the Germans, (i.e. the German Opportunist swine), are everything and that Plekhanov, Maslov and Chkheidze are *on their side.*[1]

Is this true? What do you think of it?

Greetings and best wishes,

V. Il'in

P.S. Ask Alexander to make the acquaintance of Kobezky, Kapelwej 51, Kjobenhavn VI and to get my letter from him. It is useless to put forward a kindly programme of pious wishes for peace, if simultaneously the propaganda for illegal organisation and civil war of the proletariat against the bourgeoisie is not put into the first place.

N. Lenin

P.P.S. The European War has done a great service to International Socialism in that it has clearly revealed the whole state of rottenness, baseness and swinery of Opportunism, thus giving a magnificent incentive towards cleaning up the workers' movement and ridding it of the filth which has accumulated during the scores of peaceful years.

N. Lenin

1915

227. (160 P²). TO THE SECRETARY OF THE GRANAT PUBLISHING
HOUSE IN MOSCOW

[*Berne*], *4th January, 1915*

Dear Colleague,

Yesterday I received your letter and sent you a telegram: "I consent." Although it is disappointing that the Editorial

[1] Lenin is evidently thinking of the article: Konrad Haenisch "Der Deutsche Verrat an der Internationale," in "Hamburger Echo," 8 Dec., 1914.

Board has had to cut out everything about Socialism and everything on tactics (without which Marx is not Marx), yet I was compelled to agree, because I can do nothing against the reason you put forward (i.e. "absolutely impossible").

I shall be grateful if you will send me an off-print (or a postcard saying *when* I can expect it). By the way, will there not still be time for certain corrections in the section on dialectics? Perhaps you will be good enough to write and say when exactly it is to go to the printers and what the last date is for receiving corrections. I have been studying this question of dialectics for the last six weeks and I think I could add something to it if there were time.

Also, I take the opportunity of offering my services to the editors of the Encyclopædia, if there are still some unallotted articles for the subsequent volumes. At present I am in exceptionally good circumstances in Berne with regard to German and French libraries where I can read, but I am in exceptionally bad circumstances with regard to literary work in general. It would therefore be a great pleasure to undertake articles on the subjects of political economy, politics, the labour movement, philosophy and others. My wife has written under the name of N. Krupskaya on pedagogy in "The Russian School" and "Free Education." She has made a special study of the *labour school* and the classical writers on pedagogy. She would gladly undertake articles on these questions.

At your service,

W. Ulyanow

Address: Wl. Ulyanow,
     Distelweg 11,
     Berne.

228. (85 P²). TO A. G. SHLYAPNIKOV

[Berne, end of January, 1915]

My dear Friend,

Your plan with regard to the April journey [to Russia] and your preparations for it seem to me to be quite right. Really one ought to adopt such a plan and prepare it as systematically and as thoroughly as possible.[1]

Thank you for the letters. We have written to you several times. We also sent you the lists with seals. I hope you have received them.

Today we received a copy of "Nashe Slovo" ["Our Word"] which has begun to appear in Paris instead of "Golos" whose publication has been stopped. In this issue of "Nashe Slovo" is Martov's (and Dan's) announcement about divergence from "Nasha Zarya" ["Our Dawn"].

Evidently they (the Liquidators) are going to pieces and one does not know what will happen. Axelrod is evidently "making peace" between the German Chauvinists (and those of the Bund) and the Francophiles (and Plekhanov). After Zürich Martov sang to Axelrod's tune, but now we do not know if he has gone Left for any length of time.

One of these days we shall bring out No. 37 of "The Social Democrat."

I send you warm greetings and wish you all success.

Your
Lenin

P.S. Before April we will try (together with you) to establish correspondence and some sort of links. You too must see about this *beforehand*.

229. (274 R). TO M. I. ULIANOVA

[Berne], 27th January/9th February, 1915

Darling Manyasha,

I have received from you the two small pamphlets by Oganovsky ["Why the Great War flared up"] and Maslov ["The Economic Causes of the World War"]. Very many thanks! ! Both men are bad Opportunists of the most harmful type (can there possibly be an agreement between them and Plekhanov? That is arch-bad). But it is extremely useful to

---

[1] Shlyapnikov proposed first travelling to England in order to get papers from Belgian refugees. Shlyapnikov did travel to the England and then to Russia via Norway and Sweden. He lived in Russia as a foreigner.

know their writings and I shall, therefore, be arch-grateful if you will send me such things, as well as newspaper (and periodical) cuttings, which refer to similar things. For instance, E. Smirnov [E. Gurevich, Menshevik journalist] wrote some time ago (in August or September) in "Russkiye Vedomosti," arch-basenesses on the subject of voting credits etc. I saw that, but I know nothing about his further literary activity nor of other people like him.

We are quite well off here with regard to foreign newspapers and books in libraries. We are living quite comfortably. Berne is a dull, small, but cultured little town. E. V. is ill with influenza.

An anti-Chauvinist mood is growing among the Germans; there is a split both in Stuttgart and in Frankfurt-am-Main.[1] "Lichtstrahlen"[2] in Berlin are publishing works of an anti-Chauvinist tendency.

If it is not too much trouble for you, and if you happen to be near, (please, do not go specially, it is *not at all* urgent), find out from Granat, who accepted my article [on Marx] for the Encyclopædia, if payment has been sent to M. T. Elizarov (as I asked) and if it is at all possible to get some more work for the Encyclopædia. I wrote about this to the Secretary, but he has not answered.

I greet you warmly and send greetings from myself and Nadya.

Your

V. Ulianov

230. (158 P²). TO THE EDITORS OF "NASHE SLOVO"
["OUR WORD"] IN PARIS

Berne, 9th February, 1915

Dear Comrades,

In your letter of February the 6th you suggest to us a plan for fighting "official-social patriotism" on the occasion of the

---

[1] A split between the Opportunist and the Centre-Kautskian majority in the Social Democratic Party on the one hand, and its Left Radical wing on the other.

[2] A monthly published by the Left Social Democratic Group, "I.S.D." (International Socialists of Germany).

projected London Conference of the Socialists of the "allied" countries of the Triple Entente. As you, of course, see from our Organ, "The Social Democrat," we approve of fighting it in general and are doing so. We are, therefore, very glad that you should refer to us and we accept with great pleasure your suggestion that we should discuss a plan for common action.

They say that the Conference which was intended for the 15th February (we have not received a single document about it) may be postponed until the 25th February, or even later (judging by Huysmans' letter informing us that there will be a meeting of the Executive Commission on the 20th February and of the plan to have personal conversations between the members (the Secretary) of the Executive Commission and the Socialists of England, France and Russia). It is possible that the Conference is being planned to consist not of the official members of the International Socialist Bureau, but as *private* discussions between individual "outstanding" Socialists.

Therefore this juxtaposition of a clear revolutionary and international point of view (about which you write and with which we fully sympathise) to "official-social patriotism" must be prepared *for all possible eventualities* (both in the case of a Conference of official representatives of the Parties and in case of private discussions in all forms, both for the 15th February and for a later date).

In answer to your request, we, for our part, suggest the following draft of a declaration containing such a juxtaposition (so that this declaration can be read and printed):

"The undersigned representatives of Social Democratic organisations in Russia (England etc.) proceed from the conviction that the present war is an imperialistic war, not only on the part of Germany and Austria-Hungary, but also on the part of England and France (who are acting in league with Czarism); that is to say, it is a war at a period when capitalism has reached the last stage of its development, a period when the bourgeois governments are breathing their last within national boundaries; it is a war directed exclusively towards the seizure of colonies, the plunder of competitive countries and the weakening of the proletarian movement by means of setting the proletariat of one country against the proletariat of another.

It is, therefore, the undoubted duty of Socialists in all belligerent countries immediately and decisively to bring into operation the Basle resolutions [Nov. 25, 1912], namely:

1. To break up national blocs and destroy civil peace in all countries;

2. To appeal to the workers in all the belligerent countries to wage energetic class warfare, both economic and political, against the bourgeoisie of their own particular country, a bourgeoisie that are earning incredible profits on war supplies, and are using the support of the military authorities to shut the mouths of the workers and to increase their own despotic control over them;

3. To condemn resolutely any voting of war loans;

4. To resign from the bourgeois ministries in Belgium and France and to regard entering a ministry and the voting of war loans as being the same sort of treachery to the Socialist cause as is the whole behaviour of the Austrian and German Social Democrats.

5. Immediately to stretch out a hand to the internationalist elements of German Social Democracy, who are refusing to vote for war loans and to form with them an International Committee for the purpose of agitating for the cessation of war, not in the spirit of the pacifists, the Christians and petit-bourgeois Democrats, but indissolubly linked with propaganda and the organisation of mass revolutionary actions of the proletariat against the government and bourgeoisie in each country.

6. To support all attempts at union and fraternising in the armies and in the trenches between the Socialists of the belligerent countries, despite the prohibition of the military authorities of England, Germany etc.

7. To call upon the women Socialists in the belligerent countries to increase agitation in the above-named direction.

8. To call upon the proletariat of all nations to support the struggle against Czarism and to support those Social Democrat deputies in Russia, who have not only refused to vote for credits, but also have not been deterred by the danger of perse-

cution from conducting their socialist work in the spirit of international revolutionary social democracy.

.   .   .   .

As for certain Russian Social Democrat writers who have been defending official social patriotism, (for instance Plekhanov, Alexinsky, Maslov and others) the undersigned refuse any responsibility for their activities and definitely protest against them and declare that, judging from all the facts, the Social Democrat workers of Russia do not share their point of view.

It goes without saying, that the official representative of our Central Committee in the International Socialist Bureau, Comrade Litvinov, (we are sending him your letter and a copy of our answer to it. We ask you to deal direct with him concerning all urgent matters) decides independently any question dealing with minor alterations and any steps taken in negotiations etc. We declare our *complete* solidarity with this comrade in *every* fundamental matter.

As for the Organisation Committee and the Union which are officially represented in the International Socialist Bureau, we have grounds for fearing that they support official social patriotism (in its Francophile, Germanophile form or in one which reconciles both these tendencies). In any case, we shall be glad if you will send us a reply (your corrections, counterproposals for a declaration etc.) as well as an answer from those organisations (the Organising Committee the Union etc.) to which you have referred and will refer.

With comradely greetings,

Lenin

231. (86 P²). TO A. G. SHLYAPNIKOV IN STOCKHOLM

[*Berne*], *11th February*, [*1915*]

My dear Friend,

I have received your two letters of the 4th and 5th February. Many thanks. With regard to sending "The Social Democrat" we gave your letter to the Secretary of the Expedional Commission to read. I will remind him personally tomorrow and I hope everything will be done.

The Paris people promised to send you the Plekhanov pamphlet ["On War"] and we are very surprised you have not received it. We will order it again and get a copy so as to forward it ourselves.

The two Plekhanovites about whom you wrote have been here. We talked with them. Pay attention to the little white man [A. Popov = N. Vorobiev] (they are travelling back by the same route); Plekhanov has evidently repulsed him even more than the dark man [N. Stoinov]. The latter is evidently a hopeless chatterbox. But the former is always silent and one cannot know what he is thinking.[1]

We received a letter from "Nashe Slovo" (now appearing in Paris instead of "Golos"). It contained a plan for a general protest against official social patriotism (because of a project of the London Conference of the Triple Entente Socialists). We do not know whether the Conference will take place. The other day Litvinov forwarded to us the letter from Huysmans who is behaving somewhat strangely by calling an Executive Committee of the International Socialist Bureau at the Hague for the 20th February and is organising in the same place for the 20th-25th February personal conversations (!) with the delegates from England, France and Russia. Extraordinary!! It looks like preparations for something Francophile and patriotic (by the way, you are quite right, that now there are many "files" but few Socialists. For us both Francophiles and Germanophiles are equally patriotic bourgeois or their slaves, but not Socialists. The Bundists, for instance, are generally Germanophiles and rejoice at the thought of Russia's defeat, but how are they any better than Plekhanov? Both are Opportunists and social Chauvinists, but of varying degree, and Axelrod also).

We replied to "Nashe Slovo" that we were glad to hear of its proposal and sent our draft of the declaration [see letter No. 158]. There is not much hope of agreement with them,

[1] This refers to the visit of two inter-regional Plekhanovites to all the émigré centres.

for they say Axelrod is in Paris, but Axelrod (see Nos. 86 and 87 of "Golos" and No. 37 of "The Social Democrat") is a social Chauvinist who wishes to reconcile the Francophiles and Germanophiles on the basis of social Chauvinism. We shall see which is more precious to "Nashe Slovo"—anti-Chauvinism or Axelrod's pleasantries.

I think both in Russia and throughout the world, a new fundamental grouping within Social Democracy is becoming apparent: Chauvinists ("social-patriots") with their friends and supporters, and anti-Chauvinists. Fundamentally, this division corresponds to a division between Opportunists and revolutionary Social Democrats, but it is more precise and represents, so to speak, a higher stage of development and one closer to the socialistic upheaval. Even with us the old grouping (Liquidators and supporters of "Pravda") is becoming out of date and is being replaced by a new and more rational one: social-patriots and anti-patriots. By the way, they say that Dan is a German "social-patriot" i.e. a Germanophile i.e. a supporter of Kautsky. Is this true? It looks very much like the truth. It is curious, that there is a split in the Organisation Committee along a *bourgeois* line: Francophiles (Plekhanov + Alexinsky + Maevsky + "Nasha Zarya") and Germanophiles (the Bund + Axelrod + Dan?? etc.).

If you do not get any money from the Swedes, then write: we will send you 100 francs. Think out carefully where it will be best (i.e. the most useful for work and the least dangerous for you; you must safeguard yourself!), whether to wait in London or in Norway. It is extremely important to have the transport running smoothly, if only a little at a time. You should see the Plekhanovites, who will be with you in about two or three weeks' time and come to an understanding with them about all this.

Warm greetings. I send you my wishes and hope you are keeping cheerful,

Your

Lenin

232. (87 P²). TO A. M. KOLLONTAY IN CHRISTIANIA

[Berne, Spring, 1915]

My dear Comrade,

Many thanks for all your trouble and help about which you wrote in your last letter.

Your articles in "Nashe Slovo" and "The Communist" about Scandinavian affairs have raised the following questions in my mind:

Can the position of the Left Scandinavian Social Democrats, who disapprove of the arming of the people, be appraised and considered to be right? I argued this with Z. Hoglund in 1910 [at the Copenhagen International Socialist Congress] and I tried to prove to him that it was not Left, nor revolutionary, but simply Philistinism of the provincial petit-bourgeoisie. These Scandinavian petit-bourgeois in their little kingdoms have penetrated almost to the North Pole and take pride in the fact that you can travel to them for three years and yet not reach them! How can a revolutionary class on the eve of a social revolution be against the arming of the people? It is not a struggle against militarism, but a cowardly striving to run away from the major questions of the capitalist world. How can class warfare be "recognised" without understanding the inevitability of its transformation at certain given moments into civil war?

It seems to me that one ought to collect some material about this and come out definitely against it in "The Communist"; and in order to teach the Scandinavians, you would print this later in Swedish etc.

I should like to have your detailed opinion about this.

Bruce Glasier is, in my opinion, an unsuitable collaborator. Even if he has a streak of proletarianism, he is nevertheless an unbearable Opportunist. I doubt if one could work with him; he will start crying after two days and say he has been "dragged in," that he does not want anything of the kind and cannot recognise it.

Have you seen David's book ["Die Sozialdemokratie im Weltkrieg," Berlin, 1915] and his comments on our manifesto?[1] Is there any information in the Scandinavian countries about the conflict between the two tendencies in the attitude towards war? Cannot accurate facts be gathered (comments, estimates, resolutions) with an exact juxtaposition of the *facts* regarding the tendency of both currents? Do the facts confirm (in my opinion they do), that the Opportunists taken as a current are generally more Chauvinists than revolutionary Social Democrats? What do you think? Couldn't one collect and work up such material for "The Communist"?

I send you warm greetings and best wishes.

Your,
N. Lenin

P.S. Who is this Shaw Desmond, who was lecturing in the Scandinavian countries? Could not one get hold of his lecture in English? Is he a conscious revolutionary?

233. (88 p²). TO A. M. KOLLONTAY IN CHRISTIANIA

[Zorenberg, Summer, 1915]

My dear A. M.

We are sending the money to you tomorrow. Many thanks for the news from Russia. In principle we have nothing against the agreement and we hope you will be extremely careful.

With regard to arming the people, as opposed to disarming, it seems to me that we cannot alter our programme.[2] If the words about class warfare are not an empty phrase in the Liberal sense, as it has become with the Opportunists (Kautsky and Plekhanov), then how can one retort against a historical fact—of turning this warfare under certain conditions into civil war? Further, how can an oppressed class be opposed to the idea of arming the people?

To reject that means to fall into the half-anarchist attitude towards Imperialism: that, in my opinion, can be seen in several Left partisans, even among ourselves. If Imperialism, they say,

---

[1] The manifesto on the subject of war by the C.C. of the R.S.D.L.P. was put down in David's book as folly and a crude distortion of the decisions of the International.

[2] §12 of the R.S.D.L.P. Adopted by the II Congress in 1903.

then neither the self-determination of nations, nor the arming of the people is necessary! That is a great mistake. It is just exactly for a Socialist revolution against Imperialism that both the one and the other are needed.

Is it realisable? Such a criterion is wrong. Without a revolution almost the whole programme-minimum is unrealisable. In such circumstances realisation would merely *boil down to petit-bourgeoisdom.*

It seems to me, that this question (as *all* questions of Social Democratic tactics now) can be asked *only* in connection with the evaluation (and discounting) of Opportunism. And it is clear that "disarmament" as a tactical slogan is Opportunism. And petty Opportunism at that, proving its remoteness from the struggle and a poverty of outlook.

We send you the draft (individual) of a declaration of international Left members. We beg you to translate it and to send it to the adherents of the Left in Sweden and Norway, so as to come to an understanding with them in *a businesslike way.* Send your remarks about the counter-project and *see that you get* comments from the Left partisans in Scandinavia.

Your
Lenin

234. (148 P²). TO KARL RADEK IN BERNE

[Zorenberg, End of June, 1915]

Dear Comrade,

Our letters have evidently crossed. As you were writing to me, I was writing to you (a postcard) and sending the Miscellany. I hope you have received it.

With regard to the Conference of the Left:

I have been a non-member of the International Socialist Bureau *since 1912* (since 1912 the member of the International Socialist Bureau from the Central Committee has been Maximovich [M. M. Litvinov] in London, but of course, Gregory [G. E. Zinoviev] and I will do all that is essential in the name of the Central Committee.

You write that "Grimm is doing this (= circumventing the Central Committee?) unintentionally."[1]

Hm! Hm! It does not seem credible. Is Grimm really such a child? After two Conferences in Berne?[2]

But you will be able to find out better in Berne and I should be glad if it turned out to be that I was mistaken and you were right.

And so *if* Grimm is doing *this* unintentionally, then it is a simple matter. Grimm *must write* to the Central Committee (the official address is printed in our Central Organ: Bibliothèque Russe, 7 rue Hugo de Senger 7, Genève, for the Central Committee).

(Of course, he can send it to my address: that would be more direct.)

If Grimm does *not* do this, he will be acting *dishonestly* (for to write to *London* to Maximovich means to lose time and to risk the letter not reaching him: the police would intercept it).

It is indecent for us to beg: we do not want to foist ourselves. We *cannot* do that!

Now you write: Grimm and perhaps others (perhaps?? In my opinion it is certain!) will want to alter the matter, so that only the programme of action, (better call it a programme of exhaustion, a programme of refusal to struggle, a programme of steering the workers away from the revolution, a programme of calming down the workers by Left phrases) will be brought to the fore. (It would be truer to say: squash and betray it!)

It is my opinion that the change of front on the part of Kautsky plus Bernstein and Co. (plus 500, plus 1000, plus how many more??) is simply a reversal in the policy of rotters who have sensed that the masses will not be patient any longer and they "must" turn to the Left so as to continue to cheat the masses.[3]

---

[1] R. Grimm, a Swiss Socialist, one of the organisers of the Zimmerwald Conference, wanted to prepare for the convening of the conference without the help of the Bolsheviks. But he altered his intention and the Bolshevik representative, G. Zinoviev, took part in the preliminary conferences.

[2] Two conferences in Berne: (*a*) International Women's Socialist Conference, 26-28 March, 1915; (*b*) International Socialist Conference of Youth, 5-6 April, 1915.

[3] On 20 June, 1915, Kautsky, Bernstein and Haase published a manifesto in

That is quite clear.

And Renaudel in "L'Humanité" is moving towards the Left!!

The dirty rotters will get together and say they are "against the policy of the 4th August," that they stand for "peace" against annexations and . . . and . . . by such action *they will help* the bourgeoisie to quell the beginnings of revolutionary feeling.

I conclude from your letter that you also think so.

Therefore, our programme must be:

1. To go, if we are called.

2. To unite the Left *beforehand*, i.e. the adherents of *revolutionary action* against *their own* government.

3. To present the Kautsky rotters with the draft of *our* resolution (the Dutch + ourselves + the German Left + nought, but that does not matter, for *later on* it will not be "nought" but everyone).

4. To bring forward two or three orators at the Conference (if you can manage to be there, then this will be possible).

Cannot *a few* supporters of the German Left *against* Kautsky and Co. be brought together to stand *for such* a programme?

Write and tell us what you think of the programme. Its whole point = against the dull-witted and treacherous slogan of peace.

Do come,

Your

Lenin

P.S. Is it not perfectly clear that the Organising Committee will support Kautsky and Co.??? EH!

Are you sure that Grey + Bethmann Hollweg have not "winked at" Züdekum and Vandervelde: "It is time, boys, to stand *for* peace or else there will be a revolution"???

P.P.S. (1) There is a *telephone* (No. 111) in our hotel (Hotel Marienthal). If there is anything urgent, ring up at 8.30 a.m. when I am *always* in.

P.P.S. (2) Please forward the enclosed after reading it.

which they supported the war, the condemned annexations, and appealed for the preservation of unity with the Social-Chauvinists.

235. (149 P²). TO KARL RADEK IN BERNE

[*Zorenberg, End of July, 1915*]

Dear Comrade,

I am sending you a letter about the preliminary Conference.[1]
Please make a copy for "Lichtstrahlen," or entrust it to
Wynkoop (*if you are sure* you can depend on him) to be for-
warded to them.

N.B. All this is confidential. Promise not to tell Grimm, nor
Balabanova, nor Trotsky, nor anyone at all!

Read my letter to Wynkoop and then post it. I hope you
have posted the last one? Drop me a line about this.

Either the German Left will now unite (even if it is for an
ideological action in the name of an *anonymous* group "The
Star"[2] or any other: the workers will later *adhere* to this
group), or we must ignore them.

(I understand that "Lichtstrahlen" cannot act directly. But
why should not "The Star" group consisting of X plus Y plus
Z come forward with *resolutions* or a *manifesto??* And then
privately and secretly distribute this?)

I cannot understand how you missed the preliminary Conference in Berne!?! And it was you who advised me to
attend it!

Your

Lenin

P.S. Isn't it difficult for you to read Russian? Do you understand *everything?*

P.P.S. Either send Wynkoop the Berne resolutions (translated) (if you have a copy), or send them here and we will
make a copy.[3]

It is most important for us to consult with you privately,
together with a few members of the German Left. Could
you, perhaps, arrange this? Incidentally—can you come here?

---

[1] In Berne, 11 July, 1905. On the question of convening an International Conference.

[2] "The Star" group was not formed.

[3] Resolutions of the Berne Conference of the R.S.D.L.P. sections abroad, 27
Feb.-4 March, 1915.

236. (150 p²). TO KARL RADEK IN BERNE

[Zorenberg, Before 20th August, 1915]

My dear Comrade Radek,

I have received your letter to Wynkoop and I am posting it by the first post. I am adding a postscript to it to the effect that one must set to work at once, if one wants to prepare a declaration (not to mention the new "Communist Manifesto").

We have sent (1) a manifesto (2) resolutions (3) a draft of the declaration.¹ Do hurry up and send any corrections or amendments. Hurry! ! We shall be late! !

Personally I am opposed to the participation of "Nashe Slovo" ["Our Word"], but I would not make an ultimatum of it. Why against? (1) It is perversion, because "Nashe Slovo" itself has not announced itself to be an *independent* third Party or group in Russia (apart from the Central Committee and the Organising Committee); (2) in "Nashe Slovo" there are Organising Committee members, the number of whom is not known to the public. Double representation! (Organising Committee plus "Nashe Slovo"). (3) "Nashe Slovo" stands for the Chkheidze faction (the Organising Committee plus Plekhanov, plus Alexinsky, also support it). Is that not perversion?

It is *not* comic to look upon "Lichtstrahlen" as a group and to consider it to be more important than Zetkin's group.

Borchardt plus Radek, plus the collaborators of "Lichtstrahlen" are in that group. That is sufficient.

That group has a small periodical (whereas Zetkin and Co. have not got one).

Borchardt was the first to announce in public that Social Democracy had renounced itself.² That was not propaganda, but a most important political act. *That was a fact and not a promise.*

A clear, full, exact declaration of principles is more important for us than anything (i.e. the Left). Without this all the so-

¹ Written for preliminary discussion among the Left delegates of the separate socialist parties in preparation for the Zimmerwald Conference.

² In his pamphlet: "Vor und nach dem 4 August, 1914. Hat die deutsche Sozialdemokratie abgedankt?" 1915, published by "Lichtstrahlen."

called programmes of action are mere phrases, mere deception. What came of the Zetkin resolution of action in Berne? *Nothing* in the way of action! Nothing in the way of principles! [1]

If Borchardt's group comes forward (together with us or separately) as an anonymous group ("Die Stern" ["The Star"] or "Pfeil" ["The Arrow"] or anything else) with an exact declaration of principles, plus a call to revolutionary action, then it will play a universally historic rôle.

While Zetkin and Co., who have had everything in their hands (newspapers, journals, links with the "Berner Tagwacht" and the possibility of travelling to Switzerland etc.) have done absolutely *nothing* in the last ten months towards uniting the International Left. It is a disgrace.

Best wishes.

Your

Lenin

P.S. I do *not* advise you to join up as a soldier. It would be stupid to help the enemy. You would be doing the Scheidermans a favour. Better emigrate. Yes, I swear it would be better. Left workers are desperately needed.

"The opposition in Germany is the product of a movement among the masses, but the Bolsheviks are the orientation of a small group of revolutionaries."

That is not Marxism, that is Kautskyism, or a wriggling out.

What was the Communist Manifesto of 1847 and its group? The product of a movement among the masses? Or the orientation of a small group of revolutionaries? Or was it both the one and the other?

And we, the Central Committee? Has it not been proved by R.S.D.L. faction that there is a link with the masses? And the *Petrograd* "Voice of the Proletariat"? [2] Or is there no "stirring in the masses" in Russia?

The Left in Germany will be making a historic mistake if

---

[1] K. Zetkin spoke against the draft resolution put forward by the C.C. of the R.S.D.L.P. at the International Socialist Women's Conference in Berne. (26-28 March, 1915.)

[2] An illegal Bolshevik organ of the C.C. of the R.S.D.L.P. in Petersburg, 1915.

they refuse to come forward with a declaration of principles (anonymously from "The Star" group etc. After that the workers *will join* and *think* over it) under the pretext that they (Zetkin, Laufenberg, Borchardt, Tahlheimer, Dunker! ! ! Ha! Ha!) are "the product of a stirring in the masses."

A Left declaration and programme is needed for a development of "a stirring in the masses." In view of such a stirring, this is needed. It is needed for turning the "stirring" into a "movement." It is needed for developing the "stirring" in the rotten International.

And immediately! ! !

You are definitely wrong!

P.P.S. You are not clear in your letter to Wynkoop. Is the 20th August fixed, or only suggested? Drop me a line about this *and to Gregory* (if it is urgent).

Rakovsky (see his pamphlet) ["Socialism and the War"] *supports* the defence of the Fatherland. In my opinion, we are not on the same road as such people.

237. (93 P²). TO A. G. SHLYAPNIKOV

[*Zorenberg*], *23rd August, 1915*

My dear Alexander,

It is very difficult for me to give advice from this distance concerning the plan for your journey [to Russia]. You know our financial affairs. Nadezhda Konstantinovna [Krupskaya] wrote in detail (apart from the money sent, 600 francs have been promised before the 10th October, plus another 400 francs in a month's time, making 1,000 francs in all. *So far* there is no hope of any more).

On the one hand extreme caution is necessary. Have you thoroughly good papers etc.?

On the other hand it would be undoubtedly useful for the cause if a man, who is thoroughly well informed and independent, were to travel round two or three centres now, make links, establish connections and were *immediately* to return to Sweden to hand over to us all such links and to inform us of discussions of the future position. That would be of great importance.

No. 1 of "The Communist" will appear in about eight to ten days' time; then No. 2 about eight to ten days later (or Nos. 1 and 2 will appear together). Number 44 of the Central Organ will appear in a day or two. The pamphlet [by Lenin and G. Zinoviev] about the War ["Socialism and the War"] with *all* the documents will be published in about two weeks' time. It has already been set up in type.

Events in Russia have fully confirmed our position, which those silly fools, the social-patriots (from Alexinsky to Chkheidze) have christened "defeatism." The facts have proved that we were right! Military failures are helping to shake the foundations of Czarism and are facilitating the union of revolutionary workers in Russia and other countries. They say: "What will 'you' do if 'you,' the revolutionaries, defeat Czarism?" To which I reply (a) our victory will inflame a hundredfold the movement of the Left in Germany; (b) if "we" were to defeat Czarism completely, we should offer peace to all the fighters on democratic conditions and on refusal, we should conduct a *revolutionary* war.

It is clear that the front line of "Pravda" workers, the mainstay of our Party, has survived in spite of the terrible ravages in the ranks. It would be extremely important if leading groups were to unite in two or three centres (*in absolute secrecy*), if they were to link up with us, re-establish the Bureau of the Central Committee (I believe, there already is one in Petersburg) and the Central Committee itself in Russia; if they were firmly to link up with us, (*if necessary* one or two people should be brought to Sweden for this purpose); we would send leaflets and pamphlets etc. Most important of all is the need for reliable and constant communication.

Chkheidze and Co. are obviously wriggling: they are the faithful friends of "Nashe Delo." Alexinsky is pleased with them (I hope you saw "War," Plekhanov plus Alexinsky and Co.? What a disgrace! !) And they play at being Left with the aid of Trotsky! I do not think they will deceive conscious "Pravda" workers!

Write and tell us what you have decided.

Greetings,

Your

Lenin

P.S. Will A. Kollontay agree to help us to arrange in America for an English edition of our pamphlet?

238. (97 P²). TO E. I. RIVLINA, SECRETARY OF THE LAUSANNE BOLSHEVIK SECTION

[*Zorenberg, the beginning of September, 1915*]

My dear Comrade,

I wrote to you the other day about Golet. The matter is now moving forward, so to speak, from another side. It is *not* a preliminary meeting, but the Conference itself of the Left (International) which has been fixed for the 5th September.[1] Merrheim will be present from Paris (all that is of course strictly entre nous). "Nashe Slovo" supporters will also be there. Why should not Golet and Nain also be present as representatives of Left Socialism in Switzerland? (Grimm is to be there and he is much more of a half and halfer than Golet or Nain). Please try to see both of them as soon as possible, have a frank talk with them and send me a few lines in reply as soon as you can about the mood of both these Left French Swiss. Of course you understand that the presence of French anti-Chauvinists at the Conference would be extremely important *now*, especially as Merrheim will be there. And so, answer quickly.

Greetings to Rivlin, [a Bolshevik].

Your

Lenin

239. (98 P²). TO A. G. SHLYAPNIKOV IN STOCKHOLM

[*Zorenberg, the beginning of September, 1915*]

My dear Friend,

Try to see Belenin and please tell him that he has been co-opted on to the Central Committee of the R.S.D.L.P. You will

---

[1] The International Socialist Conference in Zimmerwald, 5-8 Sept., 1915.

understand, of course, that in this matter we must maintain the maximum of secrecy and that you must "forget" about it after passing on the information to Belenin (I do not write direct to him for obvious reasons). His function on the journey is very important: Trotsky and the company of foreign lackeys of Opportunism are doing their utmost to slur over the differences of opinion and to save the Opportunism of "Nasha Zarya" by means of whitewashing and singing the praises of the Chkheidze faction (= the truest friends of "Nasha Zarya"). Groups should be created in Russia (from old, experienced, clever "Pravda" workers who have *fully* understood the war question) and the best of them (two or three) should be put on to the Central Committee. If any difficulties or doubts arise, then we should limit ourselves to creating *analogous* collegiums (e.g. a controlling all-Russia workers' group; or a Committee etc.;—it isn't the name, of course, that matters).

Your links and knowledge of old experienced workers will help you to advise Belenin, who will of course be very serious and cautious in this matter. But the most important thing of all is that he should take care of himself, going there *only for a short time* and bringing back *all the links*.

Best greetings. Write at once as soon as you receive this letter.

Your

Lenin

P.S. The pamphlet [Lenin nad Zinoviev: "Socialism and the War"] will appear earlier than I thought. I have already had some of the proofs. It will probably come out in a week or ten days, i.e. both the pamphlet and Nos. 1 and 2 of "The Communist."

There will now be three members of the Central Committee abroad; in Russia there is a number of candidates (workers) and arrested members of the Central Committee (also workers, "Pravda" leaders).

P.P.S. You will receive tomorrow a more detailed letter from Nadezhda Konstantinovna. Pay special attention to it.

240. (104 P^2). TO A. G. SHLYAPNIKOV IN STOCKHOLM

[Zorenberg,] 19th September, 1915

My dear Alexander,

We have received your letters with the good news about the smooth working of the transport and we were extremely glad. With regard to literature in Vardë, try to keep and save *everything*—send us a series of "The Proletariat" and "Vpered," pamphlets (old ones, 1905) we will also make use of them. It is worth sending them to Russia, if there is any chance of transport.[1] Yesterday I read the news about the dissolution of the Duma. It is clear that the reaction has either been frightened by the Left bloc or is speculating on some "war" chances (or on a separate peace?). Our attitude towards the Chauvinist revolutionaries (such as Kerensky and part of the Social-Democratic Liquidators or patriots) cannot in my opinion be expressed by the formula "support." The gulf between the Chauvinist revolutionaries (revolution in order to defeat Germany) and the proletarian revolutionary internationalists (revolution to awaken the proletariat of other countries so as to unite it into a general proletarian revolution) is far too wide for there to be any talk of support. We must utilise every protest (even timid and confused ones à la Gorky); we must also make use of the revolutionary work of the Chauvinists and, when the opportunity occurs, we will not refuse "combined action" (in agreement with the resolutions of our Party in 1907 at the London Congress and at our 1913 [C.C.R.S.D.L.P.] Conference) but—no further than that. In practice we will not issue any proclamation or manifestos together with the revolutionary-patriots; we shall avoid any Duma bloc with them; we will avoid any "uniting" with them at Congresses, in manifestations etc. But once the patriots agree to them, technical mutual services will probably be possible (as with the Liberals before 1905) and we will not refuse them. The relationship must be *direct* and *clear:* you

[1] In organising illegal transport from the North of Norway, Shlyapnikov discovered a stock of literature belonging to the years 1906-7. Part of it was sent over to Russia.

want to overthrow Czarism so as to defeat Germany and we are working for the international revolution of the proletariat.

We have incredibly little news from Russia. It is terribly depressing that such a comparatively simple matter as secret correspondence with Russia (*fully* possible in war time) should prove to be so unsatisfactorily organised. This is one of the most vital matters. (I hope you have agreed by letter with Nadezhda Konstantinovna in *all* details and that you will write about it to her in as much detail as possible.) The most important thing of all is to establish regular intercourse, to get two or three leading workers from Russia, if only as far as Sweden, to have a detailed conversation and correspondence, so as to reach a perfect understanding. I hope Belenin's [Shlyapnikov's] trip [to Russia] will introduce a real improvement in this sphere. At present the vital part of the work is to get one's bearings in as short a time as possible, to gather links and collect information. Without this, there is no point even in thinking of anything else.

We are considering a plan for publishing proclamations and leaflets for transport to Russia. We have not yet decided where to publish (here, or in Scandinavia); we must choose the cheapest, for the distance does not matter.

I send you best wishes and greetings,

Your

Lenin

241. (153 P²). TO KARL RADEK IN BERNE

Zorenberg (20th September, 1915)

My dear Radek,

The letter to Wynkoop has been posted.

Also a report to Gregory, together with *your* letter.

Probably you have not got *a copy of our announcement* (that we are displeased with the Manifesto [of the Zimmerwald Left] which does not go far enough)? We have handed it into the Bureau and Grimm has published it. *We must have a copy of this announcement.* Would Grimm not allow you to make a copy? If not, it is simply scandalous! ! !

And Grimm's "conspiracy"! The whole world knows about it! Those stupid Italians in "Avanti." It is a shame! A disgrace! [1]

Your
Lenin

242. (105 P[2]). TO A. G. SHLYAPNIKOV [2]

[Zorenberg,
the end of September-beginning of October, 1915]

My dear Alexander,

It is splendid that you have taken on the leaflets [for distribution in Russia]. We are drawing up a detailed plan for them and will soon send it to you and to N. I. [Bukharin]. But, you know, it is most desirable that N. I. should write two copies simultaneously (in copying pencil and with a black carbon paper) and if you (or he) would immediately send us the second copy. Leaflets are *a very* responsible matter and one of *the most* difficult forms of literature. It is therefore essential to think them out as thoroughly as possible and to consult together. Since the setting up in type and transport is slow, there will be comparatively little time lost in sending them here, and in any case it is of no importance in comparison with the importance of well thought out appeals.

How do you think of signing the leaflets? You forgot to write about this.

The idea of Kollontay's pamphlet ["Who needs the War?"] is good, but the subject is extremely difficult; it is extremely difficult to write in a popular style on such a subject. I think corrections are necessary. I have already written to her about this and have asked her to agree to alterations being made. If she agrees, I will have suggestions for corrections prepared and the matter can then go rapidly forward.

[1] All details of the organisation of the Zimmerwald Conference were published in "Avanti," with photographs even of the houses where it would take place.
[2] Shlyapnikov's pseudonym was Belenin.

As to the trip to your country[1]; the matter is delayed, first because of money difficulties (the journey is expensive and also the life there) and secondly because of police suspicion. We shall probably wait until Belenin [A. G. Shlyapnikov] gets back and we have heard his news about our native land

I greet you warmly,

Your

Lenin

243. (108 P[2]). TO A. G. SHLYAPNIKOV IN STOCKHOLM

[*Zorenberg*], *10th October, 1915*

My dear Friend,

Tomorrow we are publishing simultaneously two numbers of the Central Organ, Nos. 45 and 46 (dealing entirely with the Zimmerwald Conference) and No. 47, containing news from Russia and theses about tactics.[2] These theses contain in part the answers to questions which we touched upon in our correspondence and you in your conversations with Nikolai Ivanovich [Bukharin] etc. I will await your comments.

Have you received the *Russian* text of the pamphlet "Socialism and War"? (Alexandra Mikhailovna [Kollontay] has sent a criticism of the German text and I have sent her an answer in a detailed letter to America. If you are interested, ask her to send it to you. I wrote to her in Bergen about her leaflet ["Who needs War?"] for her consent to corrections. There was no reply. I am afraid I shall have to send it to America, but this will mean great delay.)

The news from Russia shows the growth of the revolutionary mood and movement, although it is apparently not yet the beginning of the revolution.

The most important thing for us to do now is to establish links and to make them regular (it is quite possible by correspondence: consider whether it is possible to send in a thin

---

[1] It was proposed that Lenin should leave Switzerland and settle in a neutral Scandinavian country. Shlyapnikov was to pave the way for this. The move did not take place.

[2] Written by Lenin in Oct., 1915.

binding one at a time copies of the newspaper and proclamations).

We hope that Belenin [A. G. Shlyapnikov] will succeed in
starting this. Without it, it will be useless to think of any systematically connected work.

Pay special attention to the thesis about the Council of the
Worker Deputies.[1] One must be careful with this affair: otherwise 2/300 leaders will be arrested! Without a link with the
rising the "strength" of the Council of the Worker Deputies
is an illusion. We must not fall into this illusion.

I greet you warmly,

Your

Lenin

P.S. Cannot a correspondence in chemicals be organised for
the rapid transmission to Petersburg of such articles of the Central Organ as the "Eleven Theses." Think this over carefully!

244. (109 P²). TO A. M. KOLLONTAY

[Berne], 9th November, 1915

My dear Alexandra Mikhailovna,

Only yesterday I received your letter from Milwaukee;
letters take a terrible time to come. You have still not had my
letter about Zimmerwald and all the answers to your questions
(as well as Nos. 45, 46 and 47 of "The Social Democrat"), but
I wrote that letter more than a month ago. Do at least try to
calculate where you will be (in about six weeks' time) and send
such addresses (for letters to you), so that letters may reach
you more easily.

With regard to the "Volkszeitung," Grimm of New York
answered me today that they were quite pro-Kautsky. Is that
so? I think our pamphlet in German ["Socialism and the War,"
by Lenin and Zinoviev] might help you to define the "solidarity" of internationalism. Have you got it? (500 copies were sent
to you.)

---

[1] The 4th thesis in which the workers are considered "as means of revolt, of revolutionary power."

One of these days we are going to publish (in German, and later *we hope* to publish in French, and, if we can eke out the money, also in Italian) a small pamphlet in the name of the Zimmerwald Left. Under this name we should like to put into as wide an international circulation as possible our Left Group in Zimmerwald (the Central Committee plus the Polish Social Democracy, plus the Letts, plus the Swedes, plus the Norwegians, plus one German, plus one Swiss) with *its project of the resolution and manifesto* (printed in Nos. 45-46 of "The Social Democrat"). The small pamphlet (20-30-35,000 letters [of the alphabet]) ["Internationales Flugblatt," No. 1] will contain these two documents and a short introduction. We rely on you to get it published in America and *in English* (for it is hopeless to get this done in England: it should be sent there from America) and, if possible, in other languages. This must be the first appearance of the *kernel* of the *Left* Social Democrats of *all* countries who have a clear, exact and full answer to the question: what has to be done and where to go? It is extremely important that it should be published in America and circulated as widely as possible, and that you should make firm publishing links. (N. B.   Charles Kerr in Chicago; "Appeal to Reason" in Kansas etc.) for it is arch-essential for us to appear in many languages (in this way you could do *much*).

Try to link up with these people, even by correspondence, if you are not going to Kansas. Sometimes their newspaper is *not at all bad*. Do not fail to sound them with our resolution of the "Zimmerwald Left." And who is Eugene Debs? He writes sometimes in a revolutionary manner. Is he only spineless like Kautsky? Write and say when you will next be in New York and for how many days. Try everywhere to see (if only for five minutes) the local Bolsheviks, in order to encourage them and to link them up with us.

So far as money is concerned, I regret to see from your letter, that you have not yet been able to collect any for the Central Committee. Perhaps the manifesto from the Left will help. . . .

I never doubted that Hilkvit would be on Kautsky's side and even *more Right*, for I saw him in Stuttgart (in 1907) and *heard* that afterwards he had defended the refusal to allow yellow people to enter America ("Internationalist"!) . . .

The Zimmerwald Manifesto in itself is *insufficient:* Kautsky and Co. are ready to be reconciled to it *on the condition:* "not another step further." We will *not* support this for it is *sheer hypocrisy.* So, if in America there are people who are afraid *even* of the Zimmerwald Manifesto, then ignore them and recruit only those who are *more Left than the Zimmerwald Manifesto.*

I send you warm greetings and wish you all success.

Your

Lenin

245. (112 p²). TO S. N. RAVICH IN GENEVA

[Berne, December, 1915]

My dear Comrade Olga,

Forgive me for writing on a scrap of paper. It seems to me that you have acted correctly. Truly without a break with "Nashe Delo" all the rest is sheer deception. It is as clear as daylight when you realise that in Petersburg the talemonger-okists in league with the Black Hundred have "conquered" (after falsifying the elections [of worker representatives on to military-industrial committees on 21 Nov., 1915]).

Add to the resolution [of the Geneva section of Bolsheviks] the condemnation of false *second* elections [to the Military-Industrial Committee]; and to the motives add the impossibility of participating in "the defence," since the war has an imperialistic i.e. a conquering, i.e. a grabbing, i.e. a persecuting character, (altogether I advise that the motives should be considered very carefully by "The Social Democrat," after having selected proofs from suitable articles and resolutions of the Petersburg workers).

We will pass on the latter to Inessa.

Your

Lenin

P.S. One request: Inessa said there is a young woman in Geneva who has lived in Arras. You know her. They say she knows French well. Will she undertake to translate from German to French (for Roland Holst's journal ["Vorbote," the Organ of the Zimmerwald Left], which appears here with our participation) gratis? Or for money? And for how much? Please find out.

246. (99 P²). TO A. M. KOLLONTAY IN CHRISTIANIA

[*Zorenberg, between the 8th and 13th December, 1915*]

My dear Alexandra Mikhailovna,

It will be a great pity if your trip to America falls through. We have been building not a few hopes on this journey for the publication in America of our pamphlet ("Socialism and War," which you will receive one of these days), also on your making links with the publisher, Charles Kerr in Chicago, on drawing together the internationalists, and finally on financial help which is extremely necessary to us for all that vital work in Russia about which you write (and quite rightly you emphasise its vital importance in connection with the desirability of our greater proximity to Russia: the obstacles to this in the first place are finance and in the second place the police. Can one arrive there safely . . . ?)

If the question of your trip has been definitely decided in the negative, then try to think out how you can help us (through dealings with Charles Kerr etc.) to publish our pamphlet in English. This is possible only in America. We are sending you the German edition of the pamphlet ["Socialism and War"]. Do all you can to promote its sale in Scandinavian countries (it is devilishly important for us to get back even part of the expenses incurred by it; otherwise we shall not be able to publish it in French).

Write in greater detail, more concisely and oftener (if you are not going to America), to say what concrete questions exactly are coming to the surface in Russia; who is putting such questions; how and in what circumstances? All this is extremely important for the publication of leaflets, a vital matter, you are right. The delegate *you* sent will tell you something about the

Conference of the Left and we will write to you about it (we are firmly united at this Conference and form the opposition, even though we signed the manifesto).

(No money. There is no money! That is the *main* trouble!)

Best greetings,

Your

Lenin

1916

247. (161 P²). TO A. M. GORKY IN PETERSBURG

[Berne], *11th January, 1916*

Dear Alexey Maximovich,

I am sending you the manuscript of a pamphlet ["New Facts about the Laws of the Development of Capitalism in Agriculture," by Lenin, 1914-15] to the "Letopis" ["Chronicle"] [1] address, but it is not for "Letopis." I ask you to get it published. [2]

I have tried to give as popular an exposition as possible about the new facts on America, which I am convinced are particularly useful for the popularisation of Marxism and for illustrating it. I hope I have succeeded in expounding these important facts clearly and intelligently for the new strata of the reading public, which are increasing in Russia and need to be enlightened on the economic evolution of the world.

I would also like to continue, and subsequently publish, issue No. 2—on Germany.

I am getting down to work on the pamphlet on Imperialism. [3]

As a result of the War I am in great need of earning my living by literary work and I therefore ask you if possible, and if it is not too much trouble, to speed up the publication of the pamphlet.

Kind regards,

Your

V. Il'in

Address: Mr. Wl. Ulianoff,
Seidenweg 4A,
Berne.

---

[1] A journal with Internationalist leanings.

[2] Published by "Zhizn Znaniye," 1917.

[3] This resulted in a pamphlet: "Imperialism, as the highest stage of Capitalism."

248. (114 P²). TO M. M. HARITONOV IN ZÜRICH

[Berne, 29th January, 1916]

My dear Comrade,

I am very grateful to you for your prompt and detailed reply. We shall arrive on the 4th February. If possible, find us a room on a *weekly* basis for two people, costing no more than one franc a day; best of all in a *simple* worker's family (with a stove: it may still be cold weather).

If you cannot do this, perhaps you can find a cheap hotel and send us the name (one franc a day or cheaper), where we can live until we find a room. We will discuss the date for the lecture etc., when we meet.

I hope to receive the translation from you on Monday (take the money for expenses: *express* etc., the postage etc., for we will cover it).

Best greetings,   Your

Lenin

Ulianov, Seidenweg 4A, Berne.

249. (280 R). TO HIS MOTHER

[Zürich], 28th February/12th March, 1916

Darling Mother,

I am sending you some postcards, one for Manyasha.

We are now living in Zürich, having come here to study in the local libraries. We like the lake very much and the libraries are much better than the ones at Berne, so we shall probably stay here longer than we intended. You can write to this address, for the post will always forward letters.

I hope you have no more severe frosts and that you are not freezing in a cold flat. I wish it would get warm quicker, so that you could rest after the Winter.

Nadya sends much love to all. I kiss you, my darling, and wish you good health.

Much love to Anyuta and to M. T. also.

Your

V. U.

250. (119 P²). TO A. G. SHLYAPNIKOV

[*Zürich, March, 1916*]

My dear Friend,

I should like to talk to you in greater detail about your letter and particularly about a current reproach concerning my "obstinacy."[1]

As for James [A. I. Elizarova], he never did understand politics and was always against a split. James is an excellent person, but on such subjects his judgment is seriously wrong.

The question of the split is *fundamental* for us in Russia (and also in the New International). Any yielding here would be criminal. I know quite well how many splendid people were against a split in the Duma faction (James, Galerka [M. S. Olminsky], the Petersburg "friends" among the intelligentsia). They were all a thousandfold wrong. A split was essential. A split with *Chkheidze and Co.* is *absolutely* essential now. All those who waver concerning this are the *enemies* of the proletariat and we must not give in to them.

Who is wavering? Not only Trotsky and Co. but also *Yury* [G. L. Pyatakov] plus Eugenie B. [Bosh] (why, only last Summer they were creating scenes because of Chkheidze!). Then the *Poles* (the opposition); there is a resolution in No. 5 of their "Workers' Newspaper": they are again standing *for vacillation* just as in Brussels on the 16th July 1914.[2] To be *un*yielding to them seems to be essential.

Radek is the best among them. It was useful to work *together* with him (and incidentally for the Zimmerwald Left) and we did work. But *Radek* is also *wavering*. And our tactics here are of a *dual* character (Yury plus Nikolai Ivanovich [Bukharin] did not want to understand and could not understand this: on

---

[1] Lenin was accused of obstinacy, lack of tact, etc., because of his differences of opinion with Pyatakov, Bosh, etc., on the national question, which led to a conflict in the Press resulting in the stopping of the journal "The Communist," published by the C.O., "The Social Democrat," together with Pyatakov and Bosh.

The Bureau of the C.C. of the Party in Russia passed a resolution disapproving of turning Central Committee publications into discussional ones.

[2] The Brussels Conference for re-establishing unification in the R.S.D.L.P. was convened for 16-17 July, 1914.

the one hand to *help* Radek to move to the Left and to *unite* everyone possible for the Zimmerwald Left, and on the other hand not to allow any hesitation on fundamentals.

And the fundamental was a split with the Organising Committee [the C.C. of the S.D. Mensheviks], with Chkheidze and Co.

The Poles are *wavering* and have brought out a most base resolution *after* No. 1 of "The Communist." The conclusion? To keep to "The Communist" and to open the door to *wrangling and wavering:* i.e., letters to the editors (from Radek, Bronsky, possibly Pannekuk and others); complaints, snivelling, gossip etc.

Not for anything on earth.

It is harmful to the cause.

It would mean helping the scoundrels on the Organising Committee, Chkheidze and Co.

Not for anything on earth.

"The Communist" was a temporary bloc for achieving a definite aim. The aim has been achieved: the journal has been published and the rapprochement achieved (*at that time* it was possible before Zimmerwald). Now we must proceed by *another* way, we must go further.

"The Communist" has become *harmful*. It must be *stopped* and replaced by *another:* "The Social Democrat Miscellany" (under the editorship of "*The Social Democrat*").

Only in this way can we avoid wrangling and avoid wavering.

Is there also a difference of opinion in Russia? Oh, of course! *But it is not our business to increase it.* Chkheidze and Co., and Trotsky and Co. busy themselves with increasing disagreement (that is their "profession") but our business is to continue our own policy. The fruits of *such* a work are obvious: the Petersburg workers are a hundred times better than the Petersburg intelligentsia (even when the latter are "sympathisers." . . .)

We had to make *temporary* concessions to the Three (Yury, plus Eugenie Bosh plus Nik. Iv.), because at that time it was otherwise impossible to publish the journal, (at present it is possible); but the main thing is that at that time we had not seen Eugenie Bosh and Yury at work and we could still hope that the work would lead them forward and up.

But they have gone down.

And the temporary union *must* be dissolved. It is only in this way that the *cause* will not suffer. And only in this way will *they* learn.

After all, we are not against *discussion*. We are opposed to those people, who have shown unpardonable wavering, having *editorial* rights (was it because of youth? Then let us wait and perhaps in five years' time they will have improved).

Nik. Iv. is a practising economist and *in this* we always supported him, but: (1) he is credulous towards gossip and (2) he is devilishly *unstable* in politics.

The war has pushed him towards semi-anarchistic ideas. At the conference where the Berne resolutions were carried (Spring 1915) he produced theses which were the height of stupidity (I have them!) and they are a disgrace: half anarchism.

I attacked sharply. Yury and Eugenie Bosh listened and were pleased that I permitted no falling away to the Left (they then announced their complete disagreement with Nik. Iv.).

Half a year goes by. Nik. Iv. studies economics. He does *not* interest himself in politics.

And now? On the question of self-determination he presents us with the *same kind* of rubbish. Eugenie Bosh and Yury sign it. Borrow the "theses" from Nik. Iv. and my reply.

The question is important. It is a vital question. It is linked inseparably with the question of *annexations:* one of the most burning questions of the day.

People did not think. They did not read. They did not study. They listened to Radek two or three times (he has the old "Polish" complaint: he has lost his way here) and they *approved*.

That is an absolute scandal. It is a disgrace. They are not editors. People must be refuted, shown up, they should be given time to study and to think and one ought not to hurry to wheedle them: here, take editorial rights, talk your rubbish to the workers!

If that is so, then they will *bring* the matter to polemics in the press and I will then be *compelled* to call them "Imperialist Economists" to expose their complete emptiness and complete absence of seriousness or thought. Polemics in the press will repel them *for many years*.

If however "The Communist" were to be stopped now, then they would be forced to think, and they would give up their rubbish; they would do some serious reading and become convinced. Do write a serious *pamphlet*, if you have differences of opinion in politics (which you have not studied at all). They will think about doing it, but won't do it. And in a few months' time it will fade out.

That is how it was and how it will be.

As to the question of annexation (and of self-determination) our position (resolution of 1913) has been fully confirmed by the war. And the question has become a burning one. And Radek plus the Dutch (Hörter and Pannekuk) have obviously lost their way [in the article "Summary of a Discussion on Self-determination"]. We will explain the matter clearly in the Miscellany of "The Social Democrat."

We must aim at:

(1) stopping publication of "The Communist."

(2) giving Yury plus Eugenie Bosh as *many* rights and privileges as possible in the publication of the Miscellany about the Jews (that would be harmless *here* for the cause).

Detailed conditions in a written agreement.

(3) the same in regard to their transport group (borrow their statutes from them and our corrections).

(4) we will publish the Miscellany of "The Social Democrat" under the control of the editors of "The Social Democrat."

We will invite them to collaborate. We will ask them if there are any differences of opinion. We will tell them to prepare a serious pamphlet, *which we will undertake to print* (they will not write it, they have not even begun to think seriously about the question: they have not even studied it! !).

That would be a *business-like* policy.

Eugenie Bosh was thinking of going to Russia; there she

might be useful: here there is *nothing* for her to do. She will only begin *inventing* work for herself.

Do you know this misery abroad? "Inventing" work for those who are sitting abroad? It is a terrible calamity.

Well, I must close now.

Collect all documents together and become informed. We will talk about this again and again.

Your

Lenin

P.S. I enclose a copy of my answer to N. I. Bukharin on the subject of the meaning of the new "differences of opinion."

251. (120 P²). TO A. M. KOLLONTAY IN CHRISTIANIA

[Zürich], 19th March, 1916

My dear A. M.

We have received your letter and once again congratulate you on your success.

I was devilishly angry that "noble France" had *confiscated* (fact!) a number of my registered letters to you in America. It cannot be helped! You must definitely concentrate on links with America. Did you not write and say that you had received in America No. 1 of the German "Internationales Flugblatt" and that you would try to get it published in English? And now there is *not a sound* about it. What does this mean?

Do you mean to say there were no sympathisers in America and it was impossible to get the International leaflet published in English? ? ? It is incredible.

But if that is so, it should be published in Norway (in English).

Will you undertake its translation and how much would it cost to publish it?

Next, I wrote to you in America, telling you that I had received a Socialist propaganda leaflet from Boston, Mass. (signed by twenty Socialists *with their addresses:* S. R. in Mass.).

This League is international and has a programme with obvious leanings towards the Left.

I sent them an *enormous* English letter ["A letter to the League of Socialist Propaganda in America," Lenin, Nov., 1915] (and also the International leaflet in German). There was no answer. Did "Noble France" confiscate them?

If you did not receive them and know nothing about these people, I will send you their addresses and a copy of my letter. Will you undertake to forward this to America?

What about the Socialist Labour Party? After all, they are Internationalists (even if they have a narrow sectarian colouring). Have you sent them the International leaflet? Have you any links with them?

Further, you wrote that you *had begun* conversations with *Charles* Kerr. The result? He promised to print *part* of our pamphlet [Lenin's and Zinoviev's].

And now you are silent about this. . . . How am I to interpret this?

"The International Correspondence" printed that "The New Review" in America had undertaken to print the articles of the Zimmerwald Left. Is that correct? Do you know "The New Review"?

Answer quickly and more fully. Of course you will find out and in detail all about the *direct* steamers between Norway and America.

With regard to Höglund and the Norwegians. *So far* I have not been able to find out whether they have received the International leaflet, whether they have published it in Swedish and Norwegian, and whether they have *officially* joined the Zimmerwald Left (just as Roland Holst joined the Revolutionary Socialist Union).

Please find out and see you get an answer, curse them, compel them and see it is done! Tell Bukharin to let you know what we told him in a separate letter about the Zimmerwaldites, and you, see it is carried out.

Greetings,

Your

Lenin

Address: Herrn Ulyanow, (Schuhladen Kammerer) Spiegel-gasse 12, Zürich I.

P.S. What interesting books and pamphlets have you brought back with you? Schlüter's "History of Chartism"? And what else?

I send you our "theses" from "Vorbote" No. 2.[1] Explain it to the Scandinavians.

252. (124 P²). TO V. A. KARPINSKY IN GENEVA

Zürich, 17th May, 1916

My dear V. K.

According to our agreement I am thinking of going to Geneva and Lausanne to lecture on "Two Currents in the International Labour Movement." (You said it was a better title than "Two Internationals" on which I lectured here.)

If conditions have not changed and my trip pays for itself, then please arrange so that it takes place in about a fortnight's time (*and in Lausanne on the next day*).

I shall wait for an answer.

I need some money so as to work in the Geneva (Universal) Library. Can you find out whether it closes on any other days besides holidays?

Greetings

Your

Lenin

253. (127 P²). TO A. G. SHLYAPNIKOV IN CHRISTIANIA

[Zürich, May, 1916]

My dear Alexander,

The Conference is over.[2] Its Manifesto (of the 1st May) has been published. I hope you receive the "Berner Tagwacht" or some other Swiss paper? If not, send us a line and we will send you the French text.

---

[1] "The Socialist Revolution and the Right of Nations to Self-determination."

[2] The 2nd International Socialist Conference of the adherents of Zimmerwald unification took place in Kienthal, 24-30 April, 1916; of 43 participators, 12 were Left.

Gregory [G. E. Zinoviev] is preparing a detailed letter about the Conference which will be sent to you.

In general, the accepted Manifesto is a step forward, because the French deputies (three of them, one being the half Chauvinist Brison) have accepted it. The resolution criticising pacifism and the resolution about the International Socialist Bureau with a severe criticism of it have both been accepted. All the same, in spite of the numerous deficiencies, it is a step towards a break with the Social-patriots.

The Left were stronger this time: a Serb, three Swiss, a Frenchman (not a deputy; *not* from a group, but independent) strengthened our Left. Then two Germans [B. Tallheimer and E. Meyer] (from the "International Group") supported us in the main.

Have you seen Huysmans' Manifesto? There is an obvious malicious "hint" in it about us. The "Volksfreund" (Braunschweig) sent a good reply.

With regard to the Japs [G. L. Pyatakov and E. Bosh] we have decided to make one more attempt, the last I hope, to agree: (1) all old agreements (oral) are cancelled, (2) agreement as between the editors of the Central Organ editing an issue of the paper, and the *publishers* from book to book, i.e., for each book separately, (3) to publish a number in Berne (it is obviously impossible to do this in Stockholm).

Do try and see if you can. If not, we will publish the Miscellany of "The Social Democrat." We cannot wait.

Here is the plan for No. 3:—

1. Material from Russia (up to 3 sheets).
2. Theses of the editors of the Central Organ on self-determination.
3. Lenin's article about the same.
4. The second Zimmerwald Conference—Gregory Zinoviev or Lenin.
5. Bukharin—a subject concerning economics.
6. Lyalin [G. L. Pyatakov] on high costs.
7. Alexander [A. G. Shlyapnikov]—from Russia.
8. The Serb and the Italian have promised articles.
9. Russian themes. Gregory Zinoviev.

10. Radek—continuation (is it worth it?? In my opinion, No!).

[this clause was deleted.]

10. Kollontay—from America.

11. The Lett.

12. Varin [V. Yu. Fridolin].

13. The Women's Labour Movement.

14. Bibliography.

15. About Trotsky, Martov and the Chkheidze faction.

Think it over, feel your way, find out as tactfully as possible and answer quickly.[1]

I send you greetings and wish you all success.

Your

Lenin

P.S. With regard to the proposed Jewish Miscellany,[2] (as Nadya [Krupskaya] has already written), I agree with you. Nadya has written several times to Berne about the material.

Greetings to Alexandra Mikhailovna [A. M. Kollontay].

Your

Lenin

254. (131 P[2]). TO A. G. SHLYAPNIKOV IN CHRISTIANIA

[*Zürich, June 1916*]

My dear Alexander,

There is evidently a hitch in our correspondence and a number of misunderstandings have arisen through your not having received our second letter, which was sent to Stockholm. I cannot explain in any other way how you can write that we do not answer your questions. We have answered all of them and in great detail; *you* have *not* answered us. Nadezhda Konstantinova writes to you again and again; we shall have to be patient and repeat several things we have said, so as to obtain results. It is essential to come to some understanding in our letters.

[1] Lenin's plan was rejected by the Bukharin-Pyatakov group.
[2] Based on material from Russia on the position of the Jews during the War. This Miscellany was not published.

With regard to "The Communist," you write that the split with Chkheidze does not arouse any doubts. In whom? In Bukharin and Co.!

But I wrote that it did *not* refer to Bukharin and Co., but to Radek and Co.

"The Communist" was our temporary bloc with two groups and elements (1) Bukharin and Co. (2) Radek and Co. That *could* be done so long as we kept to the same road, but now it is impossible and we must *temporarily* separate, or more exactly move away.

The Poles carried a resolution, which again showed their wavering on the question of Chkheidze. It was carried in the *Summer of 1915* (after Nos. 1-2 of "The Communist") and printed *only in 1916*. Is it practical to give them the *possibility* and the *right* (after all, they are collaborators in "The Communist"! !) to push their way into the journal and to spoil it by *wrangling*?

I do not think it is practical. It would be more useful to the cause, to take another firm (the Miscellany of "The Social Democrat") and to wait until the Poles have come to their senses (or until they withdraw towards Germany), or until the situation changes.

Next, with regard to Bukharin and Co., I shall certainly send you (but not soon, because it depends on the trip to Berne) the Spring 1915 "Theses" of Bukharin. Then you will see what it is all about: (1) in the Spring of 1915 Bukharin writes (at the Conference!) "Theses" in which it is obvious that he is getting into a bog. The Japs are *against* him (therefore we are temporarily making the maximum of allowance in "The Communist" to create a form suitable for seeing clearly whether we shall be able to overcome Bukharin's wavering in a comradely manner. Will E. B. [Bosh], who calls herself a Bolshevik, help this or not? (2) In the Summer of 1915 (or towards the Autumn) the three of them, Bukharin and the Japs, sign "Theses" on self-determination. Absolutely incorrect in our opinion and a repetition of Bukharin's mistakes. (3) In the beginning of 1916 Bukharin again returns to the ideas of the Spring 1915— "Theses" on the subject of the Dutch programme (from No. 3

Bulletin of the International Socialist Commission in Berne)！！！

The conclusion? Here too a bloc is impossible: we must wait until Bukharin's wavering has subsided. The journal as an organ of Polish-Bukharin waverings is *harmful*. In such a situation it would be harmful to keep to the old firm and not to succeed in choosing another firm (the Miscellany of "The Social Democrat").

The non-Party and non-conscientious behaviour of the Japs consists in the fact that they want to throw all rsponsibility for *their* wavering *on to us*. Forgive us, my friends, but we cannot permit this! If you want to belong to the Party, you will help us in part by giving money for the publication of the Miscellany of "The Social Democrat," in which (after all, we are not wavering) we shall dissect your faults in a comradely way *without* calling you by name and *without giving* enemies the chance of rejoicing and gloating.

Besides, if the Japs were serious towards an arch-serious question, concerning the differences of opinion (abroad only one step is needed before there is a separate faction! ! Believe me, I have been watching this for about twenty years!) they would force themselves to work on these differences of opinion, consider them carefully and study them; (they have not thought, not studied, but simply blurted out). They would expound *their* differences, either in a manuscript for a small circle of leading comrades, (who would prevent the question from coming into the open), or in a pamphlet, if they want to appear in print (they have money).

Then *they* would be responsible for their own ideas. That is essential. If you want to teach the workers new truths, *answer for them* yourselves and do not shift the responsibility on to us, do not hide (saying: "We are nothing, let Lenin and Co. be responsible to the Party for the discussion," i.e. for the gloating of enemies).

No, my friends! ! That little scheme will not work! ! I will not answer for *your* waverings. We will publish the Miscellany of "The Social Democrat" without your help, Messrs. Japs! We will allow you *a postponement*. Think the matter over, work it out, and decide finally whether you wish to take on the responsibility of another confusion or not. If you want only to set the Poles and the Dutch against us in the Russian press, we will *not* allow you to do so.

That is the position and those are my ideas. I repeat, I will certainly send you Bukharin's Spring "Theses" so that you can judge the whole position for yourself and *from documents*.

Nadezhda Konstantinova is writing to you today about self-determination. We do *not* stand for division. And what about the question of annexations? Bukharin and Co. (just as Radek, Rosa Luxembourg and Pannekuk) have not considered what it means to be against "old and new annexations" (a formula *in the Press* given by Radek?). But that *is* self-determination of nations, only expressed in *other* words.

Well, until the next time,

Your

Lenin

255. (134 P²). TO A. M. KOLLONTAY IN CHRISTIANIA

[Flums, Switzerland], 25th July, 1916

My dear A. M.

I am late in answering your letter, because we have had to move to the mountains on account of Nadezhda's illness. I quite agree with you that the rôle of the Left [of the Norwegian Social Democratic Party at the Conference of the Socialists of Neutral Countries] in the consultation with Huysmans will be informative. That is most important of all. The main thing is to make notes *there and then* and about everything; to collect all and sundry documents; not to forget for a moment the absolute necessity of getting the fullest information; to write it all down (even in brief) instantly, and on the spot, in a separate notebook—that is the only way. Grimm is not going: he has not been issued a passport, which means there will be only one from the Left. His responsibility will be all the greater. Great determination and complete awareness are necessary to conduct the policy alone. You will see if there are these qualities; if so, it would be a good thing to put several questions with regard to the voting: to approve of Zimmerwald and also of Kienthal; to condemn the Social-patriots, Hyndman and Co.; Samba and Co.; Legin and Co.; Plekhanov and Co. This could also be done in the form of questions. You will see for yourself, whether this can be realised.

Please drop me a few lines on receipt of this card.

Alexander has probably taken all the addresses and will try to find out whether anything has been printed in America about the Zimmerwald Left; he should get hold of this and link up with the Socialist Propaganda League, also with the International Socialist Review, also with "The Appeal to Reason." If you receive this card and answer it, perhaps you and I can agree by letter what can be entrusted to him.

One personal request: do you happen to have any links with publishers? I have none. I should like to have a contract for a translation, so as to earn some money, or some pedagogic literary work for Nadya (for her illness demands a lengthy stay in the mountains and that is expensive).

I send you warm greetings and also my good wishes. Nadya also sends greetings.

Your

V. Ulianov

256. (135 P²). TO G. L. SHKLOVSKY IN BERNE

[Flums, Switzerland, 4th or 5th August, 1916]

My dear G. L.

I do not know if you are in Berne. Please drop me a line as soon as you receive this letter.

(1) I have a request: I must send a manuscript ["Imperialism as the highest stage of Capitalism"] concealed inside some book bindings: 100 sheets (not pages, but sheets). *Exactly* like this one (and to the same place to which Gregory posted some).

Please order *two* books of a *suitable* size: in five or six days you will receive the manuscript. *I am in a great hurry to send it*

(I have lost my copy!!) and therefore I beg you to hurry, but if you cannot do this, then answer me as soon as possible, so that I can look for someone else through whom I can do this.

(2) Why are you silent about my papers? If you cannot do anything about them (or if it is inconvenient) do not hesitate to drop me a line. It is not worth bothering about!

(3) Have you got hold of a printed copy of the "Paper" re Ts's [?] case from Moore? *You must. Do not forget!* You must get hold of it whatever happens, or the wretch will lose it!

(4) Why has there not been an account of the money for some time? Or has so much come in that you cannot count it?

Greetings to all, beginning with Lyuda.

Your

Lenin

P.S. Please send us letters from prisoners *when you have finished with them:* one should follow their mood, opinions, demands, etc.

257. (281 R). TO M. T. ELIZAROV

Spiegelgasse, 14^{II}*, Zürich, Suisse, 7th/20th September, 1916*
My dear M. T.

Please show this postcard to Manyasha or forward it to her. Yesterday I received her message (postcard) of the 8th August and also some books, for which many thanks. The news that Anyuta is in hospital has upset me very much.[1] What is the matter? Is it the same trouble about which she wrote and for which she had to spend some time in hospital, and have an operation? Whatever it is, I hope that both she and you will consult only the very best surgeons, for you should never go to mediocre doctors in such cases. I shall wait impatiently for

[1] Anyuta was arrested on 21 July, 1916, released in October and exiled to the Astrakhan Province. On account of illness she was allowed to stay in Petersburg for a while.

frequent news, even if it is brief. Letters take a terrible time now! Very many thanks to Manyasha for all her trouble with publishers: I shall settle down and write anything, for it is devilishly expensive here and life has become damnably hard. How is Manyasha? Is she earning well? (I received 200 roubles and have already acknowledged it: I thank you once again.) If it is possible, please send once a week the Russian newspapers you have been reading, *for I do not see any at all* (it is not worth sending them oftener).

I greet you warmly and kiss Manyasha. Nadya does the same.

Your

V. Ulianov

258. (156 p²). TO FRANZ KORITSCHONER, AUSTRIAN LEFT WING SOCIAL DEMOCRAT, IN VIENNA

Zürich, 25th October, 1916

My dear Friend,

We greatly regret that so far you have not written us a single line. It is to be hoped that the big happenings in Vienna will compel you to write to us in detail.

The "Berner Tagwacht" (and other papers afterwards) published the news that 24,000 workers had struck at the Munitions Works in Speier (Austria), that Czech soldiers fired, and that 700 (seven hundred!) workers were killed. What element of truth is there in all this? Please inform us in as much detail as possible.

I would ask you to send us information about Friedrich Adler's action [attempted assassination of the Austrian Prime Minister, Count Stürg, 21 Oct., 1916]. The local papers here (The "Berner Tagwacht" and "Volksrecht"; do you receive both, or neither?) extol this act. "Avanti" (do you ever see it?) says Friedrich Adler is the author of the well-known manifesto of the Austrian Internationalists. Is that so? And how can one speak openly about it?

(1) Did Friedrich Adler mention his plan to anyone?

(2) Did he hand over to some friend his documents, letters and announcements so that they might be published later on?

(3) Is it true (as the Vienna "Arbeiter Zeitung" says) that he was in the minority everywhere (in the Railway Club and other places), and how great was that minority?

(4) Is it true that his position in the organization became "intolerable"?

(5) Did he have only seven votes to support him at the last Party Conference?

(6) At the last two meetings of trusted members [The Social Democratic Party Executive] he very bluntly attacked the Party and demanded demonstrations (and what sort of demonstrations?).

Please write as fully as possible about these questions and send more information to me about Friedrich Adler. Unless you give us any special instructions, we shall print in our newspapers everything we receive from you (and we shall also publish it in the local German press, as our editorial material).

So far as the political value of this act is concerned, we obviously keep to our confirmed opinion, based on many years' experience, that individual terroristic acts are impractical means of political strife.

"Killing is no murder" our old "Iskra" [No. 20] said about terroristic acts. We *do not at all oppose* political killing (in this sense, the servile written statements of the Opportunists in "Vorwärts" and the Vienna "Arbeiter Zeitung" are simply revolting), but as revolutionary tactics, individual attempts are both impractical and harmful. It is only a mass movement that can be considered to be a real political struggle. Individual terroristic acts can be, and must be, helpful, only when they are directly linked with the mass movement. In Russia the terrorists (against whom we always fought) made a number of such attempts, but in December, 1905, when the cause had at last reached the point of being a mass movement, a rising, and when it was necessary to help the masses to use force, then the terrorists were not there to do it. That is where the terrorists fail!

Adler would have helped the revolutionary movement far

more if, without fearing a split, he had systematically gone over to illegal propaganda and agitation. It would be a very good thing if some Left group could be found who would print a leaflet in the Vienna "Arbeiter Zeitung" and "Vorwärts," and were to justify Adler's act on moral grounds ("Killing is no murder"), but at the same time explain to the workers: not terrorism, but a systematic, prolonged, self-sacrificing work of revolutionary agitation and propaganda, demonstrations etc. etc. against the servile Opportunist party, against the Imperialists, against Governments, against war—*that* is what is needed.

Please let us know to what extent it would be correct to consider Adler's act as an act of despair. I think that politically it was such an act. He lost all faith in the Party, he could not bear the fact that it was impossible to work in such a Party, impossible to work with Victor Adler; he could not reconcile himself to the idea of a split and take upon himself the difficult task of having to struggle against the Party. And the result of his despair was—assassination.

It was an act of despair on the part of a Kautskian ("Volksrecht" says that Adler was not an adherent of the Zimmerwald Left, but rather a supporter of Kautsky).

But we revolutionaries must not despair. We are not afraid of a split. On the contrary we admit the need for a split: we explain to the masses why a split is inevitable and essential: we summon them to work against the old Party, that is to a revolutionary mass struggle.

What tendencies (or what individual shades of opinion?) are there in Vienna and Austria with regard to Adler's act?

I fear that the Austrian Government will pronounce Friedrich Adler insane, and will not allow a trial. But if he is brought to trial, then a distribution of leaflets must be organised without fail.

Write more and in greater detail and observe carefully all technical means of precaution.

Best greetings,

Your

N. Lenin

(Originally written in German.)

259. (157 p²). TO ARTUR SCHMIDT, SWISS SOCIAL DEMOCRAT

[*Zürich*], *1st December, 1916*

Dear Comrade,

Will you allow me to make a suggestion?

I must confess that yesterday I did not pay sufficient attention to one very important point in your explanations; namely, to your thought, that one of the characteristics of Switzerland is that it is very democratic (general suffrage) and that this characteristic ought to be made use of *also* in propaganda. This thought is very important and in my opinion is quite correct.

Cannot this idea be so used that our differences of opinion (which are probably inconsiderable) will disappear? For instance, if we were to put the question of a referendum *only* in this way: for a complete setting aside, or against? Then we would get a confusion of pacifist (bourgeois-pacifist etc.) and socialist votes, i.e. not a clarification of the socialist consciousness, but only its eclipse; not an application of the idea and policy of class struggle to that specific question (namely to the question of militarism), but a refusal from the point of view of class struggle on the question of militarism.

But if we were to put the question in the referendum in this way: for the expropriation of large capitalist undertakings in industry and agriculture as the *only means* of setting aside militarism completely, or against expropriation?

In that case, we in our practical policy would be saying the same thing, namely that we admit everything theoretically, namely that the complete setting aside of militarism can be considered and realised only in association with the abolition of capitalism.

Consequently it should be formulated in this way:

1. We demand an *immediate* expropriation of large undertakings, possibly in the form of a direct, combined property and income tax which would be so high, exceptionally high where large estates are concerned, that the capitalists would in fact be expropriated.

2. We announce that such a socialistic reform in Switzerland

is already now economically possible, and indirectly, and as a result of the unbearably high cost of living it is urgently necessary—and that in order to carry it through politically, Switzerland requires not a bourgeois, but a proletarian Government which would depend not on the bourgeoisie, but on the wide masses of wage-earners and the poorest strata; and that the revolutionary mass struggle whose beginning we can see for instance in the Zürich mass strikes and street demonstrations, and which has been recognised by the Aarau resolution [at the Congress of the Swiss Social Democratic Party, 21 Nov., 1915], pursues *this very task*—to put an end to the intolerable position of the masses.

3. We announce that such a reform in Switzerland would *inevitably* cause imitation and the most determined and inspired support from the working class and the exploited masses in *all* civilised countries, and that *only* in connection with such a reform will the *complete abolition of militarism*, towards which we are striving and for which the masses of Europe are instinctively thirsting, not be an empty phrase nor a pious hope, but a real practically realisable and politically obvious measure.

What do you think about this?

Do you not think that if the question were to be put in this way (in practical agitation, in parliamentary speeches and in the drafts of the initiative and referendum) we would avoid the danger of the bourgeois and "socialist" pacifists misunderstanding and misinterpreting our anti-militaristic slogan? They would say that we consider the complete abolition of militarism in *bourgeois Switzerland* with its *imperialistic* neighbours possible *without* a socialist revolution (which of course is nonsense and which we all unanimously reject).

With Party greetings,

N. Lenin

Wl. Ulyanow,
    Spiegelgasse 14 II
        bei Kammerer,
            Zürich. I.

April, 1917

[Zürich, 8th January, 1917]

My dear Comrades,

I send you *a most important* communication.

Judge for yourselves and then pass it on to Brilliant [G. V. Sokolnikov] and Guilbeaux: that is where the question will be decided as to which side they support, what they are, whether cowards or capable of fighting.

The *whole* conflict will now be transferred here.

Tell me how they reacted to it and if there is any chance of publishing a protest or an open letter.

We must make use of the fact that Nain is an unquestionable authority in French Switzerland.

Best greetings,

Your

N. Lenin

Enclosure.

On Sunday, 7th January, 1917, there was a meeting in Zürich of the Parteivorstand of the Swiss Socialist Party.

A disgraceful resolution was adopted—to postpone for an indefinite period the Party Congress which had been fixed for the 10th February, 1917, in Berne, especially for a discussion on the military question. Motives: high prices must be fought; the workers are not ready; there is no unanimity in the Commission and so on. Such motives simply ridicule the Party (in the Commission two projects have already been prepared and confidentially printed: one by Affolter, Nobs, Schmidt, Nain, and Graber *against* the defence of the Fatherland; the other by Müller, Pflüger, Huber and Klöti *for* the defence of the Fatherland.

The meeting on the 7th January was very stormy. Grimm led the Right, i.e. the Opportunists, i.e. the Nationalists; he shouted the basest phrases against "foreigners," against the *young* and he blamed them for the "split" (!!!) etc. Nain, Platten, Nobs, and Münzenberg spoke *firmly* against the postponement of the Congress. Nain frankly announced to Grimm that he was murdering himself as an International Secretary!

The accepted resolution signifies Grimm's complete treachery and a mocking of the Party on the part of Opportunist leaders, the Social Nationalists. *All* the Zimmerwald-Kienthal unification and action have in actual fact been turned into a phrase by a pack of leaders (Grimm among them) who threaten to lay down their mandates (sic!!) if the refusal to defend the Fatherland goes through, and who have decided *not to allow* this question to come up for discussion by the Party mob before the end of the War. The "Grütlianer" [Swiss Organ of the National-Democratic Grütliverein] (of the 4th and 8th January) speaks the *truth* and hits out at *such* a Party.

The whole struggle of the Left, the whole struggle *for* Zimmerwald and Kienthal have now been transferred to another sphere: the conflict against this gang of leaders who have spat at the Party. The Left ought to be collected together everywhere and the fighting methods discussed. Hurry!

Would it not be the best way of fighting (there is not a moment to lose) to pass at once at La Chaux-de-Fonds and in Geneva resolutions concerning the protest, plus open letters to Nain, and to publish them immediately? There is no doubt that "the leaders" will use all their ammunition to prevent the protest from getting into the papers.

All that has been said here should be stated in the letter and the questions asked firmly: (1) Does Nain refute these facts? (2) Does he consider it *tolerable* in a democratic party of Socialists that the decision of the Congress should be cancelled by the decision of the governing body? (3) Is it *tolerable* to conceal the voting from the Party and the *speeches* of those traitors of Socialism at the meeting of the 7th January, 1917? (4) Or that it is tolerable to make friends with a President of the International Socialist Commission (Grimm), who combines phrases of the Left with help to Swiss Nationalists, the opponents of Zimmerwald, "the defenders of the Fatherland," Pflüger, Huber and Co., in the matter of a factual breaking of the Zimmerwald decisions? (5) Or that it is tolerable to curse the German social patriots in the "Berner Tagwacht," and simultaneously to be *secretly* helping the Swiss social patriots etc.?

I repeat: they will not let it get into the papers. That is quite clear. The best way is to print an open letter to Nain above the name of some group. If this is possible, hurry and answer without delay.

261. (284 R). TO M. I. ULIANOVA

[Zürich], 2nd/15th February, 1917

Darling Manyasha,

Today I received 808 francs and besides that 500 francs on the 9th/22nd January through the Azov-Don Bank. Please write what this money is; whether from a publisher, from which one, for what, and whether it is for me. It is essential to have a statement, namely, to know exactly what is being paid for by the publisher and what is not. I cannot understand where so much money comes from; Nadya is teasing me, saying I have begun to receive a "pension." Ha! Ha! it is a good joke, for life is devilishly expensive and my capacity for work is desperately low because of my bad nerves. But joking apart, I must know exactly; please write and tell me. Most likely one (or more) letters from you have gone astray and I do not know what all this is about.

I am afraid of spending the money (sometimes a certain friend who was ill was sent money through me).

I have recently received some books from you: "Russkiye Zapiski" [a literary monthly], "Firm bread prices" [S.P.B., 1916], "Trudovoye Posrednichestvo" [M., 1917], "Tula statistics." Many, many thanks. I send warm greetings to Anyuta, M. T. and also to Mitya.

Our life goes on as usual, very quietly; Nadya is ill fairly often. The Winter was an incredibly cold one; it is still cold. How are you all? Are you all well? News from you comes very slowly.

I greet you and kiss you,

Your

V. Ul.

262. (285 R). TO M. T. ELIZAROV

[Zürich], 5th or 6th/18th or 19th February, 1917

My dear Mark Timofeich,

You will see from the enclosed (scheme of work) that Nadya is planning an edition of a "Pedagogic Dictionary" or a "Pedagogic Encyclopædia."

I am strenuously supporting this plan, which, in my opinion, will fill a very serious gap in Russian pedagogic literature; it will be a very useful work and will bring in some money, *which is arch-important for us*. With the increase in the numbers and the circle of readers the demand in Russia, *especially for "Encyclopædias"* and for similar publications, is very great and is growing rapidly. If well compiled, a pedagogic dictionary or a pedagogic encyclopædia would be a reference book and would go into a number of editions. I am quite sure Nadya will be able to complete this work, for she has studied pedagogy for many years, has written about it, and has prepared herself systematically for the task. Zürich is an exceptionally convenient centre, especially for such a work. The pedagogic museum here is the best in the world.

The income from such an undertaking would be certain.

It would be best if we could manage to publish it *ourselves* after borrowing the necessary capital or having found a capitalist who would join in the undertaking as a partner.

If that is impossible and if chasing after it would only be a waste of time—and you, of course, could see that more clearly, and you could decide the question after thinking the matter over and making enquiries—then you ought to propose the plan to some established publisher who would probably undertake it. Only the plan must not be stolen, i.e. the idea. Then you must sign an agreement with the publisher, a *very detailed agreement* in the editor's (Nadya's) name, stating *all* the conditions. Otherwise the publisher (and an old established publisher too!!) will simply take *all* the profits for himself and enslave the editor. *That does happen!*

I beg you to think over this plan thoroughly, to make enquiries, to take on the responsibility, to talk it over and to answer me in detail.

If successful answer by telegram: "Encyclopædia agreement concluded." Then Nadya will set to work seriously.

I greet you warmly,

Your

V. Ulianov

P.S. The edition—two volumes in two columns. Published in parts, 1-2 sheets at a time. Announce a *subscription*. Then money will start coming in rapidly.

263. (145 P²). TO S. N. RAVICH IN GENEVA

[*Zürich, after the 12th February, 1917*]

My dear Comrade Olga,

Many thanks for the letter about the affairs in your local Party. Truth to tell, "pessimism" often takes hold of others beside yourself.[1] The Party here is Opportunist through and through; a charitable institution for petit-bourgeois clerks.

Even the leaders who are supposed to be Left (like Nobs and Platten) are no use *at all*; especially the two I name. As we have no way of approaching the masses, nothing can be done. But without flattering myself by false hopes, it is useless to fall into pessimism: the moment is an important one and even if we can help only a little (by a couple of leaflets etc.) then that is *something*: even that will not pass unnoticed or be wasted.

I am very, very glad that you intend to help in every way with the distribution of the leaflets [in the name of the Left Zimmerwaldists]. Please do not forget to destroy the *whole* of our correspondence.

When are you having a Cantonal Conference of the Socialist Party? I have sent the draft resolution to Abramovich. Has he sent it on to you? Do you know anything (apart from the

---

[1] Ravich complained about the Opportunism of the Geneva Social Democratic organisation and their extreme Chauvinism.

Volksrecht) about the Congress of the Zürich [S.D.] Party in Töss [11 Feb., 1917]?

Who reported about the 1st February [meeting of the Zimmerwald Conference] in Olten? Only Guilbeaux and Co.? They made a terrible mistake!! They did not understand the task, they took fright!

I am not capable of reading it in French.

I send you warm greetings and wish you all success,

Greetings to Vyacheslav Alekseyevich.

Your

Lenin

P.S. And how is the referendum[1] getting on? How many signatures? Are they continuing to collect them?

264. (146 P²). TO A. M. KOLLONTAY IN CHRISTIANIA

[Zürich], 17th February, 1917

My dear A. M.

We received your letter today and were very glad to have it. For a long time we did not know that you were in America and had no letters from you, excepting one giving news of your departure from America.

I wrote to you about the 7th-8th January (the day of posting the letter from Stockholm, for when sent from here to America direct, the French intercept everything!), but this letter together with an article for "The New World" has obviously not caught you in New York.

It was pleasant to hear from you about Nikolai Ivanovich's [Bukharin] and Pavlov's [P. B. Berzin] victory in the "Novy Mir." (I receive that newspaper devilishly irregularly, obviously through the fault of the post, and not the posting of it), but it was disappointing to receive news of Trotsky's bloc against Nikolai Ivanovich. What a swine that Trotsky is! Left phrases and a bloc with the Right against the aims of the Left!! He ought to be exposed (by you) if only in a short letter to "The Social Democrat."

---

[1] "Das Referendum gegen den Parteivorstandbeschluss."

I have already received No. 1 of "The Internationalist" and was delighted. I have incomplete information about the Conference of the Socialist Labour Party and Socialist Party of the 6th-7th January, 1917. It seems that the Socialist Labour Party is throwing out the whole of its minimum programme (that is Bukharin's temptation and danger; he stumbled in 1915 on that very place!!) I am extremely sorry I cannot collect all the documents about the Socialist Labour Party (I asked Bukharin about this, but letters are obviously going astray). Do you happen to have any material? I could return it after reading it.

I am preparing (and have almost finished preparing) an article on the attitude of Marxism towards the State.[1] I have come to certain conclusions still more sharply against Kautsky than against Bukharin, (have you seen his "Nota Bene" in No. 6 of the "Jugend Internationale" and No. 2 of the Miscellany of "The Social Democrat"?[2]). The question is an extremely important one: Bukharin is much better than Kautsky, but Bukharin's mistakes can *ruin* that "just cause" in the struggle with Kautskianism.

I will send you my article on self-determination against P. Kievsky.[3] What a pity there is no money! We could then publish the Miscellany of "The Social Democrat" No. 3 (the whole material is lying ready) and No. 4 (Bukharin's article on the State which at first we declined and my article on the State).

The Zimmerwald Right has in my opinion ideologically buried Zimmerwald; Bourderon plus Merrheim in Paris voted for *pacifism* [at the Congress of the General Confederation of Labour, 24th Dec., 1916]; Kautsky did the same on the 7th January, 1917 in Berlin [at the all-German Conference of the Party opposition]; Turati (on the 17th December, 1916!!) [in his speech in the Italian Parliament] and the whole of the

[1] Lenin's notes on "Marxism in the State" were incorporated into his book "The State and Revolution."

[2] In which Bukharin criticised the Kautskian exposition of Marx's teaching about the State. It was this article that spurred Lenin to study more closely Marx's teaching about the State.

[3] Lenin's article "On the Caricature of Marxism and on 'Imperialistic Economism.' "

Italian Party also. That is the death of Zimmerwald!! In words they *condemned* social-pacifism (see the Kienthal resolution), but in deeds they have turned towards it!

Grimm has basely turned towards the Social patriots within the Swiss Party (our friend in Stockholm will send you material about this) by entering into a bloc with them on the 7th January, 1917. (The Partei Vorstandsitzung is against the Left for a postponement of the [Swiss Social Democratic Party] Congress. And now still more basely he has attacked the Left for the Begründung des Referendums (we shall send it to you) and has composed a "middle," "centre" resolution. Have you, or can you get hold of the Zürich "Volksrecht"? If not, we can send you a few copies or try to.

Tomorrow (18th February) is the Congress of the Swedish [S.D.] Party. There will probably be a split. I believe there is a devilish mess and disorder among the young people. Do you speak Swedish? Can you arrange collaboration (mine and other Left people) in the newspaper of the young Swedes?

Answer please, if only briefly, but *quickly* and regularly, for it is terribly important for us to establish regular correspondence with you.

Greetings

Lenin

THE FEBRUARY REVOLUTION AND THE PREPARATION FOR OCTOBER

1917

SUMMARY

1917

Formation of Workers' organisations, professional unions, factory committees. Eight-hour day. Increase in wages. Return of leading political S.D. emigrants. Bolshevik papers: "Pravda" in S.P.B.; "The Social Democrat" in Moscow. Menshevik papers: "Rabochaya Gazeta" in S.P.B.; "Vpered" in Moscow. Greater union in working class. An All-Russia Central Soviet of Professional Unions formed.

April: An All-Russia Congress of Soviet workers and soldier deputies.

Crisis in Provisional Government caused by Milyukov's imperialistic note. Milyukov and Guchkov resign. An All-Russia Conference of R.S.D.L.P. (Bolshevik) resolutions: (1) re war; peace without annexation or indemnities; encouragement of fraternising at the front, (2) on the agrarian question: an organised seizure of the land by the peasants; organisation of proletarian elements in the villages; formation of large model farms, (3) R.S.D.L.P. must found the III International.

May: Formation of Coalitional Provisional Government.

May-July: Wide popularity of Social Revolutionary Party.

June 17: All-Russia Congress of the Soviets of Worker and Soldier Deputies. S.R.'s and Mensheviks dominate the Congress.

July: Workers' movement against Coalition Government. Demonstrations in Petrograd.

1917

March: Lenin leaves Switzerland for Russia via Berlin.

April: Arrival in Petrograd after ten years abroad.

Addresses the masses with the slogan: "Long live the World Socialist Revolution."

Speaks at Congress.

Theses printed in "Pravda" ((1) it is essential to throw off the rags of Social Democracy and to put on the truly revolutionary clothes of Communism, (2) in the revolutionary movement Russia must abandon bourgeois parliamentary forms of State organisation. All power must be in the hands of the Soviets).

Participates in the work of the All-Russia Conference of R.S.D.L.P. (Bolshevik). Writes "Letter on Tactics."

June 4: Speaks at I Conference of Peasant Deputies on (1) the seizure of land, (2) need to organise poorest peasants, (3) organisation of model collective farms.

Writes against Imperialist bourgeoisie, the Mensheviks and Social Revolutionaries.

|

Kerensky becomes Premier. "Pravda" banned. Bolsheviks arrested (Trotsky, Kamenev, Lunacharsky, etc.).

July: Russian Army defeated in Galicia. Organisation of counter-revolutionary (bourgeois landowners) elements in country. Disorganisation in ranks of Provisional Government.

End July: VI Congress of R.S.D.L.P. (Bolsheviks). Main task to overthrow Kerensky Government; to liquidate the War; to establish Socialism in Russia.

Aug.: Government Conference in Moscow. Kornilov attempts to seize power.

Sept.: Growth of Bolshevik influence. Revolutionary majority in S.P.B. Soviet of Soldier and Worker Deputies. Trotsky elected President. Democratic Conference in S.P.B. (coalition with the bourgeoisie).

Oct. 2: Organisation of the Provisional Soviet of the Russian Republic.

Oct.: Bloc of Bolsheviks and Left S.R.'s at first meeting of Soviet of the Republic. Congress of Soviets of the Northern region. Final decision to rise and give power to Soviets during their second congress.

Organisation of military revolutionary committee attached to the S.P.B. Soviet of Worker and Soldier Deputies.

Nov. 7: Establishment of the Proletarian Dictatorship in Russia.

Lenin evades arrest. Forced to hide in S.P.B. and Finland for four months. Secret activity. Controls the Party and collaborates in semi-legal and illegal Bolshevik papers.

Writes "Lessons of the Revolution" and "The State and Revolution."

Works for overthrow of Kerensky Government to give power to the organised worker and peasant masses.

The Party C.C. disagrees with Lenin that it is time to seize power.

End Oct.: Leaves Finland and, risking being caught by Kerensky agents, comes to Petrograd to organise a rising.

265. (164 p²). TO V. A. KARPINSKY IN GENEVA

[Zürich, 19th March, 1917]

My dear Vyacheslav Alexeyevich,

I am carefully considering, and from every point of view, what will be the best way of travelling [to Russia]. The following is absolutely secret. I ask you to reply at once, and perhaps it would be best by express (let us hope we will not ruin the Party by sending a dozen or more express letters!), so as to be certain that no one has read this letter. Please procure in your name papers for travelling to France and England, and I will use *them* when passing through England and *Holland* to Russia.

I can wear a wig.

The passport photograph will be of *me* in a wig. *I* shall go to the Berne consulate to present your papers and I shall be wearing the wig.

You must then disappear from Geneva for at least two or three weeks (until you receive a telegram from me in Scandinavia). During that time you must be extremely careful and go into hiding somewhere in the mountains, where *we shall of course pay for your board and lodging*.

If you agree, begin *preparations at once* and in the most energetic (and most secret) manner, and in any case send me a line at once.　　　　Your　　　　　　　　Lenin

P.S. Think out all practical steps to be taken *in connection with this*, and write to me in detail. I write to you, because I am convinced that everything between us will remain *absolutely* secret.[1]

266. (165 p²). TO V. A. KARPINSKY IN GENEVA

[Zürich, Between the 21st and 23rd March, 1917]

Martov's plan is good.[2] We *ought* to begin working for it, only *we* (and you) cannot do this directly. *We* would be sus-

---

[1] The plan mentioned in this letter was not realised.

[2] At the meeting of the representatives of Russian political parties in Geneva on 19 March, 1917, Martov proposed a plan to procure a pass for political emi-

pected. Apart from Martov, non-Party Russian and Russian patriots should appeal to Swiss Ministers (and influential people, such as lawyers etc., which can be done also in Geneva), with a request that they should discuss this with the representative of the German Government in Berne. We cannot participate either directly or indirectly; our participation would *ruin* everything. But the plan in itself is *very* good and *quite* right.

267. (166 P²). TO V. S. GANETSKY IN CHRISTIANIA

[*Zürich, 23rd/24th March, 1917*]

Note.

Wire to "Pravda," giving them an address for a reply. I have just read extracts from the Central Committee's manifesto.[1] Best wishes! Long live the proletarian militia which is preparing peace and socialism!

268. (167 P²). TO V. A. KARPINSKY IN GENEVA

[*Zürich, 24th March, 1917*]

My dear Comrade,

I have sent you (by Inessa [I. Armand]) copies of two of my articles for "Pravda," for your information and our mutual agreement.[2]

I must have them back on *Monday;* if necessary, send them express and take them to the railway station.

Be careful of a bloc with the "Nachalo"[3] people: we are

grants to Russia via Germany in exchange for interned German civilians. This plan was accepted by the C.C. of the R.S.D.L.P.

[1] The manifesto of the Russian Social Democratic Labour Party "To all Citizens of Russia" was issued and distributed as a leaflet on 26 February/11 March, 1917, at the height of the revolutionary conflict in the streets of Petrograd. It was also printed in "Pravda," No. 1, 5 March, 1917.

[2] Lenin's "Letters from Afar," a series of articles on the February-March revolution, written in Switzerland before he left for Russia. The first letter was printed in "Pravda" on 3, 4 April, 1917.

[3] A group of S.D. Internationalists publishing the newspaper "Nachalo" in Paris, 30 Sept., 1916-23 March, 1917, in place of "Nashe Slovo," which was banned. A. Lunacharsky, G. Sokolnikov, D. Manilsky, etc., collaborated in it.

against any rapprochement with other parties, we stand for warning the workers *against* Chkheidze. Definitely! Chkheidze is obviously wavering: see how he is praised by "Le Temps" of the 22nd March, and many others. We stand *for* the Central Committee in Russia, *for* "Pravda," *for* our own Party, *for* the proletarian militia which is preparing peace and socialism.

Greetings,

Your

Lenin

W. Uljanoff,
    Spiegelgasse 14 II
        Zürich. I.

269. (168 P²). TO V. A. KARPINSKY IN GENEVA

[Zürich, 25th March, 1917]

My dear Comrade,

I have sent to you by Inessa [I. Armand] copies of two of my letters to "Pravda." I hope you have fulfilled my request and posted them back by *express* today (Sunday), or that you will do so tomorrow.

After Tuesday (in the evening I am to lecture here [on "The Tasks of the R.S.D.L.P. in the Russian Revolution"]), I will send you a copy of letter No. 3. I think it will then be easy for us to agree on tactics.

Lunacharsky wrote to me suggesting a "consultation," and I replied that I was agreeable to having a talk with him. (He will be in Zürich.) I agreed to this *only* on condition that the workers were warned *against* Chkheidze's waverings. He (Lunacharsky) *remained silent.*

This means it will only be a *personal* conversation.

Chkheidze is obviously wavering: on the 22nd March "Le Temps" *praises* him, but on the 24th March, they *curse* him. The position is clear!

I am afraid that you have been in too great a hurry in drawing up a general resolution.[1] I sent it today to "Pravda,"

---

[1] Of the Geneva Bolshevik section drawn up for the proposed meeting with the "Vpered" group.

together with my article, and addressed it to: Herrn Fürsten-berg, Boulevard Hotel, Christiania. You can send articles there, explaining that the articles are for "Pravda," and that I have given you this address; so far as articles on principles are con-cerned, it would be better if you and I were first to come to an agreement.

"Pravda" no doubt needs articles. At any rate I am writing and continuing to write for it, *and I advise all friends to do the same.*

I am afraid you are also in too great a hurry to unite with the "Vpered" ["Forward"] people.[1]

The end of the resolution is good. (I had time only to *scan* it before sending it on), but the beginning (about democracy in general) seemed to me to be very bad.

With regard to uniting with "Vpered," I sent a telegram to Christiania to the members of our Party who were leaving: "Our tactics: absolute mistrust, no support of new govern-ment, Kerensky particularly suspect; to arm proletariat only guarantee; immediate election Petrograd Duma; *no rapproche-ment with other Parties.*"

The last is a sine qua non condition.

We do not trust Chkheidze.

Our deputies and Kamenev are *already* in Petersburg, *or* will be one of these days.[2] The Central Committee [of the R.S.D.L.P.] is in Petersburg (there were extracts from its manifesto in the "Frankfurter Zeitung": *lovely!*) "Pravda" is there. We stand for preserving *that* Party *absolutely,* we are against any uniting with the Organisation Committee.

(The Organisation Committee is probably *not* in Petersburg, for the "Frankfurter Zeitung" and the "Vossische Zeitung" have given in detail Chkheidze and Co.'s proclamation of the 16th March, and there is *not a word* about the Organisation Committee.[3])

---

[1] On the receipt of Lenin's letter, negotiations for uniting were broken off.

[2] Lenin means the return of the exiled members of the Bolshevik faction of the IV State Duma, sentenced in 1915 for organising an illegal S.D. Conference and underground S.D. work.

[3] Evidently the proclamation of the Petrograd Soviet of Worker and Soldier Deputies, 14 March, 1917.

It is for the elections to the Constituent Assembly (or for overthrowing Guchkov's and Milyukov's Government), that we *need* a special Party, our own, which in my opinion has *fully* justified itself throughout the years 1915-1917.

And so? Do the "Vpered" people wish to join this Party *honestly?*

Good!

They do not?

Well, I am neither going to bargain, nor make concessions. Talk to them frankly and *more* than once, and send me a line, so that I receive it on Tuesday (or at the latest on Wednesday morning).

Would you undertake to type a copy in duplicate (or only one copy) of my manuscript of 500 pages (in my handwriting) *for a fee not lower than last time?* [1] I would have it published at once in Petersburg. Reply.

Greetings   Your
                                        Lenin

P.S. Lyudmila [L. Stal'] has *left* Stockholm. Do not write to the Stockholm address.

P.P.S. Are you and Olga [S. P. Ravich] going to Russia, if an opportunity occurs, and when? Who else will go from Geneva?

270. (169 P²). TO Y. S. GANETSKY IN STOCKHOLM

Telegram from Berne.   [*28th March, 1917*]

Berlin permit inadmissible for me. Either Swiss Government will be granted railway carriage to Copenhagen or will come to agreement about exchange all Russian emigrants for interned Germans.

271. (170 P²). TO Y. S. GANETSKY IN STOCKHOLM

Telegram.   [*30th March, 1917*]

Your plan impossible. England will never allow me transit, but will sooner intern me. Milyukov will deceive us. Only hope

---

[1] Lenin's book, "The Agrarian Programme of Social Democracy in the First Russian Revolution, 1905-7," published in 1917.

is to send somebody Petrograd and insist on exchange interned
Germans through Soviet Workers' Deputies. Wire.

Ulianov

272. (171 P²). TO THE NATIONAL COUNCILLOR GRIMM IN BERNE
Telegram.   [*31st March, 1917*]

Our Party definitely decided accept offer for Russian emigrants to pass through Germany and to organise transit at once.
At present we number over ten passengers.

We absolutely cannot agree to further delay. Protest strongly
against it and are travelling alone. We insistently beg you
to end negotiations and, if possible, to send us decision tomorrow.

Gratefully,

Lenin, Zinoviev, Ulianova

273. (286 P²). TELEGRAM NO. 148. TO A. I. ELIZAROVA AND
M. I. ULIANOVA

Shirokaya, 48/9 flat 24, Petrograd

Blank No. 71.   Rec. 2/April, 1917. 20 hrs. 8 mins.

Military censor No. 87

Petrograd. Torneo. 148. 13. 218. 12. Nazen PGD.
Arriving Monday Night 11. Tell "Pravda."

Ulianov

274. (172 P²). TO THE BOLSHEVIK SECTION IN ZÜRICH

[*Berne, 3rd April, 1917*]

My dear Friends,

I enclose the resolution of the Central Committee of our
Party.[1] (The Karpinskys, after making two copies of this resolution, must *immediately* return it to me.) Have a copy made

---

[1] About the immediate travelling of political emigrants to Russia via Germany.

(*for yourselves*) *at once*, and send it *express by the first train* (*take it to the station*) to the Karpinskys, *and also enclose this letter of mine.*

Inform Lausanne (Hoberman[1]) separately.

I would add that I consider the Mensheviks, who have ruined the common cause, are scoundrels of the worst kind, who are afraid of "public opinion," i.e. of the social patriots!![2] I (and Zinoviev) intend to travel, *whatever happens.*

Find out exactly (1) who is going and (2) how much money there is.

This information should be sent at once to Radomyslsky, Neufeldstrasse 27, Berne.

We have *already* got a fund of over 1,000 francs to cover the journey. We are thinking of making Wednesday, 4th April, the day for leaving.

Everyone should *immediately* get passports from the Russian Consul, according to their place of residence.

Greetings,

Your

Lenin

P.S. Send a copy of this at once to Abraham [A. Skovno] and his wife. I enclose 100 francs, which you asked Gregory to lend you.

275. (173 p²). TELEGRAM TO Y. S. GANETSKY IN STOCKHOLM

[*6th April, 1917*]

Have been inexplicably delayed. Mensheviks demand sanction of Worker Deputies' Council. Send somebody immediately Finland or Petrograd to discuss with Chkheidze how far possible. Belenin's opinion desirable. Wire People's House, Berne.

Ulianov

---

[1] Social Democrat, member of a Bolshevik section, arrived in Russia together with Lenin.

[2] The Mensheviks did not approve of the political emigrants travelling to Russia immediately, and proposed waiting for sanction to travel via Germany from the Soviet of Worker Deputies.

276. (174 P²). TELEGRAM TO HENRI GUILBEAUX IN GENEVA

[*Berne, 6th April, 1917*]

Leaving tomorrow midday for Germany.[1] Platten accompanying train. Request you come at once. We will cover expenses. Bring Romain Rolland if he agrees on principle. Do all you can to bring Nain and Graber.

Wire People's House.

Ulianov

277. (175 P²). TO V. A. KARPINSKY IN GENEVA

[*Petrograd*], *12th April, 1917*

My dear Friend,

I hope this letter will reach you, and also the newspapers that are being sent to you. I say "I hope," because the difficulties of communicating with people outside Russia are incredible. We were allowed into the country, but were met with frenzied persecution, and so far have not received any books, manuscripts, or letters. Evidently the military censorship is working wonderfully—even too assiduously, for you know, of course, that we did not and could not hear anything about the war.

Please stop copying the Agrarian manuscript, for I have *found* a copy here already set up in type; only the conclusion is missing, namely where it says "All the peasants and the proletariat are against private ownership of land. . . ."

You will oblige me if you will make four or five copies of these words down to the end and send them (1) to me personally, (2) to "Pravda," Moika 32, (3) to the address given to you for Stockholm. Perhaps I shall receive one of these copies.

Send me a postcard care of "Pravda," or better to Elizarov M. T. (for V. I.), Shirokaya 48, Flat 24, Petrograd, saying whether you have received this letter and when you posted the copies of the conclusion.

---

[1] Lenin and a group of political émigrés (19 Bolsheviks, 6 Bundists, 3 adherents of the internationalist newspaper "Nashe Slovo") left Berne on 7th April. The group left Switzerland on 8th April, 1917.

We arrived quite safely. Milyukov would not allow Platten to enter Russia.

The atmosphere here is one of frenzied persecution of us by the bourgeoisie. Among the workers and *soldiers*, there is sympathy. The Social Democrats are supporting "revolutionary defence" (they have something to defend now—to defend the republic from Wilhelm). Chkheidze and Co. and Steklov (leaders of the Soviet of Worker and Soldier Deputies in Petersburg) have completely gone over to "revolutionary defence." Chkheidze is in a bloc with Potresov. All are fighting and screaming for the "unity" of the whole of Russian Social Democracy; of course we are against this.

The All-Russia Conference of Bolsheviks (our Party) will take place in Petersburg on the 22nd April, 1917.[1]

Drop me a line to say whether our "farewell letter"[2] has been published, in which languages, and how it is selling.

Please write to say if you have received the newspapers (I am sending you a batch of "Pravda" and cuttings from various newspapers). Keep Paris and the whole of Switzerland better informed.

Greetings,

Your

V. Ulianov

278. (176 P²). TO Y. S. GANETSKY AND K. B. RADEK
IN STOCKHOLM

[*Petrograd*], *12th April, 1917*]

My dear Friends,

So far nothing has come; absolutely nothing. We have received neither letters, parcels, nor money from you.[3] Only two telegrams from Ganetsky. We are sending two batches of "Pravda," one for you and one for Karpinsky, (M. Karpinsky, Bibliothèque Russe, 7, Rue Hugo de Senger, Genève (Genf)

---

[1] It took place on 24-29 April, 1917.

[2] "A farewell letter to Swiss workers" was printed in "Jugend Internationale," No. 8, 1 May, 1917.

[3] The money belonging to the C.C. of the R.S.D.L.P. and left abroad, which Lenin evidently required in Russia for Party aims.

Suisse) and two batches of cuttings, one for you and the other for Karpinsky.

Send a postcard or telegram (to M. T. Elizarov (for V. I.), Shirokaya Ulitsa 48, Flat 24, Petrograd) acknowledging the receipt of this letter and newspapers. Steinberg[1] has arrived and has promised to get the packets that have been sent to us. We will see if he will manage this.

If you receive the newspapers, you will be able to understand the position after reading them.

In case the newspapers do not reach you, I will tell you everything in brief. The bourgeoisie (Plekhanov) are attacking us frantically for having passed through Germany. They are trying to stir up the soldiers against us. So far they have not succeeded: we have supporters, and loyal ones. There is a desperate Chauvinist fever raging among the Social Revolutionaries and Social Democrats; it has taken the form of "revolutionary defence" (they have something to defend now—to defend the republic from Wilhelm). We are being frantically attacked for being against unity; whereas the masses support the union of all Social Democrats, we are against.

Chkheidze has gone over completely to "revolutionary defence"; he has joined *Potresov*. They all stand for the Liberty Loan. We are the only ones against it: i.e., the supporters of "Our Word," *Larin* and a few of *Martov's* friends.

We are calling an All-Russia Conference of Bolsheviks for the 22nd April, 1917. We hope fully to straighten out the policy of "Pravda" which has been leaning towards Kautskianism.[2]

Do write some articles for "Pravda" on foreign policy— arch-short and in the spirit of "Pravda." (We have very very little space and are struggling for enlargement.) Also archshortly on the German revolutionary movement and on the Press of the Left.

---

[1] A Russian engineer living in Stockholm, an intermediary for receiving letters.

[2] L. Kamenev, who had returned from Siberian exile to Petrograd before Lenin's arrival, was at that time one of the editors of "Pravda." He did not share Lenin's position (a struggle for a direct going over to Socialistic revolution). Kamenev tended more to favour a limitation of the tasks of the working class within the confines of a bourgeois-democratic revolution.

Write also a letter about the Swedish Left. We have heard that the Chauvinist Branting is attacking *Radek*.

The Soviet of Worker and Soldier Deputies concluded an *agreement* at the beginning of the revolution with the Provisional Government to *support* the latter. There is a "contact commission": the Soviet "controls" the Provisional Government.

The position is arch-complicated and arch-interesting. We are publishing small pamphlets on tactics [Letters on tactics, Letter No. 1]. The Soviet wants a general Socialist International Congress. We want a Congress of the Left against Social Chauvinists and against "the Centre."

Warm greetings and wishes. Write oftener. Be extremely careful and accurate in your dealings.

Your

V. Ulianov

279. (APPENDIX R. IV, PAGE 448). TO M. I. ULIANOVA

[*Stirsudden, June-July, 1917*]

Darling Manyasha,

Thanks for the letter. Please forgive me for not answering by return. I am so "drunk" with the Summer rest and with doing nothing (I am resting as I have not rested for ages) that I keep putting off all important and unimportant work.

I am against the boycott of the Third Duma and a small article I have just finished writing on this subject will soon be coming out. In my opinion such a slogan ought not to be repeated outside the struggle with the first constitutional illusions. The new enthusiasm (perhaps in connection with the July strike of the Moscow textile-workers—a strike of up to 400,000 men is expected), must be expanded, prepared, and turned into a general one; but it is out of place to proclaim a boycott. We must not forswear it; if the occasion arises in the moment of enthusiasm we will support a boycott. But to proclaim one now would be either premature bravado or an uncritical repetition of slogans that have a glorious revolutionary past. This, briefly, is the argument I am developing in print. It will probably be published in about a fortnight.

Write and tell me how you are living and whether you are happy. Greetings to Mark and to all friends.

We are having a wonderful rest and are thoroughly idle.

I kiss you warmly,

Your

V. Ulianov

280. (177 p²). TO L. B. KAMENEV

July, 1917

Strictly "entre nous": if I am done in, please publish my notebook "Marxism and the State."[1]

It is held up in Stockholm. A blue binding. All the quotations are taken from Marx and Engels, as well as Kautsky versus Pannekuk. There are a number of notes and remarks. They need to be collated. I think it could be published after, say, a week's work. I think it is important, because Plekhanov and Kautsky are not the only ones to have blundered. One condition: all this must remain absolutely "entre nous."

281. (287 R). TO M. I. ULIANOVA

[*Helsingfors, August, 1917*]

Darling Manyasha,

I am sending much love and best wishes. I am living well here and have settled down to write a work on the State ["The State and Revolution"], which has long been interesting me. I want to give you some advice: you really must go away for treatment. You should take advantage of the present time when you are comparatively free and simultaneously anxious, to cure both your leg and your nerves. I beg you: *do* go without fail and at once. You can take with you a translation or

---

[1] A note to Kamenev, written when Lenin's life was in danger. He was at that time in hiding in Finland. His notebooks on "Marxism and the State" were brought to him, and he then wrote his book "The State and Revolution."

some fiction to help you bear the tedium which to a certain extent is inevitable during treatment. But you must go. Please fulfil this request for me and write me something in reply. I embrace you warmly.

Your,

Ulianov

282. (288 R). TO MIMOSA (M. I. ULIANOVA)

[Helsingfors, 2nd August-September, 1917]

My dear darling Mimosa,

I beg you to go for the treatment; do not put it off, you must not lose time. And when you return it will be *easy* to arrange all sorts of work. You must go without fail.

The Beer[1] theme is excellent. Try to get Schlüter[2] on Chartism (in German); it came out after Beer and corrects that Opportunist. You could write an arch-good pamphlet based on Beer *and Schlüter*. Send me a reply.

"Party Congresses" is also a good subject (apart from *protocols* you will need various pamphlets. I happen to have Lenin's "report" on the Stockholm Congress, but that is all. Too little! The titles of these I do not remember exactly). If you write it, send me the rough draft, we will discuss it.

I embrace you warmly,

V. Ulianov

283. (178 P[2]). TO THE BUREAU OF THE CENTRAL COMMITTEE ABROAD (IN STOCKHOLM)

Helsingfors, 30th, 31st August; 2nd, 7th September, 1917
17th/30th August, 1917

My dear Friends,

It is with great difficulty, and after an enforced interval of several weeks, that I believe we shall be able to renew our

---

[1] Lenin's sister was proposing to translate Beer's book on the Labour Movement.
[2] Hermann Schlüter: "Die Chartistenbewegung," Berlin.

correspondence. Of course, to do this successfully, you must do your utmost to see that you organise it from your side.

The base slander, raised by the bourgeoisie, that Ganetsky, Kollontay, and many others, are spying, or aiding it, is, of course, a low means of hiding the attack on the Internationalists on the part of our brave "Republicans," who wish to differentiate themselves profitably from Czarism by slander.[1]

(1) I read somewhere in a Russian newspaper that Ganetsky and Radek are coming forward with a denial. I do not know whether this is true, but it is essential. First of all, Radek must write to Paris and obtain the protocols (of the various factions of the R.S.D.L.P.) of his last Paris [Party] trial. Lunacharsky, in chastising the slanderers, described this trial in "Novaya Zhizn" ["New Life," No. 60], but that is not enough. He must try to get the protocols, or at least a full account of the Court proceedings, and if it is not possible to publish it, then to have a few copies typed, and to send them here. If the protocols or the sentence cannot be secured, it would help to have a written description of the trial made by some Parisians, who took part in the trial, and to publish, say, a small pamphlet in Russian (there is a Russian printing press in Christiania) in order to refute this disgusting slander by documents. We can manage to send on the pamphlet; extracts from it must appear in the "Arbeiter Politik," in "Politiken," in "Demain" etc.

(2) It is equally essential for Ganetsky to refute the slander by documentary evidence, by publishing the financial report of his business and his "affairs" with Sumenson (what sort of a man is Sumenson? It is the first time I hear of him!) and with Kozlovsky (it would be desirable for the report to be checked and witnessed by a solicitor or a few Swedish socialists, Members of Parliament). It is also essential to print the text of the telegrams (they have already appeared in some Russian newspapers, e.g. "Russkaya Volya" ["The Russian Will"]),

---

[1] The bourgeois press accused Radek, Ganetsky and Kollontay, members of the C.C. of the R.S.D.L.P. abroad, of being agents in the pay of the German Government. Alexinsky printed the text of telegrams sent by Ganetsky and others from Petrograd and attempted to represent these telegrams as being sent in code as German agents.

in "Bez Lishnikh Slov" ["Without Superfluous Words"] and others, but probably not in full) and each telegram should be analysed and explained. A pamphlet ought to be brought out at once against this monstrous Dreyfusism and slander, and without sparing labour, trouble or money, so as to brand the slanderers, and to help those who have been arrested on account of the slander.

(3) In what state are the money affairs of the Bureau abroad, which was appointed by our Central Committee? The July persecutions have shown quite clearly that our Central Committee cannot help (at any rate I think not). Write and tell me whether you have managed to collect any money through the Swedish Left, and can the Bureau continue to exist? And the bulletin [of the C.C. of the R.S.D.L.P.]? How many issues have been published, and in how many languages? Has Guilbeaux received them all? Have you a complete file of "Demain"? Is the bulletin being sent to North and South America? Write fully about all this.

(4) By the way, I do not remember who told me, but I think it was someone in Stockholm, that Moor, [Swiss Socialist, who offered the Bolsheviks money, but was refused] appeared after Grimm, and independently of him. It does not surprise me that this scoundrel Grimm, as a Centre-Kautskian, should prove himself to be capable of such a scandalous rapprochement with his "own" Minister: the man who does not break definitely with the Social Chauvinists always risks falling into such a disgraceful position. But what is Moor like? Has it been completely and absolutely proved that he is honest? Has he never had any direct, or indirect, hobnobbing with German Social Imperialists? If it is true that Moor is in Stockholm, and if you are acquainted with him, then I beg you insistently to adopt all measures to check this carefully, and by documentary evidence. There must be no room for the shadow of a doubt or rumour etc. I very much regret that the Zimmerwald Commission did not condemn Grimm more severely: it ought to have been more severe.[1]

[1] Robert Grimm, the Secretary of the Swiss Socialist Party during the War was accused by the International Socialist Commission in Berne, that without its knowl-

(5) I was, and I undoubtedly remain, against participation in the [International Socialist] Stockholm Conference. I must remark that I am writing the whole of this letter unofficially, for I have had no chance of consulting the Central Committee nor even of getting into touch with them. Therefore, in answering me in detail, please append to your letter an official, detailed, businesslike and documented account, namely your own (as well as of the whole Bureau) report for the Central Committee. I will forward it.

And so, I am absolutely against participation in the Stockholm Conference. I consider Kamenev's action [1] (have you seen "Novaya Zhizn"? You must subscribe to it) to be the height of folly and baseness, and I have written about it to the Central Committee and also to the Press. Fortunately, Kamenev was speaking solely for himself and was disavowed by the other Bolshevik.

I consider it would be direct treachery to participate in the Stockholm Conference, or any other, together with the Ministers (and scoundrels) Chernov, Tseretelli, Skobelev and their Parties, and if anyone does participate, I shall publish this opinion in the Press. If (judging from the report of the social Chauvinist Rozanov), they have managed in the Zimmerwald Commission to reject half, or almost half reject, Stockholm, then that is excellent. But "half or almost half" is no use, and all this "half" social Chauvinist Zimmerwald gang, which depends on the Italians and the Ledeburiantzy, who desire union with the Social Chauvinists is a most harmful element.

(6) We are making a gigantic and unpardonable mistake by delaying or postponing the calling of a Conference of the Left for founding the Third International. It is now that we are by duty bound to call such a Conference, when Zimmerwald is so scandalously hesitating, or is compelled to be inactive, and there is still a legal (almost legal) Internationalist Party in

---

edge he had taken upon himself to sound the ground for German conditions for peace, and when in Russia in 1917 he exchanged telegrams about that with the Swiss Minister Hoffmann. Grimm was pronounced as acting in contradiction to the Zimmerwald movement.

[1] Kamenev approved of the Stockholm Conference.

Russia of more than 200,000 (240,000) members, (a Party which exists nowhere else in the world in wartime). And it would be simply criminal if we were *too late* to do this (the Bolshevik Party in Russia is being daily driven more and more underground).

Money will be found for the Conference. There is a possibility of bringing out several numbers of its bulletin. There is a centre for it in Stockholm. There is French support ("Demain") and English support (the Socialist *Labour* Party of America—their delegate is Reinstein. I have no idea what sort of a fellow he is: according to the newspapers he welcomed the unifying Congress of the Mensheviks, which means he is suspect. The other day he was in Petersburg and will probably go to Stockholm). However, *apart from* the Socialist *Labour* Party of America, there is also English support; Tom Mann in England and the minorities in the British Socialist Party and Scottish Socialists and the International in America.

It would be criminal to postpone now the calling of a Left Conference.

It would be immeasurably stupid to "wait" for a "large" number of participators, and to be embarrassed by the fact that at present there are "few," for at present such a Conference would be a force in the realm of *ideas,* quite independent of the number of participators, whereas later it might be *silenced*.

The Bolsheviks of the Polish Social Democracy, the Dutch, the "Arbeiter Politik" and "Demain"—this is a sufficiently large *nucleus*. If one were to act energetically several Dutch (Trier and others who have left the Party of that scoundrel Stawning) could be added to it. Also some young Swedish people (against who *we* are committing a sin, because we are *not leading* them and they *ought to be led*), some Bulgarians, the Left from Austria (Franz Koritschoner); some friends of Loriot in France; some members of the Left in Switzerland ("The Youth International") and in Italy; as well as those aforenamed elements in the Anglo-American movement.

The resolutions of the Bolshevik Conference (24th/29th April, 1917) and of the Congress (17th July, 1917—see

"Novaya Zhizn"), the draft of a new programme of the same Party—that is sufficient *ideological basis* (with the addition of "Vorbote," "Tribune," "Arbeiter Politik" and others) to appear before the whole world with clear-cut replies to questions of Imperialism, and a condemnation of the Social Chauvinists and Kautskians.

Such a Conference must immediately be convened. Its temporary Bureau should be established. Its appeal and draft resolutions should be printed in three languages for distribution to the Parties—once again I repeat: I am deeply convinced that if we do not do this *at once*, we shall make our own work in the future infinitely more difficult, and it will enormously help the "amnesty" of the traitors to Socialism.

(7) The ministerialism of the Russian Menshevik-Zimmerwaldists must be thoroughly made use of for putting an ultimatum to Zimmerwald in general: either a break with the Brantings, Huysmans and Co., or we withdraw at once. By the way, is the "Arbeiter Politik" waging a war against Zetkin and against the Braunschweiger "Volksfreund," on account of the fact that these scoundrels, because of intrigue, have been whitewashing and upholding Russian Mensheviks, Chkheidze and Co., who have turned out to be absolute swine, like Samba, Renaudel, Thomas, and Co.?

Is it possible that until now Mehring has also not understood the sordidness of Chkheidze, Tsereteli, Skobelev and Co.?

(8) It is essential to organise the despatch of your letters to me here—I hope to receive one by return, and *just as* full of detail as mine is (otherwise I refuse to correspond). Also some literature: from the middle of June, copies of "Arbeiter Politik," "Demain," "Kampf" (Duisburg), "Weekly People" (Socialist Labour Party), "Leipziger Volkszeitung," "Neue Zeit," "The Call" and others, "Spartacus," the publications of Loriot and his friends, "Avanti" etc. etc. You might begin even by sending cuttings.

(9) You must send to me here, and weekly if possible, firstly, articles for the provincial and Petersburg Party Press (surveys of the Left Movement abroad and facts, facts, facts); secondly, printed sheets (4, 8, 16 small pages) for publishing small

pamphlets, *facts* about the crash of the International, the disgrace of the Social Chauvinists, the disgrace of the Kautskians
and also about the growth of the Left movement (if only four
small pamphlets of 16-32 pages on each of these subjects).
Facts and again facts! There is a possibility of our being able
to have them published. Reply at once if you can undertake
this. When forwarding by our method (there cannot now be
any question of legal postage), I do not think it matters in
which language you write; *it is all the same.*

(10) I hope you have a complete file of "Pravda." Subscribe to "Novaya Zhizn." Write to me at once if you have
not got "Rabochy i Soldat" ["The Worker and Soldier"],
(closed down) "Proletarskoye Delo" ["The Proletarian
Cause"] (Kronstadt) and "The Social Democrat" (Moscow)
and then I will send them to you as soon as a new way has been
set going, and is being tested for the first time by means of this
letter.

P.S. 18th August.

I have just received Nos. 1, 2 and 4 of the new newspaper
"The Proletariat," the Central Organ. Of course it will soon
be suppressed. I will try to send it to you. I am sending you
Nos. 1-7.

20th August.

I have still not managed to send this letter, and will probably
not be able to do so just yet. It is therefore turning into something of a diary, instead of a letter! It cannot be helped. You
must be patient and persistent if you want to have dealings
with the Internationalists in the "freest" Imperialist Republic.
I saw in "Izvestia" ("News") today that the news sheet of
the Stockholm Information Bureau of the Soviet of the Worker
and Soldier Deputies is appearing weekly in Stockholm. Try
to send me *complete files* of all the Stockholm editions. *We see
nothing.*

25th August (7th September).

I think I shall be able to send this letter tomorrow. Do your
utmost to organise despatch from your side. Answer at once
and without fail, if only briefly, to the address (in your *own*
country) which the comrade (or his friend), who will hand

you this letter, will give you. He will also hand over the cipher to you. I am writing a few words in cipher as an experiment, and I would ask you to answer them in the same cipher.

P.S. Write also a small pamphlet of 16-32 pages on the Russian Secret Diplomatic Agreements: briefly, concisely, facts and more facts! such and such an agreement; such and such a date! the month, the year, its contents, a survey of such agreements. Write briefly and with more facts. Answer me whether you will do this, and when you will send it. I close: for goodness' sake, let us have a conference of the Left and called at once! A Bureau of the Left, a bulletin of the Bureau, and fix a second Conference in six to eight weeks' time.

Greetings,
Lenin

284. (274 P²). TO FINNISH COMRADES IN HELSINGFORS (MANNER, SIROL, KUUSINEN, VALIIPAS AND VIIK)[1]

[Petrograd], 11th November, 1917

Dear Comrades,

I was very glad to hear from my Finnish friends that you are at the head of the revolutionary wing of the Finnish Social Democratic Labour Party and are fighting for the proletarian Socialist Revolution. I can confidently state in the name of the revolutionary proletariat of Russia that the great organising talent of the Finnish workers, their high level of development and the long political school of democratic institutions will help them to realise successfully a socialistic re-organisation. We count upon the brotherly help of the revolutionary social democracy of Finland.

Long live the International Socialist Revolution.

With best wishes,
N. Lenin

---

[1] Sent by Lenin in the days of the revolutionary movement which had developed in Finland under the influence of the October Revolution in Russia.

THE SOVIET PERIOD

1917– 1923

SUMMARY

| THE RUSSIAN REVOLUTIONARY MOVEMENT | LENIN'S LIFE |

1917

Nov. 8: II Congress of Soviets of Worker and Soldier Deputies. (Coalition of Bolsheviks and Left S.R.'s form a majority.) Seizure of Winter Palace and arrest of Kerensky Ministers. First sitting of the All-Russia Central Executive Committee: Kamenev President.

Dec. 24: Armistice with Germans signed in Brest Litovsk.

1917

Lenin made President of Council of People's Commissars created by the Congress as Central Executive Power.

1918

Civil War.

Jan.: III Congress of Soviets of Worker and Soldier Deputies.
Trotsky conducts peace negotiations with Germans at Brest Litovsk.

Feb.: Breakdown of negotiations. General demobilisation of Russian Army declared. German offensive on the Russian Front.

March: Critical position of Soviet Republic. All-Russia Central Executive Committee accepts German peace terms. Brest Litovsk agreement signed. VII Congress of Russian Communist Party (Bolshevik); main questions: Brest Litovsk peace negotiations and election of a Commission for revising the Party programme.

End March: IV Congress of Soviets (ratification of Brest Litovsk agreement; sanction to transfer capital to Moscow; election of new Central Executive Committee).

April: Overthrow of Ukrainian Rada (Parliament).

Summer: Czecho-Slovaks seize middle Volga district.
Allies seize North Russia.

1918

Shot at in Petrograd—unhurt. Lenin active at Congress.

Speaks on war and peace. Urges peace. Struggles with Left Communism (Bukharin). Writes numerous articles. Soviet of People's Commissars and Lenin move to Moscow.

THE RUSSIAN REVOLUTIONARY MOVEMENT   LENIN'S LIFE

July: V Congress of Soviets (break with Left S.R.'s. Confirmation of constitution of the R.S.F.S.R.).

Aug.: Kazan taken by Czecho-Slovaks.

Sept.: Red and White terror.

Nov. 11: Armistice and end of European War.

VI Congress of Soviets.

Dec.: Kolchak seizes Perm and moves towards West.

Moscow: Shot at by Social Revolutionary—Kaplan.

Speaks on "Year of Revolution," the international situation. Creation of Soviet of Worker and Peasant Defence: Lenin made President.

1919

Jan.: Versailles Peace Conference.

Feb.: Formation of Ukrainian Soviet Republic.

March: I Congress of III International.

III Congress of Russian Communist Party (Bolshevik).

April: Kolchak advance on Eastern front. Volga region threatened. Mobilisation of Communists. Denikin advance on Southern front.

July: Red Army captures Ekaterinburg and Chelyabinsk.

Aug.: Manifesto to workers of Siberia re overthrow of Kolchak.

Sept.: Red Army abandons Kiev and Kursk.

Oct.: Denikin's Army within 15 miles of Orel.

Yudenich approaches S.P.B.

Red Army victory at Orel.

Nov.: Red Army occupies Omsk and Kursk.

Dec.: Fuel crisis. Growing dissolution of armies of Kolchak, Denikin and Yudenich.

VII Congress of Soviets. (Work on re-establishing the economic life of the Republic: Addenda to constitution of R.S.F.S.R., election of new Central Executive Committee.)

1919

Lenin presides at I Congress. His theses: "The Bourgeois and Proletariat Democracy."

Lenin's letter to S.P.B. workers re Kolchak menace.

Active throughout the year against counter-revolution.

THE RUSSIAN REVOLUTIONARY MOVEMENT	LENIN'S LIFE

1920

1920

Final liquidation of Kolchak and Yu-denich armies. Creation of Labour Corps. III Congress of the Soviets of National Economy (problems of re-establishing transport).

Speaks at Central Executive Committee on international situation and the imme-diate economic tasks.

Feb.: Negotiations with European powers begin re renewal of trade relations with Russia. Peace with Esthonia. I Session of the new All-Russia Central Executive Committee.

March: Liquidation of the Northern Front (return of Archangel and Mur-mansk).
Liquidation of the Southern Front (cap-ture of Rostov). Poland and Latvia agree to have peace negotiations.
March 29-April 5: Congress of the Rus-sian Communist Party.

Speaks at the Congress of the Cossacks and at Moscow Soviet of Worker Depu-ties. Also at meeting of celebration of first year of III International; and at a meeting in honour of Sverdlov. Addresses the III All-Russia Congress of Water Transport Workers. Active at IX Con-gress of the Russian Communist Party. Makes speeches, including concluding speech on the tasks of the Party.

April: Poland attacks Soviet Russia. General Wrangel's White Guard attacks in the Crimea.
July-Aug.: II Congress of the Comintern held in Petrograd and Moscow.
End 1920: Wrangel routed. War with Poland ends.
VIII Congress of Soviets.

April: Celebration of his 50th birthday. Writes "Left Wing Communism—an in-fantile disorder."
Writes most of the resolutions and theses. Reports on the international situation. Writes "Letter to the German and French Workers."
Concentrates on economic reconstruction, especially electrification.

1921

1921

March: The Kronstadt mutiny. X Con-gress of the Party.
New Economic Policy restores union be-tween proletariat and peasantry.

Under his leadership Congress agrees to New Economic Policy as the road to Socialism.

April: Moscow Party officials meeting.
May: All-Russia Party Conference.

Speaks on the Tax in kind.

June-July: III Congress of the Com-munist International.

Speaks on N.E.P.

Oct.: II All-Russia Congress of Political Education Departments. Moscow Party Conference.

Dec.: IX Congress of Soviets.

Symptoms of illness.

THE RUSSIAN REVOLUTIONARY MOVEMENT   LENIN'S LIFE

1922

1922

March: Speech at meeting of the Communist faction of the Metal-workers re decision that the Party's retreat would now cease.

End March: XI Party Congress (last Congress at which Lenin speaks).

Makes Central Committee Report on the first year of the New Economic Policy. Sclerosis of the brain develops. Continues work. Writes articles and letters.

End May: Hæmorrhage of the brain.

Summer: Condition improves.

Oct.: Works again at Council of People's Commissars and on the Party Central Committee.

End Oct.: Speaks at Session of Central Executive Committee of Soviets.

Nov. 18: Reports at IV Congress of Comintern.

Nov. 20: Last speech at the Plenum of Moscow Soviet: advocates turning N.E.P. Russia into Socialist Russia.

Dec. 16: Second hæmorrhage of brain. Paralysis of right hand and right leg. Dictates articles, "Pages from a Diary," etc.

1923-1924
Jan.: Illness.

Jan. 21, 1924: 6.50 p.m.
Lenin dies.
Lenin buried in the Red Square, Moscow.

285. (179 P²). TO THE PRÆSIDIUM OF THE MOSCOW SOVIET
OF WORKER AND SOLDIER DEPUTIES [1] IN MOSCOW

Telegram from Petrograd.   [*19th November, 1917*]

All power is in hands of Soviets. Confirmation not required. Your dismissal of one [official] and appointment of another is law.

[1] Sent in answer to a telegram asking for confirmation of the dismissal of a commissar.

286. (216 P²). TO A. G. SHLYAPNIKOV AND
F. E. DZERZHINSKY

[Petrograd], 14th/23rd December, 1917

The bearer of this letter, Comrade Vorobiev, is a delegate from the Urals and has excellent recommendations from the local organisation. The whole situation in the Urals is very acute: the governing bodies of the works here (in Petrograd) must be *arrested* at once. They must be threatened with trial (revolutionary court) for creating a crisis in the Urals and all the Ural works must be *confiscated*.

Prepare draft regulations as soon as possible.[1]

Lenin

1918

287. (247 P²). TO THE GENERAL ARMY CONGRESS ON
DEMOBILISATION

[Petrograd, between the 1 & 3 January, 1918]

Comrade Podvoisky has handed me your invitation, and I must ask you to excuse me and not take it in bad part that I am compelled to limit myself to a letter to you. I welcome the conviction that the *great task of creating a Socialist army* will, despite all the difficulties of the present moment, be solved and *successfully solved by you*. We are experiencing possibly one of the most critical periods of the revolution, when the Soviet power is being threatened, both by an outside enemy, the Imperialists of Germany and other countries, and by the enemy within—counter revolution, which hides itself behind the slogan "All power to the Constituent Assembly."

And this crisis too we will overcome. There is not a shadow of doubt about it! The power won by the Soviets will remain in the hands of the Soviets. The Socialist Revolution has begun, and it will go farther towards victory, both in Russia and throughout the whole world.

With best wishes for success and for courage in your work,

Yours,

Lenin

---

[1] Money was not sent from the Petrograd headquarters to pay the Ural workers. In December, 1917, the Ural works were nationalised.

288. (248 P²). TO V. A. ANTONOV-OVSEYENKO [1]
IN KHARKOV
Telegram.

[Petrograd, 20th Dec./between the 3 & 10 January, 1918]

Heartily welcome energetic activity and merciless struggle against Kaledinites. Fully approve resisting local supporters who have apparently misled certain Bolsheviks. Particularly approve and welcome arrest of sabotage millionaires in Ist and IInd class railway carriages. Advise you send them six months forced labour in mines. Once again congratulate you on determination and condemn waverers.

Lenin

289. (249 P²). TO THE NAVAL REVOLUTIONARY COMMITTEE

[Petrograd], 15th January, 1918

I ask you to adopt special measures to put 2,000 sailors immediately at the disposal of Comrade Ter-Arutvunants [2] for military operations against the bourgeois Rada. [3]

Lenin

290. (255 P²). TO V. A. ANTONOV-OVSEYENKO
Telegram. Urgent.   *[Petrograd, 23 February, 1918]*

Today at all costs Rostov must be taken. [4]

Lenin

[1] On Jan. 3, 1918, workers from the Kharkov factories appealed to Antonov-Ovseyenko to help them to obtain their pay before the Christmas holidays. As the Revolutionary Committee was apathetic, Antonov-Ovseyenko summoned 15 of the leading capitalists of Kharkov and demanded that they should produce one million roubles to provide this pay and threatened them with deportation to the mines. The money was produced and the capitalists set free.

[2] M. K. Ter-Arutyunants, communist. In 1918 member of the Revolutionary Committee at G.H.Q., and commander of the field staff attached to the G.H.Q.

[3] In Nov., 1918, the Central Rada—the supreme Organ of power in the Ukrainian Republic—was antagonistic to the Soviets, and actively anti-Bolshevik. All negotiations failed and on 7 Jan., 1918, Soviet military forces in the Ukraine attacked and occupied Kiev on the 8th Feb. and overpowered the Central Rada.

[4] The White forces were defeated and Rostov was taken by the Reds on Feb. 24.

291. (256 P²). TO V. A. ANTONOV-OVSEYENKO, ROSTOV ON DON

Telegram.[1]   *Petrograd, 28 February, 1918*

Warm greetings to all our devoted fighters for Socialism. Greetings to the revolutionary Cossacks. In answer to your telegram from Novocherkassk we say: let the empowered Congress of the Town and Village Soviets of the whole Don Region work out its own agrarian measures and present them for the Sovnarkom's confirmation. That would be better. I have nothing against autonomy for the Don Region. Geographical boundaries of that autonomous region must be determined by agreement with the inhabitants of the adjacent districts and the autonomous republic of the Donets Basin. We cannot send you a delegate. All here are up to their eyes in work. Ask you to send representative to Sovnarkom, or appoint somebody chosen by you.

                                                            Lenin-Stalin

292. (180 P²). TO THE TASHKENT CONGRESS OF THE SOVIETS
OF THE TURKESTAN REGION

                                    [Moscow], 22nd April, 1918

You may be sure, Comrades, that the Sovnarkom will uphold the autonomy of your region on Soviet lines; we welcome your first efforts, and are deeply convinced that you will cover the whole region with a network of Soviets and that you will act in contact with the existing Soviets.

We would ask you to send a Commission to us, in Moscow, for the convening of the Executive Congress of the Soviets, for the mutual examination of the question concerning the relationship between the empowered Organ of your region and the Council of National Commissars.

In welcoming your Congress, we hope you will worthily fulfil the task laid upon it by history.

                                                        Lenin and Stalin

---

[1] Sent in answer to a telegram reporting negotiations with delegates from the Don Region who raised the question of autonomy.

293. (181 P²). TO D. I. KURSKY

A Note.   [*Not later than the 8th May, 1918*]

It is essential to introduce a bill *immediately* and with demonstrative swiftness, that the penalty for bribery (perjury, bribery, collusion etc. etc.) must be *not less* than ten years' imprisonment, and added to that, ten years of hard labour.

294. (182 P²). TO G. E. ZINOVIEV IN PETERSBURG[1]

[*Moscow*], *14th June, 1918*

Comrade Zinoviev,

Every attempt must be made at once to move from Petersburg *hundreds* of agitators. This is extremely important, and must be done before the Congress of the Soviets and the *whole* military and food situation renders it even more urgent. Money will be found for this, so do not stint it. We (and Tsyurupa) discussed this in detail with Sviatersky. You must see that this is done.

Greetings,

Lenin

295. (257 P²). TELEGRAM (BY TELEPHONE)

[*Moscow*], *6th July, 1918*

To all Regional Committees of the Russian Communist Party, to all Regional Sovdeps and to all Staffs of the Red Army.

About three o'clock this afternoon two bombs were thrown in the German Embassy, seriously wounding Mirbach. This is the obvious work of Monarchists, or those provocators, who want to drag Russia into a war in the interests of Anglo-French Capitalists who have also bribed the Czecho-Slovaks. Mobilise all forces. Immediately set afoot everything for catching the

---

[1] The V Congress of the Soviets took place in Moscow in July, 1918. There was sharp conflict between the Bolsheviks and the S.R.'s, who wanted the war with Germany to continue.

culprits. Stop *all* motor cars and detain them for triple checking. President of the Council of People's Commissars.[1]

V. Ulianov (Lenin)

296. (258 P²). TO THE MOSCOW SOVIET, THE WORKER-PEASANT DEPUTIES

Telegram (by telephone).　　　　[*Moscow, 7th July, 1918*]

To be passed on to all Regional, Village and District Sovdeps of the Moscow Province.

Scattered bands of Left Social Revolutionaries, who have risen against Soviet power, are at large in the neighbourhood. Leaders of these adventurers are running away. Adopt all measures to catch and detain those who have dared to rise against Soviet power. Hold up all motor cars. Keep all the level crossings shut on the highroads. Concentrate near to these level crossings armed squadrons of local workers and peasants. Information to hand that one armoured car belonging to rebels has escaped out of the town. Adopt all measures to capture it.

President of the Sovnarkom.

Lenin

297. (262 P²). TO M. S. KEDROV (BOLSHEVIK) IN VOLOGDA

Telegram.　　　　　　　*Moscow, 12th August, 1918*
Secret.

The harm done by your departure is proved by the absence of a leader when English began moving along Dvina. You must strenuously make up lost time, link up with Kotlas, send aeroplanes there at once, and at all costs organise defence of Kotlas.

President of the Sovnarkom.

Lenin

[1] Council of People's Commissars, Sovet Narodnyst Kommissarov, or, in short, Sovnarkom.

298. (264 P²). TO M. S. KEDROV IN VOLOGDA

[Moscow], 29th August, 1918

Comrade Kedrov,

You send me few facts. Send reports at *every possible opportunity*.

What fortifications have been built?

Along which line?

What points along the railway line have been *safeguarded* by mines so that in case of a large scale advance of the Anglo-French we can blow up and seriously destroy such and such a number (give exact number, what and where) of bridges, miles of railway, passes through bogs, etc. etc.

Have you safeguarded Vologda sufficiently from the menace of the White Guards? It would be unpardonable if you were to show weakness or negligence in this matter.

Greetings,

Lenin

299. (183 P²). TO THE NARKOMS [NATIONAL COMMISSARS]

[Moscow, 29th August, 1918]

I permit myself to send the following requests, concerning the fulfilment of the decisions of the Council of National Commissars, made on the 29th August, on the subject of *weekly reports:*

It is essential that in the reports, which ought to be *as popular as possible,* the following points should be noted: (a) the improvement in the conditions of the masses (increase in pay for the workers; elementary school teachers etc.) (b) the participation of workers in the Government (the outstanding individual workers and workers' organisations etc.) also (c) of the poorest peasants, and those who assisted the Soviet authorities in their struggle against the Kulaks; (d) the expropriation of landowners, capitalists, merchants, financiers etc.

The main task is to show *concretely*, by means of facts, *exactly how* the Soviet authority took definite steps (the *first*) towards Socialism.

Lenin

300. (265 P²). TO THE FIFTH ARMY HEADQUARTERS IN SVIYAZHSK [1]

Telegram. *Moscow, 8th September, 1918*

Thanks. Excellent progress towards recovery. Convinced that quelling of Kazan Czechs and White Guards and their bloodthirsty Kulak supporters will be a model of mercilessness.

Best greetings,
Lenin

301. (275 P²). TO Y. A. BERZIN IN BERNE

[*Moscow*], *20th September, 1918*

Dear Comrades,

Today's "Pravda" prints extracts from Kautsky's article against Bolshevism (Sozialistische Auslandspolitik).

Kautsky's disgraceful rubbish, childish patter and basest Opportunism raise the question: why are we doing nothing to fight Kautsky's theoretical debasement of Marxism?

How can it be tolerated that even such people as Mehring and Zetkin defend themselves from Kautsky "morally" (if I may put it in this way) rather than theoretically? . . . Has Kautsky really found nothing better to do than to write against the Bolsheviks?

Is that a reason? How can we weaken our position in this way? After all, it means we are putting a weapon into Kautsky's hands.

While what we really ought to do is to write that Kautsky

---

[1] In answer to a telegram wishing Lenin a speedy recovery after the Right S.R., F. Kaplan, shot him in the throat and lung on 30 August, 1918.

has absolutely misunderstood and twisted in a purely opportunist manner:

Marx's teaching about the State;
  ″   ″   ″   ″ dictatorship of the proletariat;
  ″   ″   ″   ″ bourgeois democracy;
  ″   ″   ″   ″ parliamentarianism;
  ″   ″   ″   ″ rôle and importance of the com-
                                   mune, etc.

We should adopt the following measures:

1. To talk seriously and in detail with the Left (Sparta-
kovtsy etc.) compelling them to come out in the Press with a
theoretical announcement of principle stating that on the question of dictatorship Kautsky is talking base Bernsteinism and
not Marxism.

2. To publish as soon as possible and in German my book
"State and Revolution."

3. To supply it with a publisher's foreword something like
this:

> "The publisher considers it absolutely vital that the
> volume should appear at this moment particularly in view
> of the complete distortion of Marxism on similar questions
> in Kautsky's latest works where he substitutes the point of
> view of the dictatorship of the proletariat by base social lib-
> eralism in the spirit of Bernstein and other Opportunists."

4. If it is not possible to publish pamphlets rapidly, then a
notice should be inserted in the Left newspapers similar to the
publisher's foreword.

Please send me (to me personally) Kautsky's pamphlet
(about the Bolsheviks, the dictatorship, etc.) as soon as it
appears.

Also, collect for me all Kautsky's articles about the Bolsheviks ("Democracy and Dictatorship" end 1917 or beginning
1918; also articles from "Soz. Auslandspolitik," August, 1918)
and any other of his articles that have appeared.

Best wishes,

Lenin

302. (277 P²). TO A. A. JOFFE, RUSSIAN AMBASSADOR IN
BERLIN

Telegram by telephone.   [*Moscow, 23rd October, 1918*]

Give our warmest greetings without delay to Karl Liebknecht.
The release from prison of the representative of revolutionary
workers of Germany is the sign of a new epoch, an epoch of
triumphant Socialism, which is opening out now both for Germany and the whole world.

In the name of the Central Committee of the Russian Communist Party (Bolsheviks)—Lenin, Sverdlov and Stalin.

303. (184 P²). TO M. F. VLADIMIRSKY (OR TO SOME OTHER
MEMBER OF THE PRÆSIDIUM OF THE MOSCOW SOVIET OF
DEPUTIES)

Moscow, 27th October, 1918

The bearers are comrades from Viborg. Please receive them
at once. They comment upon the *excessive formalities* required
before being allowed to enter the Soviet Union; also the incredible pettiness of the control and the writing of quite unnecessary permits. Cannot this matter be simplified?

Greetings,
Lenin

304. (278 P²). TO V. V. VOROVSKY IN STOCKHOLM

Telegram.   [*Moscow, 10th November, 1918*]

Today news has been received from Germany of the triumph
of the revolution in Germany. At first Kiel informed us by
radio that the power had passed into the hands of the Soviet
of workers and sailors; next, Berlin sent us the following:
"Greetings, freedom and peace for all. Berlin and surroundings
in the hands of the Soviet of Worker and Soldier Deputies." . . .
German soldiers have arrested at the front a peace delegation

of the old German Government and have begun peace negotiations with French soldiers.

President of the Sovnarkom.

305. (279 p²). TO V. V. VOROVSKOY IN STOCKHOLM

Telegram.   [*Moscow, 10th November, 1918*]

According to latest information German soldiers have arrested
delegation of German generals who had gone to negotiate an
armistice. German soldiers have entered into direct negotiations
with French soldiers. Kaiser Wilhelm has abdicated. Chancellor
Prince Baden has resigned. New Chancellor will be the Government Social Democrat, Ebert. There is a general strike in all
large towns of Southern Germany. Entire German Fleet is on
side of the revolution. All German ports of North and Baltic
Seas are in hands of German revolutionary Fleet. We received
a radio telegram from the Kiel Soviet of Soldier Deputies addressed to the International Proletariat saying that the Red
Flag is flying over the German Fleet and that the funeral of
those who fell fighting for freedom will take place today. Probably all this will be concealed from the German soldiers on the
Eastern Front—the Ukraine. Bring these facts before German
soldiers by all the means at your disposal.

Lenin

1919

306. (185 p²). TO THE KURSK SUPREME COMMISSION

Telegram.   [*Moscow*], *6th January, 1919*

Immediately arrest Kogan, member of Kursk Central Buying
Commission, for failing to help 120 starving Moscow workers,
and for allowing them to go away empty-handed. Publish this
in newspapers and leaflets, so that all workers of the Central
Buying Commission and Supply Organisations may know that
suppression will be severe, even shooting, for a formal and bu-

reaucratic attitude towards work, and for not helping starving workers.

The President of the Sovnarkom.

Lenin

307. (266 p²). TO E. M. SKLYANSKY

Note. [*Moscow, 25th April, 1919*]

A *fierce* telegram must be sent *today*, signed by you and me, both to the General Headquarters and the C. in C. of Western Front, ordering them to develop the *maximum* of energy and *speed* in the capture of Vilna.

308. (269 p²). TO L. B. KAMENEV

[*Moscow, 16th May, 1919*]

The cessation of mobilisation among the workers of the Donets Basin is absolutely inadmissible in view of the present situation at the front.[1] The Council of Defence considers the Donets Basin is exceptionally important and has, therefore, determined to release from mobilisation only miners, even in those undertakings which at present, for one reason or another, are not producing coal. By this means we shall in any case preserve and safeguard the coal industry from catastrophe. When these exceptional conditions have passed, this action will allow of the re-establishment of coal production. No other privileges whatsoever of release from conscription are possible.

President of the Council of Defence.

Lenin

309. (289 R). TO N. K. KRUPSKAYA[2]

(*Moscow*), *9th July, 1919*

Darling Nadyushka,

I was very glad to receive news from you. I had already sent one telegram to Kazan, and not having received a reply, sent

---

[1] In the Ukraine the White Army was particularly active during May, 1919.

[2] This is the only personal letter which Krupskaya has from Lenin. They seldom lived apart. They corresponded much when Lenin was in prison, during his first year of exile, and when she was in exile in Ufa. But the letters were chiefly chemical letters, destroyed at once on reading. In 1919 Krupskaya was travelling on a propaganda steamer "The Red Star" on the Volga and the Kama.

another one to Nizhny from where they replied today that "Krasnaya Zvezda" has to be in Kazan on the 8th July and will stay there not less than 24 hours. I asked in that telegram if it would be possible to give Gorky a cabin on the "Krasnaya Zvezda." He is arriving here tomorrow and I would very much like to get him out of Petrograd where his nerves have gone to pieces and he is depressed. I hope you and the other comrades will be glad to be travelling with Gorky. He is a very nice fellow; a little capricious, but that is a trifling matter.

I read the letters begging for help which are sometimes sent to you, and I try to do what I can.

Mitya has gone to Kiev: I believe the Crimea is again in the hands of the Whites.

Our life goes on as usual: we rest in "our" villa on Sundays. Trotsky has recovered, he has gone to the South, I hope he will pull up. I expect improvements from the replacement of the Commander-in-Chief Vatsetis by S. S. Kamenev (from the Eastern front).

We have given Pokrovsky (M. N.) [the historian] two months' leave: we want to appoint Ludmila Rudolfovna Menzhinsky [Social Democrat, Bolshevik] as substitute, although that is not decided yet, *but not* Pozner [in the Narkompros].

I embrace you warmly, I ask you to write and to telegraph oftener.

Your

V. Ulianov

Obey the doctor: eat and sleep more, then you will be *quite* fit for work by the Winter.

310. (272 P²). TO G. N. KAMINSKY, D. P. OSKIN AND
I. V. MEZHLAUK IN TULA

Moscow, 20th October, 1919

Comrades!

At present Tula is exceptionally important—even apart from the proximity of the enemy, the importance of Tula to the Republic is enormous.

Every effort must, therefore, be made to encourage friendly work and to concentrate upon military work and military supply work.

I very much regret your and Seligman's differences of opinion with Peterson (he is an important and most devoted worker) and I think that Seligman is to blame here, for if an irregularity was noticeable, it ought to have been straightened out at once (and it was not difficult to do this) without bringing it to a conflict. In future, the slightest irregularity should be settled and brought to the notice of the Centre in time, without allowing a conflict to develop.

Work in Tula must be energetically increased and put entirely on a military footing. The decree about curtailing the civil control will be published one of these days; it should not only be observed, but applied arch-conscientiously and assiduously. The masses in Tula are far from being all on our side. Hence the urgent need for greater intensity in work among the soldiers, reserves, workers and the female workers.

If you have not sufficient strength, then write and we will send you help from Moscow.

Look after the defence and watch it closely: are blockhouses being built? Is the work slackening? Have you sufficient material? Workers? Are the Red Army soldiers learning? Are their supplies in order? All these and similar questions must be allotted for special observation to efficient people and devoted Party comrades.

You are held wholly responsible for the success of this work or for its failure (if you do not do this in time, or do not refer to the Centre). The moulding of the Army is exceptionally important.

If we capture Orel,[1] work must not slacken, but must be increased tenfold, for without that, we shall not be victorious, and if we stop our advance, it will be our death.

Read this letter to all responsible workers and members of the Party and inform me regularly, but very briefly, of what is actually being done.

With Communist greetings,

V. Ulianov (Lenin)

[1] Orel was taken by the Red Army on 20 Oct., 1919.

LENIN, KRUPSKAYA AND HIS SISTER

LENIN AND STALIN, SUMMER, 1922

1920

311. (189 P²). TO M. P. TOMSKY

Moscow, 16th January, 1920

To Comrade Tomsky with a request to bring it before the V.Ts.S.P.S.[1] and the Communist Faction in the V.Ts.S.P.S.

My dear Comrades,

I send you information about the amazing procrastination, casualness, bureaucratism and inefficiency, shown in a most important *practical* matter.[2]

I have never doubted that there is still a great deal of bureaucratism in each of our Commissariats.

But I did not expect that there would be so much bureaucratism in the Professional Unions.

It is a terrible scandal. Do read through all the documents to the Communist Faction, and work out *practical* measures for fighting bureaucratism, procrastination, slackness and inefficiency.

Please do not refuse to inform me of the result.

Melnichansky[3] *himself* telephoned to me about the 10,000 metal workers. I complained about this to the N.K.P.S. and now Melnichansky has got me into this fix.

With Communist greetings,

V. Ulianov (Lenin)

312. (190 P²). TO I. V. STALIN

[Moscow], 24th January, 1920

Copies to be sent to Avanesov, Tomsky and Kiselev, Member of the Præsidium of the Vsetsik.

On the basis of the directive, given by the Central Committee, I think that all three projects ought to be amalgamated into one.

In my opinion, the following should be added:

1. The "Section" of the Worker-Peasant inspection, attached to the Goskon [State Control], should be temporary, with the

---

[1] V.Ts.S.P.S., Initials of the Russian name for The All-Union Central Council of Trade Unions.

[2] A fuel shortage caused almost all metallurgical undertakings to be closed down, and this threw 34,200 workers out of employment.

[3] From 1917 to 1926, at first Secretary, then President of the M.G.S.P.S.

object of introducing the worker-peasant inspection *into all* sections of the Goskon, and then for it to cease to function as a separate section.

2. The object: to pass the *whole* of the toiling masses, both men and (*particularly*) women, through participation in the worker-peasant inspection.

3. To compile lists (according to the constitution) locally, and to exclude those who are serving etc, and the rest in turn should all be passed through participation in the worker-peasant inspection.

4. To make this participation varied according to the stage of development of the participators, beginning with the rôle of "eavesdropper," or witness, or a hired informant or a learner, for those workers and peasants, who are illiterate and undeveloped, and ending with full privileges (or almost all) for the literate, educated, and those who in one way or another have been tested.

5. Particular attention should be paid (and organised with exact rules) to the introduction of a *wider* control of the worker-peasant inspection over the checking of provisions, goods, stores, ammunition, raw materials, fuel etc. etc. (especially workers' kitchens etc.) It is absolutely essential to make use of women, indeed every woman for this.

6. It is necessary to establish a gradual interest among the women, so that there need not be any confusion in encouraging these masses of participators. It is also essential to consider carefully the kind of participators (two to three, and occasionally more, but only in special circumstances, so that those who are working are not unnecessarily removed from their work).

7. Detailed instructions must be worked out.

8. The workers in the Goskon must be compelled (by special instructions) firstly, to attract to their activities representatives, or groups, of the worker-peasant inspection, and secondly, to lecture to non-Party Conferences of workers and peasants (lectures according to a specially agreed programme; popular and on the principles and methods of the Goskon; or the lectures might be substituted by the reading of a pamphlet which we will publish i.e. the Goskon. Stalin and Avanesov will publish

it with the special aid of the Party, and also a commentary on this pamphlet).

9. To call up peasants *gradually* (and they must be non-Party peasants) to participate in the Central Goskon: one might begin with one or two from each Province (if it is impossible to get more), and then later to *expand* this according to transport and other conditions; also for non-Party workers.

10. To introduce gradually the checking of participation of the masses in the Goskon on the part of those workers, through the Party and through Professional Unions i.e. to check whether everybody is participating and what is the result of such partici-pation from the point of view of teaching the participators the business of Government.

Lenin

313. (191 P^2). TO THE MEMBERS OF THE COUNCIL OF DEFENCE

[*Moscow*], *1st February*, [*1920*]

The railway transport position is catastrophic. Bread transport to Moscow has ceased. Special measures are essential to save the situation. The following measures should be passed (and others of a similar character carefully considered) for two months (February and March):

1. *Decrease* the individual bread ration for those workers, who are not transport workers; *increase* it for transport workers. Let thousands perish, but the country must be saved.

2. Take 3/4ths of the responsible workers from all depart-ments, except from the People's Commissariats for war and food, for two months, and use them for railway transport and repair. Close down correspondingly (or decrease tenfold) for two months the work of the other Commissariats.

3. Place 30-50 versts along both sides *of the railway, under martial law*, so as to mobilise workers for the clearing of the track, and transfer 3/4ths of the responsible workers from the Volust[1] and Uezd Executive Committees of that whole province to the volosti of that region.

President of the Council of Defence.

V. Ulianov (Lenin)

---

[1] Volust is a small administrative division including several villages, uezd is a larger administrative division.

314. (221 P²). TO V. V. ADORATSKY IN KAZAN

Moscow, 6th April, 1920

Comrade Adoratsky,

I have passed it on to Comrade Hodorovsky asking him to help you with regard to rations, fuel etc.

He has promised to do this. Write to me when you get an opportunity (better through soldiers):

1. Has anything been done to help you in the way of rations? Fuel?

2. Is there anything else you need?

3. Can you collect any material for the *History of the Civil War and the History of the Soviet Republic?* Can this material be collected in Kazan? Can I help you?

Files of "Izvestia" and "Pravda"?

Is there much missing?

Can I help by sending you what is missing?

Please write *and send me your address.*

Greetings from,

Lenin

315. (192 P²). TO V. P. MILYUTIN

[Moscow, May, 1920]

Note:

We cannot suffer this indefiniteness a *single day longer.* If anyone protests, then report it *at once* to the S.N.K.[1] (otherwise you will be culpable).

Have signed a statement agreeing with German delegates, that we have announced to them, that we do not *guarantee* food supplies, clothing, or housing, to be better than those supplied to the rest, and to the *rank and file* of the Russian workers.

316. (273 P²). TO THE ARMY REVOLUTIONARY COMMITTEE OF THE AZERBAIDZHAN SOVIET REPUBLIC IN BAKU

Telegram.   *Moscow, 9th May, 1920*

The Sovnarkom welcomes the liberation of the toiling masses

---

[1] S.N.K., Sovnarkom, Council of People's Commissars.

in the independent Azerbaidzhan Republic and expresses its firm conviction that under the leadership of its Soviet Government the independent Republic of Azerbaidzhan together with the R.S.F.S.R. will defend and save its freedom and independence from the enemy of the enslaved masses of the East from Imperialism.

Long live the independent Soviet Republic of Azerbaidzhan.

Long live the Union of the Workers and Peasants of Azerbaidzhan and Russia.

President of the Council of People's Commissars of the R.S.F.S.R.

Lenin

317. (280 P²). TO A. S. SERAFIMOVICH, A PROLETARIAN WRITER, A BOLSHEVIK

[Moscow], 21st May, 1920

My dear Comrade,

My sister has just told me of the terrible misfortune which has befallen you.[1] Allow me to send you my very sincere condolences and wish you courage and strength. I am deeply sorry that I have been unable to realise my wish to see you oftener and to get to know you better. But your writings and what my sister has told me about you have inspired in me a deep sympathy towards you, and I should like to tell you how *necessary* your work is to the workers and to all of us and how essential it is for you to have courage at this moment so as to struggle and overcome your grief and to *force yourself* to return to work.

Forgive me for writing in a hurry.

Once again my sympathy,

Your

Lenin

318. (196 P²). TO S. I. BOTIN

[Moscow], 4th June, 1920, 11.30 p.m.

Comrade Botin,

When you came to see me today, I had only two minutes to spare, for I was torn away from an important meeting.

---

[1] His son was killed in the Civil War.

Now I have a free quarter of an hour, and I can (and must) tell you more clearly and fully, that mistakes have obviously been allowed to occur, and that these mistakes must be rectified frankly, honestly and decisively. Otherwise, a most serious piece of work will be spoilt.

One mistake was that there was mistrust shown towards the specialist, which prevented him from at once saying everything and using his experience. Secondly, all the hard preparatory work was done by you, and so took you away from your real work; whereas, the whole mass of this preparatory work ought to be given to mechanics, fitters, electro-technicians, of whom dozens can be found. And in order to separate your real work from the preparatory or subsidiary work, the constant advice of a specialist is necessary.

You have now promised me to trust the specialist fully, and I believe you are quite convinced of his Party loyalty and absolute devotion to the Revolution. I must, therefore, ask you to fulfil your promise to me in full; otherwise mistakes will inevitably be repeated. From tomorrow, you will show everything to the specialist and tell him everything (while the assistants are bringing up the railway waggons and are doing the preparatory work). Then the tests will be conducted with the specialist and without any hitch.

Please reply that you promise to do this.

Greetings,

Lenin

319. (223 P²). TO GOSIZDAT (STATE PUBLISHING HOUSE) AND
TO E. A. PREOBRAZHENSKY AND N. I. BUKHARIN

Moscow, 8th August, 1920

Both in our own and in foreign newspapers (not only Communist, but the *bourgeois* papers of *various* countries) there accumulates *weekly* a gigantic amount of material, *especially relating to the foreign policy* of the Entente.

This extremely valuable material is lost, so far as Communist agitation is concerned. (See also "Bulletin of the N. K. Foreign Department.")

I suggest that a Commission be formed to collate this material and for the *monthly* publication of small pamphlets.

Their contents: *facts* about the foreign policy of the Entente (plunder, wars, risings and *financial* strangulation).

The number of copies: the least possible, for the main purpose will be the translation *into other languages.*

A Sub-Commission consisting of a few professors must (under strict control) collect *everything* valuable, *especially from bourgeois newspapers* (which best denounce their rivals).

A Commission consisting of *Party* comrades will read the manuscripts of the professors, will correct them, and will *compel* the professors to correct them.

Newspapers get lost; the pamphlets, however, will be kept and they will *help our comrades abroad.*

Please reply,

Lenin

320. (281 p²). TO THE LIBRARY OF THE RUMYANTSEV MUSEUM

[*Moscow, 1st September, 1920*]

If, according to regulations, reference books cannot be borrowed, could I not be allowed to borrow for reference purposes some books for one evening, say a night, after the library has closed? *I would return them by the morning:*

1. Two of the *best* and most complete *Greek* dictionaries: Greek-*German;* Greek-French; Greek-Russian; or Greek-English.

2. The best *philosophical* dictionaries: dictionaries of philosophical terms: German (Eisler, I think); English (Baldwin, I believe); French (I think Franck—if nothing newer); Russian (whichever one you have of the new ones); Radlov's and others.

3. The History of Greek Philosophy:

    a. Tseller—complete and newest edition.

    b. Gomperz—the Viennese philosopher "Griechische Denker."

321. (193 P²). A NOTE TO A. I. ELIZAROVA

[Moscow, Autumn, 1920]

The basic principle of Government in the spirit of all the decisions of the Russian Communist Party and the Central Soviet institutions is that a definite person is wholly responsible for conducting a definite piece of work.

I have been conducting the work (for such and such a length of time) and I am responsible. A certain person is in my way, since he is not responsible and is not in control.

That is confusion! That is chaos! It is the interference of a person *unsuitable* for responsible work, and I demand his *removal*.

322. (225 P²). TO THE MINERS IN CHEREMKHOVSK, (EASTERN SIBERIA)

Moscow, 15th September, 1920

My dear Comrades,

I thank you with all my heart for your greetings of August 2nd, 1920, which were passed on to me by Comrade Ivan Yac. Il'in. The conversation with Comrade Il'in about your energetic work in the Siberian mines and his description of the gradual development of conscious discipline among the workers, (who are working from now on for themselves and not for the capitalists), gave me enormous pleasure.

The most gratifying part of your message was the expression of deep conviction in a complete and final victory of the Soviet authorities over landowners, capitalists and every kind of exploiter, as well as your unswerving will and determination to overcome all obstacles and difficulties. It is from such firmness of purpose in the working, labouring masses that I and every single Communist draw our conviction in the inevitable world victory of the workers and the workers' cause.

With comradely greetings and good wishes for speedy success,

Your warmly devoted

V. Ulianov (Lenin)

323. (282 P²). TO THE PRÆSIDIUM OF THE PETROGRAD SOVIET
OF THE WORKER, PEASANT AND COMMUNIST DEPUTIES

Moscow, 21st October, 1920

Dear Comrades,

In my opinion, I feel convinced it would not be wrong to arrange in Petrograd (a town which has plenty of accommodation) an extra room or laboratory in which scholars could study. Indeed, you ought to arrange for this on your own initiative.

I beg you to see to this; but if you disagree, do not refuse to write me a few words at once, so that I may see where the obstacle lies.

With Communist greetings,

V. Ulianov (Lenin)

324. (226 P²). TO COMRADE M. N. POKROVSKY

Moscow, 5th December, 1920

Comrade M. N.,

I do congratulate you on your success: your new book, "The History of Russia in its Briefest Outline" pleased me immensely. An original construction and exposition. I read it with very great interest. I think it should be translated into other European languages.

I would make one small comment: if it is to be a *text book* (and it must be) it ought to have a chronological index. I will explain: (1) a column of dates, (2) a column of bourgeois evaluation of these dates (given briefly); (3) a column giving your, Marxist, evaluation of these dates, *giving references to pages in your book.*

Students must know *both* your book and its *index,* in order that there should be no *superficiality,* that they should *know the facts* and be able to compare the old learning with the new. Tell me what is your opinion of this addition.

With comradely greetings,

Your

Lenin

1921

325. (228 P²). TO G. M. KRZHIZHANOVSKY

[Moscow, 19th/22nd February, 1921]

Secret.

Gleb Maximilianovich,

Please look through and note the contents. Return it secretly and at once.

Milyutin writes rubbish about the Plan.[1] The greatest danger of all is to bureaucratise this matter of a plan of State economy.

That is a great danger. Milyutin does not see it.

I am very much afraid that, even though you approach the matter from another angle, *you too do not see it*. We are poor, starving, ruined beggars.

A complete, a complete and real plan for us now would be a bureaucratic Utopia.

Do not run after it!

The most important parts of it should be taken bit by bit, and the minimum number of enterprises should be organised, at once, without delaying a day or even an hour.

We will talk about this personally before you make your statement.

Think it over,

Lenin

326. (230 P²). TO N. I. BUKHARIN

[Moscow, March/April, 1921]

The question is *also* theoretically interesting. The proletarian State holds in its power factories, railways, foreign trade, (i.e., the material basis). Result: the *goods stock* is in its hands, as well as its wholesale transport (railway).

What is the proletarian State power doing with this stock?

It is selling it:

(a) To workers and employees for money, or in return for

---

[1] V. P. Milyutin read a paper before the Socialist Academy on the methods of working out a single economic plan.

their labour, without money, and (b) to the peasants in return *for bread*.

How does it sell it? Through whom? Through a *commission agent* (= the salesman) for a percentage commission.

It shows preference to co-operation (by trying to organise the whole population).

Why is that *impossible?* But that is *Capitalism* plus Socialism.[1]

327. (231 P²). TO G. M. KRZHIZHANOVSKY

Moscow, 12th April, 1921

Gleb Maximilianovich,

Yesterday I had a talk with Smilga. He is supposed to be having a talk with you today.

The question of the main lines of the State Plan, not as an institution but as a *plan*, is urgent.

Now you know the Prodnalog [Food tax] and other decrees. That is the policy. But you must calculate more accurately (in case of different harvests) how much it can yield.

Fuel is also an extremely urgent matter. The timber transport has broken down. A bad harvest with such a Spring will dislocate the bringing up of supplies.

Let Ramzin and Co. send me *brief* totals in a day or so: three sets of figures (wood, coal and petrol); half yearly, 1918? 1919? 1920? *particularly* 1921 and the plan for 1922. Also the fuel plan for 1920. Four sets of figures: (1) what was intended; (2) what was received; (3) how the intended amounts were to be allotted (giving only the main headings); (4) how the supply received was allotted.

Send these by Thursday morning. I shall make my decisions concerning foreign trade in accordance with your answers.

See that this is done today; we will discuss it tomorrow.

Greetings,
Lenin

---

[1] This note was written at a meeting of the Politbureau, when concrete measures with regard to going over to a New Economic Policy were discussed. Bukharin did not see the danger of the revival of capitalism on the part of the small traders. He did not think it was Capitalism + Socialism.

328. (233 p²). TO COMRADE ZINOVIEV FOR THE NON-PARTY
CONFERENCE OF THE PETROGRAD WORKERS

[Moscow, 10th/21st April, 1921]

Comrades,

I much regret that I was unable to accept your suggestion to come to Petrograd. I welcome with all my heart the non-Party Conference and your work. It is at this moment, when the bourgeoisie of the whole world is conducting an outrageous campaign of lies against Soviet Russia and trying to break our foreign trade agreements, it is just at this moment that the help of the non-Party masses and collaboration with them is particularly important. The workers and peasants have, after the Kronstadt events, begun to understand better than before, that any shifting of power in Russia would be to the advantage of the White Guards; it is not for nothing that Milyukov, and all the clever leaders of the bourgeoisie, have welcomed the Kronstadt slogan "Soviets without Bolsheviks."

Once again I send greetings to the non-Party Conference, wishing you all success in your work, and in particular I would ask you to pay attention to the need for singling out at once, and constantly bringing forward more and more non-Party workers and peasants in the matter of agricultural development. A regional agricultural centre has been established in Petrograd; you must get this work to progress. Local workers receive more rights, more initiative. Non-Party workers must set to work and produce more and more men.

Greetings,

Lenin

329. (235 p²). TO M. P. PAVLOVICH [1]

Moscow, 31st May, 1921

Comrade Pavlovich,

I have made arrangements for the publication (in Petrograd) of an atlas ["A Universal Geographical Atlas"].

---

[1] M. P. Pavlovich (M. L. Weltman's literary pseudonym), Social Democrat, Menshevik, Communist after 1917. Since 1921 member of the Collegium of the National Commissariat for dealing with the question of nationalities, President of the Scientific Association of Oriental Studies.

It is most important to add some maps showing Imperialism. Would you undertake to do this?

For instance (1) Colonial possessions 1876-1914-1921, including, with special marking, the half-colonial countries (Turkey, Persia, China etc); (2) brief statistics concerning Colonies and Half-Colonies; (3) a map of financial dependencies—for instance plus or minus, with a figure (millions or milliards of francs) showing how much each country owes, or is owed. Also comparative figures for 1876-1914-1921 (if we are to take 1876 as the culmination point of pre-monopolistic capitalism); (4) railways of the world, showing by special marks in each country to whom most of the railways belong: to the English, French, North America etc. Would it be too confusing? We can find suitable methods. The main thing is to mark the predominating facts as precisely as possible. (5) The main sources of raw material for which there is such competition (oil, ore etc), also giving the percentages or values (viz. so many millions of francs), which belong to each country.

We must insert such maps into *text books*, giving of course brief explanatory notes. We can give you an assistant statistician.

Please reply if you can undertake this work, and how and when.

With Communist greetings,

The President of the Council of National Commissars.

V. Ulianov (Lenin)

330. (198 P²). TO L. M. HINCHUK

[Moscow], 29th July, 1921

Comrade Hinchuk,

They tell me you are going away. For how many months?

Before you leave, you must officially provide a substitute and inform me unofficially to which of the Communists in the Tsentrosoyuz [1] (*fully* experienced, and two or three men) I can refer.

Next: you must inform me *very briefly*, before you leave,

---

[1] The All-Union Consumers' Association.

when the machinery of co-operation will at last begin to function.

This is what I want to know:

1. How many shops, (co-operatives) and consequently your commercial agents, are there in the volosti (in such and such a Province), and in how many are there no such shops? And how many shops to each volust?

2. How many of the shops (agents) give accurate answers to questions from the Centre and send reports? Once a week or fortnightly?

3. How many regional shops have received goods? What kind of goods? (Give the briefest replies). Salt? Paraffin? Manufactured goods? Etc.

4. How many replies are there concerning the amount of surplus (perhaps received in exchange for certain things) and raw material which the peasants have? Bread? Other provisions? Raw materials, etc.?

5. How much has been exchanged during the period reported on? What has been exchanged and for what?

In my opinion, so long as there are no such reports received, there is *nothing*. Only talk. I await a reply.

With Communist greetings,

Lenin

331. (236 p²). TO V. V. ADORATSKY

Moscow, 2nd August, 1921

I have looked through the preface. It is difficult to judge, because it is unfinished. It looks as though it ought to be shortened and more clearly formulated, after giving the formulation full consideration.[1]

The *really* outstanding quotations from the letters should be collated with quotations from *other* works by Marx, and with "*Capital*" (for instance, on the subject of "equality," there are most important ones in "Capital"). If you were to take a

---

[1] This refers to V. V. Adoratsky's foreword to the Marx-Engels correspondence, published in Russia in 1922. The initiative to publish the most important letters belongs to Lenin, who entrusted this task to Adoratsky.

question, say "X," then you ought to give quotations from the letters on that question, so-and-so from Marx's other works, so-and-so from "Capital."

I have had time only to glance at the letters. Of course you will have to cut the material considerably, link it up, space it out, think it over two or three times and then give *brief* comments. There is evidently more work than it seemed at first.

A chronological arrangement would seem to be the most convenient (perhaps you are right).

With Communist greetings,
                                          Your
                                                      Lenin

P.S. I am on leave. Not well. I cannot see you. If you have finished the text book, you must push it forward.[1] Probably it would be quickest to do it through Mikhail Nikolaevich Pokrovsky.

332. (240 p[2]). TO G. M. KRZHIZHANOVSKY

[Moscow, 1921]

Gleb Maximilianovich!

This idea has just come to me: there must be propaganda for electricity. How? Not only in words, but in deeds.

What does this mean? Most important of all—to popularise it. To do this, we must at once work out a *plan* for putting electricity into every single house in the R.S.F.S.R.

And this must be for a long time ahead, because for some time to come we shall not have sufficient wiring etc. for 20 million (or is it 40 million?) bulbs. All the same, a plan is necessary *at once*, even though it covers a number of years.

That comes first. Secondly, we must immediately work out an *abridged* plan; and then thirdly, and this is the most important of all, we must succeed in stimulating both the *competitive instinct* and *initiative of the masses*, so that they will set to work at once.

---

[1] "A course on the main questions of Marxism," publ. in 1922 and "Karl Marx's Scientific Communism," publ. in 1923.

Could not the following plan (for instance) be drawn up at once?

1. All volosti (rural districts—10/15,000) to be supplied with electric light within one year.

2. All hamlets (half-a-million to a million, and probably not more than three quarters of a million), within two years.

3. First of all—the reading-room huts and the Sovdep (two electric bulbs).

4. Electric light standards to be made *immediately*, and in such and such a way.

5. Insulators to be manufactured *immediately*, and *by us* (ceramic factories—I suppose local and small ones?) to be made in such and such a way.

6. *Copper* for wiring? *Collect it yourselves* in each volost (rural district) and local district (a little hint at church bells, etc).

7. Electrical training to be organized in such and such a way. Cannot something *like this* be thought out, worked out in detail and *decreed?*

Yours,

Lenin

333. (201 p²). TO A. S. KISELEV, COPIES TO BE SENT TO COM-
RADES BOGDANOV, UNSKLIEDT, AVANESOV AND KURSKY

[*Moscow*], *15th September, 1921*

I would draw your attention to a note by Mihels in No. 203 of "Izvestia" of the 13th September [called "Pauper Million-aires"].

The author writes that since 1918 there have been 2½ million poods [1 pood = 40 English pounds] of the most valuable metal freight lying almost in a bog, neither checked nor guarded, which is being plundered and allowed to go to waste.

Please have this statement verified immediately, and if it is correct, take proper steps at once for the metal to be checked, guarded etc., and discover, and severely punish the culprits.

Send me a detailed written report, giving the names and

LENIN WITH A NEPHEW AT GORKI, 1922

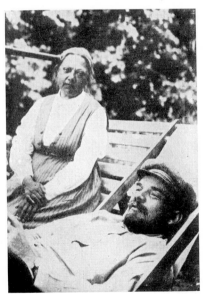

LENIN AND KRUPSKAYA

occupations of the culprits concerned in this scandal, and inform the Council of Labour and Defence.

Please carry out this instruction without delay.

President of the Council of National Commissars.

V. Ulianov (Lenin)

334. (204 p²). TO N. A. SEMASHKO

Moscow, 24th October, 1921

Comrade Semashko,

Having today signed the decision of the Maly S.N.K. to
vote two milliard roubles (I believe that is correct, although I
do not remember the actual figure) for the cleaning of Moscow,
and having read the regulations of the Narkomsdrav [1] about the
week of dwelling-house resanitation ("Izvestia," 12th July), I
have come to the conclusion that my suspicions (concerning
the complete rottenness in the way the whole of this business
is being organised) is increasing.

Milliards of roubles will be taken, pilfered and stolen, and
the work will not be done.

We must get model (or to begin with *tolerable*) cleanliness in
Moscow, for there can be no greater disgrace than the "Soviet"
dirt, which is to be found in first class houses. It simply cannot
be imagined. And what is it like in those houses which are not
first class?

Please send me a report, brief, but accurate and businesslike,
showing what was the result of the week devoted to cleaning.
Can you tell me of one single Province, where something was
done, that was not inefficient?

Further, what is being done (and what has been done) in
Moscow? Who is responsible for this work? Are they mere
clerks with pompous Soviet titles who understand nothing, do
not know their jobs, and can only sign bits of paper? Or are
there some *efficient* people in charge? And who are they?

The most important thing of all is to see that there are reliable people, who can take on responsibility.

What is being done to encourage personal responsibility?

[1] People's Commissariat for Health.

Who inspects the work? Inspectors? And how many are there? Who are they?

Detachments of youth? (Komsomol?) Are there any? How many? Where and how have they proved themselves?

What other means are there for *real* control?

Is money being spent on buying valuable things (Carbolic? Cleaning implements? How much has been bought?), or is the money going towards the maintenance of official do-nothings?

President of the Sovnarkom,

V. Ulianov (Lenin)

335. (206 P²). TELEGRAM (BY 'PHONE) TO V. A. AVANESOV, D. I. KURSKY AND A. D. TSYURUPA

[Gorki, 13th December, 1921]

I suspect a little military trick on the part of Osinsky and Bogdanov, who in my absence today have brought up the question of rescinding the decisions of the Council of Labour and Defence concerning the bringing to book of people guilty of the delay over the production of Fowler ploughs.

Please take note of this and use your influence against rescinding the decisions of the Council of Labour and Defence. There is no doubt as to who is guilty of causing the delay, but from the point of view of principles, it is essential that such matters should not be left within the confines of bureaucratic institutions, but should be brought into the light of a Court, not so much for the sake of administering severe punishment (it might be sufficient to reprimand them, but for the sake of publicity and to destroy the general conviction that the guilty cannot be punished.

Lenin

1922

336 (283 P²). TO V. A. KARPINSKY

[Moscow], 26th January, 1922

Comrade Karpinsky,

Would you write to me briefly (say, two or three short pages maximum) telling me how many letters have been sent in by peasants to "Bednota" ["Poverty"]? What is important (or particularly important) and new in these letters?

What is their tone?

The burning questions of the day?

Cannot I receive letters once in two months? (The next one by March 15th, 1922?).

a. The average number of letters?

b. Their tone?

c. The most important burning questions of the day.

With Communist greetings,

Lenin

337. (241 P²). TO I. I. SKVORTSOV-STEPANOV

Moscow, 19th March, 1922

Comrade Stepanov,

I have just finished looking through 160 pages of your book [On the Electrification of the R.S.F.S.R.]. Just as I swore madly at you (almost to an outrageous degree) for being capable of sitting for months over a refutation of Cunow,[1] so now I am delighted with this book. Yes, it *is* a book! It is a model of how a Russian savage should be taught from the very beginning, but taught not merely "half science" but the *whole subject*.

Write another (after a *thorough* rest); a similar little volume on the history of religion and *against every* religion (among them Kantianism and any other refined idealism, or refined agnosticism) with a survey of material on the history of atheism and on the *links* between the Church and the bourgeoisie.

Once again, greetings and congratulations on your magnificent success.

Your

Lenin

P.S. Page 97 is incorrect. "Respondek" is wrong.[2] I advise you to look up the original source and have it verified. I

[1] "Religionsgeschichtliche Streifzüge," 1913.

[2] A table from D. G. Respondek's work "Weltwirtschaftlicher Stand und Aufgaben der Elektroindustrie," Berlin, 1920.

append a letter to Popov. You can send it off through my secretary.

P.P.S. I am sending the preface to the Secretary.[1]

338. (212 P[2]). TO I. V. STALIN, THEN NATIONAL COMMISSAR OF RABKRIN THE WORKER AND PEASANT INSPECTION

[Moscow, 21st March, 1922]

I have had a talk with Tsyurupa and Rykov.[2] I hope the work will go well. By the way, the question concerns your Narkomat.[3] The main task for Tsyurupa and Rykov is (and must continue so) to see that the work is carried out and to see to the selection of people.

Helpers are needed. The Narkomat management alone is not enough for this and it is not rational to increase it. I expressed the opinion that we must make use of Rabkrin for this (direct help to Tsyurupa and Rykov for checking the work and supervision of the lower strata workers in the People's Commissariat). I want to know if you approve; if yes, then your written agreement with the substitutes is necessary, and I should like to take part in drawing up this agreement.

The object: to train from among the best workers of Rabkrin whom Tsyurupa and Rykov are selecting with your approval, those who will be particularly reliable and will do the following both swiftly and properly (you and both the substitutes will test them by *practical* instructions):

a. to see that the work is done.

b. to check the work.

c. to check the correct working of the administration in this or that Narkomat, Department, Mossoviet or Petrosoviet etc.

d. to give instructions *how* the work is to be organised.

These people will work by reporting *personally* on the progress and results of the work to the substitutes and to you. They

---

[1] Lenin's preface to Skvortsov-Stepanov's book on the electrification of the R.S.F.S.R.

[2] A. Tsyurupa and A. Rykov substituted the President of the Council of People's Commissars.

[3] Narkomat, the People's Commissariat.

must be selected *very* slowly so that only after repeated tests they will be made so to speak inspectors and instructors with special powers; their number will be *gradually* increased to a dozen or so. These in turn will bring about the entry of non-Party workers and peasants into the Rabkrin.

If you approve, send a copy of this to Tsyurupa and Rykov with your comments. If you have any objections, then send me a line at once (or telephone). I should like to mention this in my speech at the Congress.

Lenin

339. (242 P²). TO G. M. KRZHIZHANOVSKY

Moscow, 6th April, 1922

Gleb Maximilianovich!

Yesterday Martens[1] told me that the presence of an unheard of wealth of iron had been "proved" (you said "almost") in the Kursk Province.

If this is true, should not the following be carried out *this Spring:*

1. To lay down the necessary narrow gauge railway.

2. To prepare the nearest peat bog (or bogs?) for building an electrical station.

If you do not think these schemes are superfluous, then write to Martens (also a few words to me).

Martens wants to go there in about three weeks' time. I have written to Rykov and Tsyurupa, saying he is to be given another engineer from Gosplan.

All this should be carried out *most* energetically. I am much afraid that without triple control, the matter will be forgotten. When I go away, do not forget that Rykov and Tsyurupa have my letter about this.

Your,

Lenin

---

[1] Communist, engineer, President of the Scientific-Technical Department of the Supreme Council of National Supremacy.

340. (243 P²). TO I. I. SKVORTSOV-STEPANOV

[*Moscow, 15th November, 1922*]

My dear Ivan Ivanovich,

I have read your article on "Specialists" ["Pravda," No. 244].

I disagree on two points:

First, at the beginning (third column): "The proletarian dictatorship will fail if, firstly . . . (that is correct), and secondly "if these specialists are not their own specialists, namely those who realise that their task is to consolidate and develop the dictatorship of the proletariat."

The underlined is wrong. We will not get such specialists for a long time, not until the *bourgeois* specialists have disappeared, also the *petit-bourgeois* specialists, and certainly not before *all* the specialists become *Communists*. Meanwhile, the proletarian dictatorship must not fail. The *lesser* condition is sufficient, namely, the first. The second does not ruin us. It is sufficient "to have it under control."

For a long time to come there will be doubts, uncertainty, suspicion, treachery etc. The second condition will last until the *end* of the dictatorship, and it is, therefore, *not a condition of the dictatorship.*

And the second point at the end of the article—sections II and III *from the end*—"class struggle is no uglier than the attitude expressed towards it."

This is wrong. It is *wrong,* and not only ugly: it is worse than ugly, it is *scientifically inaccurate*. It is *not* class struggle.

Further. "A scientific laboratory is a united collective acting in agreement, in solidarity and is conscious in all its elements."

Wrong. That cannot happen before the *abolition of classes.*

It is sentimental and not scientific for you to say: "*share*" all *before* the abolition of classes. That is wrong. It will degenerate into examples of 1918: first-aid men demand from the doctors "to share" all (scientific knowledge).

That is both wrong and harmful in practice.

Example: The Politbureau and its *female secretaries*. "Share everything" (scientific)? You yourself will not insist on that. You have been carried away by your thoughts.

Best wishes,

Your

Lenin

Index of Letters *

(TO WHOM WRITTEN)

* Reference is by letter rather than by page number.

479

Index of Names and Places